DIEGO JOURDAN PEREIRA
LARGE-PRINT
BIBLE POWER PUZZLES

LEARN THE WORD OF GOD
THROUGH THE POWER OF PUZZLES

Good Books®

BIBLE POWER PUZZLES

Copyright © 2020 by Diego Jourdan Pereira

Unless otherwise noted, all Scripture quotations are taken from the Christian Standard Bible ®, Copyright © 2017 by Holman Bible Publishers. Used by permission.
Christian Standard Bible ® and CSB ® are federally registered trademarks of Holman Bible Publishers.

Good Books books may be purchased in bulk at special discounts for sales promotion, corporate gifts, fund-raising, or educational purposes. Special editions can also be created to specifications. For details, contact the Special Sales Department, Good Books, 307 West 36th Street, 11th Floor, New York, NY 10018 or info@skyhorsepublishing.com.

Good Books is an imprint of Skyhorse Publishing, Inc.®, a Delaware corporation.

Visit our website at www.skyhorsepublishing.com.

10 9 8 7 6 5 4 3 2 1

Library of Congress Cataloging-in-Publication Data is available on file.

Cover and interior design by Diego Jourdan Pereira
Mechanical design by Kai Texel

ISBN: 978-1-68099-610-4

Printed in China

CONTENTS

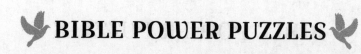

Dedicated to the memory of
Melvin Donnell Taylor Lopez
(1941 - 2012)

 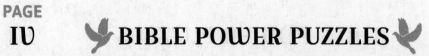

INTRODUCTION

Born from a traditionally Waldensian-Methodist family, I was baptized a Lutheran, raised Catholic, and for the longest time remained strictly an atheist, until my aunt Lissy and her husband Don (whom this book is dedicated to) kindly mailed me a copy of the red-letter Holman *Christian Standard Bible* ® at one of the lowest points in my life. As I read through its pages, my proud, self-reliant armor began to slowly crack.

Dialing down on my atheism I turned agnostic, but that wasn't enough. Arrogance kept me stumbling and falling as I took the longest-possible road back home, but the more I read the Good Book, the more it became obvious I would never be able to stand upright and walk straight unless held by a frame made from the very God I was seeking.

So in addition to reading the Scripture in the abstract I decided to try and *live* it for a change, and found that the more I did just that, the less distracted by false attractions and the more focused on the path to the Father I got—a path which has led me, through comic books and woodcut printmaking, into puzzle-craft!

In fact, I like to picture the Creator as an avid puzzlist as well, so this book is first and foremost an offering, not to curry favor (Christ took care of that already), but as a child would present Dad with his latest handmade craft, hoping He appreciates intent rather than results. As far as the latter go, however, I trust this book will provide senior adults many hours of uplifting, wholesome, and free from eye-strain (hence the *large-print*) fun, with an assorted variety of Bible-based puzzles (quotes coming straight from my beloved *CSB* ®), which get progressively more demanding but, as in life, answers will always be found in the Word of God!*

—Diego Jourdan Pereira

* If in a hurry, check the Solutions section starting on page 501!

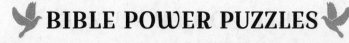

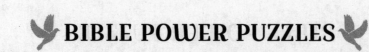

WORD-SEARCH

CONTAINED WITHIN THIS PUZZLE YOU MUST FIND ALL
CAPITALIZED WORDS FROM THE VERSES BELOW.

```
M Y G Z R E A R T H J
U Z R Z L E U J E E M
L S O N S J T B R V Y
T F U H B D H G R R W
I R N I Q I O U O I C
P U D F E A R N R D I
L I V I N G I D O X F
Y T Y S I K T E A A H
R F X H S K Y R Z U H
L U I V W A V O Z J G
R L W C R E A T U R E
```

"**GOD** blessed **NOAH** and his **SONS** and said to them,
'Be **FRUITFUL** and **MULTIPLY** and fill the **EARTH**.
The **FEAR** and **TERROR** of **YOU** will be
in every **LIVING CREATURE** on the earth,
every **BIRD** of the **SKY**,
every creature that crawls on the **GROUND**,
and all the **FISH** of the **SEA**.
They are placed **UNDER** your **AUTHORITY**.'"

CRISS-CROSS

USE THE DEFINITIONS BELOW TO FIND THE WORDS AND GUESS THE THEME.

ACROSS:

1. Elder of the "sons of thunder".
4. Brother of Peter.
5. Denied Jesus three times.
7. The beloved disciple.
8. First name Nathanael.
10. Known as the Zealot.
11. Betrayed Christ.

DOWN:

1. Known as Thaddaeus.
2. The 13th apostle.
3. Was a tax collector.
6. He came from Bethsaida.
7. —the Less, son of Alphaeus.
9. Refused to believe without seeing.

SUDOKU

MATCH THE HIGHLIGHTED NUMBER SEQUENCE TO THE CHAPTER AND VERSE BELOW.

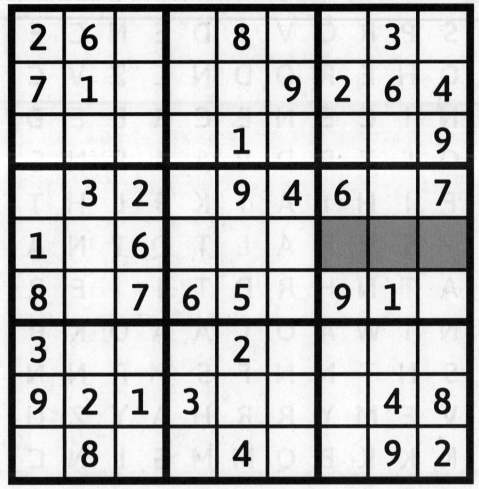

2	6			8			3	
7	1				9	2	6	4
				1				9
	3	2		9	4	6		7
1		6						
8		7	6	5		9	1	
3				2				
9	2	1	3				4	8
	8			4			9	2

2 TIMOTHY _ : _ - _

"Preach the word; be ready in season and out of season; rebuke, correct, and encourage with great patience and teaching. For the time will come when people will not tolerate sound doctrine, but according to their own desires, will multiply teachers for themselves because they have an itch to hear what they want to hear. They will turn away from hearing the truth and will turn aside to myths. But as for you, exercise self-control in everything, endure hardship, do the work of an evangelist, fulfill your ministry."

DEFINITION SEARCH

FIND ALL WORDS PLACED HORIZONTALLY, VERTICALLY, OR DIAGONALLY, AND MATCH THEM TO THE DEFINITIONS BELOW.

```
S P R O V I D E N C E
O H E R O D N L Z V C
N I C E N E C R E E D
O L T P D V A J E N S
F I H I A I K S L H T
M S V P A L T Q T N A
A T N H R D T I I E R
N I W A O L A A O K R
S N T N N F S M R N N
V E M Y R R H A Y Z U
K K K B Q M M G L N C
```

- Brother of Moses.
- First man.
- Sacrificial structure.
- Fallen angel.
- Celebration of the Resurrection.
- Version.
- Visit of the Magi.
- Came from Adam's rib.
- To believe.
- Tried to kill Jesus as a baby.
- From Ash Wednesday to Holy Saturday.
- Symbolized by a winged lion.
- Third gift from the Magi.
- 325 AD statement of belief (2 w.).
- Ancient occupier of Canaan.
- God's manifest care and support.
- Holy person.
- Estrangement from god.
- Expression which affirms Christ's humanity (3 words).
- Shone on Bethlehem.

PARABLES

"You are the salt of the earth. But if the salt should lose its taste, how can it be made salty? It's no longer good for anything but to be thrown out and trampled under people's feet."

Matthew 5:13

WHAT DOES IT MEAN?

....
....
....
....
....
....
....

WHAT DOES IT MEAN?

....
....
....
....
....
....
....

"Why do you look at the splinter in your brother's eye but don't notice the beam of wood in your own eye?"

Matthew 7:3

"No one patches an old garment with unshrunk cloth, because the patch pulls away from the garment and makes the tear worse. And no one puts new wine into old wineskins. Otherwise, the skins burst, the wine spills out, and the skins are ruined. But they put new wine into fresh wineskins, and both are preserved."

Matthew 9:16-17

WHAT DOES IT MEAN?

....
....
....
....
....
....
....

THE RIGHT ONE

REWRITE THE LIST IN THE CORRECT ORDER.

1. Leviticus	1.
2. 1 Samuel	2.
3. Judges	3.
4. Numbers	4.
5. Genesis	5.
6. Exodus	6.
7. Ruth	7.
8. Deuteronomy	8.
9. Joshua	9.
10. 2 Samuel	10.

QUOTES

IDENTIFY THE PROPER BOOK, CHAPTER, AND VERSE THESE BIBLE QUOTATIONS BELONG TO.

"For God loved the world in this way: He gave His One and Only Son, so that everyone who believes in Him will not perish but have eternal life."

BOOK:
....

CHAPTER:
....

VERSE:
....

BOOK:
....

CHAPTER:
....

VERSE:
....

"'For I know the plans I have for you'—this is the LORD'S declaration— 'plans for your welfare, not for disaster, to give you a future and a hope.'"

"We know that all things work together for the good of those who love God, who are called according to His purpose."

BOOK:
....

CHAPTER:
....

VERSE:
....

UNSCRAMBLE
REARRANGE ONE WORD AT THE TIME, IN THE SAME ORDER THEY'RE PRESENTED, TO REVEAL THE PRECISE VERSE FROM THE SCRIPTURE.

1. YB HIST VEONEERY LIWL WONK HATT OYU REA YM CIPSIDLES, FI OYU VELO NEO NOAHERT.

....

....

....

....

2. VEMORE HET DALSSAN MORF YORU ETFE, OFR EHT CELAP HEWRE YUO REA DINGSTAN SI LYOH UGROND.

....

....

....

....

3. SELBSED EB HET ORLD, HOW SHA TON FELT OUY THOWIUT A MIFALY DEREMERE DATYO. YAM SHI MENA COBEME LWEL WNKNO NI RASIEL.

....

....

....

....

4. I LIWL CLGIN OT YM HOTEUSENSRIGS NAD VERNE TEL TI OG. IM SCIENCECON LIWL TON CUCASE EM SA GONL SA I VELI!

....

....

....

....

"'Ask and it will be given to you. Seek and you will find. Knock and the door will be opened to you.

For everyone who asks receives, and the one who seeks finds, and to the one who knocks, the door will be opened.

For every activity there is a right time and procedure, even though a person's troubles are heavy on him.

If you then, who are evil, know how to give good gifts to your children, how much more will your Father in heaven give good things to those who ask Him.

Therefore, whatever you want others to do for you, do also the same for them, for this is the Law and the Prophets.'"

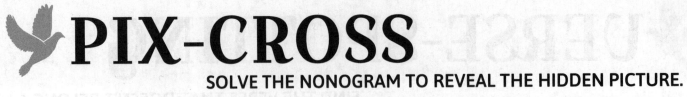

PIX-CROSS

SOLVE THE NONOGRAM TO REVEAL THE HIDDEN PICTURE.

										2
										2
										2
										2
										2
										2
										2
										2
										2
										2
0	0	0	0	10	10	0	0	0	0	0

WORD-SEARCH

CONTAINED WITHIN THIS PUZZLE YOU MUST FIND THE CAPITALIZED WORDS FROM THE VERSES BELOW.

```
F  S  J  R  P  F  X  M  X  F  Y
B  N  E  D  E  F  G  Q  I  A  T
O  L  S  O  S  A  F  R  A  I  D
A  W  U  U  W  I  C  H  L  T  Z
T  A  S  B  A  H  N  H  I  H  C
X  T  U  T  L  A  A  K  E  M  O
J  E  C  E  K  N  F  T  T  D  M
U  R  M  X  I  D  W  X  D  E  M
O  O  W  I  N  D  L  O  R  D  A
C  U  F  Z  G  P  E  T  E  R  N
E  S  T  R  E  N  G  T  H  P  D
```

"Immediately **JESUS** spoke to them. 'Have courage! It is I. Don't be afraid.'
'Lord, if it's you,' **PETER** answered **HIM**, **'COMMAND** me to come to you on the
WATER.'
He said, **'COME**.'
And climbing out of the **BOAT**, Peter started **WALKING** on the water and came
toward Jesus. But when he saw the **STRENGTH** in the **WIND**, he was **AFRAID**, and
beginning to **SINK** he cried out, **'LORD**, save me!'
Immediately Jesus **REACHED OUT** his **HAND**, caught hold of him, and said to him,
'You of little **FAITH**, why did you **DOUBT**?'"

CRISS-CROSS

USE THE DEFINITIONS BELOW TO FIND THE WORDS AND GUESS THE THEME.

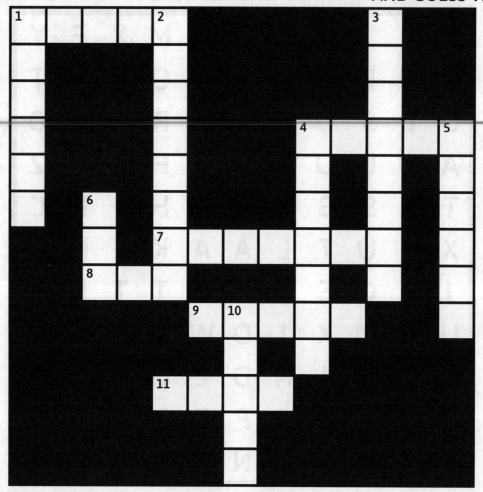

ACROSS:
1. Wrestled with God.
4. Brother of Gad.
7. Son of Hagar.
8. Father of Hushim.
9. Defiled by Shechem.
11. Traded his birthright for pottage.

DOWN:
1. Sold into slavery by his brothers.
2. Jacob's 12th son.
3. Son of Bilhah.
4. God promised him numerous offspring.
5. Persuaded his brothers not to kill Joseph.
6. Son of Zilpah.
10. Almost sacrificed by his father.

SUDOKU

MATCH THE HIGHLIGHTED NUMBER SEQUENCE TO THE CHAPTER AND VERSE BELOW.

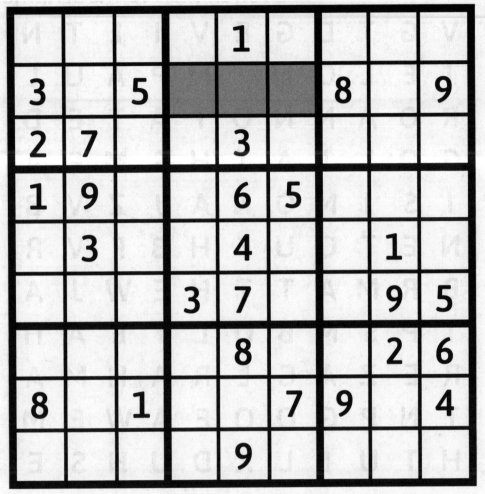

NUMBERS _ : _ - _

"'Speak to the Israelites and tell them: When a man or woman makes a special vow, a Nazirite vow, to consecrate himself to the Lord, he is to abstain from wine and beer. He must not drink vinegar made from wine or from beer. He must not drink any grape juice or eat fresh grapes or raisins. He is not to eat anything produced by the grapevine, from seeds to skin, during the period of his consecration.'"

DEFINITION SEARCH

FIND ALL WORDS PLACED HORIZONTALLY, VERTICALLY, OR DIAGONALLY,
AND MATCH THEM TO THE DEFINITIONS BELOW.

```
V G T D G E V I L T N
I E L O H I M P A U L
R O A N N O T A T E D
G O L I A T H S M E A
I S I M O N A J Z V B
N E T Q U F H B F V R
B R M A T T H E W J A
I P S M B O L Y E A H
R E Z A G L R A H M A
T N P G O O E A W E M
H T U I L X D U H S E
```

- Commanded by God to sacrifice his son.
- Contains additional notes.
- One of God's Hebrew names.
- Eldest son of Isaac.
- Morally objectionable.
- Abstaining from food.
- Yahweh.
- Precious metal.
- Giant Philistine warrior slain by David.
- Brother of John.
- Pentateuch.
- Wise men who visited baby Jesus.

- Author of the first Gospel.
- Apostle of the Gentiles.
- Tempted Eve.
- Forced to carry Jesus' cross.
- Firm and dependable.
- 613 of these in the Torah.
- Conception without a human father (2 w.).

PARABLES

WHAT DOES IT MEAN?

....
....
....
....
....
....
....

"You are the light of the world... No one lights a lamp and puts it under a basket, but rather on a lampstand, and it gives light for all who are in the house."
Matthew 5:14-15

WHAT DOES IT MEAN?

....
....
....
....
....
....
....

"The harvest is abundant, but the workers are few. Therefore, pray to the Lord of the harvest to send out workers into his harvest."
Matthew 9:37-38

WHAT DOES IT MEAN?

....
....
....
....
....
....
....

"The kingdom of heaven is like a mustard seed that a man took and sowed in his field. It's the smallest of all the seeds, but when grown, it's taller than the garden plants and becomes a tree, so that the birds of the sky come and nest in its branches."
Matthew 13:31-32

THE RIGHT ONE

REWRITE THE LIST IN THE CORRECT ORDER.

11. **Esther**	11.
12. **1 Chronicles**	12.
13. **Psalms**	13.
14. **Ezra**	14.
15. **2 Chronicles**	15.
16. **1 Kings**	16.
17. **Proverbs**	17.
18. **Job**	18.
19. **Nehemiah**	19.
20. **2 Kings**	20.

QUOTES

"I am able to do all things through him who strengthens me."

BOOK:
....

CHAPTER:
....

VERSE:
....

BOOK:
....

CHAPTER:
....

VERSE:
....

"In the beginning God created the heavens and the earth."

"Trust the Lord with all your heart, and do not rely on your own understanding..."

BOOK:
....

CHAPTER:
....

VERSE:
....

UNSCRAMBLE

REARRANGE ONE WORD AT THE TIME, IN THE SAME ORDER THEY'RE PRESENTED, TO REVEAL THE PRECISE VERSE FROM THE SCRIPTURE.

1. EH LYRUT SI NA LITERAESI NI HOWM THEER SI ON CEDETI.

....

....

....

....

2. FI ORUY THROBER NISS INAGAST OYU, OG DAN BUKEER IHM NI VATERIP. FI EH TENLISS OT OYU, OYU VEHA OWN ORUY THROBER.

....

....

....

....

3. THIW ATREG WERPO HET SOPATLES REWE VINGGI SETMONITY OT HET RUSERIONERCT FO HET ROLD SUJES...

....

....

....

....

4. WOH GOLN ILWL OYU VERWA WENBEET OWT NIOOPINS? FI HET ROLD SI DOG, WOLLOF MIH.

....

....

....

....

VERSE-SPOTTING

FIND THE VERSE THAT DOESN'T BELONG.

"In the beginning was the Word, and the Word was with God.

He was with God in the beginning.

All things were created through him, and apart from him not one thing was created that has been created. In him was life, and that light was the light of men.

God saw that the light was good, and God separated the light from the darkness.

That light shines in the darkness, and yet the darkness did not overcome it."

PIX-CROSS

SOLVE THE NONOGRAM TO REVEAL THE HIDDEN PICTURE.

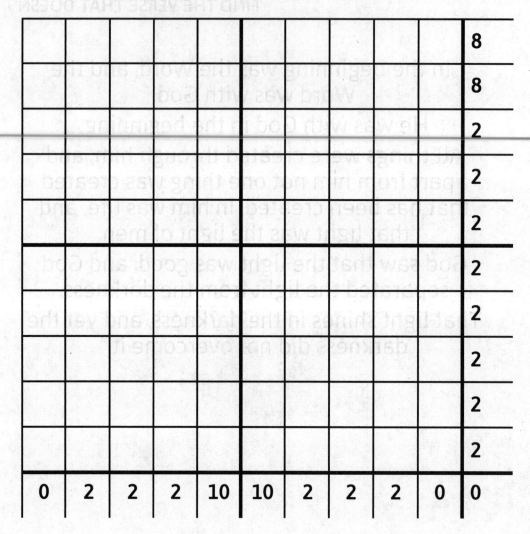

										8
										8
										2
										2
										2
										2
										2
										2
										2
										2
0	2	2	2	10	10	2	2	2	0	0

WORD-SEARCH

CONTAINED WITHIN THIS PUZZLE YOU MUST FIND THE CAPITALIZED WORDS FROM THE VERSES BELOW.

```
W O M B R S H A V E D
I Y L E A V E H B L T
P S X T S Q F E L L N
R O B E D H G Y E I A
V Z V A H R N V S F K
Z I E M G D V M S E E
G H Z T O R E S E H D
V L K O U U O P D L V
M O T H E R J U P O J
P S O T A K E S N R O
W O R S H I P E D D B
```

"Then **JOB STOOD** up, **TORE** his **ROBE**, and **SHAVED** his **HEAD**.
He **FELL** to the **GROUND** and **WORSHIPED**, saying:
'**NAKED** I came from my **MOTHER**'s **WOMB**,
and naked I will **LEAVE** this **LIFE**.
The **LORD GIVES**, and the Lord **TAKES** away.
BLESSED be the name of the Lord.'
Throughout all this Job did not sin or blame God for anything."

CRISS-CROSS

USE THE DEFINITIONS BELOW TO FIND THE WORDS AND GUESS THE THEME.

ACROSS:
6. Mother of Tubal-cain.
7. Lamech's wife.
8. Lamech's father.
9. He was the first shepherd.
12. Ancestor of all musicians.
13. Son of Seth.
14. Son of Enos.

DOWN:
1. Longest-living patriarch in the Bible.
2. First to take two wives.
3. Murdered his brother.
4. Lived 895 years.
5. Third son of Adam and Eve.
10. Son of Cain.
11. Kenan's grandson.
12. Brother of Jubal.

SUDOKU

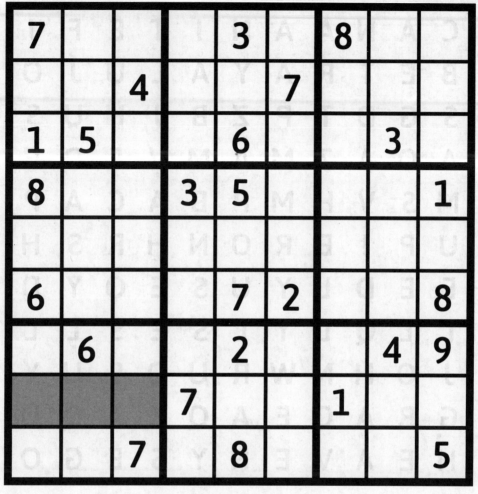

7				3		8		
		4			7			
1	5			6			3	
8			3	5				1
6				7	2			8
	6			2			4	9
			7			1		
		7		8				5

ACTS _ : _ - _

"...and requested letters from him to the synagogues in Damascus, so that if he found any men or women who belonged to the Way, he might bring them as prisoners to Jerusalem. As he traveled and was nearing Damascus, a light from heaven suddenly flashed around him."

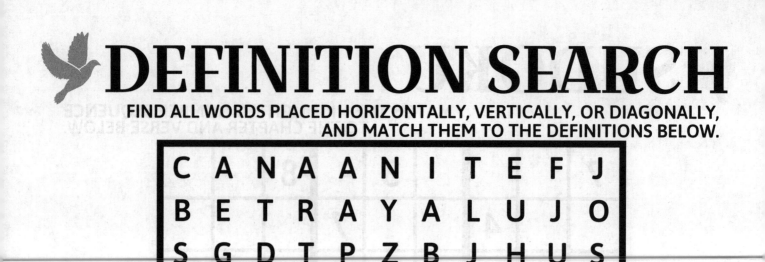

DEFINITION SEARCH

FIND ALL WORDS PLACED HORIZONTALLY, VERTICALLY, OR DIAGONALLY, AND MATCH THEM TO THE DEFINITIONS BELOW.

```
C A N A A N I T E F J
B E T R A Y A L U J O
S G D T P Z B J H U S
A O A Z M A M V F D E
M S V H M P B A C A P
U P I E R O N H R S H
E E D L Y U S E O Y D
L L Q L Y L S E S L L
J O H N W R U Q S U Y
G R A C E A Q K A Q U
H E A V E N Y S E G O
```

- Treason.
- Ancient Semitic inhabitant of Palestine.
- Jesus was nailed to one.
- King—.
- The story of Christ.
- State of sanctification by God.
- Abode of God and the angels.
- Opposite of Heaven.
- Sacred.
- —the Baptist.
- Foster father of Jesus.
- —Iscariot.
- Author of the third Gospel.
- —Magdalene.
- Led the Israelites out of Egypt.
- Anointed Saul as king.
- Adversary of God.
- King of the Israelites before David.
- Line of Scripture text.
- "I am the —, the truth, and the life."

PARABLES

"Therefore, everyone who hears these words and acts on them will be like a wise man who built his house on the rock. The rain fell, the rivers rose, and the winds blew and pounded that house. Yet it didn't collapse, because its foundation was on the rock. But everyone who hears these words of mine and doesn't act on them will be like a foolish man who built his house on the sand. The rain fell, the rivers rose, the winds blew and pounded that house, and it collapsed. It collapsed with a great crash." **Matthew 7:24-28**

WHAT DOES IT MEAN?

....
....
....
....
....
....
....

WHAT DOES IT MEAN?

....
....
....
....
....
....
....

"To what should I compare this generation? It's like children sitting in the marketplaces who call out to other children: We played the flute for you, but you didn't dance; we sang a lament, but you didn't mourn!"
Matthew 11:16-17

"Learn this lesson from the fig tree: As soon as its branch becomes tender and sprouts leaves, you know that summer is near. In the same way, when you see these things happening, recognize that he is near—at the door."
Mark 13:28-29

WHAT DOES IT MEAN?

....
....
....
....
....
....
....
....

THE RIGHT ONE

REWRITE THE LIST IN THE CORRECT ORDER.

21. **Amos**	21.
22. **Jeremiah**	22.
23. **Hosea**	23.
24. **Ezekiel**	24.
25. **Ecclesiastes**	25.
26. **Daniel**	26.
27. **Joel**	27.
28. **Isaiah**	28.
29. **Lamentations**	29.
30. **Song of Songs**	30.

QUOTES

IDENTIFY THE PROPER BOOK, CHAPTER, AND VERSE THESE BIBLE QUOTATIONS BELONG TO.

"'Your name will no longer be Jacob,' he said. 'It will be Israel because you have struggled with God and with men and have prevailed.'"

BOOK:
....

CHAPTER:
....

VERSE:
....

BOOK:
....

CHAPTER:
....

VERSE:
....

"Lord God, please remember me. Strengthen me, God, just once more. With one act of vengeance, let me pay back the Philistines for my two eyes."

"Lord, do not hold this sin against them!"

BOOK:
....

CHAPTER:
....

VERSE:
....

UNSCRAMBLE

REARRANGE ONE WORD AT THE TIME, IN THE SAME ORDER THEY'RE PRESENTED, TO REVEAL THE PRECISE VERSE FROM THE SCRIPTURE.

1. SITH SI YM VANTSER; I THENSTRENG IHM, SITH SI YM SENCHO NEO; I THELIDG NI IHM.

....

....

....

....

2. HOW YAM CENDAS OT HET TAINNUMO FO HET ROLD? HOW YAM ANDST NI IHS LYHO CELAP?

....

....

....

....

3. HET ROLD POPATEDIN A ERGAT SHIF OT LOWLAWS HAJON, DAN HAJON SAW NI HET LYBEL FO HET SHIF THERE YSAD NAD THERE THINGS.

....

....

....

....

4. TUB OWE OT OYU HOW REA CHIR, ROF OYU VEHA CEIREVED OYUR FORTMOC.

....

....

....

....

VERSE-SPOTTING

FIND THE VERSE THAT DOESN'T BELONG.

"They came to Jerusalem, and he went into the temple and began to throw out those buying and selling. He overturned the tables of money changers and the chairs of those selling doves, and would not permit anyone to carry goods through the temple.

He found a fresh jawbone of a donkey, reached out his hand, took it, and killed a thousand men with it.

He was teaching them: 'Is it not written, My house will be called a house of prayer for all nations? But you have made it a den of thieves!'"

PIX-CROSS

SOLVE THE NONOGRAM TO REVEAL THE HIDDEN PICTURE.

										2
										2
										2
										2
										10
										10
										2
										2
										2
										2
2	2	2	2	10	10	2	2	2	2	0

WORD-SEARCH

CONTAINED WITHIN THIS PUZZLE YOU MUST FIND THE CAPITALIZED WORDS FROM THE VERSES BELOW.

```
R A S H A M E D E J E W
E R B A R B A R I A N S
V V O W R I T T E N N O
E S E M O F O O L I S H
A A S V E A N W H U T S
L L G O S P E L O I E I
E V E R Y O N E A V G P
D A N I S B T F E E R O
Q T M N W H G I Y R E W
W I S E G U L O J L E E
I O I I Q E W R D L K R
L N R O B L I G A T E D
```

"I am **OBLIGATED** both to Greeks and **BARBARIANS**, both to the **WISE** and the **FOOLISH**. So I am eager to preach the **GOSPEL** to you also who are in **ROME**. For I am not **ASHAMED** of the gospel, because it is the **POWER** of **GOD** for **SALVATION** to **EVERYONE** who **BELIEVES**, first to the **JEW**, and also to the **GREEK**. For in it the righteousness of God is **REVEALED** from **FAITH** to faith, just as it is **WRITTEN**: *The* **RIGHTEOUS** *will live by faith.*"

CRISS-CROSS

USE THE DEFINITIONS BELOW TO FIND THE WORDS AND GUESS THE THEME.

ACROSS:

1. Grandfather of Zerubbabel.
3. Son of Eliud.
7. Abiud's father.
9. Great-grandfather of Matthan.
11. Eliakim's father.
12. Son of Achim.

DOWN:

1. Married Mary.
2. Joseph's father.
4. Zadok's father.
5. Son of Jeconiah.
6. Grandfather of Joseph.
8. Great-grandfather of Achim.
10. Son of Azor.

SUDOKU

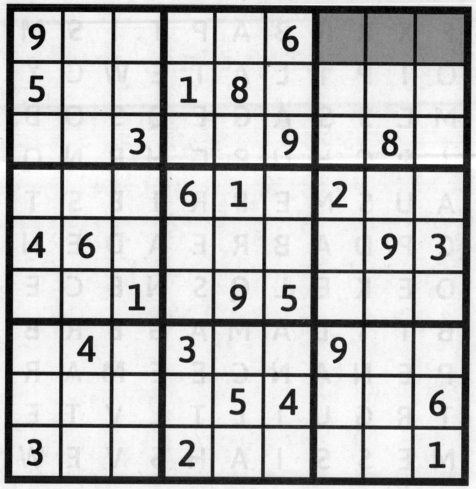

REVELATION _ : _ - _

"Then I saw in the right hand of the one seated on the throne a scroll with writing on both sides, sealed with seven seals. I also saw a mighty angel proclaiming with a loud voice, 'Who is worthy to open the scroll and break its seals?'"

DEFINITION SEARCH

FIND ALL WORDS PLACED HORIZONTALLY, VERTICALLY, OR DIAGONALLY, AND MATCH THEM TO THE DEFINITIONS BELOW.

```
F  X  R  R  B  A  P  T  I  S  M
O  I  P  I  L  A  T  E  W  C  Y
M  E  S  S  A  G  E  Q  S  O  B
J  P  C  H  U  R  C  H  R  N  Q
A  U  S  M  E  P  R  I  E  S  T
C  P  D  A  B  R  E  A  D  E  H
O  E  K  E  L  Q  S  N  E  C  E
B  T  I  L  A  M  A  G  E  R  B
P  E  N  A  N  C  E  E  M  A  R
T  R  G  U  I  L  T  L  V  T  E
M  E  S  S  I  A  H  S  V  E  W
```

- God's messengers.
- Sacrament of cleansing, admission, and adoption by water immersion.
- Jesus broke it.
- Body of Christians.
- To render holy.
- —of men.
- Remorse.
- Official language of Israel.
- Son of Abraham and Hagar.
- Son of Isaac and Rebecca.
- Kingdom of Judah.
- Eleventh and twelfth books in the OT.
- Divine communication.
- Promised redeemer.
- Voluntary self-punishment.
- A.K.A. Cephas.
- Washed his hands.
- Religious leader.
- Religious ode.
- Restore the worth of.

PARABLES

"'The kingdom of God is like this,' he said. 'A man scatters seed on the ground. He sleeps and rises night and day; the seed sprouts and grows, although he doesn't know how. The soil produces a crop by itself—first the blade, then the head, and then the full grain on the head. As soon as the crop is ready, he sends for the sickle because the harvest has come.'"

Mark 4:26-29

WHAT DOES IT MEAN?

....
....
....
....
....
....

WHAT DOES IT MEAN?

....
....
....
....
....
....
....
....

"A man had a fig tree that was planted in his vineyard. He came looking for fruit on it and found none. He told the vineyard worker, 'Listen, for three years I have come looking for fruit on this fig tree and haven't found any. Cut it down! Why should I even waste the soil?' But he replied to him, 'Sir, leave it this year also, until I dig around it and fertilize it. Perhaps it will produce fruit next year, but if not, you can cut it down.'"

Luke 13:6-9

WHAT DOES IT MEAN?

....
....
....
....
....
....
....
....

"'I am the bread of life', Jesus told them. 'No one who comes to me will ever be hungry, and no one who believes in me will ever be thirsty again.'"

John 6:35

THE RIGHT ONE

REWRITE THE LIST IN THE CORRECT ORDER.

31. **Nahum**	31.
32. **Obadiah**	32.
33. **Haggai**	33.
34. **Zechariah**	34.
35. **Micah**	35.
36. **Zephaniah**	36.
37. **Malachi**	37.
38. **Jonah**	38.
39. **Habakkuk**	39.

QUOTES

IDENTIFY THE PROPER BOOK, CHAPTER, AND VERSE THESE BIBLE QUOTATIONS BELONG TO.

"So give your servant a receptive heart to judge your people and to discern between good and evil..."

BOOK:
....

CHAPTER:
....

VERSE:
....

BOOK:
....

CHAPTER:
....

VERSE:
....

"It is better to listen to rebuke from a wise person than to listen to the song of fools..."

"Whoever does the will of God is my brother and sister and mother."

BOOK:
....

CHAPTER:
....

VERSE:
....

UNSCRAMBLE

REARRANGE ONE WORD AT THE TIME, IN THE SAME ORDER THEY'RE PRESENTED, TO REVEAL THE PRECISE VERSE FROM THE SCRIPTURE.

1. TOND ROWRY TUBOA THANINGY, TUB NI VEREYTHNIG HOUGHRT RAPERY NAD TITONIPE THIW THIGNVIKANSG, TENPRES OYUR QUERSETS OT OGD.

....
....
....
....

2. OG, THEFORERE, NAD KEMA SCESIPIDL FO LAL TINANOS, TIZBAPING HETM NI HET MENA FO HET HETFAR NAD FO HET NOS NAD FO HET LYOH PIRIST...

....
....
....
....

3. ROF OYU REA VEDAS YB CEGRA THUGHRO THAIF, NAD HIST SI TON MORF SELOURYVES...

....
....
....
....

4. TUB HET TUFRI FO HET RITPIS SI VELO, OJY, EPACE, TIENPACE, DINKSNES, DOGOSNES, HAITFULNESFS, GELENESNTS, NAD FELS-TONCROL.

....
....
....
....

VERSE-SPOTTING

"Then his mother and brothers came to him, but they could not meet with him because of the crowd.

He was told, 'Your mother and your brothers are standing outside, wanting to see you.'

But he replied to them, 'I will execute severe vengeance against them with furious rebukes. They will know that I am the LORD when I take my vengeance against them.'"

PIX-CROSS

SOLVE THE NONOGRAM TO REVEAL THE HIDDEN PICTURE.

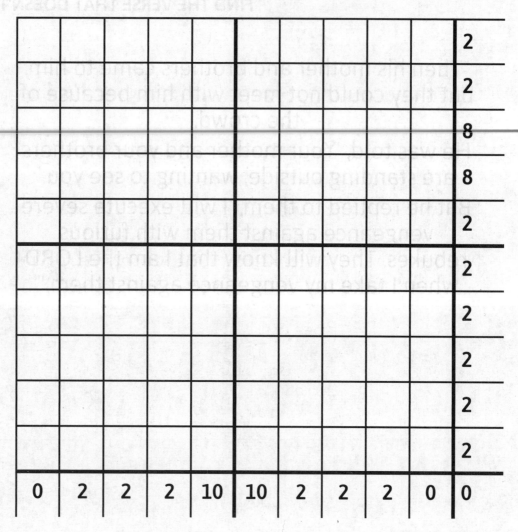

										2
										2
										8
										8
										2
										2
										2
										2
										2
										2
0	2	2	2	10	10	2	2	2	0	0

WORD-SEARCH

CONTAINED WITHIN THIS PUZZLE YOU MUST FIND THE CAPITALIZED WORDS FROM THE VERSES BELOW.

```
B O L O M D H T I V S
I C A S O A E K I Y W
R C U R U N A X T M E
T A G L R C L I E I E
H S H O N E V N M B P
P I W V Z I E W B Y G
E O C E T V J Z R X A
A N R C A W P L A N T
C O A E S E A R C H H
E M H C S T O N E S E
E V E R Y T H I N G R
```

"There is an **OCCASION** for **EVERYTHING**, and a **TIME** for every **ACTIVITY** under **HEAVEN**: a time to give **BIRTH** and a time to die; a time to **PLANT** and a time to uproot; a time to kill and a time to **HEAL**; a time to tear down and a time to build; a time to **WEEP** and a time to **LAUGH**; a time to **MOURN** and a time to **DANCE**; a time to throw **STONES** and a time to **GATHER** stones; a time to **EMBRACE** and a time to avoid embracing; a time to **SEARCH** and a time to count as lost; a time to keep and a time to throw away; a time to tear and a time to sew; a time to be silent and a time to speak; a time to **LOVE** and a time to hate; a time for war and a time for **PEACE**."

CRISS-CROSS

USE THE DEFINITIONS BELOW TO FIND THE WORDS AND GUESS THE THEME.

ACROSS:
2. Son of Naggai.
4. Great-grandfather of Jesus.
6. Grandson of Esli.
7. Mary's father-in-law.
9. Son of Naggai.
11. A carpenter by trade.

DOWN:
1. Father of Melchi.
2. Son of Amos.
3. Father of Esli.
4. Son of Jannai.
5. Father of of Jannai.
8. Father of Amos.
10. Great-grandfather of Joseph.

SUDOKU

HEBREWS _ : _ - _

"Now every house is built by someone, but the One who built everything is God. Moses was faithful as a servant in all God's household, as a testimony to what would be said in the future. But Christ was faithful as a Son over His household. And we are that household if we hold on to our confidence and the hope in which we boast."

DEFINITION SEARCH

FIND ALL WORDS PLACED HORIZONTALLY, VERTICALLY, OR DIAGONALLY, AND MATCH THEM TO THE DEFINITIONS BELOW.

```
C O N T R I T I O N T T
S O L O M O N M L G C B
C H A P T E R I U I H Z
Q A Z A L M A C C Q R Z
N R A R G S P H I L I P
I M R A A S T A F L S R
T O U B L S U E E H T O
H N S L I A R L R U M P
O Y E E L J E H O V A H
M I N D E X I N G R S E
A A S C E N S I O N R C
S H E P H E R D I W L Y
```

- Rising of the body of Jesus into heaven.
- Numbered subdivision of the Bible.
- Celebration of the birth of Christ.
- Sorrow for sin.
- An area of northern Israel where Jesus' ministry took place.
- Compatibility in opinion and action.
- Assortment and classification of Bible contents.
- Name for God in the OT, transliterated from consonants YHVH.
- Raised from the dead by Jesus.
- Master of Hell.
- Leader of God's armies against Satan's forces.
- Stories told by Jesus to convey his messages.
- From the same city as Andrew and Peter.
- Prediction uttered under divine inspiration.
- Futurist Christian doctrine popularized by John N. Darby.
- Abel's trade.
- Wise king of Israel in the OT.
- Called Didymus ("twin").

PARABLES

"Every kingdom divided against itself is headed for destruction, and no city or house divided against itself will stand. If Satan drives out Satan, he is divided against himself. How then will his kingdom stand?"

Matthew 12:25-26

WHAT DOES IT MEAN?

....
....
....
....
....
....
....

WHAT DOES IT MEAN?

....
....
....
....
....
....
....
....

"When you give a lunch or a dinner, don't invite your friends, your brothers or sisters, your relatives, or your rich neighbors, because they might invite you back, and you would be repaid. On the contrary, when you host a banquet, invite those who are poor, maimed, lame, or blind. And you will be blessed, because they cannot repay you; for you will be repaid at the resurrection of the righteous."

Luke 14:12-14

WHAT DOES IT MEAN?

....
....
....
....
....
....
....

"What father among you, if his son asks for a fish, will give him a snake instead of a fish? Or if he asks for an egg, will give him a scorpion? If you then, who are evil, know how to give good gifts to your children, how much more will the heavenly Father give the Holy Spirit to those who ask him?"

Luke 11:11-13

THE RIGHT ONE

REWRITE THE LIST IN THE CORRECT ORDER.

1. Mark	1.
2. Acts	2.
3. Luke	3.
4. Romans	4.
5. Galatians	5.
6. John	6.
7. Matthew	7.
8. 1 Corinthians	8.
9. Ephesians	9.
10. 2 Corinthians	10.

QUOTES

"As for you, lift up your staff, stretch out your hand over the sea, and divide it so the Israelites can go through the sea on dry ground."

BOOK:

....

CHAPTER:

....

VERSE:

....

BOOK:

....

CHAPTER:

....

VERSE:

....

"The Lord is my rock, my fortress, and my deliverer, my God, my rock where I seek refuge..."

"I chose you before I formed you in the womb; I set you apart before you were born. I appointed you a prophet to the nations."

BOOK:

....

CHAPTER:

....

VERSE:

....

UNSCRAMBLE

REARRANGE ONE WORD AT THE TIME, IN THE SAME ORDER THEY'RE PRESENTED, TO REVEAL THE PRECISE VERSE FROM THE SCRIPTURE.

1. REFOREETH, HERSBROT NAD TERSSIS, NI WEVI FO HET MIESCER FO OGD, I GERU OYU OT TENPRES OYUR DIEOB SA A VINGLI CASFIRICE...

....
....
....
....

2. I MA HET OGOD HESERDPH. I NOWK YM WON, NAD YM WON NOWK EM...

....
....
....
....

3. ROF I MA THIW OYU, NAD ON NEO ILWL YAL A DANH NO OYU OT THUR OYU, SECAUBE I VEHA NAMY PLEOPE NI SITH TICY.

....
....
....
....

4. ROF MODEFRE, HIRSTC TES SU REFE. DANST MIRF HENT NAD TOND MITUBS NIAGA OT A OKEY FO RYVELAS.

....
....
....
....

VERSE-SPOTTING

FIND THE VERSE THAT DOESN'T BELONG.

"Now Israel loved Joseph more than his other sons because Joseph was a son born to him in his old age, and he made a robe of many colors for him.

There was an opening in the center of the robe like that of body armor with a collar around the opening so that it would not tear.

When his brothers saw that their father loved him more than all his brothers, they hated him, and could not bring themselves to speak peaceably to him."

PIX-CROSS

SOLVE THE NONOGRAM TO REVEAL THE HIDDEN PICTURE.

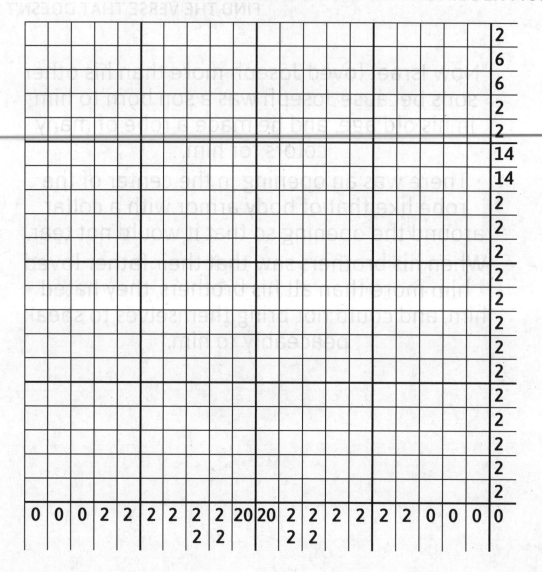

																				2
																				6
																				6
																				2
																				2
																				14
																				14
																				2
																				2
																				2
																				2
																				2
																				2
																				2
																				2
																				2
																				2
																				2
0	0	0	2	2	2	2	2 2	2 2	20	20	2 2	2 2	2	2	2	2	0	0	0	0

WORD-SEARCH

CONTAINED WITHIN THIS PUZZLE YOU MUST FIND THE CAPITALIZED WORDS FROM THE VERSES BELOW.

```
S U F F E R I N G N C
C Z I A N Y O N E X H
H F A I T H P V T L E
U L S I N G I C D N E
R O S H E G M A Q J R
C R B S R S C L O S F
H D I O S D A L H I U
U R F U I P R A Y C L
A N O I N T I N G K E
S A V E S E L D E R S
P R A I S E S K F Z S
```

"Is **ANYONE** among you **SUFFERING**? He should **PRAY**. Is anyone **CHEERFUL**? He should **SING PRAISES**. Is anyone among you **SICK**? He should **CALL** for the **ELDERS** of the **CHURCH**, and they are to pray over him, **ANOINTING** him with **OIL** in the name of the **LORD**. The prayer of **FAITH** will **SAVE** the sick person, and the Lord will **RISE** him up; if he has committed **SINS**, he will be **FORGIVEN**."

CRISS-CROSS

USE THE DEFINITIONS BELOW TO FIND THE WORDS AND GUESS THE THEME.

ACROSS:

1. Slept in the lion's den.
4. The Lord touched his mouth.
6. Prophesied that Bethlehem would be the birthplace of the Messiah.
7. Openly questioned the workings of God.
8. Ordered the deaths of 450 priests of Baal.
11. First of the prophets to put in writing the messages he has received.
12. Warned against arrogance.

DOWN:

2. The first part of his book is an acrostic.
3. Prophesied the Lord's judgement.
4. Spent 3 days and 3 nights in the belly of a large fish.
5. Lived as an exile in Babylon.
9. Son of Amoz.
10. He married Gomer, daughter of Diblaim.

SUDOKU

MATCH THE HIGHLIGHTED NUMBER SEQUENCE TO THE CHAPTER AND VERSE BELOW.

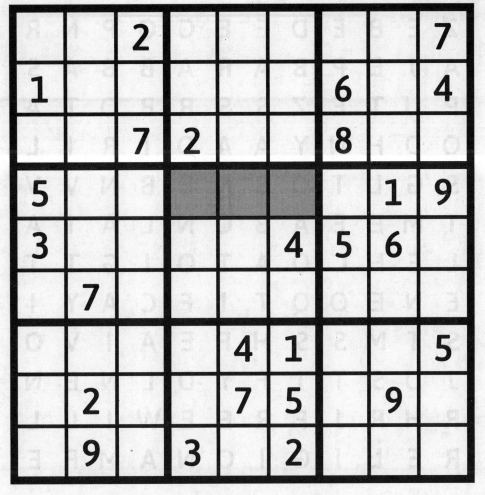

PSALMS _ : _ - _

"Be gracious to me, Lord, for I am weak;
heal me, Lord, for my bones are shaking;
my whole being is shaken with terror.
And You, Lord—how long?"

DEFINITION SEARCH

FIND ALL WORDS PLACED HORIZONTALLY, VERTICALLY, OR DIAGONALLY, AND MATCH THEM TO THE DEFINITIONS BELOW.

```
Z E B E D E E G Q P N R
A J E P B A R A B B A S
P U T E Z S S R B O T A
O D H N Y A A D I R I L
S G L T Q B N E B N V V
T M E E A B C N L A I A
L E H C O A T O I G T T
E N E O Q T I F C A Y I
S T M S S H F E A I V O
J U S T I F Y D L N E N
R H R J F R E E W I L L
R E L I G I O N A M F E
```

- Primary disciples of Jesus.
- The crowd chose to release him instead of Jesus.
- Birthplace of Christ.
- In accordance to the Bible.
- Rebirth in Christ (2 words).
- Voluntary choice (2 words).
- Idyllic place where God placed Adam (3 words).
- Final —.
- Clear away.
- Gospel scene of the birth of Jesus.
- Outpouring of the Holy Spirit to the Apostles.
- Services, rituals, and rules of a belief system.
- It is only found through Jesus.
- Make holy.
- Father of James and John.

PARABLES

"A man was going down from Jerusalem to Jericho and fell into the hands of robbers. They stripped him, beat him up, and fled, leaving him half dead. A priest happened to be going down that road. When he saw him, he passed by on the other side. In the same way, a Levite, when he arrived at the place and saw him, passed by on the other side. But a Samaritan on his journey came up to him, and when he saw the man, he had compassion. He went over to him and bandaged his wounds, pouring on olive oil and wine. Then he put him on his own animal, brought him to an inn, and took care of him.

The next day he took out two denarii, gave them to the innkeeper, and said, 'Take care of him. When I come back I'll reimburse you for whatever extra you spend.'

Which of these three do you think proved to be a neighbor to the man who fell into the hands of the robbers?"

Luke 10:30-36

WHAT DOES IT MEAN?

....
....
....
....
....
....
....
....
....
....
....
....
....
....
....
....

WHAT DOES IT MEAN?

....
....
....
....
....
....
....
....
....

"It is not those who are well who need a doctor, but those who are sick. I didn't come to call the righteous, but sinners."

Mark 2:17

THE RIGHT ONE

REWRITE THE LIST IN THE CORRECT ORDER.

11. **1 Timothy**	11.
12. **Titus**	12.
13. **Philippians**	13.
14. **Philemon**	14.
15. **James**	15.
16. **1 Thessalonians**	16.
17. **Hebrews**	17.
18. **Colossians**	18.
19. **2 Timothy**	19.
20. **2 Thessalonians**	20.

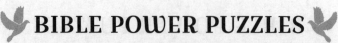

QUOTES

"How will it be known that I and your people have found favor with you unless you go with us?..."

BOOK:
....

CHAPTER:
....

VERSE:
....

BOOK:
....

CHAPTER:
....

VERSE:
....

"Above all, maintain constant love for one another, since love covers a multitude of sins."

"Don't be afraid, but keep on speaking and don't be silent."

BOOK:
....

CHAPTER:
....

VERSE:
....

UNSCRAMBLE

REARRANGE ONE WORD AT THE TIME, IN THE SAME ORDER THEY'RE PRESENTED, TO REVEAL THE PRECISE VERSE FROM THE SCRIPTURE.

1. I VEHA ENBE FICICRUED WHIT THIRSC, NAD I ON GERNOL VEIL, TUB THIRSC VEILS NI EM.

....

....

....

....

2. FI EW SECONFS URO NISS, EH SI THAIFULF NAD TEGHSOURI OT VEGIROF SU URO NISS NAD OT SENALEC SU MORF LAL NUTEGHSOURISNES.

....

....

....

....

3. I MA HET YAW, HET THURT, NAD HET FELI. ON EON SECOM OT HET THAERF PEXTEC THUORGH EM.

....

....

....

....

4. TUB OGD VESPRO SHI WON VELO ROF SU NI HATT HLEIW EW REWE SILTL NERNISS, THIRSC EDDI ROF SU.

....

....

....

....

"As soon as Martha heard that Jesus was coming, she went to meet him, but Mary remained seated in the house. Then Martha said to Jesus, 'Lord, hear my prayer; let my cry for help come before you. Do not hide your face from me in my day of trouble. Listen closely to me; answer me quickly when I call.'

'Your brother will rise again,' Jesus told her.

Martha said to him, 'I know that he will rise again in the resurrection at the last day.'

Jesus said to her, 'I am the resurrection and the life. The one who believes in me, even if he dies, will live. Everyone who lives and believes in me will never die. Do you believe this?' 'Yes, Lord,' she told him, 'I believe you are the Messiah, the Son of God, who comes into the world.'"

PIX-CROSS

SOLVE THE NONOGRAM TO REVEAL THE HIDDEN PICTURE.

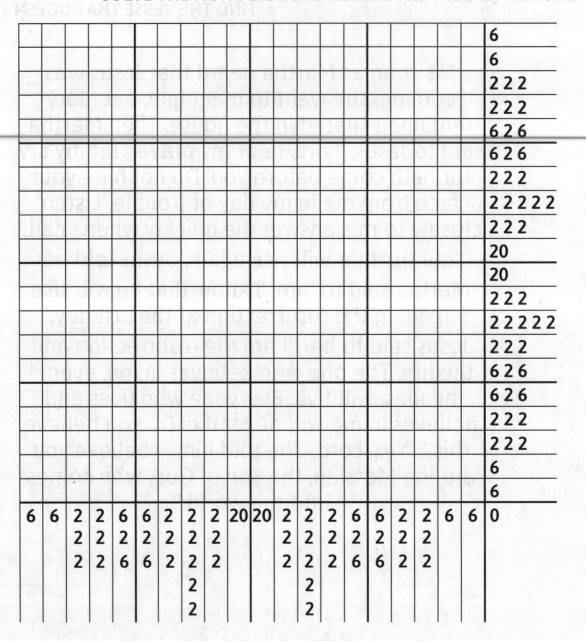

WORD-SEARCH

CONTAINED WITHIN THIS PUZZLE YOU MUST FIND THE CAPITALIZED WORDS FROM THE VERSES BELOW.

```
B L O S S O M S A D U
A P P E A R N O A A V
R L G W I N T E R R S
I B E A U T I F U L I
S E R D G H M T B I N
E T N K O E E P U N G
C A B D N A W A Y G I
L P N E E R I S R H N
K H M K J D Z T A T G
C O U N T R Y S I D E
C Q A A C O O I N G L
```

"**ARISE**, my **DARLING**.
Come **AWAY** my **BEAUTIFUL** one.
For now the **WINTER** is **PAST**; the **RAIN** has **ENDED** and **GONE** away.
The **BLOSSOMS APPEAR** in the **COUNTRYSIDE**.
The **TIME** of **SINGING** has **COME**, and the turtledove's **COOING** is **HEARD** in our **LAND**."

CRISS-CROSS

USE THE DEFINITIONS BELOW TO FIND THE WORDS AND GUESS THE THEME.

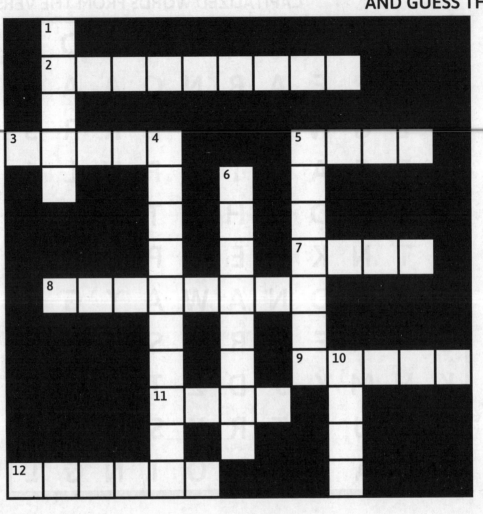

ACROSS:

2. Son of judge Gideon.

3. Murdered King Elah and all his family.

5. Fell on his sword to avoid capture in battle.

7. Built the city of Samaria.

8. The hand he pointed against a man of God withered.

9. Killed by Baasha at Gibbethon.

11. Son of Baasha.

12. Reigned in Tirzah for 24 years.

DOWN:

1. Arranged the death of Uriah the Hittite.

4. Proclaimed king by Abner.

5. Prayed the Lord for discernment and wisdom.

6. First king of the Kingdom of Judah.

10. Married Jezebel, who persuaded him against the Lord.

SUDOKU

MATCH THE HIGHLIGHTED NUMBER SEQUENCE
TO THE CHAPTER AND VERSE BELOW.

LUKE _ : _ - _

"The scribes and Pharisees were watching him closely, to see if he would heal on the Sabbath, so that they could find a charge against him. But he knew their thoughts and told the man with the shriveled hand, 'Get up and stand here.' So he got up and stood there."

LEVEL
1

🕊 **BIBLE POWER PUZZLES** 🕊

PAGE
063

DEFINITION SEARCH

FIND ALL WORDS PLACED HORIZONTALLY, VERTICALLY, OR DIAGONALLY, AND MATCH THEM TO THE DEFINITIONS BELOW.

```
K  P  U  R  G  A  T  O  R  Y  S  E  O  Y
I  D  D  E  L  W  L  K  E  C  D  T  R  M
N  M  P  P  Z  C  A  C  G  D  E  E  I  I
G  L  J  E  Z  Z  S  B  E  R  U  R  G  M
D  E  E  N  A  C  T  W  N  E  T  N  I  M
O  V  R  T  B  M  S  F  E  I  E  A  N  O
M  I  U  A  G  D  U  M  R  F  R  L  A  R
O  T  S  N  L  D  P  I  A  D  O  L  L  T
F  I  A  C  J  J  P  R  T  V  N  I  S  A
G  C  L  E  M  S  E  A  I  S  O  F  I  L
O  U  E  N  Y  T  R  C  O  F  M  E  N  I
D  S  M  L  Z  G  U  L  N  R  Y  J  W  T
A  F  O  R  G  I  V  E  N  E  S  S  P  Y
L  H  O  J  E  S  U  S  C  H  R  I  S  T
```

- Fifth book of the Old Testament.
- Continued life after death (2 words).
- Act of pardon.
- Third person of the Trinity (2 words).
- Perpetual life which only God possesses.
- The city of David, a.k.a. Zion.
- Our Lord and Savior (2 words).
- Realm where people enjoy the blessings of the Lord's rule (3 words).
- Final meal that Jesus shared with his Apostles (2 words).
- Third book of the Old Testament.
- Jesus performed them.
- Adam and Eve's disobedient arrogance (2 words).
- Expiatory state as believed by some Christians to occur after death.
- The work of God in a believer's life.
- Turning away from sin.

PARABLES

WHAT DOES IT MEAN?

....

....

....

....

....

....

"Truly I tell you, anyone who doesn't enter the sheep pen by the gate but climbs in some other way is a thief and a robber. The one who enters by the gate is the shepherd of the sheep. The gatekeeper opens it for him, and the sheep hear his voice. He call his own sheep by name and leads them out."

John 10:1-3

WHAT DOES IT MEAN?

....

....

....

....

....

....

....

"Truly I tell you, I am the gate for the sheep. All who came before me are thieves and robbers, but the sheep didn't listen to them.

I am the gate. If anyone enters by me, he will be saved and will come in and go out and find pasture."

John 10:7-9

WHAT DOES IT MEAN?

....

....

....

....

....

....

"I am the good shepherd. I know my own and my own know me, just as the Father knows me, and I know the Father. I lay down my life for the sheep. But I have other sheep that are not from this sheep pen; I must bring them also, and they will listen to my voice. Then there will be one flock, one shepherd."

John 10:14-16

THE RIGHT ONE

REWRITE THE LIST IN THE CORRECT ORDER.

21. 1 John	21.
22. Jude	22.
23. 2 Peter	23.
24. Revelation	24.
25. 3 John	25.
26. 1 Peter	26.
27. 2 John	27.

QUOTES

IDENTIFY THE PROPER BOOK, CHAPTER, AND VERSE
THESE BIBLE QUOTATIONS BELONG TO.

"...Am I my brother's guardian?"

BOOK:

CHAPTER:

....

VERSE:

....

BOOK:

....

CHAPTER:

....

VERSE:

....

"...Look, I am the one who has sinned; I am the one who has done wrong. But these sheep, what have they done? Please let your hand be against me and my father's family."

"Offenses will certainly come, but woe to the one through whom they come!"

BOOK:

CHAPTER:

....

VERSE:

....

UNSCRAMBLE

REARRANGE ONE WORD AT THE TIME, IN THE SAME ORDER THEY'RE PRESENTED, TO REVEAL THE PRECISE VERSE FROM THE SCRIPTURE.

1. NAD HET CEPAE FO OGD, CHIHW PASURSSES LAL STANNUDERDING, LLIW DARGU RUYO HASRET NAD DIMNS NI HIRSTC SUJES.

....
....
....
....

2. OD TON EB DIFRAA RO DEGACOURSID, ROF HET ROLD OYUR OGD SI THIW OYU HEVERREW OYU OG.

....
....
....

3. ... SEOTH HOW URSTT HET ROLD ILWL WEREN THREI THERNSTG; HETY ILWL RASO NO NIGWS KELI GLEASE...

....
....
....
....

4. LAL TUREPRISC SI DEPIRSIN YB OGD NADSI FIROPTEBLA FRO ICHANGTE, ROF KINGBURE, ROF RECCORTING, ROF NINIGRAT NI RISENGHOUSSET...

....
....
....

VERSE-SPOTTING

FIND THE VERSE THAT DOESN'T BELONG.

"When Joshua was near Jericho, he looked up and saw a man standing in front of him with a drawn sword in his hand. Joshua approached him and asked, 'Are you for us or for our enemies?'

'Neither', he replied. 'Don't let your heart be troubled. Believe in God; believe also in me.'

The Joshua bowed with his face to the ground in worship and asked him, 'What does my lord want to say to his servant?'"

PIX-CROSS

SOLVE THE NONOGRAM TO REVEAL THE HIDDEN PICTURE.

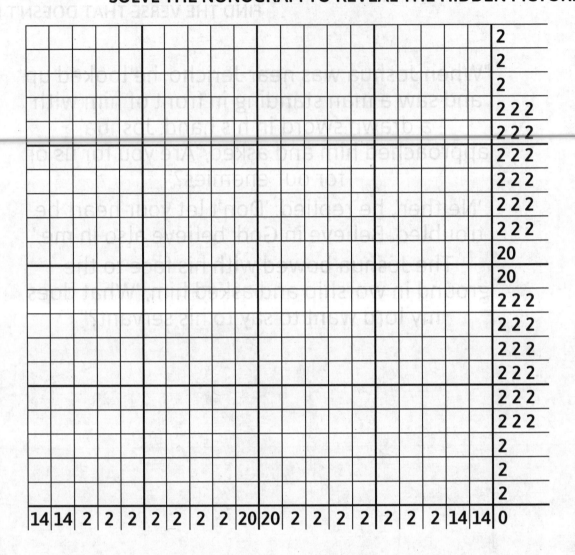

Row clues (top to bottom):
2
2
2
2 2 2
2 2 2
2 2 2
2 2 2
2 2 2
2 2 2
20
20
2 2 2
2 2 2
2 2 2
2 2 2
2 2 2
2 2 2
2
2
2

Column clues (left to right):
14 14 2 2 2 2 2 2 2 20 20 2 2 2 2 2 2 2 14 14 0

WORD-SEARCH

CONTAINED WITHIN THIS PUZZLE YOU MUST FIND THE CAPITALIZED WORDS FROM THE VERSES BELOW.

```
T H I R S T Y B W O D
W J E S H U R U N F L
O N E L M Q S E G F O
R S D K P A S C G S R
D E P I I O K R A P D
F R V O H M B E R R T
O V P C U O W T R I F
R A A Q C R U W R N E
M N W A T E R I O G A
E T J F I N P B U M R
D B L E S S I N G G B
```

"This is the **WORD** of the **LORD** your **MAKER**, the **ONE** who **FORMED** you from the **WOMB**: He will **HELP** you.

Do not **FEAR**, **JACOB** my **SERVANT**, **JESHURUN** whom I have **CHOSEN**.

For I will **POUR WATER** on this **THIRSTY** land and streams on the dry ground; I will pour out my **SPIRIT** on your descendants and my **BLESSING** on your **OFFSPRING**."

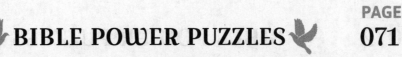

CRISS-CROSS

USE THE DEFINITIONS BELOW TO FIND THE WORDS AND GUESS THE THEME.

ACROSS:

3. Ruled over the Kingdom of Israel for 41 years (number at the end).

4. Grandson of Solomon.

8. Killed by his officer Pekah in Samaria.

9. Succeeded by his brother Joram.

10. Overthrown by Hoshea.

12. Removed the sacred pillar of Baal his father made.

13. The king of Aram destroyed most of his army.

DOWN:

1. Killed Tiphsah's pregnant women.

2. Caught in a conspiracy and imprisoned.

5. Visited prophet Elisha at his deathbed.

6. Killed by Menahem.

7. Son of Jeroboam II.

11. Eliminated Baal worship from Israel.

SUDOKU

MATCH THE HIGHLIGHTED NUMBER SEQUENCE TO THE CHAPTER AND VERSE BELOW.

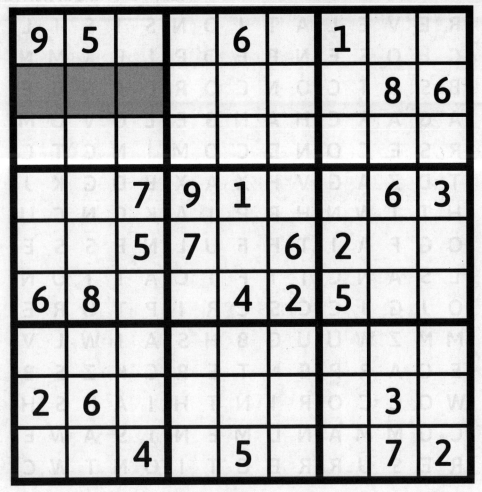

JEREMIAH _ : _ - _

"This is the word that came to Jeremiah from the LORD: 'Stand in the gate of the house of the LORD, and there call out this word: Hear the word of the LORD, all you people of Judah who enter through these gates to worship the LORD.'"

DEFINITION SEARCH

FIND ALL WORDS PLACED HORIZONTALLY, VERTICALLY, OR DIAGONALLY,
AND MATCH THEM TO THE DEFINITIONS BELOW.

```
R E V E L A T I O N S I S I L
C H O S E N P E O P L E K M N
B S N T C O N C O R D A N C E
A G A R C H A N G E L O V O M
R S E C O N D C O M I N G T C
T D Z A G V H X A X B D G K J
H T T W N H R P I A K C N C U
O G F A I T H F U L N E S S E
L S A N C T I F I C A T I O N
O J G J C C S C R I P T U R E
M M Z W U U G B H S A I W L V
E C A R P E N T E R C K Z S B
W O C C O R I N T H I A N S H
C O M M A N D M E N T S A W E
R E S U R R E C T I O N T W C
```

- Re: 1 John 2: 22.
- High-ranking angel.
- A friend of apostle Philip, identified as Nathanael in the gospel of John.
- Joseph's craft.
- Israelites and Christians (2 words).
- Ten were given to Moses.
- Harmony between facts and teachings.
- Residents of Corinth.
- Roman torture and execution method inflicted upon Jesus.
- Quality of being steadfast.
- Rising of Christ on the third day after his crucifixion.
- Last book of the New Testament.
- Process of making something holy.
- The Christian holy writings.
- Christ's return as judge of all mankind (2 words).

PARABLES

WHAT DOES IT MEAN?

....
....
....
....
....
....

"You can't make the wedding guests fast while the groom is with them, can you? But the time will come when the groom will be taken from them—then they will fast in those days."

Luke 5:34-35

WHAT DOES IT MEAN?

....
....
....
....
....
....
....
....
....
....

"The kingdom of heaven is like a treasure, buried in a field, that a man found and reburied. Then in his joy he goes and sells everything he has and buys that field."

Matthew 13:44

"Again, the kingdom of heaven is like a merchant in search of fine pearls. When he found one priceless pearl, he went and sold everything he had and bought it."

Matthew 13:45-46

WHAT DOES IT MEAN?

....
....
....
....
....
....
....

THE RIGHT ONE

REWRITE THE LIST IN THE CORRECT ORDER.

1. No coveting of his good or his goods.	1.
2. No taking away of a neighbor's life.	2.
3. No desecration of God's day.	3.
4. No taking away his good name.	4.
5. No image of God.	5.
6. No taking away of his wife, his dearest good.	6.
7. No dishonoring God's representatives (parents).	7.
8. No dishonoring God's name.	8.
9. No other gods.	9.
10. No taking away his goods.	10.

PAGE
076

 BIBLE POWER PUZZLES

LEVEL
1

QUOTES

"We will worship the Lord our God and obey him."

BOOK:
....

CHAPTER:
....

VERSE:
....

BOOK:
....

CHAPTER:
....

VERSE:
....

"You observe my travels and my rest; you are aware of all my ways."

"You are mistaken, because you don't know the Scriptures or the power of God."

BOOK:
....

CHAPTER:
....

VERSE:
....

UNSCRAMBLE

REARRANGE ONE WORD AT THE TIME, IN THE SAME ORDER THEY'RE PRESENTED, TO REVEAL THE PRECISE VERSE FROM THE SCRIPTURE.

1. TUB EKES SIRTF HET DOMKING FO OGD NAD SIH RISENGHOUSSET, NAD LAL ESETH NIGSTH ILWL EB VIDEPROD ROF OYU.

....
....
....
....

2. ... PEEKING URO YEES NO SUJES, HET CERUOS NAD FECTERREP FO URO THIAF.

....
....
....

3. HEUBLM OYURVELESS, FOREERETH, DERNU HET THIGMY NADH FO OGD, OS AHTT EH YAM XELTA OYU TA HET PEROPR METI...

....
....
....
....

4. ROF EW REA SIH MANOWRKHIPS, TEDREAC NI HIRSTC SUJES ROF ODOG KORWS, CHIHW OGD PAREPRED HADEA FO METI ROF SU OT OD.

....
....
....

VERSE-SPOTTING

FIND THE VERSE THAT DOESN'T BELONG.

"After this, Jesus crossed to the sea of Galilee (or Tiberias). A huge crowd was following him because they saw the signs that he was performing by healing the sick. Jesus went up a mountain and sat down there with his disciples.

Now the Passover, a Jewish festival, was near. So when Jesus looked up and noticed a huge crowd coming toward him, he asked Philip, 'Quick! Knead three measures of fine flour and make bread.'

He asked this to test him, for he himself knew what he was going to do."

PIX-CROSS

SOLVE THE NONOGRAM TO REVEAL THE HIDDEN PICTURE.

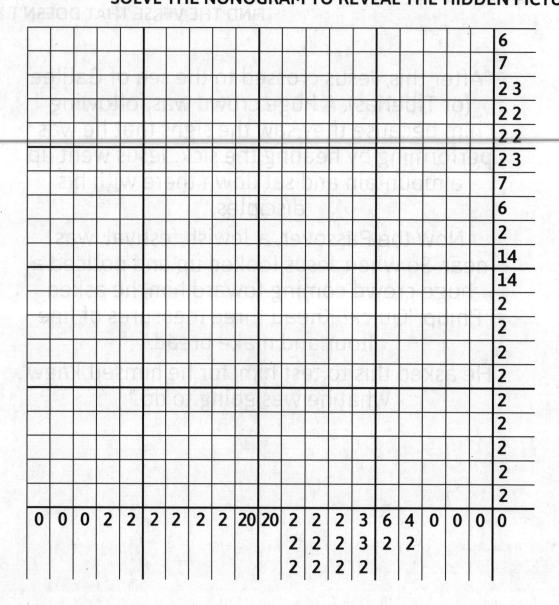

WORD-SEARCH

CONTAINED WITHIN THIS PUZZLE YOU MUST FIND THE CAPITALIZED WORDS FROM THE VERSES BELOW.

```
E G R A C I O U S N E S S
A V O A D P E T I T I O N
S E E O N P R D A F L X M
G V G R O Y S A R T S A Y
Z E U L Y K T P Y Q Z P K
R R V Q O O J H Z E Y R C
E Y R H X R N G I S R E C
Q T P N Z N D E Y N X S B
U H Q E X N O A D X G E K
E I Z A G Y W O R R Y N N
S N Y R V L A G A I N T O
T G Y E A R E J O I C E W
T H A N K S G I V I N G N
```

"**REJOICE** in the **LORD ALWAYS**. I will **SAY** it **AGAIN**: Rejoice! Let your **GRACIOUSNESS** be **KNOWN** to **EVERYONE**. The Lord is **NEAR**. Don't **WORRY** about **ANYTHING**, but in **EVERYTHING**, through **PRAYER** and **PETITION** with **THANKSGIVING, PRESENT** your **REQUEST** to **GOD**."

CRISS-CROSS

USE THE DEFINITIONS BELOW TO FIND THE WORDS AND GUESS THE THEME.

ACROSS:

2. Built the Upper Gate of the Temple of Jerusalem.

5. Killed by his servants, who in turn were killed by the common folk.

7. Executed by order of the priest Jehoiada.

9. Sacrificed his son in the fire.

10. Son of Asa.

11. Became king when he was 7 years old.

DOWN:

1. Struck with leprosy for disobeying God.

2. Commissioned Temple repairs.

3. Prophets Hosea and Micah lived during his reign.

4. Believed in astrology.

6. Shot in his chariot.

8. Received a letter from Elijah condemning him.

9. Sought only the aid of physicians to heal his foot.

SUDOKU

MATCH THE HIGHLIGHTED NUMBER SEQUENCE TO THE CHAPTER AND VERSE BELOW.

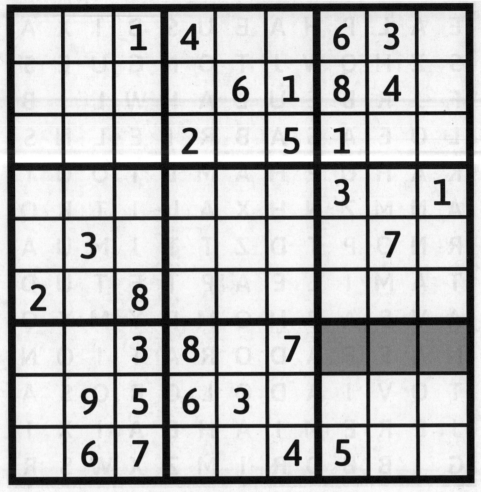

1 TIMOTHY _ : _ - _

"If you point these things out to the brothers and sisters, you will be a good servant of Christ Jesus, nourished by the words of the faith and the good teaching that you have followed. But have nothing to do with pointless and silly myths. Rather, train yourself in godliness. For the training of the body has limited benefit, but godliness is beneficial in every way, since it holds promise for the present life and also for the life to come. This saying is trustworthy and deserves full acceptance."

DEFINITION SEARCH

FIND ALL WORDS PLACED HORIZONTALLY, VERTICALLY, OR DIAGONALLY,
AND MATCH THEM TO THE DEFINITIONS BELOW.

```
E A L P H A E U S B I X A
S Z H Q W J T O N G U E S
F J R B E U L A H W L I B
L O E A G A B R I E L N S
K A H U P H A M L I O U Y
A N M Z N H X A U I T R Q
R N O P T D Z T T I M U A
T A M I L E A P T E T U D
A V B A B H O M P Y M Y O
N A F F A D O R A T I O N
T Q V I A D O L O R O S A
J E R E M I A H B A I X I
G I B B O R I M Z X W S R
```

- Plural form of "adon" ("Lord").
- Worship given to God alone.
- Assuming the parenting of another.
- Father of Matthew and James.
- Chief artisan who made the Tabernacle.
- Married
- One of Paul's converts in Athens.
- OT book continuing Chronicles.
- Angel who brought important messages to Daniel, Zechariah, and Mary.
- Mighty men.
- Son of Benjamin.
- Second among the major prophets.
- Managed the household of Herod Antipas.
- Levitical town allotted to the descendants of Gershon.
- Instrument for artificial lighting.
- Raised from the dead by Peter.
- Greek follower and helper of Paul.
- Gift of —.
- Traditional route of Jesus to Golgotha (Latin, 2 words).

PAGE
084

BIBLE POWER PUZZLES

LEVEL
1

PARABLES

"He told a parable to those who were invited, when he noticed how they would choose the best places for themselves: 'When you are invited by someone to a wedding banquet, don't recline at the best place, because a more distinguished person than you may have been invited by your host. The one who invited both of you may come and say to you, 'Give your place to this man,' and then in humiliation, you will proceed to take the lowest place.

But when you are invited, go and recline in the lowest place, so that when the one who invited you comes, he will say to you, 'Friend, move up higher.' You will then be honored in the presence of all the other guests."

Luke 14:7-10

WHAT DOES IT MEAN?

....

....

....

....

....

....

....

....

WHAT DOES IT MEAN?

....

....

....

....

....

....

....

....

"...every teacher of the law who has become a disciple in the kingdom of heaven is like the owner of a house who brings out of his storeroom treasures new and old."

Matthew 13:52

THE RIGHT ONE

1. Jesus Himself.	1.
2. Lazarus after three days, by Jesus.	2.
3. Many holy people after Jesus died on the cross.	3.
4. Man raised after touching Elisha's bones.	4.
5. Dorcas by Peter.	5.
6. Widow of Nain's son, by Jesus.	6.
7. Eutychus, by Paul.	7.
8. Shunammite woman's son, by Elisha.	8.
9. Jairus' daughter, by Jesus.	9.
10. Widow of Zarephath's son, by Elijah.	10.

QUOTES

"...I will go down to Sheol to my son, mourning..."

BOOK:

....

CHAPTER:

....

VERSE:

....

BOOK:

....

CHAPTER:

....

VERSE:

....

"The LORD will reign forever and ever!"

"God arises. His enemies scatter, and those who hate him flee from his presence."

BOOK:

....

CHAPTER:

....

VERSE:

....

UNSCRAMBLE

REARRANGE ONE WORD AT THE TIME, IN THE SAME ORDER THEY'RE PRESENTED, TO REVEAL THE PRECISE VERSE FROM THE SCRIPTURE.

1. ON TATTINOPEM SHA MECO PUNO OYU CEPEXT THAW SI MONOMC OT MAHUTINY.

....

....

....

....

2. MECO OT EM, LAL FO OYU HOW REA RYAWE NAD DEBURNED, NAD I ILWL VEGI OYU SETR.

....

....

....

....

3. WON THIAF SI HET ARELITY FO HAWT SI PEDOH ROF, HET FOPRO FO HAWT SI TON ESEN.

....

....

....

....

4. REREFOHET, FI OYNENA SI NI HRISTC, EH SI A WEN ECRATION; HET LOD SAH SEDSAP YAWA, NAD ESE, HET WEN SAH MECO!

....

....

....

....

VERSE-SPOTTING

"When they had crossed over, Elijah said to Elisha, 'Tell me what I can do for you before I am taken from you.'

So Elisha answered, 'Please, let me inherit two shares of your spirit.'

Elijah replied, 'You have asked for something difficult. If anyone wants to follow me, let him deny himself, take up his cross daily, and follow me.'

As they continued walking and talking, a chariot of fire with horses of fire suddenly appeared and separated the two of them.

Then Elijah went up into heaven in the whirlwind. As Elisha watched, he kept crying out, 'My father, my father, the chariots and horsemen of Israel!'"

PIX-CROSS

SOLVE THE NONOGRAM TO REVEAL THE HIDDEN PICTURE.

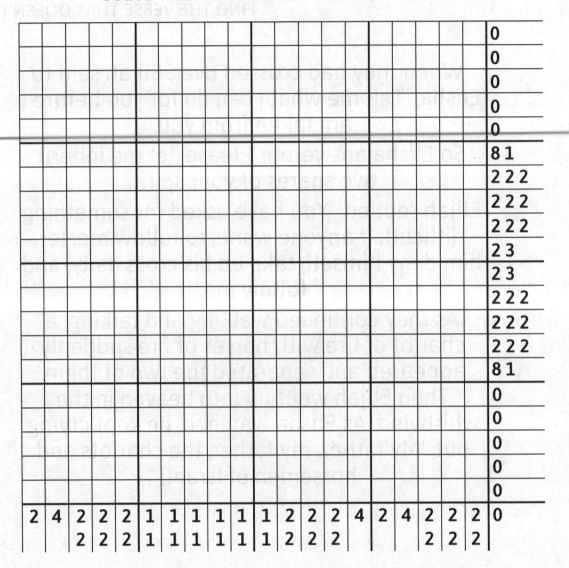

WORD-SEARCH

CONTAINED WITHIN THIS PUZZLE YOU MUST FIND THE CAPITALIZED WORDS FROM THE VERSES BELOW.

```
C Z V P E H U M B L E Z
B L E S S E D E E N J L
M S X F M E R C Y C A H
E B U F L U P Q I R T T
R V E F P W U J E R S N
C R L X I C E G A R E F
I M O U R N N E I V S I
F P O O R U H H A W P L
U V D C H D T E P F I L
L R R Q O G H A R L R E
K I N G D O M R L I I D
Y C O M F O R T E D T F
```

"**BLESSED** are the **POOR** in **SPIRIT**, for the **KINGDOM** of **HEAVEN** is theirs.
Blessed are those who **MOURN**, for they will be **COMFORTED**.
Blessed are the **HUMBLE**, for they will **INHERIT** the **EARTH**.
Blessed are those who **HUNGER** and **THIRST** for **RIGHTEOUSNESS**, for they will be **FILLED**.
Blessed are the **MERCIFUL**, for they will be shown **MERCY**.
Blessed are the **PURE** of **HEART**, for they will see **GOD**."

CRISS-CROSS

USE THE DEFINITIONS BELOW TO FIND THE WORDS AND GUESS THE THEME.

ACROSS:

1. The Israelites rejected him at first.
4. Samuel's second evil son.
7. Deborah's general.
8. Spoke to an angel under an oak.
10. The first judge.
11. Realized the Lord's call for Samuel.
13. Samuel's first-born evil son.
15. Wife of Lappidoth.
17. The strongest judge.

DOWN:

1. Judged Israel for 22 years.
2. Murdered 69 out of his 70 brothers.
3. Killed 600 Philistines with a cattle prod.
5. Had 40 sons and 30 grandsons who rode on 70 donkeys.
6. Was also a prophet.
9. Lived in the hill country of Ephraim.
12. Had 30 sons and 30 daughters.
14. He was left-handed.
16. Originally from Zebulun.

SUDOKU

MATCH THE HIGHLIGHTED NUMBER SEQUENCE TO THE CHAPTER AND VERSE BELOW.

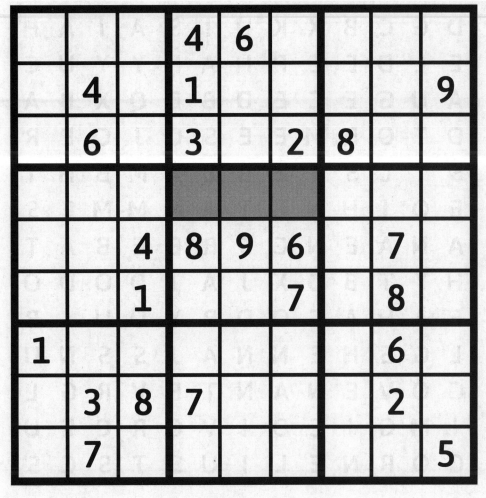

2 SAMUEL _ : _ - _

"All the tribes of Israel came to David at Hebron and said, 'Here we are, your own flesh and blood. Even while Saul was king over us, you were the one who led us out to battle and brought us back. The LORD also said to you, 'You will shepherd my people Israel, and you will be ruler over Israel.'

So all the elders of Israel came to the king at Hebron. King David made a covenant with them at Hebron in the LORD's presence, and they anointed David king over Israel."

DEFINITION SEARCH

FIND ALL WORDS PLACED HORIZONTALLY, VERTICALLY, OR DIAGONALLY, AND MATCH THEM TO THE DEFINITIONS BELOW.

```
D G C B X K U I S A I A H
E L D E E P H A H Y Y U C
A U G E C E D B D Q X B A
D T O R M E E S O J C E R
S T L S I E B L A M B H I
E O I H N L T A M M M E S
A N A E N C S R B E B A T
H Y T B O X J A I D O D O
E A H A C O D R Y U U I B
L G E H E N N A J S S N U
C O V E N A N T E V R G L
I M G I C D I V O R C E U
C O R N E L I U S T S C S
```

- Mount —.
- One of Paul's disciples in Rome.
- Hagar wandered the wilderness there.
- Method of execution suffered by John the Baptist.
- Devout and God-fearing centurion.
- A pact between God and men, and vice-versa.
- — —Scrolls (2 words).
- Raised a mob against Paul.
- Forgive us our —...
- Public dissolution of marriage.
- Grandfather of judge Tola.
- One of Caleb's concubines.
- Likened to hell.
- Opposite of abstinence.
- Killed by David using a slingshot.
- Freedom from guilt.
- Prophesied four reigns of kings of Judah.
- —of God.

PARABLES

"For the kingdom of heaven is like a landowner who went out early in the morning to hire workers for his vineyard. After agreeing with the workers on one denarius, he sent them into his vineyard for the day. When he went out about nine in the morning, he saw others standing in the marketplace doing nothing. He said to them, 'You also go to my vineyard, and I'll give you whatever is right.' So off they went. About noon and about three, he went out again and did the same thing. Then about five he went and found others standing around and said to them, 'Why have you been standing here all day doing nothing?' 'Because no one hired us,' they said to him. 'You also go to my vineyard,' he told them. When evening came, the owner of the vineyard told his foreman, 'Call the workers and give them their pay, starting with the last and ending with the first.' When those who were hired about five came, they each received one denarius. So when the first ones came, they assumed they would get more, but they also received a denarius each. When they received it, they began to complain to the landowner: 'These last men put in one hour, and you made them equal to us who bore the burden of the day and the burning heat.' He replied to one of them, 'Friend, I'm doing you no wrong. Didn't you agree with me on a denarius? Take what's yours and go. I want to give this last man the same as I gave you. Don't I have the right to do what I want with what is mine? Are you jealous because I'm generous?'

So the last will be first, and the first last."

Matthew 20:1-16

WHAT DOES IT MEAN?

. . . .
. . . .
. . . .
. . . .
. . . .
. . . .
. . . .

WHAT DOES IT MEAN?

. . . .
. . . .
. . . .
. . . .
. . . .
. . . .
. . . .
. . . .

"A prophet is not without honor except in his hometown and in his household."

Matthew 13:57

THE RIGHT ONE

REWRITE THE LIST IN THE CORRECT ORDER.

1. "Eli, Eli, lema sabachthani?"	1.
2. "Father, into your hands I entrust my spirit."	2.
3. "It is finished."	3.
4. "Truly I tell you, today you will be with me in paradise."	4.
5. "I'm thirsty."	5.
6. "Father, forgive them, because they do not know what they are doing."	6.
7. "Woman, here is your son." "Here is your mother."	7.

QUOTES

"The one who loves silver is never satisfied with silver, and whoever loves wealth is never satisfied with income. This too is futile."

BOOK:

....

CHAPTER:

....

VERSE:

....

BOOK:

....

CHAPTER:

....

VERSE:

....

"Be silent, and come out of him!"

"Take this man away! Release Barabbas to us!"

BOOK:

....

CHAPTER:

....

VERSE:

....

UNSCRAMBLE

REARRANGE ONE WORD AT THE TIME, IN THE SAME ORDER THEY'RE PRESENTED, TO REVEAL THE PRECISE VERSE FROM THE SCRIPTURE.

1. PEEK OYUR FELI REFE MORF HET VELO FO NOMEY.

....
....
....
....

2. YM CERAG SI FIFUSCIENT ROF OYU, ROF YM WOPER SI FECPERTED NI ASWEKNES.

....
....
....
....

3. FI OYU FESNOCS WHIT OYUR THOUM, "SUJES SI ORLD," NAD LEVEBEI NI OYUR THARE HATT OGD SEDAIR IHM MORF HET DADE, OYU ILWL EB VEDAS.

....
....
....
....

4. OD TON AREF, ROF I MA WHIT OYU; OD TON EB RAFAID, ROF I MA OYUR OGD.

....
....
....

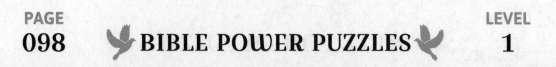

VERSE-SPOTTING

FIND THE VERSE THAT DOESN'T BELONG.

"When Herod was about to bring him out for trial, that very night Peter, bound with two chains, was sleeping between two soldiers, while the sentries in front of the door guarded the prison. Suddenly an angel of the Lord appeared, and a light shone in the cell. Striking Peter on the side, he woke him up and said, 'Quick, get up!' And the chains fell off his wrists. 'Get dressed,' the angel told him, 'and put on your sandals.' And he did. 'The LORD is with you, valiant warrior' he told him. So he went out and followed, and he did not know that what the angel did was really happening, but thought he was seeing a vision."

PIX-CROSS

SOLVE THE NONOGRAM TO REVEAL THE HIDDEN PICTURE.

Row clues
1
1
1
1
5
1
1
2 2 1 2 3
2 2 1 2 5
2 2 1 2 3 2
2 2 1 2 2
2 2 1 2 3
2 9 4
2 9 3
2 2 2 2
2 2 2 2
2 2 2 2
2 2 2 2 3
2 2 2 5
2 2 2 3

Column clues:

13	13	0	0	13	13	1 2	1 2	14	1 2	1 2	13	13	0	3 2	5 3	3 2 2	2 2 3	3 7	2 5	0

WORD-SEARCH

CONTAINED WITHIN THIS PUZZLE YOU MUST FIND ALL CAPITALIZED WORDS FROM THE VERSES BELOW.

```
N B O J A O C F A I T H F U L
A Y Q F V P Q K P A T H S D T
N V I N M S X N A U F E Z I F
C O M P A S S I O N R V A G Y
F U T D K G R Y K N O W N C X
C L V R M L I C O E L Z A S H
X R E B E L L I O N E S R Y Q
F Q S U T M T O N O T P T P S
X C Y C M A E C R W J I I S V
R J T W V P B M M B U O E N W
A P A L O V E P B Q O N A R G
B A A O V Y I Q I E D U K K N
C S H R T R U T H O R S S H O
H E E D O A N S O L N Z H S H
G A W G C A C G U I D E J B Z
```

"Make your **WAYS KNOWN** to me, **LORD**; teach me your **PATHS**.
GUIDE me in your **TRUTH** and **TEACH** me, for you are the God of my **SALVATION**;
I **WAIT** for you all day long.
REMEMBER, Lord, your **COMPASSION** and your **FAITHFUL LOVE**, for they have existed from **ANTIQUITY**.
Do not remember the sins of my **YOUTH** or my acts of **REBELLION**;
in **KEEPING** with your faithful love, remember me because of your **GOODNESS**, Lord."

CRISS-CROSS

USE THE DEFINITIONS BELOW TO FIND THE WORDS AND GUESS THE THEME.

ACROSS:
1. Died at age 910.
4. Died at age 930.
7. Died at age 912.
9. Died at age 962.
10. Died at age 969.

DOWN:
2. Died at age 905.
3. Died at age 950.
5. Died at age 895.
6. Died at age 777.
8. Taken by God at age 365.

SUDOKU

MATTHEW _ : _ - _

"When he came down from the mountain, large crowds followed him. Right away a man with leprosy came up and knelt before him, saying, 'Lord, if you are willing, you can make me clean.' Reaching out his hand, Jesus touched him, saying, 'I am willing; be made clean.' Immediately his leprosy was cleansed."

DEFINITION SEARCH

FIND ALL WORDS PLACED HORIZONTALLY, VERTICALLY, OR DIAGONALLY, AND MATCH THEM TO THE DEFINITIONS BELOW.

```
A Z R I E L H D X C A M M Y S
J B T F N X A E G Y P T F U F
T A Z O E D W Y C M O S T A F
R R X R L W R W L M Q C C H O
U I B E E Q T A R M I P O I R
M M E S A U B I B D G E L M T
P A N K Z E S B E J M S O E U
E T O I A X Q N R T C I S L N
T H N N R H E I N O H X S E A
X E I I T B X R I E E M I C T
M A I S R E U H C L R E A H U
S B N L H H A Y E B U X N Y S
R U R W N Y G K Q G B E S T I
E Z I E X L U Q B R I F H S R
J I B K P L U U R Q M U A I L
```

- Helping David cost him his life.
- Went before the cart that carried the Ark of the Covenant.
- Home town of the man who buried Jesus in his own tomb.
- Chief of the half-tribe of Menasseh.
- Zechariah's thanksgiving hymn (Latin).
- Supplied provisions for Solomon (2 w.).
- Original name of Benjamin (2 words).
- Daughter of Herod Agrippa I.
- Father of Ezekiel.
- Guardian angels.
- People from the ancient city of Colosse.

- Mount at the foot of which Jacob's well was located.
- Country in the NE corner of Africa.
- Sixth son of Benjamin.
- One of seventy elders chosen by Moses.
- Aaron's first-born.
- Prepuce.
- Prominent member of the Corinthian church.
- "Jesus Nazarene King of the Jews" (Latin abbr.).
- Instrument used to signal the beginning of battle.

PARABLES

"A man planted a vineyard, put a fence around it, dug out a pit for a winepress, and built a watchtower. Then he leased it to tenant farmers and went away.

At harvest time he sent a servant to the farmers to collect some of the fruit of the vineyard from them. But they took him, beat him, and sent him away empty-handed. Again he sent another servant to them, and they hit him on the head and treated him shamefully. Then he sent another, and they killed that one. He also sent many others; some they beat, and others they killed.

He still had one to send, a beloved son. Finally he sent him to them, saying, 'They will respect my son'. But those tenant farmers said to one another, 'This is the heir. Come, let's kill him, and the inheritance will be ours.' So they seized him, killed him, and threw him out of the vineyard.

What then will the owner of the vineyard do? He will come and kill the farmers and give the vineyard to others.

Haven't you read this Scripture:

The stone that the builders rejected has become the cornerstone. This came about from the Lord and is wonderful in our eyes?"

Mark 12:1-11

WHAT DOES IT MEAN?

. . . .
. . . .
. . . .
. . . .
. . . .
. . . .
. . . .
. . . .
. . . .
. . . .

WHAT DOES IT MEAN?

. . . .
. . . .
. . . .
. . . .
. . . .

"Or what king, going to war against another king, will not first sit down and decide if he is able with ten thousand to oppose the one who comes against him with twenty thousand? If not, while the other is still far off, he sends a delegation and asks for terms of peace. In the same way, therefore, every one who does not renounce all his possessions cannot be my disciple."

Luke 14:31-33

THE RIGHT ONE

REWRITE THE LIST IN THE CORRECT ORDER.

1. **Anointing of the Sick**	1.
2. **Holy Orders**	2.
3. **Confession**	3.
4. **Marriage**	4.
5. **Holy Communion**	5.
6. **Confirmation**	6.
7. **Baptism**	7.

QUOTES

IDENTIFY THE PROPER BOOK, CHAPTER, AND VERSE THESE BIBLE QUOTATIONS BELONG TO.

"I will gladly go with you, but you will receive no honor on the road you are about to take, because the LORD will sell Sisera to a woman."

BOOK:

....

CHAPTER:

....

VERSE:

....

BOOK:

....

CHAPTER:

....

VERSE:

....

"Yet I prefer to speak to the Almighty and argue my case before God."

"Tabitha, get up."

BOOK:

....

CHAPTER:

....

VERSE:

....

UNSCRAMBLE

REARRANGE ONE WORD AT THE TIME, IN THE SAME ORDER THEY'RE PRESENTED, TO REVEAL THE PRECISE VERSE FROM THE SCRIPTURE.

1. TEL SU KEMA AMN NI RUO AMIGE, CORCADING OT RUO NESILKES.

....

....

....

....

2. KETA PU YM KEOY NAD LAREN ROMF EM, CAUBESE I MA WOLYL NAD HEBLUM NI HARET, NAD OYU ILWL NIFD TRES ROF OYUR USOLS.

....

....

....

....

3. I VEHA LODT OYU HESET HINGST OS HATT NI EM OYU YAM VEHA PACEE.

....

....

....

....

4. TI SI TON ROF OYU OT WONK MESIT RO REIODPS HATT HET THERFA SAH TES YB SIH WON THAUROITY.

....

....

....

....

VERSE-SPOTTING

FIND THE VERSE THAT DOESN'T BELONG.

"At dawn he went to the temple again, and all the people were coming to him. He sat down and began to teach them.

Then the scribes and the Pharisees brought a woman caught in adultery, making her stand in the center. 'Teacher,' they said to Him, 'this woman was caught in the act of committing adultery. In the law Moses commanded us to stone such women. So what do you say?' They asked this to trap him, in order that they might have evidence to accuse Him.

Jesus stooped down and started writing on the ground with his finger. When they persisted in questioning him, he stood up and said to them, 'The one without sin among you should be the first to throw a stone at her.'

Then he stooped down again and continued writing on the ground. When they heard this, they left one by one, starting with the older men. Only he was left, with the woman in the center. When Jesus stood up, he said to her, 'Rise, plead your case before the mountains, and let the hills hear your complaint.'"

PIX-CROSS

SOLVE THE NONOGRAM TO REVEAL THE HIDDEN PICTURE.

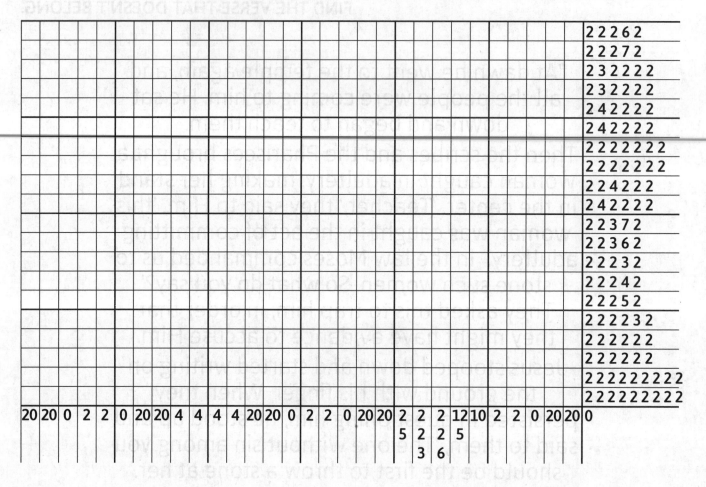

Column clues (left to right):

20, 20, 0, 2, 2, 0, 20, 20, 4, 4, 4, 4, 20, 20, 0, 2, 2, 0, 20, 20, (2 5 3), (2 2 2 3), (2 2 6), (12 5), 10, 2, 2, 0, 20, 20, 0

Row clues (top to bottom):

| 2 2 2 6 2 |
| 2 2 2 7 2 |
| 2 3 2 2 2 2 |
| 2 3 2 2 2 2 |
| 2 4 2 2 2 2 |
| 2 4 2 2 2 2 |
| 2 2 2 2 2 2 2 |
| 2 2 2 2 2 2 2 |
| 2 2 4 2 2 2 |
| 2 4 2 2 2 2 |
| 2 2 3 7 2 |
| 2 2 3 6 2 |
| 2 2 2 3 2 |
| 2 2 2 4 2 |
| 2 2 2 5 2 |
| 2 2 2 2 3 2 |
| 2 2 2 2 2 2 |
| 2 2 2 2 2 2 |
| 2 2 2 2 2 2 2 2 |
| 2 2 2 2 2 2 2 2 |

WORD-SEARCH

CONTAINED WITHIN THIS PUZZLE YOU MUST FIND ALL CAPITALIZED WORDS FROM THE VERSES BELOW.

```
H E L P Q F A E B I L L O W S
L A W I V S W V A G Z C N U F
R W T B W N Q T N H M I R R T
A N S W E R E D I I D C X B L
W Z E L C S E A S O I L S R K
J L H X R U B Z H Q S S O E X
U J I R I V I T E M T U V A W
K C X H E A R T D Q R H E K H
I D D E D G W D L J E C R E E
K H E T H R E W S L S S C R A
S J V P X O M S P H S H A S R
I A O N T M R M V Y K E M X D
G Q I U Z H E Y D G K O E N K
H Z C J A T S M C A L L E D T
T X E V M F E D E E P F Z N I
```

"I **CALLED** to the Lord in my **DISTRESS**, and he **ANSWERED** me.
I **CRIED OUT** for **HELP** from **DEEP** inside **SHEOL**; you **HEARD** my **VOICE**.
You **THREW** me into the **DEPTHS**, into the **HEART** of the **SEAS**, and the current **OVERCAME** me. All your **BREAKERS** and your **BILLOWS** swept over me.
But I said, 'I have been **BANISHED** from your **SIGHT**, yet I will look once more toward your holy **TEMPLE**.'"

CRISS-CROSS

USE THE DEFINITIONS BELOW TO FIND THE WORDS AND GUESS THE THEME.

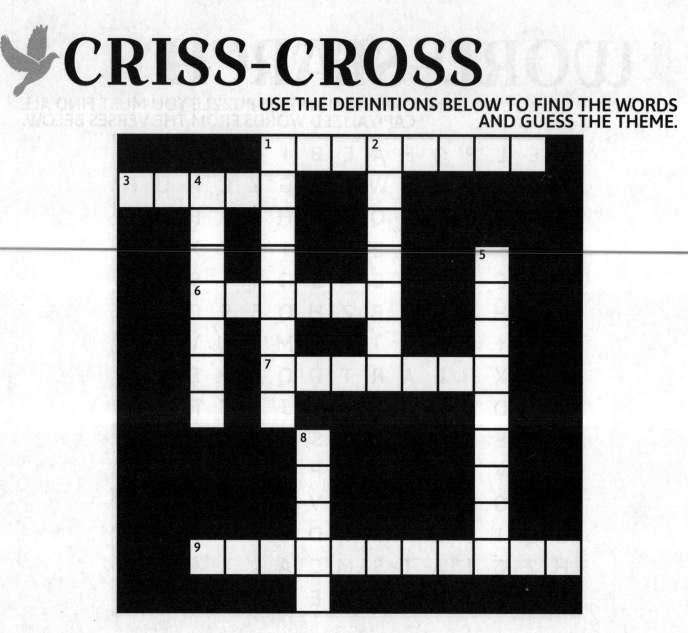

ACROSS:
1. Priest at Solomon's court.
3. Solomon's adviser.
6. Secretary of Solomon.
7. Son of Zadok.
9. Solomon's court historian.

DOWN:
1. Manager of forced labor.
2. Solomon's palace butler.
4. Army commander.
5. Brother of Ahijah.
8. Father of Azariah.

SUDOKU

**MATCH THE HIGHLIGHTED NUMBER SEQUENCE
TO THE CHAPTER AND VERSE BELOW.**

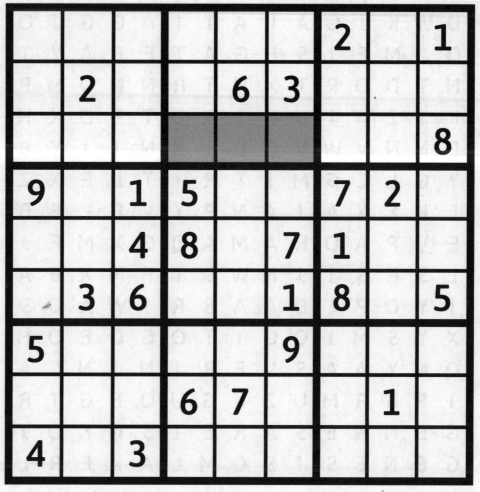

LUKE _ : _ - _

"Summoning the Twelve, he gave them power and authority over all the demons, and to heal diseases. Then he sent them to proclaim the kingdom of God and to heal the sick."

LEVEL
2

🕊 **BIBLE POWER PUZZLES** 🕊

PAGE
113

DEFINITION SEARCH

FIND ALL WORDS PLACED HORIZONTALLY, VERTICALLY, OR DIAGONALLY,
AND MATCH THEM TO THE DEFINITIONS BELOW.

```
D W K J G A L A T I A G G J O
O A M F I S H G A T E E A Y T
N T D D P T X H T R N N D M P
K I Z W I U K J A O T T D K H
E N N V W V O E I B N I I Y B
Y G L C G M I T R I T L E X Z
F K E X A J A N P Y V E L F B
E V P A O R A M A Q G X M F J
L S R S I J N W D T F M X B A
I Y O P L D A A B R I W A D S
X Y S M J O O I T O G O E O H
Q N Y A A S V E R I N I N C A
I P G R M U Z K G U O E G T R
G E N N E S A R E T S N K O J
G E N E S I S O M L A K E R L
```

- Condemned in Deuteronomy 18:10-11.
- Luke the evangelist's profession.
- Saul's head shepherd.
- Jesus rode one.
- Held Paul for two years.
- Likely the NW wall of Jerusalem (2 w.).
- One of the twelve spies sent by Moses to spy the land of Canaan.
- Roman province in NC Asia Minor.
- Originally called "Bereshit."
- Jesus reached this plain after feeding the 5,000.
- Non-Jewish person.
- Becoming a deity in the flesh.
- Supernatural work of the Holy Spirit.
- Jesus brought his daughter back to life.
- May have been Jesus' oldest brother.
- Ancient missing book mentioned twice in the OT.
- Used by Samson as a weapon.
- Apostolic preaching of the Gospel (Greek).
- —of fire.
- Hansen's disease.

PARABLES

"What man among you, who has a hundred sheep and loses one of them, does not leave the ninety-nine in the open field and go after the lost one until he finds it? When he has found it, he joyfully puts it on his shoulders, and coming home, he calls his friends and neighbors together, saying to them, 'Rejoice with me, because I have found my lost sheep!'"

Luke 15:4-6

WHAT DOES IT MEAN?

....

....

....

....

....

....

....

....

WHAT DOES IT MEAN?

....

....

....

....

....

....

....

....

....

"Or what woman who has ten silver coins, if she loses one coin, does not light a lamp, sweep the house, and search carefully until she finds it? When she finds it, she calls her friends and neighbors together, saying, 'Rejoice with me, because I have found the silver coin I lost!'"

Luke 15:8-9

WHAT DOES IT MEAN?

....

....

....

....

....

....

....

....

"Again, the kingdom of heaven is like a large net thrown into the sea. It collected every kind of fish, and when it was full, they dragged it ashore, sat down, and gathered the good fish into containers, but threw out the worthless ones."

Matthew 13:47-48

THE RIGHT ONE

REWRITE THE LIST IN THE CORRECT ORDER.

1. Cast two demons out of two men.	1.
2. A woman was healed from bleeding by touching his robe.	2.
3. Cast out a demon.	3.
4. Healed many people and cast out demons.	4.
5. Cleansed a leper.	5.
6. Healed two blind men.	6.
7. Forgave and healed a paralytic.	7.
8. Healed a man with a shriveled hand.	8.
9. Healed a centurion's servant.	9.
10. Cast a demon out of a blind-mute man.	10.
11. Raised a girl from the dead.	11.
12. Calmed the windstorm.	12.

QUOTES

IDENTIFY THE PROPER BOOK, CHAPTER, AND VERSE THESE BIBLE QUOTATIONS BELONG TO.

BOOK:
....

"For many are invited, but few are chosen."

CHAPTER:
....

VERSE:
....

BOOK:
....

CHAPTER:
....

"Nothing that goes into a person from outside can defile him but the things that come out of a person are what defile him."

VERSE:
....

BOOK:
....

"Truly I tell you, if anyone keeps my word, he will never see death."

CHAPTER:
....

VERSE:
....

UNSCRAMBLE

REARRANGE ONE WORD AT THE TIME, IN THE SAME ORDER THEY'RE PRESENTED, TO REVEAL THE PRECISE VERSE FROM THE SCRIPTURE.

1. ROF OGD SAH TON NEVIG SU A TIRIPS FO RAFE, TUB NEO FO WERPO, VELO, NAD DUNSO DUGEJMNTE.

....

....

....

....

2. TEY EH FLESMIH REBO RUO NESSISCK, NAD EH RIRACED RUO NIPAS...

....

....

....

....

3. EH DAME HET NEO HOW IDD TON KWON NIS OT EB NIS ROF SU, OS HATT NI MIH EW THIGM COBEME HET THERIGUSOSENS FO OGD.

....

....

....

....

4. WON YAM HET OGD FO PEHO ILFL OYU THIW LAL YOJ NAD CEAPE SA OYU LIVEEBE OS HATT OYU YAM FLOVERWO THIW PEHO...

....

....

....

....

VERSE-SPOTTING

"Now a man from the family of Levi married a Levite woman. The woman became pregnant and gave birth to a son; when she saw that he was beautiful, she hid him for three months. But when she could no longer hide him, she got a papyrus basket for him and coated it with asphalt and pitch. She placed the child in it and set it among the reeds by the bank of the Nile. Then his sister stood at a distance in order to see what would happen to him.

Pharaoh's daughter went down to bathe at the Nile while her servant girls walked along the riverbank. She saw the basket among the reeds, sent her slave girl, took it, opened it, and saw him, the child—and there he was, a little boy, crying.

The child grew up and became spiritually strong, and he was in the wilderness until the day of his public appearance to Israel."

PIX-CROSS

SOLVE THE NONOGRAM TO REVEAL THE HIDDEN PICTURE.

	1 1	12	1 1	1	0	0	8 2	2 2	2 1	1 1	2 2	2 2	1 1	1 1	2 2	2 2	3 3	4	3 3	3 2	2 2	1 1	8	2 2	2 2	1 1	1 1	2 2	2 2	1 1
0
0
0
0
0
0
0
0
0
3 4 2 2 4
1 2 2 2 2 2 2
1 2 2 2 2 2 2
1 1 1 1 1
1 1 3 1
1 1 1 1
1 1 1 1
1 1 3 1
1 1 1 1 1
1 2 2 2 2 2 2
1 2 2 2 2 2 2
3 4 2 2 4
0
0
0
0
0
0
0
0
0
0

WORD-SEARCH

CONTAINED WITHIN THIS PUZZLE YOU MUST FIND ALL
CAPITALIZED WORDS FROM THE VERSES BELOW.

```
S B X E O L R C I H T I O
O U R H H E D D D O T N R
U R N T G M I E P I P D C
N D M N K H S F H N U I H
D E A Z D S C L S I N G E
N N W N E S I O W Q I N A
E D A R N U P O R U S A L
S H P P N N L D A I H T T
S W K W H K I E T T U I H
B O O Y E M N D H I I O E
U D D S A T E N J E O N A
B O H C V B O N E S W S D
B I W V Y O A R R O W S B
```

"Lord, do not **PUNISH** me in your **ANGER** or **DISCIPLINE** me in your **WRATH**.
For your **ARROWS** have **SUNK** into me, and your **HAND** has **PRESSED DOWN** on me.
There is no **SOUNDNESS** in my **BODY** because of your **INDIGNATION**; there is no
HEALTH in my **BONES** because of my **SIN**.
For my **INIQUITIES** have **FLOODED** over my **HEAD**; they are a **BURDEN** too **HEAVY**
for me to bear."

CRISS-CROSS

USE THE DEFINITIONS BELOW TO FIND THE WORDS AND GUESS THE THEME.

ACROSS:

1. Son of Paruah.
4. Served in Ephraim.
5. Served in Benjamin.
7. Son of Uri.
8. Son of Ahilud.
9. Married Tapath.
10. Solomon's deputy in four districts.

DOWN:

2. Married Basemath.
3. Son of Iddo.
4. Deputy over 60 walled cities.
6. Deputy in Arubboth.
8. Deputy in Asher and Bealoth.

SUDOKU

							4	5
	5	6	4		9			8
				2	9			
	7			1	8	4		
1								3
		3	9	5			2	
			1					
5			6		4	1	3	
8	6							

JUDGES _ : _ - _

"Now announce to the troops: 'Whoever is fearful and trembling may turn back and leave Mount Gilead.' So twenty-two thousand of the troops turned back, but ten thousand remained.

Then the Lord said to Gideon, 'There are still too many troops. Take them down to the water, and I will test them for you there. If I say to you, This one can go with you, he can go. But if I say about anyone, This one cannot go with you, he cannot go.'"

DEFINITION SEARCH

FIND ALL WORDS PLACED HORIZONTALLY, VERTICALLY, OR DIAGONALLY, AND MATCH THEM TO THE DEFINITIONS BELOW.

```
F K U D F T D E H D Y W J J P
C H I X C E D S A C I W H E U
O L Q L N R U U N P N V A Z D
B K L A E N E X N J Y S N F M
Z C R P I A K D A W I G U Y W
S A E L K F B V H I P K K I C
H E R M O G E N E S T A K E X
K H N U V Q A K I S H B A B Y
L E X T A L I O N I S Z H R E
P D K G J L K A D M I E L F L
L I B E R T Y A M Y I E O L Y
L P F C D C F C D P T L U O F
U E W A D U L T E R Y U H O A
P D V Z L A Q S N I V Q M D T
X O T I N L C I T Q B Z U M E
```

- Account of the early Church, attributed to Luke.
- Intercourse between a married person w/ someone other than his/her spouse.
- The —, also know as the first sin.
- Destiny.
- Deluge.
- Mother of Samuel.
- Feast of Dedication (Hebrew)
- Father of Lot.
- Abandoned Paul.
- God struck Jacob here.
- Native town of Benaiah.
- Returned from exile with Zerubabbel.
- Guardian.
- Instrument for moving the bolt of a lock.
- David's first son by Abigail.
- Father of King Saul.
- The tax collector known as Matthew.
- "An eye for an eye" rule (Latin, 2 words).
- The opposite of enslavement.
- Friend of Paul during his second imprisonment.

PARABLES

"The kingdom of heaven is like a king who gave a wedding banquet for his son. He sent his servants to summon those invited to the banquet, but they didn't want to come. Again, he sent out other servants, and said, 'Tell those who are invited: See, I've prepared my dinner; my oxen and fattened cattle have been slaughtered, and everything is ready. Come to the wedding banquet.' But they paid no attention and went away, one to his own farm, another to his business, while the rest seized his servants, mistreated them, and killed them. The king was enraged, and he sent out his troops, killed those murderers, and burned down their city.Then he told his servants, 'The banquet is ready, but those who were invited were not worthy. Go then to where the roads exit the city and invite everyone you find to the banquet.' So those servants went out on the roads and gathered everyone they found, both evil and good. The wedding banquet was filled with guests. When the king came in to see the guests, he saw a man there who was not dressed for a wedding. So he said to him,

'Friend, how did you get in here without wedding clothes?' The man was speechless. Then the king told the attendants, 'Tie him up hand and foot, and throw him into the outer darkness, where there will be weeping and gnashing of teeth.' For many are invited, but few are chosen."

Matthew 22:2-14

WHAT DOES IT MEAN?

....
....
....
....
....
....
....
....
....

WHAT DOES IT MEAN?

....
....
....
....
....
....
....

"Two men went up to the temple to pray, one a Pharisee and the other a tax collector. The Pharisee was standing and praying like this about himself: 'God, I thank you that I'm not like other people —greedy, unrighteous, adulterers, or even like this tax collector. I fast twice a week; I give a tenth of everything I get.' But the tax collector, standing far off, would not even raise his eyes to heaven but kept striking his chest and saying, 'God, have mercy on me, a sinner!'" **Luke 18:10-13**

THE RIGHT ONE

REWRITE THE LIST IN THE CORRECT ORDER.

13. Walked on water.	13.
14. Transfigured in front of Peter, James, and John.	14.
15. Healed two blind men.	15.
16. Many healed by touching the end of his robe.	16.
17. Resurrected!	17.
18. Healed crowds.	18.
19. Cast a demon out of a Canaanite woman's daughter.	19.
20. Withered a fig tree.	20.
21. Cast a demon out of an epileptic boy.	21.
22. Fed 4,000.	22.
23. Fed 5,000.	23.

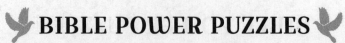

QUOTES

"Look, today I set before you a blessing and a curse: there will be a blessing, if you obey the commands of the LORD your God I am giving you today, and a curse if you do not..."

BOOK:

....

CHAPTER:

....

VERSE:

....

BOOK:

....

CHAPTER:

....

VERSE:

....

"Now you can see that the king is leading you. As for me, I'm old and gray, and my sons are here with you. I have led you from my youth until now."

"What is truth?..."

BOOK:

....

CHAPTER:

....

VERSE:

....

UNSCRAMBLE

REARRANGE ONE WORD AT THE TIME, IN THE SAME ORDER THEY'RE PRESENTED, TO REVEAL THE PRECISE VERSE FROM THE SCRIPTURE.

1. I MA HET SURECTRIONER NAD HET FELI. HET NEO HOW LEVESBEI NI EM, VENE FI EH SEDI, ILWL VELI.

....

....

....

....

2. WON THOWIUT THAIF TI SI SIBLEPOMIS OT ASELEP OGD, CENIS HET NEO HOW WARDS AREN OT MIH TUSM LEVEBEI HATT EH SISTXE NAD HATT EH WARREDS THESO HOW KESE MIH.

....

....

....

....

3. LURYT I LETL OYU, NEYONA HOW HARES YM DORW NAD LEVESBEI MIH HOW TENS EM SAH TERNELA FELI...

....

....

....

....

4. DERSICON TI A TERAG YOJ, YM THERROBS NAD SERSTIS, HENEREVW OYU CENERIEXPE SARVIOU LASTRI...

....

....

....

....

VERSE-SPOTTING

FIND THE VERSE THAT DOESN'T BELONG.

"Then their whole assembly rose up and brought Him before Pilate. They began to accuse Him, saying, 'We found this man misleading our nation, opposing payment of taxes to Caesar, and saying that He Himself is the Messiah, a king.'

So Pilate asked Him, 'Are you the King of the Jews?' He answered him, 'You say so.'

Pilate then told the chief priests and the crowds, 'No one will be executed this day, for today the LORD has provided deliverance in Israel.'

But they kept insisting, 'He stirs up the people, teaching throughout all Judea, from Galilee where He started even to here.'"

PIX-CROSS

SOLVE THE NONOGRAM TO REVEAL THE HIDDEN PICTURE.

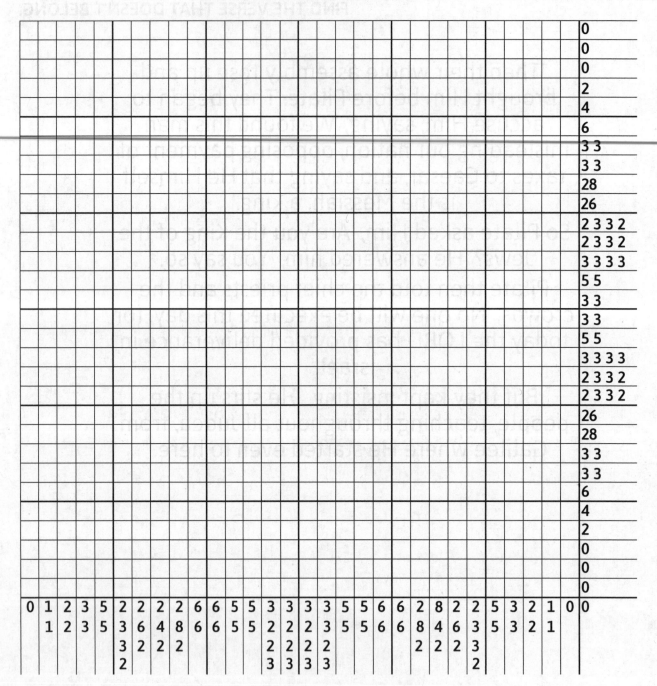

WORD-SEARCH

CONTAINED WITHIN THIS PUZZLE YOU MUST FIND ALL
CAPITALIZED WORDS FROM THE VERSES BELOW.

```
M I N D S B O W L L I F E
U D R U N K E N N E S S E
U N C P D H F L Q L S H S
W Y E O F Y Z J H I T M C
Z O E X M A L I G R R A A
G H R N P E C N A R E D P
U L P R J E I E Y T N X E
A W I M I S C A M A G G N
R I H V U E O T T P T J A
D L V O E I S S E J H P L
T L R T I M E S H D A Z E
K A D U L L E D D R L V R
C P R A Y I N G T A M Y T
```

"Be on your **GUARD**, so that your **MINDS** are not **DULLED** from **CAROUSING**, **DRUNKENNESS**, and **WORRIES** of **LIFE**, of that day will come on you **UNEXPECTEDLY** like a **TRAP**. For it **WILL COME** on all who **LIVE** on the **FACE** of the whole **EARTH**. But be **ALERT** at all **TIMES**, **PRAYING** that you may have **STRENGTH** to **ESCAPE** all these things that are going to take place and to **STAND** before the Son of Man."

CRISS-CROSS

USE THE DEFINITIONS BELOW TO FIND THE WORDS AND GUESS THE THEME.

ACROSS:

1. Agonized in prayer for the Colossians.

5. Onesimus was his slave.

7. Sold his land and laid the money at the apostles' feet.

9. Wrote the Epistle to the Romans at Paul's dictation.

10. Sent twice to Ephesus by Paul.

13. Son of Pyrrhus.

14. Spent time in prison with Paul.

17. Allowed Paul to preach at his home.

DOWN:

2. Imprisoned with Paul at Philippi.

3. Son of a Gentile father and a Jewish mother.

4. Slave of Philemon.

6. Wife of Aquila.

8. Husband of Priscilla.

10. The Jews thought Paul had taken him into the temple.

11. Sailed to Cyprus with Barnabas (Latin).

12. One of Paul's companions in Greece.

15. Organized the Church in Crete.

16. Baptized by Paul in Corinth.

SUDOKU

MATCH THE HIGHLIGHTED NUMBER SEQUENCE TO THE CHAPTER AND VERSE BELOW.

	3	7					4	
				4		9		
1			6	8				
	4				7	1		3
			8		4			
5		8	2				7	
				2	6			5
		3		5				
	2							

1 CORINTHIANS _ : _ - _

"Now about food sacrificed to idols: We know that 'we all have knowledge.' Knowledge puffs up, but love builds up. If anyone thinks he knows anything, he does not yet know it as he ought to know it. But if anyone loves God, he is known by Him. About eating food sacrificed to idols, then, we know that 'an idol is nothing in the world,' and that 'there is no God but one.'"

DEFINITION SEARCH

FIND ALL WORDS PLACED HORIZONTALLY, VERTICALLY, OR DIAGONALLY,
AND MATCH THEM TO THE DEFINITIONS BELOW.

```
J A D D U A I C H A B O D
C H R O N I C L E S E C T
S F I S R A E L Y M Z I J
I N H E R I T A N C E T K
J A E L C H E E K B B I N
E H F K M R N N R C T Z O
T R U J A A S I E L J E W
H R A B T P T D R E E N L
R I E R B R I L P A Z S E
O K A T A B N E E N R H D
U K C H A R I O T S E I G
P N B C N I D U S N E P E
M I D O L A T R Y K L G M
```

- Turn the other —.
- Used by Pharaoh's army to pursue Moses.
- Two OT books retelling 2 Samuel and 1-2 Kings after the Babylonian exile.
- Paul's was Roman.
- Pure and/or chaste according to Mosaic law.
- Paul sailed past it on the way to Rome.
- One of the sons of David born in Jerusalem.
- His mother died giving birth to him.
- Lazy.

- The worship of manmade images.
- The prodigal son squandered it.
- Jacob's God-given name.
- Son of Abner.
- Israelite leader who sealed a covenant with Nehemiah.
- Wife of Heber, the Kenite.
- Also called Reuel.
- Ahinoam may have been from this town.
- Levitical town in the territory of Naphtali.
- Babylon watercourse where Nebuchadnezzar settled Jewish exiles.
- The tree of —.

PARABLES

"A man had two sons. The younger of them said to his father, 'Father, give me the share of the estate I have coming to me.' So he distributed the assets to them. Not many days later, the younger son gathered together all he had and traveled to a distant country, where he squandered his estate in foolish living. After he had spent everything, a severe famine struck that country, and he had nothing. Then he went to work for one of the citizens of that country, who sent him into his fields to feed pigs. He longed to eat his fill from the pods that the pigs were eating, but no one would give him anything. When he came to his senses, he said, 'How many of my father's hired workers have more than enough food, and here I am dying of hunger! I'll get up, go to my father, and say to him, *Father, I have sinned against heaven and in your sight. I'm no longer worthy to be called your son. Make me like one of your hired workers.*' So he got up and went to his father. But while the son was still a long way off, his father saw him and was filled with compassion. He ran, threw his arms around his neck, and kissed him. The son said to him, 'Father, I have sinned against heaven and in your sight. I'm no longer worthy to be called your son.' But the father told his servants, 'Quick! Bring out the best robe and put it on him; put a ring on his finger and sandals on his feet. Then bring the fattened calf and slaughter it, and let's celebrate with a feast, because this son of mine was dead and is alive again; he was lost and is found!' So they began to celebrate.

Now his older son was in the field; as he came near the house, he heard music and dancing. So he summoned one of the servants and asked what these things meant. 'Your brother is here,' he told him, 'and your father has slaughtered the fattened calf because he has him back safe and sound.' Then he became angry and didn't want to go in. So his father came out and pleaded with him. But he replied to his father, 'Look, I have been slaving many years for you, and I have never disobeyed your orders, yet you never gave me a young goat so I could celebrate with my friends. But when this son of yours came, who has devoured your assets with prostitutes, you slaughtered the fattened calf for him.' 'Son,' he said to him, 'you are always with me, and everything I have is yours. But we had to celebrate and rejoice, because this brother of yours was dead and is alive again; he was lost and is found.'"

Luke 15:11-32

WHAT DOES IT MEAN?

....

....

....

....

....

....

....

....

....

THE RIGHT ONE

1. Healed many people and cast out demons.	1.
2. Calmed the windstorm.	2.
3. Cast out a demon.	3.
4. Healed a man with a shriveled hand.	4.
5. Healed Simon's mother-in-law.	5.
6. Fed 5,000.	6.
7. Raised Jairus' daughter from the dead.	7.
8. Forgave and healed a paralytic.	8.
9. Cleansed a leper.	9.
10. A woman was healed from bleeding by touching his robe.	10.
11. Cast many demons ("Legion") out of one man.	11.

QUOTES

BOOK:

....

"...Speak, for your servant is listening."

CHAPTER:

....

VERSE:

....

BOOK:

....

CHAPTER:

....

"...Then I fell on my knees, and spread out my hands to the LORD, my God."

VERSE:

....

BOOK:

....

"The one who has two shirts must share with someone who has none, and the one who has food must do the same."

CHAPTER:

....

VERSE:

....

UNSCRAMBLE

REARRANGE ONE WORD AT THE TIME, IN THE SAME ORDER THEY'RE PRESENTED, TO REVEAL THE PRECISE VERSE FROM THE SCRIPTURE.

1. OS OGD RECAEDT NAM NI SIH WON MAGEI...

....
....
....
....

2. HEREREFOT, SA OGD'S HOSCEN NEOS, LHOY NAD AREDLY VEDOL, TUP NO PAMOCNOISS, SENKINDS, HILIMUTY, TELSGENSEN, NAD TIPANECE...

....
....
....
....

3. TEL SU NUR THIW ANCENEDUR HET CERA HATT ESLI REFOBE SU, EPIKENG RUO YEES NO SUJES...

....
....
....
....

4. HEREREFOT FESCONS OYUR NISS OT NEO THERONA NAD RAYP ROF NEO THERONA, OS HATT OYU YAM EB HELEDA.

....
....
....
....

VERSE-SPOTTING

"The Lord hates six things; in fact, seven are detestable to him: arrogant eyes, a lying tongue, hands that shed innocent blood, a heart that plots wicked schemes, feet eager to run to evil, a lying witness who gives false testimony, and one who stirs up trouble among brothers.

Let no one deceive you with empty arguments, for God's wrath is coming to the disobedient because of these things.

Therefore, do not become their partners. For you were once darkness, but now you are light in the Lord."

PIX-CROSS

SOLVE THE NONOGRAM TO REVEAL THE HIDDEN PICTURE.

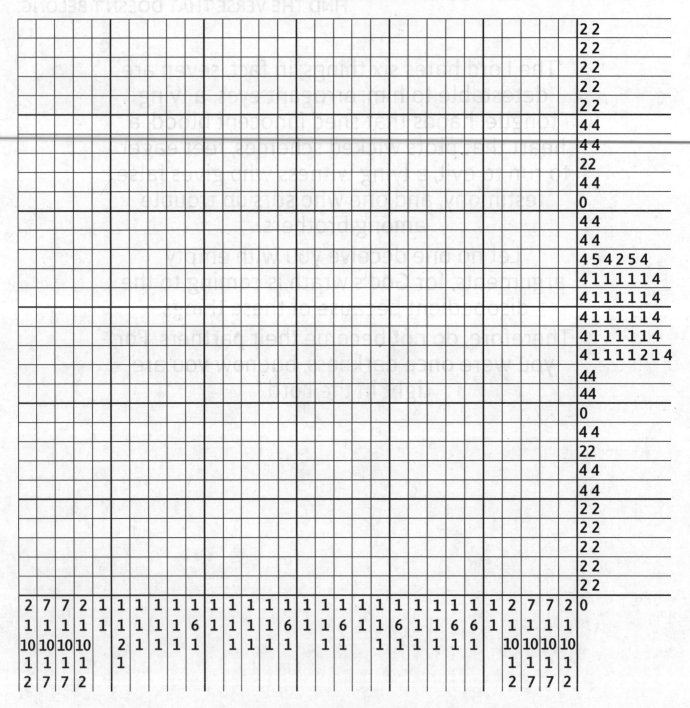

WORD-SEARCH

```
R G F U L F I L L E D S E
S I N C E U W R Z Z E L E
Y K E W U T A T H D O F H
M F P T H I N G A H S A A
R I Z L W A N M W E O I X
N Y P R O M I S E X R L G
E V E R Y T H I N G P E O
T M Q W P V I O Z K H D I
T T Q A Y G L D R G O D N
P N N Y O O A B O U T Z G
F B O I U O T S O U L I W
Y K N O W D E E A R T H J
A H E A R T D J S G O B N
```

"I am now **GOING** the **WAY** of the **WHOLE EARTH**, and you **KNOW** with all your **HEART** and all your **SOUL** that **NONE** of the **GOOD** promises the Lord your **GOD** **MADE** to you has **FAILED**. **EVERYTHING** was **FULFILLED** for **YOU**; not one **PROMISE** has failed. **SINCE** every good **THING** the Lord has promised has come **ABOUT** , so he will bring on you every bad thing until he has **ANNIHILATED** you from this good land the Lord your God has given you."

CRISS-CROSS

USE THE DEFINITIONS BELOW TO FIND THE WORDS AND GUESS THE THEME.

ACROSS:

1. Sent along with Timothy to Macedonia.
7. Became a Christian before Paul.
9. Hosted Paul and Silas at Thessalonica.
10. Paul sent her greetings in Colossians 4:15.
11. Possibly the first convert in Europe.
12. A disciple of Paul, who lived in Troas.
14. Servant of the Church in Cenchreae.
15. Greeted by Paul in Romans 16:9.

DOWN:

2. Paul taught at his school.
3. Took care of Paul while in prison.
4. Fellow prisoner alongside Paul.
5. Christian teacher in Colosse.
6. For a time he was so sick, he nearly died.
8. Deserted Paul and left for Thessalonica.
11. Possibly a relative of Paul.
13. Believed by some to be Philemon's wife.

SUDOKU

MATCH THE HIGHLIGHTED NUMBER SEQUENCE TO THE CHAPTER AND VERSE BELOW.

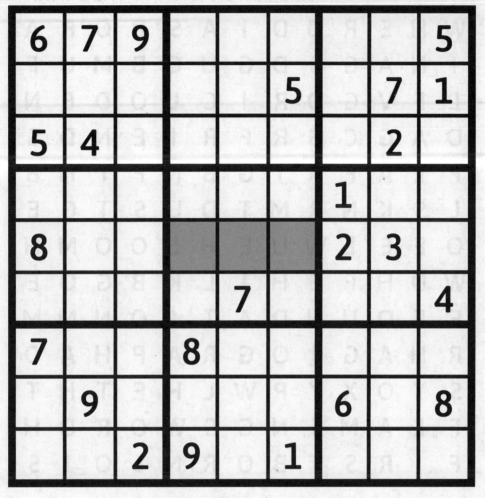

COLOSSIANS _ : _ - _

"Masters, deal with your slaves justly and fairly, since you know that you too have a Master in heaven. Devote yourselves to prayer; stay alert in it with thanksgiving. At the same time, pray also for us that God may open a door to us for the word, to speak the mystery of Christ, for which I am in chains, so that I may make it known as I should. Act wisely toward outsiders, making the most of the time. Let your speech always be gracious, seasoned with salt, so that you may know how you should answer each person."

DEFINITION SEARCH

FIND ALL WORDS PLACED HORIZONTALLY, VERTICALLY, OR DIAGONALLY, AND MATCH THEM TO THE DEFINITIONS BELOW.

```
W H E R O D I A S P O R A
I N A G S D G U C B M U F
L F V G D R I C L O D E N
D A G C G R F R I E N D S
F L A F A I G B N F Y H B
L S K N R M T D U S T G E
O E E L W U E H L O O M H
W D H F E H I L K B G O E
E F O U N D A T I O N M M
R H A G I O G R A P H A O
S Y O X Y P W L H E T H T
F L A M I N G S W O R D H
F I R S T B O R N L O I S
```

- Beast mentioned in the book of Job.
- Easier for it to go through the eye of a needle.
- Lions' dwelling.
- Most common Roman coin from the time of Jesus.
- Dispersion of the Jews outside of Palestine.
- The apostles were to shake it off their feet when leaving a place of rejection.
- —prophet.
- Eldest son.
- A cherubim wielded it to guard the way to the tree of life (2 words).
- Beat severely with a whip.
- Basis on which something stands.
- Lazarus, Mary, Martha, and Jesus were —.
- Forbidden —.
- Mother of Adonijah.
- OT's sacred writings (Greek).
- Had John the Baptist beheaded.
- Ancestor of the Hittites.
- Mother of Eunice.
- Machine for weaving thread or yarn.
- They don't labor or spin thread.

PARABLES

"There was a rich man who would dress in purple and fine linen, feasting lavishly every day. But a poor man named Lazarus, covered with sores, was lying at his gate. He longed to be filled with what fell from the rich man's table, but instead the dogs would come and lick his sores.

One day the poor man died and was carried away by the angels to Abraham's side. The rich man also died and was buried. And being in torment in Hades, he looked up and saw Abraham a long way off, with Lazarus at his side. 'Father Abraham!' he called out, 'Have mercy on me and send Lazarus to dip the tip of his finger in water and cool my tongue, because I am in agony in this flame!'

'Son,' Abraham said, 'remember that during your life you received your good things, just as Lazarus received bad things, but now he is comforted here, while you are in agony. Besides all this, a great chasm has been fixed between us and you, so that those who want to pass over from here to you cannot; neither can those from there cross over to us.' 'Father,' he said, 'then I beg you to send him to my father's house—because I have five brothers—to warn them, so they won't also come to this place of torment.'

But Abraham said, 'They have Moses and the prophets; they should listen to them.'

'No, father Abraham,' he said. 'But if someone from the dead goes to them, they will repent.'

But he told him, 'If they don't listen to Moses and the prophets, they will not be persuaded if someone rises from the dead.'" **Luke 16:19-31**

WHAT DOES IT MEAN?

....

....

....

....

....

....

"Which one of you having a servant tending sheep or plowing will say to him when he comes in from the field, 'Come at once and sit down to eat'? Instead, will he not tell him, 'Prepare something for me to eat, get ready, and serve me while I eat and drink; later you can eat and drink'? Does he thank the servant because he did what was commanded? In the same way, when you have done all that you were commanded, you should say, 'We are worthless servants; we've only done our duty.'" **Luke 17:7-10**

WHAT DOES IT MEAN?

....

....

....

....

....

....

12. Resurrected!	12.
13. Healed a blind beggar.	13.
14. Transfigured in front of Peter, James, and John.	14.
15. Fed 4,000.	15.
16. Cast a demon out of a Gentile woman's daughter.	16.
17. Walked on water.	17.
18. Many healed by touching the end of his robe.	18.
19. Healed a deaf, speech-impaired man.	19.
20. Healed a blind man.	20.
21. Cast a demon out of an epileptic boy.	21.
22. Withered a fig tree.	22.

QUOTES

"Get up and go on your way. Your faith has saved you."

BOOK:

CHAPTER:

VERSE:

BOOK:

CHAPTER:

VERSE:

"Do whatever he tells you..."

"...What God has made clean, do not call impure."

BOOK:

CHAPTER:

VERSE:

UNSCRAMBLE

REARRANGE ONE WORD AT THE TIME, IN THE SAME ORDER THEY'RE PRESENTED, TO REVEAL THE PRECISE VERSE FROM THE SCRIPTURE.

1. EW LAL TWEN TRAYSA KELI HESEP; EW LAL VEHA NEDRUT OT URO WON YAW; NAD HET ROLD SAH HEDSINPU MIH ROF HET TYNIIQUI FO SU LAL.

....

....

....

....

2. PENTER NAD EB TIBAPZED, CHAE FO OYU, NI HET MENA FO SUJES HIRSTC ROF HET VEFORGINESS FO RUO NISS...

....

....

....

....

3. EH CIREXESED SIH WERPO NI HIRSTC YB SINAIRG MIH MORF HET DADE NAD TEASING MIH TA SIH HIRGT NI HET EVEHANS...

....

....

....

....

4. ROF YM KEYO SI SAEY NAD YM DENBUR SI HILTG.

....

....

....

....

VERSE-SPOTTING

"On the third day a wedding took place in Cana of Galilee. Jesus' mother was there, and Jesus and his disciples were invited to the wedding as well. When the wine ran out, Jesus' mother told Him, 'They don't have any wine.' 'What has this concern of yours to do with you and me, woman?' Jesus asked. 'My hour has not yet come.'

'How long are you going to be drunk? Get rid of your wine!' his mother told the servants.

Now six stone water jars had been set there for Jewish purification. Each contained twenty or thirty gallons.

'Fill the jars with water,' Jesus told them. So they filled them to the brim."

PIX-CROSS

SOLVE THE NONOGRAM TO REVEAL THE HIDDEN PICTURE.

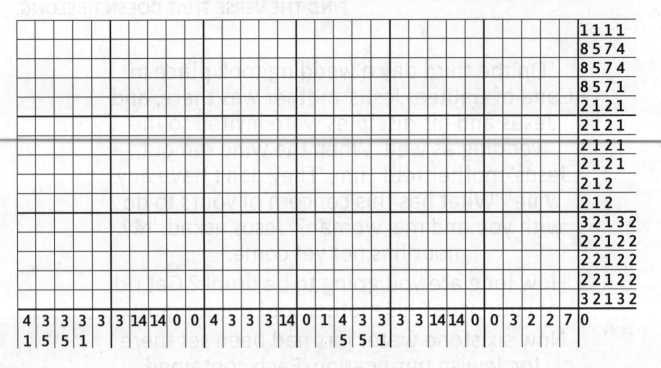

Row clues (top to bottom):
1 1 1 1
8 5 7 4
8 5 7 4
8 5 7 1
2 1 2 1
2 1 2 1
2 1 2 1
2 1 2 1
2 1 2
2 1 2
3 2 1 3 2
2 2 1 2 2
2 2 1 2 2
2 2 1 2 2
3 2 1 3 2

Column clues (left to right):
4 1 / 3 5 / 3 5 / 3 1 / 3 / 3 / 14 / 14 / 0 / 0 / 4 / 3 / 3 / 3 / 14 / 0 / 1 / 4 5 / 3 5 / 3 1 / 3 / 3 / 14 / 14 / 0 / 0 / 3 / 2 / 2 / 7 / 0

WORD-SEARCH

CONTAINED WITHIN THIS PUZZLE YOU MUST FIND ALL
CAPITALIZED WORDS FROM THE VERSES BELOW.

```
L F A L S E H O O D F A L
D O X C V I M M O R A L I
O O V I D O L A T E R S F
U N G E F G R V N T R E E
T Y G S S H U Y A U I N J
S B J A Y D L K E F G E Y
I S L T T L P N J D H N O
D V I E A E O G S O T T B
E C T U S Y S S R O B E S
W W X W R S L W D X Q R N
A E Y E P X E N T H O S E
S C V O M U R D E R E R S
H E S O R C E R E R S T T
```

"**BLESSED** are **THOSE** who **WASH** their **ROBES**, so that they may have the **RIGHT** to
the **TREE** of **LIFE** and may **ENTER** the **CITY** by the **GATES**. **OUTSIDE** are the **DOGS**,
the **SORCERERS**, the **SEXUALLY IMMORAL**, the **MURDERERS**, the **IDOLATERS**, and
EVERYONE who **LOVES** and practices **FALSEHOOD**."

CRISS-CROSS

USE THE DEFINITIONS BELOW TO FIND THE WORDS AND GUESS THE THEME.

ACROSS:

3. His insensitivity triggered a civil war.

4. Led a revolt against Moses.

6. Raped his half-sister.

7. Narcissistic son of David.

10. King of Sodom.

11. Ordered the slaughter of 85 godly priests.

12. Carried out the order to kill 85 godly priests.

13. Threatened to gouge the right eye of all Israelites living in Jabesh.

DOWN:

1. Many scholars believe him to be the Pharaoh of the Exodus (number at the end).

2. Murdered his brother.

5. Proclaimed king after the death of Gideon.

8. Cursed David.

9. Betrayed Christ.

SUDOKU

MATCH THE HIGHLIGHTED NUMBER SEQUENCE TO THE CHAPTER AND VERSE BELOW.

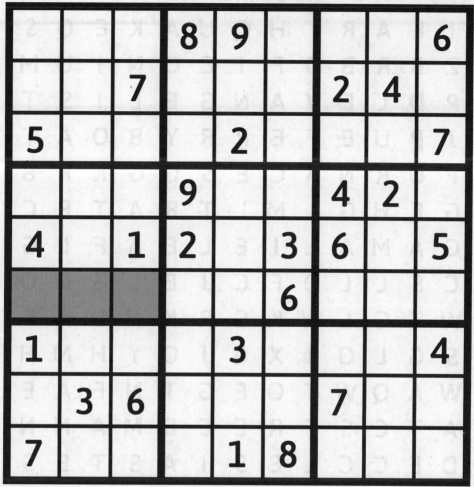

			8	9				6
		7				2	4	
5				2				7
			9			4	2	
4		1	2		3	6		5
					6			
1				3				4
	3	6				7		
7				1	8			

LEVITICUS _ : _ - _

"If your offering is a grain offering prepared on a griddle, it is to be unleavened bread made of fine flour mixed with oil. Break it into pieces and pour oil on it; it is a grain offering. If your offering is a grain offering prepared on a pan, it is to be made of fine flour with oil. When you bring to the LORD the grain offering made in any of these ways, it is to be presented to the priest, and he will take it to the altar."

DEFINITION SEARCH

FIND ALL WORDS PLACED HORIZONTALLY, VERTICALLY, OR DIAGONALLY,
AND MATCH THEM TO THE DEFINITIONS BELOW.

```
I E A R T H Q U A K E Q S
Z B R B D F I C O N I U M
P D L E V A N G E L I S T
J P U E F E R R Y B O A T
F U R N A C E S G G K K B
G E H G L M L T R A T E C
G A M A L I E L E A F L G
C S L L O F C J E L G D O
W T G L W K G R K N O A S
S G L O I X G J O Y H M H
W A Q W T O E G T N F A E
A T C S F R E E D M A N N
D E C C L E S I A S T E S
```

- Field of blood.
- One freed Paul and Silas from prison.
- Located between the Horse Gate and the Muster Gate (2 words).
- Also known as Qoheleth.
- Altar built by the Reubenites and the Gadites.
- Preacher of the Gospel.
- —ground.
- Shimei and Ziba used one to cross the Jordan to meet King David (2 words).
- Emancipated slave.
- Tower of the —.
- Led a revolt against Abimelech.

- Urged the Sanhedrin caution when dealing with the apostles.
- Brother of Seneca.
- Built by Haman to execute Mordecai.
- The gift of tongues without Love (a/t Paul).
- Jacob and his family settled there.
- Herod the —.
- Most common European language during the time of Jesus.
- Manasseh was unable to drive the Canaanites from this city.
- Paul and Barnabas visited this town after being expelled from Antioch.

PARABLES

"For it is just like a man about to go on a journey. He called his own servants and entrusted his possessions to them. To one he gave five talents, to another two talents, and to another one talent, depending on each one's ability. Then he went on a journey. Immediately the man who had received five talents went, put them to work, and earned five more. In the same way the man with two earned two more. But the man who had received one talent went off, dug a hole in the ground, and hid his master's money.

After a long time the master of those servants came and settled accounts with them. The man who had received five talents approached, presented five more talents, and said, 'Master, you gave me five talents. See, I've earned five more talents.' His master said to him, 'Well done, good and faithful servant! You were faithful over a few things; I will put you in charge of many things. Share your master's joy!'

Then the man with two talents also approached. He said, 'Master, you gave me two talents. See, I've earned two more talents.' His master said to him, 'Well done, good and faithful servant! You were faithful over a few things; I will put you in charge of many things. Share your master's joy!'

The man who had received one talent also approached and said, 'Master, I know you. You're a harsh man, reaping where you haven't sown and gathering where you haven't scattered seed. So I was afraid and went off and hid your talent in the ground. See, you have what is yours.'

But his master replied to him,

'You evil, lazy servant! If you knew that I reap where I haven't sown and gather where I haven't scattered, then you should have deposited my money with the bankers, and I would have received my money back with interest when I returned.'

'So take the talent from him and give it to the one who has ten talents. For to everyone who has, more will be given, and he will have more than enough. But from the one who does not have, even what he has will be taken away from him. And throw this good-for-nothing servant into the outer darkness, where there will be weeping and gnashing of teeth.'"

Matthew 25:14-30

WHAT DOES IT MEAN?

....
....
....
....
....
....
....
....
....
....
....
....
....

THE RIGHT ONE

REWRITE THE LIST IN THE CORRECT ORDER.

1. Cleansed a leper.	1.
2. Raised a widow's son from the dead.	2.
3. Healed a centurion's servant.	3.
4. Healed a man with a shriveled hand.	4.
5. Healed Simon's mother-in-law.	5.
6. Cast many demons ("Legion") out of one man.	6.
7. Calmed the windstorm.	7.
8. Forgave and healed a paralytic.	8.
9. Healed many people and cast out demons.	9.
10. Made Simon Peter catch a large number of fish.	10.
11. Healed Simon's mother-in-law.	11.
12. Cast out a demon.	12.

QUOTES

"Saul, Saul, why are you persecuting me?"

BOOK:

....

CHAPTER:

....

VERSE:

....

BOOK:

....

CHAPTER:

....

VERSE:

....

"Aeneas, Jesus Christ heals you. Get up and make your bed."

"...Won't you ever stop perverting the straight paths of the Lord?"

BOOK:

....

CHAPTER:

....

VERSE:

....

UNSCRAMBLE

1. ...CESIN HEYT CEVIREED HET ROWD THIW AGERANESES NAD MAXENIED HET PRICSURETS LIADY OT ESE FI HESET GHITNS REWE OS.

....

....

....

....

2. NAD YM OGD ILWL PLYPUS LAL OYUR EDENS CORNCADIG OT SIH CHERIS NI LORGY NI HIRSTC SUJES.

....

....

....

....

3. NI HET NIGNIGBEN SAW HET ROWD, NAD HET ROWD SAW THIW OGD, NAD HET ROWD SAW OGD.

....

....

....

....

4. OD OYU TON KWON HATT OYUR DYBO SI A LEPEMT FO HET LYHO TIRPIS, HOW SI NI OYU, MOHW OYU VEHA CEVIREED MORF OGD?

....

....

....

....

VERSE-SPOTTING

FIND THE VERSE THAT DOESN'T BELONG.

"Absalom was riding on his mule when he happened to meet David's soldiers. When the mule went under the tangled branches of a large oak tree, Absalom's head was caught fast in the tree. The mule under him kept going, so he was suspended in midair.

One of the men saw him and informed Joab. He said, 'I just saw Absalom hanging in an oak tree!' 'You just saw him!' Joab exclaimed. 'Why didn't you strike him to the ground right there? I would have given you ten silver pieces and a belt!'

The man replied to Joab, 'Even if I had the weight of a thousand pieces of silver in my hand, I would not raise my hand against the king's son.' So he threw the silver into the temple and departed."

PIX-CROSS

SOLVE THE NONOGRAM TO REVEAL THE HIDDEN PICTURE.

Row clues (top to bottom):
- 4
- 4
- 2
- 2 2 2 2 2 2 2 2
- 2
- 2 2 2 2 2 2 2 2
- 2 2 2 2 2 2 2 2
- 2 2 2 2 2 2 2 2
- 2 2 2 8 2 2 2
- 2 2 2 6 2 2 2
- 2 2 3 2 3 2 2
- 2 2 1 2 2 2
- 2 2 10 2 2
- 3 3 2 3 3
- 2 16 2
- 2 12 2
- 4 4 4
- 4 2 4
- 14
- 10
- 2
- 2
- 4
- 6
- 8
- 10
- 12
- 14
- 14
- 8

Column clues (left to right):
| 1 3 | 1 7 | 6 | 3 | 1 5 4 | 1 7 2 | 4 2 | 1 4 3 2 | 1 6 2 2 2 | 3 2 2 3 | 1 3 3 2 2 4 | 1 4 2 2 6 | 2 2 2 2 7 | 2 2 2 3 2 8 | 30 | 30 | 2 2 2 3 2 8 | 2 2 2 2 7 | 1 4 2 2 6 | 1 3 3 2 2 4 | 3 2 2 3 | 1 6 2 2 2 | 1 4 3 2 | 4 2 | 1 7 2 | 1 5 4 | 3 | 6 | 1 7 | 1 3 | 0 |

WORD-SEARCH

CONTAINED WITHIN THIS PUZZLE YOU MUST FIND ALL CAPITALIZED WORDS FROM THE VERSES BELOW.

```
B C I E S Y I G C B A L P E L
Y R Y J U V N C R O S V D L A
P R Z I L H H F I U X A A R C
E S O B T A I N M N E M V E Z
K T K W O A D Z I D K M I M D
N C E O N G O D N W U S D E E
O S W R M B H L A P G R D M L
E F M Q N D G A L N X N Q B E
A N G F P A A O I R E R D E C
J X D Y B R L H S C M T A R T
C E H U E M T R S P G C D H D
D Y S F R I S E N L E L Y R O
Y G F U Z E D Y G S U L O U K
N U P X S C H R I S T W R R J
S A L V A T I O N V S H K X Y
```

"**REMEMBER JESUS CHRIST, RISEN** from the **DEAD** and **DESCENDED** from **DAVID**, according to my **GOSPEL**, for which I **SUFFER** to the point of being **BOUND** like a **CRIMINAL**. But the **WORD** of **GOD** is not bound. This is why I **ENDURE** all **THINGS** for the **ELECT**: so that they also may **OBTAIN SALVATION**, which is in Christ Jesus, with **ETERNAL GLORY**."

CRISS-CROSS

USE THE DEFINITIONS BELOW TO FIND THE WORDS AND GUESS THE THEME.

ACROSS:

1. Defenestrated by her eunuch servants.

3. Usurper and killer of pregnant women.

5. Pierced Absalom's chest with three spears.

6. Had the prophet Jeremiah beaten.

9. Ordered the slaughter of babies in and around Bethlehem (3 words)

10. Attempted to sabotage the rebuilding of Jerusalem's walls.

DOWN:

1. Conspired against Solomon.

2. Mocked the Lord.

4. Divorced his wife to marry his niece (2 w.).

7. Plotted to have John the Baptist beheaded.

8. Killed his six brothers and some of their children.

9. Planned the first genocide against the Jews.

SUDOKU

MATCH THE HIGHLIGHTED NUMBER SEQUENCE TO THE CHAPTER AND VERSE BELOW.

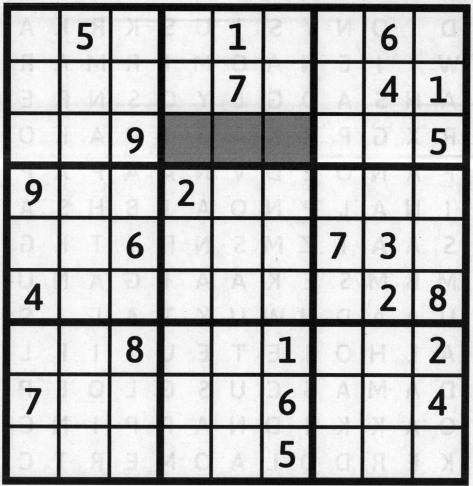

ISAIAH _ : _ - _

"And one called to another:

'Holy, holy, holy is the LORD
of Armies;
his glory fills
the whole earth.'

The foundations of the doorways shook at the sound of their voices, and the temple was filled with smoke."

DEFINITION SEARCH

FIND ALL WORDS PLACED HORIZONTALLY, VERTICALLY, OR DIAGONALLY,
AND MATCH THEM TO THE DEFINITIONS BELOW.

```
D I O N Y S I U S K R K A
W I I E N A O M I R M A R
A H S A D G L Y O S N R E
R X G P R K A G I P A K O
F A N O E D V N A A P A P
I N A L P N O A J B H S A
S A A I Z M S N R I T K G
M B M S E K A A I G A N U
U A A D N W U K T A L I S
A L H O I E T E U I I F L
D A M A S C U S G L O E P
O A K K I D N A P P I N G
K E R D O L A O M E R T C
```

- Intelligent and beautiful wife of Nabal.
- Son of Caleb.
- Paul stood in the middle of it and addressed the crowd.
- En route there, Paul was converted.
- Known as "the Aeropagite."
- Belief in and/or reverence for devils.
- Commission to preach the Gospel given to Paul.
- Condition referred to in Leviticus 21:20.
- Pagan astronomical deity.
- Judge Jair was buried there.
- Settlement in the South of Judah.
- King of Elam.
- Abducting a person against their will.
- Abraham took one along to sacrifice his son.
- Solomon imported horses from there.
- Ammonite mother of Rehoboam.
- Surly and mean descendant of Caleb.
- Wife of Elimelech.
- His tribe furnished 53,400 soldiers at Kadesh Bernea.
- First point of Europe touched by Paul.

PARABLES

"At that time the kingdom of heaven will be like ten virgins who took their lamps and went out to meet the groom. Five of them were foolish and five were wise. When the foolish took their lamps, they didn't take oil with them; but the wise ones took oil in their flasks with their lamps. When the groom was delayed, they all became drowsy and fell asleep.

In the middle of the night there was a shout: 'Here's the groom! Come out to meet him.'

Then all the virgins got up and trimmed their lamps. The foolish ones said to the wise ones, 'Give us some of your oil, because our lamps are going out.'

The wise ones answered, 'No, there won't be enough for us and for you. Go instead to those who sell oil, and buy some for yourselves.'

When they had gone to buy some, the groom arrived, and those who were ready went in with him to the wedding banquet, and the door was shut.

Later the rest of the virgins also came and said, 'Master, master, open up for us!'

He replied, 'Truly I tell you, I don't know you!'

Therefore be alert, because you don't know either the day or the hour."

Matthew 25:1-13

WHAT DOES IT MEAN?

....
....
....
....
....
....
....
....
....
....
....
....

WHAT DOES IT MEAN?

....
....
....
....
....
....
....
....

"A creditor had two debtors. One owed five hundred denarii, and the other fifty. Since they could not pay it back, he graciously forgave them both. So, which of them will love him more?"

Luke 7:41-42

THE RIGHT ONE

13. Transfigured in front of Peter, James, and John.	13.
14. Raised Jairus' daughter from the dead.	14.
15. Cast a demon out of an epileptic boy.	15.
16. Healed a swollen man.	16.
17. Healed a blind beggar.	17.
18. Cast a mute demon out of a man.	18.
19. Resurrected!	19.
20. Fed 5,000.	20.
21. Healed ten lepers.	21.
22. Regrew the high priest's servant's ear.	22.
23. Healed a bent and disabled woman.	23.
24. A woman was healed from bleeding by touching his robe.	24.

QUOTES

"If a man seduces a virgin who is not engaged, and he sleeps with her, he must certainly pay the bridal price for her to be his wife."

BOOK:

....

CHAPTER:

....

VERSE:

....

BOOK:

....

CHAPTER:

....

VERSE:

....

"Why have you beaten your donkey these three times? Look, I came out to oppose you, because I consider what you are doing to be evil."

"Prophesy! Who is it that hit you?"

BOOK:

....

CHAPTER:

....

VERSE:

....

UNSCRAMBLE

REARRANGE ONE WORD AT THE TIME, IN THE SAME ORDER THEY'RE PRESENTED, TO REVEAL THE PRECISE VERSE FROM THE SCRIPTURE.

1. HIST SI WHO EW VEHA MECO OT WONK VELO: EH DILA WOND SIH FELI ROF SU.

....

....

....

....

2. WHO OGOD NAD SANPLEAT TI SI NEWH THERROBS VELI HERTEGTO NI HONMARY!

....

....

....

....

3. CEPAE I VEALE HITW OYU. YM CEPAE I VEGI OT OYU.

....

....

....

....

4. ROF HET ROWD FO OGD SI VINILG NAD FECFETIVE NAD HARPERS NATH YNA BLEDOU-GEDDE WORDS...

....

....

....

....

VERSE-SPOTTING

"The next day, John was standing with two of his disciples. When he saw Jesus passing by, he said, 'God himself will provide the lamb for the burnt offering, my son.'

The two disciples heard him say this and followed Jesus. When Jesus turned and noticed them following him, he asked them, 'What are you looking for?'

They said to Him, 'Rabbi' (which means 'Teacher'), 'where are you staying?'

'Come and you'll see,' he replied. So they went and saw where he was staying, and they stayed with him that day. It was about four in the afternoon."

PIX-CROSS

SOLVE THE NONOGRAM TO REVEAL THE HIDDEN PICTURE.

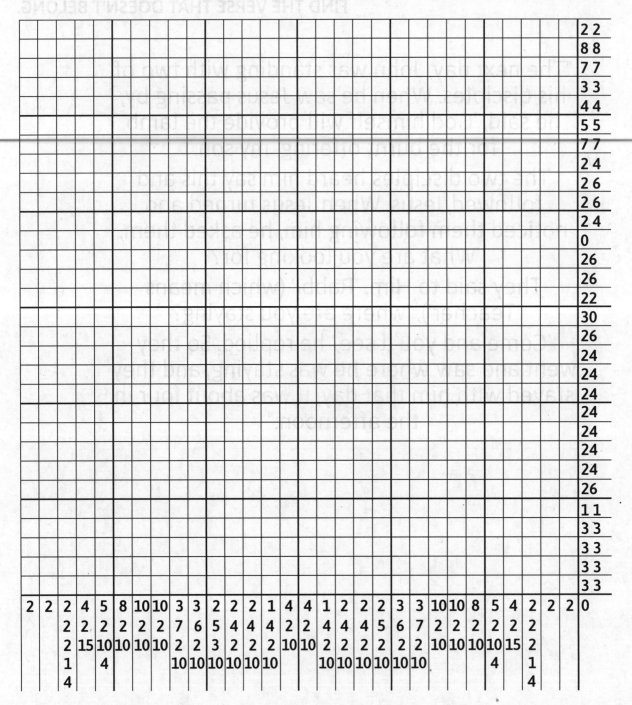

WORD-SEARCH

CONTAINED WITHIN THIS PUZZLE YOU MUST FIND ALL CAPITALIZED WORDS FROM THE VERSES BELOW.

```
F M W W L G E L I P S Z H
E R O P K K E E P C Z A G
B L O C A R E F U L Y G C
S Q L M G Y Q Z S L O A W
R R S C O U N T E D U I C
E B Z R K W X E D G R N O
F E F E R D R O Z X L S M
R C L Q W F G Y D I B T E
A A O U Q B N V K L U S S
I U R I Y W H A T E V E R
N S D R G S H H D V V O W
V E I E Z P R O M I S E D
C R N J L Y Y P O S I N Z
```

"If you **MAKE** a **VOW** to the **LORD** your **GOD**, do not be **SLOW** to **KEEP** it, **BECAUSE** he will **REQUIRE** it of you, and it will be **COUNTED AGAINST** you as **SIN**. But if you **REFRAIN FROM** making a vow, it will not be counted against you as sin. Be **CAREFUL** to do **WHATEVER COMES** from your **LIPS**, because you have **FREELY** vowed what you **PROMISED** to the Lord **YOUR** God."

CRISS-CROSS

USE THE DEFINITIONS BELOW TO FIND THE WORDS AND GUESS THE THEME.

ACROSS:

2. Married Azubah, Jerioth, Ephrath, Ephah, and Maachah.

6. Fathered Jether, Mered, Epher, and Jalon.

8. Married Judith and Basemath at age 40.

9. Allied with kings Asa and Baasha.

12. Had eight wives at the very least.

13. Had sixty children.

15. Married Sarah, Hagar, and Keturah.

16. Married Hannah and Peninnah.

17. Had forty sons.

DOWN:

1. Had seventy sons.

3. Son of Omri.

4. Used vessels looted from the Temple as wine cups.

5. Married Leah, Rachel, Bilhah and Zilpah.

7. Father of Tekoa.

10. Son of Adah and Esau.

11. Married to fourteen women.

14. King David's seer.

SUDOKU

2 CORINTHIANS _ : _ - _

"Now concerning the ministry to the saints, it is unnecessary for me to write to you. For I know your eagerness, and I boast about you to the Macedonians: 'Achaia has been ready since last year', and your zeal has stirred up most of them."

DEFINITION SEARCH

FIND ALL WORDS PLACED HORIZONTALLY, VERTICALLY, OR DIAGONALLY,
AND MATCH THEM TO THE DEFINITIONS BELOW.

```
G H B B I T T E R W A T E R Z
E N L L G L O S S O L A L I A
R H A A V U R X X S E U R B Q
W O S S R E T R I B U T I O N
B S T P H B L Z N L E S L A L
I P U H R I V V A B C P Y S Z
T I S E H N N A Z L G I K T X
U T N M U O B G V U R S I B P
M A X Y S R P W O E C N R I R
E L H R U G T E R F U P M B E
N I O G S I J H G G T Y E L U
C T P A C H A I A L V E B I M
J Y H N Y I B V Y O P E A A
E K R S E U M M P E Y R U T H
B O A N E R G E S B O D Y B H
```

- Corinth was its capital.
- Plural of *byblos* (Greek).
- Expressing disrespect for God.
- Concoction forced upon women suspected of adultery (2w.).
- Tar pitch.
- Herod Agrippa's chamberlain.
- Color on the fringe of every Hebrew garment.
- To show off.
- Temple of the Holy Spirit.
- "Sons of Thunder"
- Allegory of remorsefulness (3 words).
- God's majestic splendor.
- Gift of tongues (Greek).
- Second son of Naphtali.
- Uzziah conquered it with the help of God.
- His end was prophesied by Jeremiah.
- Together with Faith and Love, it is considered one of the main Christian virtues.
- Kindness in welcoming guests or strangers.
- Punishment for wrongdoing.
- Concubine of Nahor.

PARABLES

"Listen! Consider the sower who went out to sow. As he sowed, some seed fell along the path, and the birds came and devoured it. Other seed fell on rocky ground where it didn't have much soil, and it grew up quickly, since the soil wasn't deep. When the sun came up, it was scorched, and since it had no root, it withered away. Other seed fell among thorns, and the thorns came up and choked it, and it didn't produce fruit. Still other seed fell on good ground and it grew up, producing fruit that increased thirty, sixty, and a hundred times." **Mark 4:3-8**

WHAT DOES IT MEAN?

....
....
....
....
....
....
....
....

WHAT DOES IT MEAN?

....
....
....
....
....
....
....
....

"What do you think? A man had two sons. He went to the first and said, 'My son, go work in the vineyard today.' He answered, 'I don't want to,' but later he changed his mind and went. Then the man went to the other and said the same thing. 'I will, sir,' he answered, but he didn't go. Which of the two did their father's will?"

Matthew 21:28-31

WHAT DOES IT MEAN?

....
....
....
....
....
....
....

"Be ready for service and have your lamps lit. You are to be like people waiting for their master to return from the wedding banquet so that when he comes and knocks, they can open the door for him at once."

Luke 12:35-36

THE RIGHT ONE

REWRITE THE LIST IN THE CORRECT ORDER.

1. Gave the apostles a large catch of fish.	1.
2. Walked on water.	2.
3. Healed a man born blind.	3.
4. Showed knowledge of a woman's sinful life.	4.
5. Turned water into wine at a wedding.	5.
6. Raised Lazarus from the dead.	6.
7. Fed 5,000.	7.
8. Healed an official's son.	8.
9. Healed a disabled man.	9.
10. Judas and the soldiers fall back.	10.
11. Resurrected!	11.

QUOTES

IDENTIFY THE PROPER BOOK, CHAPTER, AND VERSE THESE BIBLE QUOTATIONS BELONG TO.

"If those who do not deserve to drink the cup must drink it, can you possibly remain unpunished?..."

BOOK:
....

CHAPTER:
....

VERSE:
....

BOOK:
....

CHAPTER:
....

VERSE:
....

"What then? Should we sin because we are not under the law but under grace? Absolutely not!"

"For me, to live is Christ and to die is gain."

BOOK:
....

CHAPTER:
....

VERSE:
....

UNSCRAMBLE

REARRANGE ONE WORD AT THE TIME, IN THE SAME ORDER THEY'RE PRESENTED, TO REVEAL THE PRECISE VERSE FROM THE SCRIPTURE.

1. ON NEO SAH TERAGRE VELO HANT HIST: OT YAL WOND SIH FELI ROF SIH ENFRIDS.

....

....

....

....

2. KINDAMN, EH SAH LODT HACE FO OYU THAW SI OGDO NAD THAW TI SI HET ORLD QUIERERS FO OYU...

....

....

....

....

3. OS THIAF MESCO MORF THAW SI DERAH, NAD THAW SI DERAH MESCO THUGHRO HET SAGEMES TABOU HRISTC.

....

....

....

....

4. TUB OT LAL HOW IDD CEIVERE MIH, EH VEGA HEMT HET THRIG OT EB DRECHILN FO OGD...

....

....

....

....

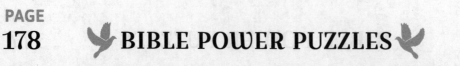

VERSE-SPOTTING

"Just one thing: With one act of vengeance, let me pay back the Philistines for my two eyes. Then, whether I come and see you or I am absent, I will hear about you that you are standing firm in one spirit, in one accord, contending together for the faith of the gospel, not being frightened in any way by your opponents. This is a sing of destruction for them, but of your salvation—and this is from God."

PIX-CROSS

SOLVE THE NONOGRAM TO REVEAL THE HIDDEN PICTURE.

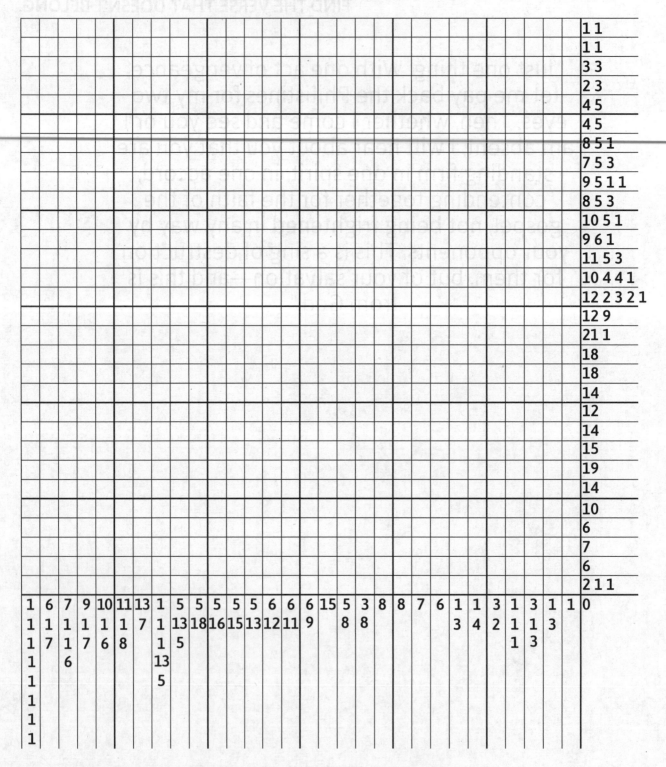

WORD-SEARCH

CONTAINED WITHIN THIS PUZZLE YOU MUST FIND ALL CAPITALIZED WORDS FROM THE VERSES BELOW.

```
F Z H R J H M M G G A Z H
K L U R L E N W O W Z B R
G C E I J A K E E X A L T
D P V E O R D N A E Y T R
G E Y P Y T W R D R P H E
D G F M I S E R A B L E S
H L A U G H T E R W J R I
A S I N N E R S K B M E S
N K G A C Z T G Z V O F T
D P L W S U B M I T U O Q
S X O C L E A N S E R R F
V Y O P U R I F Y Q N E I
H U M B L E G K K Y R R I
```

"**THEREFORE**, **SUBMIT** to God. **RESIST** the **DEVIL**, and he will **FLEE** from you. **DRAW NEAR** to God, and he will draw near to you. **CLEANSE** your **HANDS**, **SINNERS**, and **PURIFY** your **HEARTS**, you double-minded. Be **MISERABLE** and **MOURN** and **WEEP**. Let your **LAUGHTER** be turned to mourning and your **JOY** to **GLOOM**. **HUMBLE** yourselves before the Lord, and he will **EXALT** you."

CRISS-CROSS

USE THE DEFINITIONS BELOW TO FIND THE WORDS AND GUESS THE THEME.

ACROSS:

1. Had 700 wives.
7. Installed as king of Judah by Nebuchadnezzar II.
8. Reigned eight years in Jerusalem.
9. Had four wives.
10. Was deported to Babylon.
11. Had 18 wives.

DOWN:

2. Married Adah and Zillah.
3. Also married an Ethiopian woman.
4. Married Maachah and Zelophehad.
5. His second wife was named Atarah.
6. Divorced both Hushim and Baara.
10. His sons rode thirty donkeys.

SUDOKU

MATCH THE HIGHLIGHTED NUMBER SEQUENCE TO THE CHAPTER AND VERSE BELOW.

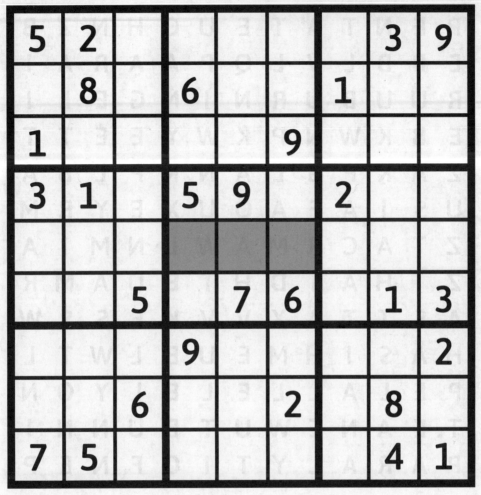

5	2						3	9
	8		6			1		
1				9				
3	1		5	9		2		
		5		7	6		1	3
		9						2
		6			2		8	
7	5						4	1

1 PETER _ : _ - _

"Therefore, rid yourselves of all malice, all deceit, hypocrisy, envy, and all slander. Like newborn infants, desire the pure milk of the word, so that you may grow up into your salvation, if you have tasted that the Lord is good."

DEFINITION SEARCH

FIND ALL WORDS PLACED HORIZONTALLY, VERTICALLY, OR DIAGONALLY,
AND MATCH THEM TO THE DEFINITIONS BELOW.

```
P E N T A T E U C H N Z B
E B B L V L Q P A A R A I
R U U B U R N I N G E L I
E B K W N P K W Y E E T T
Z A K P G L A N K P L B A
U S I A F A O U X E Y R M
Z T A C R M A W L N M I A
Z I H A I D H T E U A M R
A S T T A X V V K E S S W
H A S I H M E U B L W T L
P E L A L L E L E L Y O N
T E A N E W U T B U N N I
P A R A L Y T I C F N E P
```

- Sulfur.
- Egyptian city called Pi-Beseth.
- Son of Heman.
- Leader who sealed the covenant with Nehemiah.
- —bush.
- "God most high" (Hebrew, 2 words).
- Number of apostles before Matthias.
- Judge and high priest from Shiloh.
- Commander of 200,000 archers.
- Paul blinded him.
- Also know as Naarai.
- Its capital was Laodicea.

- Sergius —.
- Jesus both forgave and healed one.
- Port city of Lycia.
- First five books of the Bible.
- Founded Gedor with Jered.
- Place where God struck someone dead for touching the Ark (2w.).
- Witness statement.
- Disguised herself as a prostitute.

PARABLES

"There was a rich man who received an accusation that his manager was squandering his possessions. So he called the manager in and asked, 'What is this I hear about you? Give an account of your management, because you can no longer be my manager.'

Then the manager said to himself, 'What will I do, since my master is taking the management away from me? I'm not strong enough to dig; I'm ashamed to beg. I know what I'll do so that when I'm removed from management, people will welcome me into their homes.'

So he summoned each one of his master's debtors. 'How much do you owe my master?' he asked the first one.

'A hundred measures of olive oil,' he said.

'Take your invoice,' he told him, 'sit down quickly, and write fifty.'

Next he asked another, 'How much do you owe?'

'A hundred measures of wheat,' he said.

'Take your invoice,' he told him, 'and write eighty.'

The master praised the unrighteous manager because he had acted shrewdly. For the children of this age are more shrewd than the children of light in dealing with their own people."

Luke 16:1-8

WHAT DOES IT MEAN?

....
....
....
....
....
....
....
....
....
....
....
....

WHAT DOES IT MEAN?

....
....
....
....
....
....
....
....

"There was a judge in a certain town who didn't fear God or respect people. And a widow in that town kept coming to him, saying, 'Give me justice against my adversary.'

For a while he was unwilling, but later he said to himself, 'Even though I don't fear God or respect people, yet because this widow keeps pestering me, I will give her justice, so she doesn't wear me out by her persistent coming.'"

Luke 18:2-5

THE RIGHT ONE

REWRITE THE LIST IN THE CORRECT ORDER.

1. Destruction of Sodom and Gomorrah.	1.
2. The ten plagues of Egypt.	2.
3. The flood.	3.
4. Birth of Isaac.	4.
5. The waters of Marah sweetened.	5.
6. Aaron's rod changed into a serpent.	6.
7. Creation.	7.
8. The Red Sea parted.	8.
9. Manna fell from heaven.	9.
10. Lot's wife turned into a pillar of salt.	10.
11. The burning bush.	11.
12. The confusion of tongues.	12.

QUOTES

"...I have healed this water. No longer will death or unfruitfulness result from it."

BOOK:
....

CHAPTER:
....

VERSE:
....

BOOK:
....

CHAPTER:
....

VERSE:
....

"Preserve justice and do what is right, for my salvation is coming soon, and my righteousness will be revealed."

"Your faith has saved you. Go in peace."

BOOK:
....

CHAPTER:
....

VERSE:
....

UNSCRAMBLE

1. SEDSELB SI HET NEO HOW DUNERES LASTRI, SEBECAU HWEN EH SAH DOTOS HET SETT EH ILWL CEVIERE HET WORNC FO FELI...

....

....

....

....

2. ... TEL SU WARD RANE THIW A URET HARTE NI LULF RASUSACEN FO THIAF, THIW RUO HARTES KLEDPRINS CANLE...

....

....

....

....

3. ROF HIST RYVE ONSARE, KEMA REEVY FORFET OT PLEPUSMENT OYUR THIAF THIW SODOGNES, SODOGNES THIW LEDGELODWONK...

....

....

....

....

4. I MA RESU FO HIST, HATT EH HOW TEDTARS HET DOGO KWOR NI OYU ILWL RYRAC TI NO OT PLETIONMOC TILNU HTE YAD FO HIRSTC SUJES.

....

....

....

....

VERSE-SPOTTING

FIND THE VERSE THAT DOESN'T BELONG.

"Suddenly, a hand touched me and set me shaking to my hands and knees. He said to me, 'Daniel, you are a man treasured by God. Understand the words that I'm saying to you. Stand on your feet, for I have now been sent to you.' After he said this to me, I stood trembling. 'Don't be afraid, Daniel,' he said to me, 'I know your works, your labor, and your endurance, and that you cannot tolerate evil people. I have come because of your prayers. But the prince of the kingdom of Persia opposed me for twenty-one days. Then Michael, one of the chief princes, came to help me after I had been left there with the kings of Persia. Now I have come to help you understand what will happen to your people in the last days, for the vision refers to those days.'

While he was saying these words to me, I turned my face toward the ground and was speechless."

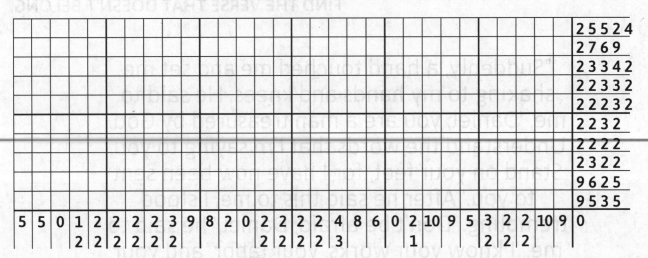

Row clues (right side):
- 2 5 5 2 4
- 2 7 6 9
- 2 3 3 4 2
- 2 2 3 3 2
- 2 2 2 3 2
- 2 2 3 2
- 2 2 2 2
- 2 3 2 2
- 9 6 2 5
- 9 5 3 5

Column clues (bottom):

5	5	0	1	2	2	2	2	3	9	8	2	0	2	2	2	2	4	8	6	0	2	10	9	5	3	2	2	10	9	0
			2	2	2	2	2	2			2		2	2	2	2	4	3			2	1			3	2	2			
			2	2	2	2	2	2					2	2	2	2					1				2	2	2			

WORD-SEARCH

CONTAINED WITHIN THIS PUZZLE YOU MUST FIND ALL CAPITALIZED WORDS FROM THE VERSES BELOW.

```
F I G H T P E T I T I O N
U P H O L D N W U G U V W
D L L N Y D E H N S B H R
I N O A E C M E A S N A E
R O R R N B I R G W E O G
E P Y V D H E E A H K N I
C K U N Q N S V I Y N F D
T V N A M E Z E N E G H Y
I C X C L T U R S Y K E C
O M P P L B Z O T U W A A
N W M I I Z H I A P H V U
N E U L Q C C Q X M E E S
T B B I P E O P L E N N E
```

"**WHEN** your **PEOPLE** go out to **FIGHT AGAINST** their **ENEMIES**, **WHEREVER** you **SEND** them, and they **PRAY** to the **LORD** in the **DIRECTION** of the **CITY** you have **CHOSEN** and the **TEMPLE** I have **BUILT** for your **NAME**, may you **HEAR** their prayer and **PETITION** in **HEAVEN** and **UPHOLD** their **CAUSE**."

CRISS-CROSS

USE THE DEFINITIONS BELOW TO FIND THE WORDS AND GUESS THE THEME.

ACROSS:

1. Made silver shrines of Artemis.
7. She was a tentmaker.
8. A carpenter by trade.
11. Son of Meonothai.
12. Worked as a tentmaker with his wife.
13. Chief artisan of the Tabernacle.

DOWN:

2. Carried out repairs on the house of the temple servants.
3. The first blacksmith.
4. Father of Joab.
5. Master of carpentry, weaving, and embroidery.
6. Grandfather of Joab.
9. Born from a family of craftsmen.
10. A skilled tentmaker.

SUDOKU

MATCH THE HIGHLIGHTED NUMBER SEQUENCE TO THE CHAPTER AND VERSE BELOW.

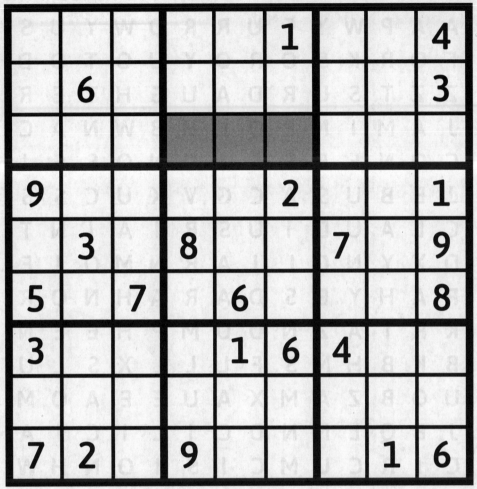

ECCLESIASTES _ : _ - _

"It is better to go to a house of mourning than to go to a house of feasting, since that is the end of all mankind, and the living should take it to heart.
Grief is better than laughter, for when a face is sad, a heart may be glad.
The heart of the wise is in a house of mourning, but the heart of fools is in a house of pleasure."

DEFINITION SEARCH

FIND ALL WORDS PLACED HORIZONTALLY, VERTICALLY, OR DIAGONALLY,
AND MATCH THEM TO THE DEFINITIONS BELOW.

```
A A P W Y F U R R O W Y U S
F O R K S O R O Y U O T D D
Z Z T S U R D A U G H T E R
J A M I N E Q L H B W N A C
C O N F E S S I O N O S E I
J E B U S A C G V K U C S S
C L A U D I U S R I A I N T
D X Y N C L J A R N M O J E
P A H Y B S D A R A H N O R
K R T A Z N D U M P H E E N
B K B H M S F L L L X S L U
U O B Z A M X A U E E A O M
J B Q L N N D C I L I C I A
C I R C U M C I S I O N H W
```

- It's main city was Tarsus.
- Surgical removal of the foreskin.
- Joseph was cast into one.
- A severe famine happened during his reign.
- Admission of guilt.
- Second son of Haman put to death by the Jews.
- —the Great.
- Ancestor of a group of Solomon's servants.
- Female offspring.
- Son of Eliab, brother of Abiram.

- Hung on the front mast of a ship.
- Bezalel made bronze ones.
- Metal smelting oven.
- Long trench made with a plow.
- Levite helper of Ezra.
- Clan leader of the tribe of Simeon.
- Former name of Jerusalem.
- King of Madon.
- Minor prophet, son of Pethuel.

PARABLES

"For this reason, the kingdom of heaven can be compared to a king who wanted to settle accounts with his servants. When he began to settle accounts, one who owed ten thousand talents was brought before him. Since he did not have the money to pay it back, his master commanded that he, his wife, his children, and everything he had be sold to pay the debt.

At this, the servant fell facedown before him and said, 'Be patient with me, and I will pay you everything.' Then the master of that servant had compassion, released him, and forgave him the loan. That servant went out and found one of his fellow servants who owed him a hundred denarii. He grabbed him, started choking him, and said, 'Pay what you owe!'

At this, his fellow servant fell down and began begging him, 'Be patient with me, and I will pay you back.' But he wasn't willing. Instead, he went and threw him into prison until he could pay what was owed. When the other servants saw what had taken place, they were deeply distressed and went and reported to their master everything that had happened.

Then, after he had summoned him, his master said to him, 'You wicked servant! I forgave you all that debt because you begged me. Shouldn't you also have had mercy on your fellow servant, as I had mercy on you?'

And because he was angry, his master handed him over to the jailers to be tortured until he could pay everything that was owed."

Matthew 18:23-34

WHAT DOES IT MEAN?

....
....
....
....
....
....
....
....
....
....
....
....
....
....
....
....
....
....
....
....
....
....
....
....

THE RIGHT ONE

REWRITE THE LIST IN THE CORRECT ORDER.

13. Jordan river parted.	13.
14. The bronze serpent healed the people.	14.
15. Aaron's rod budded at Kadesh.	15.
16. Fire consumed 250.	16.
17. People consumed by fire.	17.
18. Fire devoured Nadab and Abihu.	18.
19. Water sprouted from a rock.	19.
20. Korah and company swallowed by the earth.	20.
21. Miriam contracted leprosy.	21.
22. 14,700 slain by a plague.	22.
23. Water sprouted from the rock in Zin.	23.
24. Balaam's donkey spoke.	24.

QUOTES

"The flesh of his foreskin must be circumcised on the eighth day."

BOOK:

....

CHAPTER:

....

VERSE:

....

BOOK:

....

CHAPTER:

....

VERSE:

....

"His power will be great, but it will not be his own..."

"...The kingdom of the world has become the kingdom of our Lord and of his Christ, and he will reign forever and ever."

BOOK:

....

CHAPTER:

....

VERSE:

....

REARRANGE ONE WORD AT THE TIME, IN THE SAME ORDER THEY'RE PRESENTED, TO REVEAL THE PRECISE VERSE FROM THE SCRIPTURE.

1. ROF HET ORLD SAH POPANITED HET SIBSELNG—FELI REFOREVREMO.

....

....

....

....

2. HEREREFOT, TEL SU PACHAPRO HET THEORN FO CEGRA THIW LOBDNESS, OS HATT EW YAM CEIREVE CYREM NAD DINF CEGRA...

....

....

....

....

3. KETA THELIGD NI HET ROLD NAD EH ILWL VEGI OYU OYUR ARHET'S SIRESED.

....

....

....

....

4. ROF OGD IDD TON NEDS SIH NOS TONI HET ORLDW OT DEMCONN HET ORLDW, TUB OT VESA HET ORLDW HUORGTH MIH.

....

....

....

....

VERSE-SPOTTING

FIND THE VERSE THAT DOESN'T BELONG.

"When those around him saw what was going to happen, they asked, 'Lord, should we strike with the sword?' Then one of them struck the high priest's slave and cut off his right ear.

But Jesus responded, 'No more of this!' And touching his ear, He healed him. Then Jesus said to the chief priests, temple police, and the elders who had come for Him, 'You come against me with sword, spear, and javelin, but I come against you in the name of the Lord of Armies, the God of the ranks of Israel—you have defied him.'"

PIX-CROSS

SOLVE THE NONOGRAM TO REVEAL THE HIDDEN PICTURE.

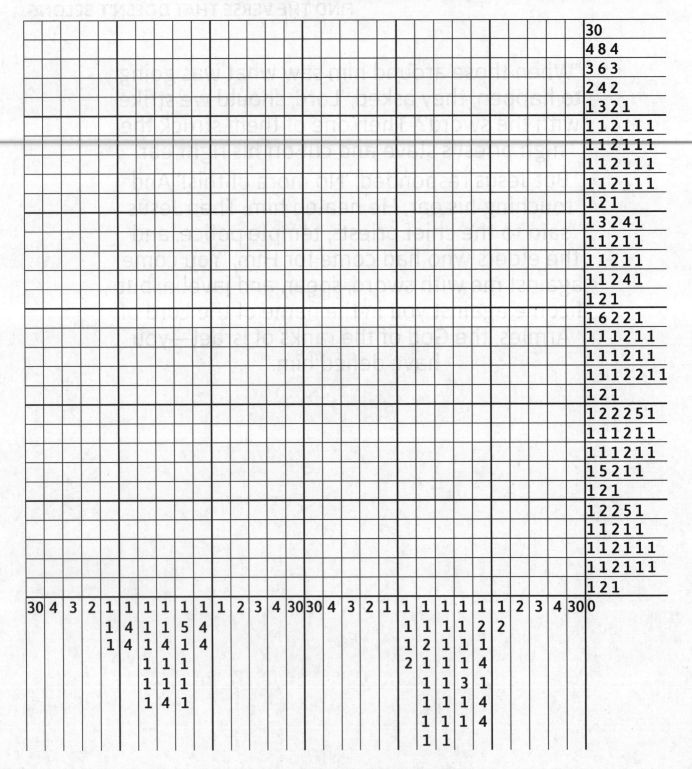

WORD-SEARCH

```
W I T H H E L D P E O P L E M
K O M W G K W W P Q R D Z K O
W O D W O Z B N K K W Y C M T
K M C O R R O S I O N B O C H
L N L N D W K P M S P B M P E
O W H Z S I W E O X G Y E D A
U E F K E T R T R Y H O E A T
T A G A I N S T R S O W V S E
C L O T H E S R S E C J A G N
R T U E I S X M T D A L E H S
Y H R L C S J Y O L G S S B I
V X I F I W F I R E O E U A L
X A M I S E R I E S L H T R V
W R O T T E D W D F D M X U E
O U P R V P N R I C H D Z C R
```

"**COME** now, you **RICH PEOPLE**, **WEEP** and **WAIL** over the **MISERIES** that are coming on you. Your **WEALTH** has **ROTTED**, and your **CLOTHES** are **MOTH-EATEN**. Your **GOLD** and **SILVER** are corroded, and their **CORROSION** will be a **WITNESS AGAINST** you and will **EAT** your **FLESH** like **FIRE**. You have **STORED** up **TREASURE** in the **LAST** days. **LOOK**! The pay that you **WITHHELD** from the **WORKERS** who mowed your fields cries out, and the **OUTCRY** of the harvesters has reached the ears of the Lord of Hosts."

CRISS-CROSS

USE THE DEFINITIONS BELOW TO FIND THE WORDS AND GUESS THE THEME.

ACROSS:
1. Enlisted Barak to defeat Sisera.
7. Mother of Ishmael.
8. Gave birth to fraternal twins.
12. Anxious sister of Lazarus.
13. Jewish wife of Persian king Xerxes.
14. Set her baby adrift in a basket.
18. Married Jacob through deceit.
19. Served God day and night.
20. Mother of Samuel.
21. Wife of Aquila.
22. Betrayed Samson's love.

DOWN:
2. Mother of John the Baptist.
3. Harbored Hebrew spies.
4. Aaron and Moses' sister.
5. Visited by angel Gabriel.
6. Created by God.
9. Had an affair with King David.
10. Mother of Isaac.
11. Persecuted Elijah.
15. Wife of Ananias.
16. Wife of Felix.
17. Resurrected by Peter.

SUDOKU

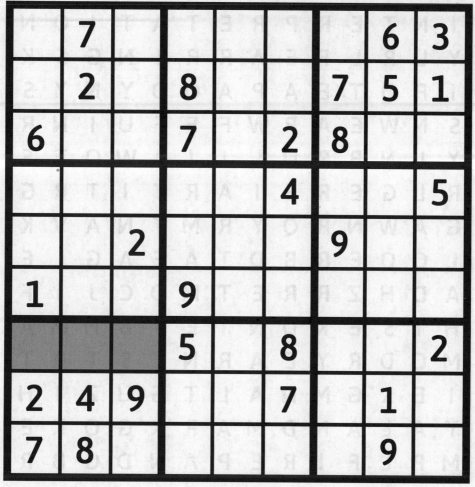

1 PETER _ : _ - _

"In the same way, wives, submit yourselves to your own husbands so that, even if some disobey the word, they may be won over without a word by the way their wives live when they observe your pure, reverent lives. Don't let your beauty consist of outward things like elaborate hairstyles and wearing gold jewelry or fine clothes, but rather what is inside the heart—the imperishable quality of a gentle and quiet spirit, which is of great worth in God's sight.

For in the past, the holy women who put their hope in God also adorned themselves in this way, submitting to their own husbands, just as Sarah obeyed Abraham, calling him lord. You have become her children when you do what is good and do not fear any intimidation."

DEFINITION SEARCH

FIND ALL WORDS PLACED HORIZONTALLY, VERTICALLY, OR DIAGONALLY,
AND MATCH THEM TO THE DEFINITIONS BELOW.

```
I N T E R P R E T A T I O N
Y U R L F E A R R I N G S K
I R Q T E A P A O D Y N Y S
S N W E A P W F F U I N R
Y L N B R U L I I A W O T F
R L G E R E I A R T I T R G
G A W N R Q Y R M T N A V K
L O O E R B D T A E A G L E
A D H Z R R E T M D C J I F
H I S E K D N I E J B H M A
M C D R Y E A R N E S T R T
I E K G M N A L T G U Z I H
Y A L A N D M A R K G Q K E
M P L F I R E P A N D G B R
```

- John the Evangelist's symbol.
- Boys wore them in the Old Testament.
- Pray in —.
- Israelites were defeated here twice.
- Tower of —.
- —of God.
- Abba.
- —calf.
- Container for carrying live or dead coals.
- Sky expanse.
- Son of Bani.
- True self (2 words).
- Hermeneutics.
- Smallest letter (Greek).
- One of David's mighty warriors.
- Goliath's brother.
- Father of Jabal and Jubal.
- OT book coming after Jeremiah.
- A mark showing the boundary of a piece of land.
- Wealthy city in Asia Minor.

WORD WHEEL

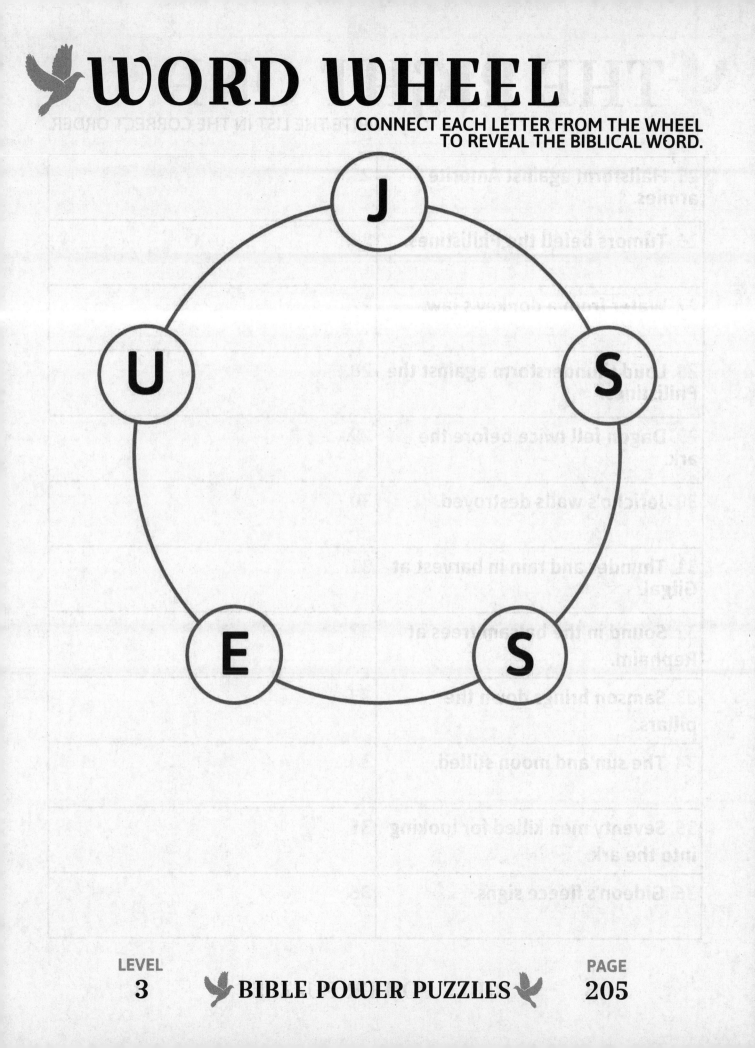

25. Hailstorm against Amorite armies.	25.
26. Tumors befell the Philistines.	26.
27. Water from a donkey's jaw.	27.
28. Loud thunderstorm against the Philistines.	28.
29. Dagon fell twice before the ark.	29.
30. Jericho's walls destroyed.	30.
31. Thunder and rain in harvest at Gilgal.	31.
32. Sound in the balsam trees at Rephaim.	32.
33. Samson brings down the pillars.	33.
34. The sun and moon stilled.	34.
35. Seventy men killed for looking into the ark.	35.
36. Gideon's fleece signs.	36.

CHRISTIAN QUOTES

"Faith is to believe what you do not see; the reward of this faith is to see what you believe."

AUTHOR:

....
....

AUTHOR:

....
....

"We must remember that Satan has his miracles, too."

"Science can purify religion from error and superstition. Religion can purify science from idolatry and false absolutes."

AUTHOR:

....
....

OPPOSITES

UNSCRAMBLE THE LETTERS TO FORM PAIRS OF BIBLICAL ANTONYMS AND ANTAGONISTS.

1. DOOG	≠	1. VILE
1.	≠	1.

2. NIS	≠	2. TUVIRE
2.	≠	2.

3. CHALEMI	≠	3. CIREFUL
3.	≠	3.

4. SESOM	≠	4. HORAHAP
4.	≠	4.

MATCHMAKER

CONNECT THE SITUATION DESCRIBED TO ITS CORRESPONDING BIBLE BOOK, CHAPTER, AND VERSES.

TEMPTATION OF JESUS	MATTHEW 20:29-34
TAMAR IN DISGUISE	DEUTERONOMY 20
RULES OF WAR	1 SAMUEL 10:1
SAUL ANOINTED KING	LUKE 4:1-13
JEHOIADA'S COVENANT	DANIEL 6:19-24
A WORD SPOKEN	PROVERBS 25:11
DANIEL'S RELEASE	2 KINGS 11:17-20
TWO BLIND MEN HEALED	GENESIS 38:12-19

PIX-CROSS

SOLVE THE NONOGRAM TO REVEAL THE HIDDEN PICTURE.

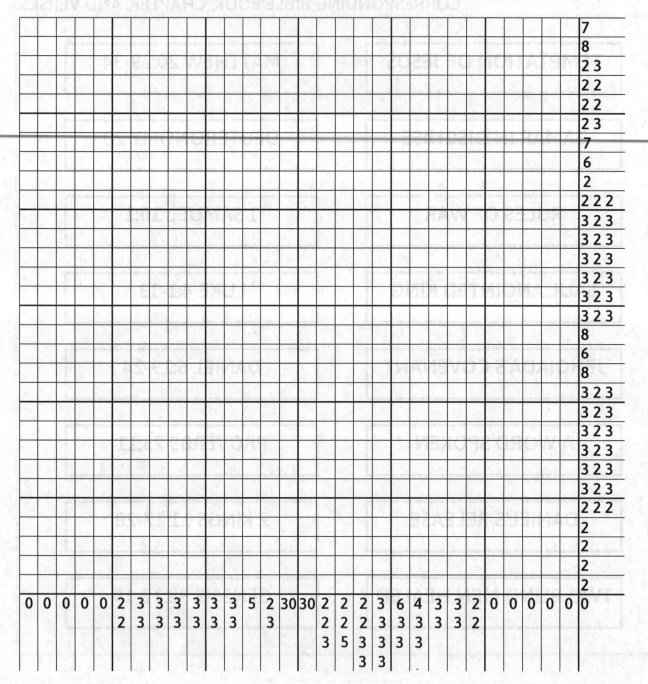

																								7
																								8
																								2 3
																								2 2
																								2 2
																								2 3
																								7
																								6
																								2
																								2 2 2
																								3 2 3
																								3 2 3
																								3 2 3
																								3 2 3
																								3 2 3
																								3 2 3
																								8
																								6
																								8
																								3 2 3
																								3 2 3
																								3 2 3
																								3 2 3
																								3 2 3
																								3 2 3
																								2 2 2
																								2
																								2
																								2
																								2

Column clues:
0 0 0 0 0 2/2 3/3 3/3 3/3 3/3 3/3 3/3 5 2/3 30 30 2/2/3 2/2/5 2/2/3/3 3/3/3/3 6/3/3 4/3/3 3/3 3/3 2/2 0 0 0 0 0 0

WORD-SEARCH

CONTAINED WITHIN THIS PUZZLE YOU MUST FIND ALL CAPITALIZED WORDS FROM THE VERSES BELOW.

```
F Y G Y S G J S C H E M I N G
K P V D A Y M D T L H S U S S
E R R W M H O X P D E A W M P
B O V E H Y T O P U A O S O B
W T N O H E E E G L R F X B M
F E K A I P N N R R A L Q I E
S C C R D C O X A R V C A W Q
H T U R E T E Z H I O L E A D
A F B I T T E R S W O R D S M
R H Y Z Y S H O O T I N G M L
P G W O J C O N C E A L E D I
E V I L D O E R S V R C P P F
N A N G U I S H Z I B I N U E
S Y E R V F B I T L N D O V I
U B L A M E L E S S U T F M Y
```

"God, **HEAR** my **VOICE WHEN** I am in **ANGUISH**.
PROTECT my **LIFE** from the **TERROR** of the **ENEMY**.
HIDE me from the **SCHEMING** of **EVIL PEOPLE**, from the **MOB** of **EVILDOERS**, who
SHARPEN their **TONGUES** like **SWORDS** and **AIM BITTER WORDS** like **ARROWS**,
SHOOTING from **CONCEALED PLACES** at the **BLAMELESS**..."

CRISS-CROSS

USE THE DEFINITIONS BELOW TO FIND THE WORDS AND GUESS THE THEME.

ACROSS:

2. Wife of Hosea.
6. Daughter of Haran.
7. Second wife of King Rehoboam.
8. Wife of Josiah.
11. Ethiopian queen.
12. Second daughter of Job.
17. Aaron's wife.
19. Daughter of Caleb.
20. Wife of Shaharaim.
21. Daughter of Hosea.

DOWN:

1. One of Job's daughters.
3. Daughter of Saul and wife of David.
4. Daughter of Jacob.
5. One of King David's wives.
7. Saul's oldest daughter.
9. Sister of David.
10. Wife of Abraham.
13. Mother of Manasseh.
14. Grandmother of Timothy.
15. Killed by Phineas.
16. Sister of Tubal-cain.
18. Heroine who killed Sisera.

SUDOKU

MATCH THE HIGHLIGHTED NUMBER SEQUENCE
TO THE CHAPTER AND VERSE BELOW.

1					2	5	6	9
6	3					8	7	
2		7						
			2		5			3
		8					5	
		6	4			7		
				9				
		3					1	
				1		2	9	

LAMENTATIONS _ : _ - _

"Judah has gone into exile following affliction and harsh slavery;
she lives among the nations but find no place to rest.
All her pursuers have overtaken her in narrow places.
The roads to Zion mourn, for no one comes to the appointed festivals.
All her gates are deserted; her priests groan, her young women grieve, and she
herself is bitter."

LEVEL
3

BIBLE POWER PUZZLES

PAGE
213

DEFINITION SEARCH

FIND ALL WORDS PLACED HORIZONTALLY, VERTICALLY, OR DIAGONALLY, AND MATCH THEM TO THE DEFINITIONS BELOW.

```
N  Y  R  J  I  I  G  G  A  I  U  S  X  I
W  H  T  X  W  M  L  A  Z  W  F  C  I  Q
G  A  E  N  I  M  A  D  B  D  U  A  S  W
A  D  Z  L  W  E  G  G  U  B  G  E  W  H
L  A  A  A  E  R  T  B  E  G  A  T  G  A
E  D  B  G  X  M  A  C  A  R  S  I  A  L
E  E  D  A  U  Z  X  H  G  E  Y  I  L  L
D  Z  I  D  P  C  I  J  C  A  J  Z  A  E
K  E  E  H  I  Z  J  N  R  G  A  S  T  L
I  R  L  A  H  A  I  G  H  D  D  L  I  U
S  N  I  M  O  D  B  Q  A  A  B  X  A  J
T  J  D  D  R  O  Q  D  H  A  B  M  N  A
H  A  D  I  D  K  O  Z  W  E  S  O  S  H
D  I  M  M  A  N  U  E  L  Y  T  H  R  C
```

- Betrayed by Zebul.
- Joshua was buried North of here.
- Volunteered to settle in Jerusalem.
- Semitic god of fortune.
- He was baptized by Paul.
- One of the letters written by Paul.
- Name given by Jacob to a heap of stones.
- Tributary of the Euphrates.
- Son of Rehob.
- Town resettled by Jews after the Exile.
- Minor Bible prophet.
- Brother of Shem and Japheth.
- To praise (Greek).
- One of the sons of Heber (a/t 1 Chronicles 7:35).
- Popular Eastern Christogram (Greek abbr.).
- Jewish seer and genealogist.
- Religious —.
- God is with us (Hebrew).
- Father of Zadok.
- Intercourse among blood-relatives.
- Asian country named twice in the Bible.
- Son of Haggedolim.
- Son of Nathan.
- Refused to support Adonijah.

WORD WHEEL

CONNECT EACH LETTER FROM THE WHEEL TO REVEAL THE BIBLICAL WORD.

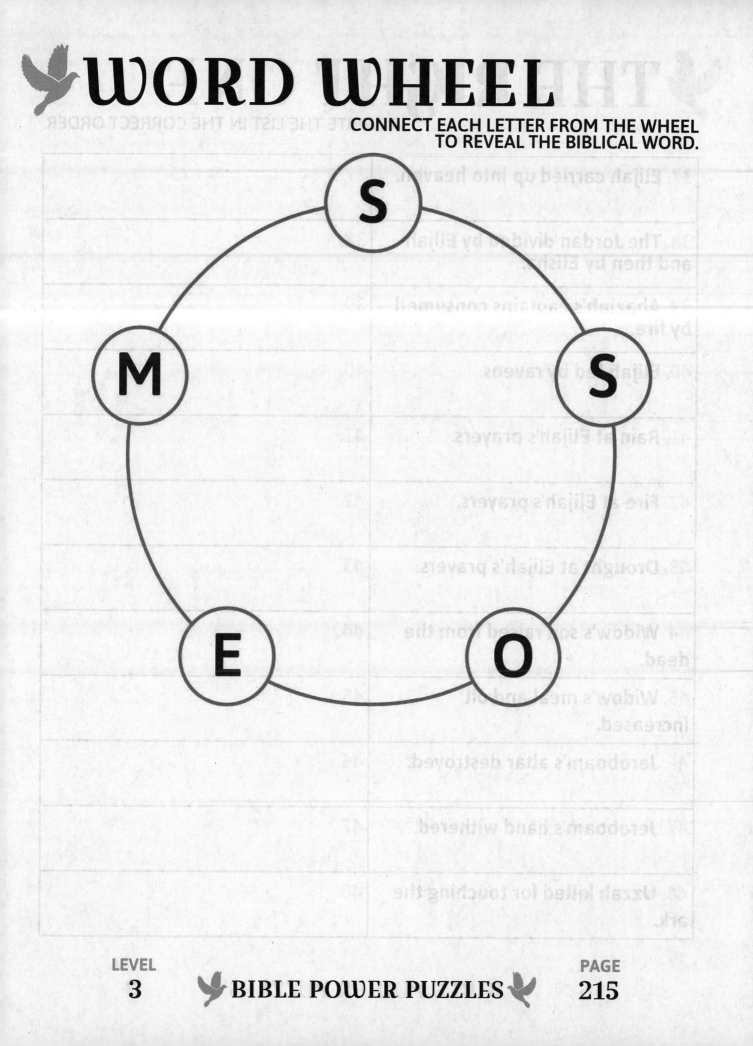

THE RIGHT ONE

REWRITE THE LIST IN THE CORRECT ORDER.

37. Elijah carried up into heaven.	37.
38. The Jordan divided by Elijah and then by Elisha.	38.
39. Ahaziah's captains consumed by fire.	39.
40. Elijah fed by ravens.	40.
41. Rain at Elijah's prayers.	41.
42. Fire at Elijah's prayers.	42.
43. Drought at Elijah's prayers.	43.
44. Widow's son raised from the dead.	44.
45. Widow's meal and oil increased.	45.
46. Jeroboam's altar destroyed.	46.
47. Jeroboam's hand withered.	47.
48. Uzzah killed for touching the ark.	48.

CHRISTIAN QUOTES

FROM CHURCH FATHERS TO MODERN CHRISTIAN THINKERS, IDENTIFY THE AUTHOR OF EACH QUOTE.

"...my conscience is captive to the Word of God. I cannot and I will not recant anything, for to go against conscience is neither right nor safe. Here I stand, I cannot do otherwise, God help me. Amen."

AUTHOR:

....

....

AUTHOR:

....

....

"For Jesus Christ I am prepared to suffer still more."

"God cannot give us a happiness and peace apart from Himself, because it is not there. There is no such thing."

AUTHOR:

....

....

OPPOSITES

UNSCRAMBLE THE LETTERS TO FORM PAIRS OF BIBLICAL ANTONYMS AND ANTAGONISTS.

1. **DISAOREH** ≠ 1. **JNOH HET TISTBAP**

1. ≠ 1.

2. **RENGEISOTY** ≠ 2. **DEGRE**

2. ≠ 2.

3. **LEBA** ≠ 3. **NIAC**

3. ≠ 3.

4. **CEGANRORA** ≠ 4. **MILITHUY**

4. ≠ 4.

MATCHMAKER

CONNECT THE SITUATION DESCRIBED TO ITS CORRESPONDING BIBLE BOOK, CHAPTER, AND VERSES.

MIRIAM PUNISHED	PSALM 23:1-6
THE GOOD SHEPHERD	MARK 3:13-19
PETER'S VISION	2 SAMUEL 16:5-13
SHIMEI CURSES DAVID	ESTHER 2:21-23
STEPHEN FORGIVES	JONAH 4:6-11
JESUS APPOINTS TWELVE	NUMBERS 12:10-15
JONAH'S PLANT	ACTS 7:60
MORDECAI SAVES THE KING	ACTS 10:9-16

PIX-CROSS

SOLVE THE NONOGRAM TO REVEAL THE HIDDEN PICTURE.

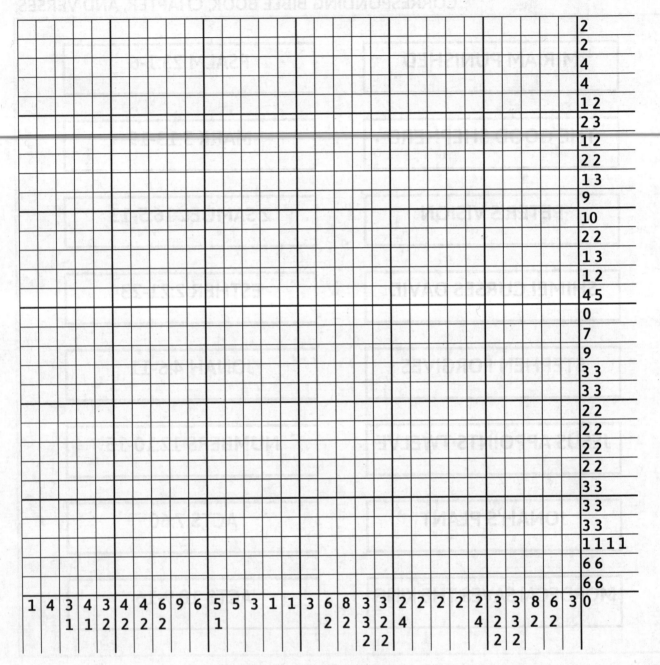

Row clues (top to bottom):

2
2
4
4
1 2
2 3
1 2
2 2
1 3
9
10
2 2
1 3
1 2
4 5
0
7
9
3 3
3 3
2 2
2 2
2 2
2 2
3 3
3 3
3 3
1 1 1 1
6 6
6 6

Column clues (left to right):

1 | 4 | 3 1 | 4 1 | 3 2 | 4 2 | 4 2 | 6 2 | 9 | 6 | 5 1 | 5 | 3 | 1 | 1 | 3 | 6 2 | 8 2 | 3 3 2 | 3 2 2 | 2 4 | 2 | 2 | 2 | 2 4 | 3 2 2 | 3 3 2 | 8 2 | 6 2 | 3 | 0

WORD-SEARCH

CONTAINED WITHIN THIS PUZZLE YOU MUST FIND ALL CAPITALIZED WORDS FROM THE VERSES BELOW.

```
M C U X H E A R T S Z L R U L
U T U Y P G W F W S A Z F D M
R J V B E P L A E U S T U J T
D N F O O S Y L X S X H L Y H
E D U L P L I E E N E I U P E
R E T P L F S N W W V N D A F
S C P K E C H F X E O G C D T
J E E D H S G R E E D S C U S
A I R Q I W I T H I N I O L S
V T S L D L Z P A E C N M T L
T H O U G H T S P K S V E E A
X O N X T H E S E R A K S R N
F I M M O R A L I T I E S I D
Q G S S E I B W H A T D P E E
E J O A C T I O N S Q F E S R
```

"**WHAT COMES OUT** of a **PERSON** is what **DEFILES** him. For from **WITHIN**, out of **PEOPLE**'s **HEARTS**, come **EVIL THOUGHTS**, **SEXUAL IMMORALITIES**, **THEFTS**, **MURDERS**, **ADULTERIES**, **GREED**, evil **ACTIONS**, **DECEIT**, self-indulgence, **ENVY**, **SLANDER**, **PRIDE**, and **FOOLISHNESS**. All **THESE** evil **THINGS** come from within and defile a **PERSON**."

CRISS-CROSS

USE THE DEFINITIONS BELOW TO FIND THE WORDS AND GUESS THE THEME.

ACROSS:

1. Daughter of Etam.
4. Mother of Uzziah.
6. Wife of Elkanah.
11. Mentioned in Acts 17:34.
13. Mother of Michal.
14. First convert after the resurrection.
15. Lois' daughter.
17. Daughter of Elon.
18. Wife of Mered.

DOWN:

1. Mother of Adoniyah.

2. Midwife who saved Hebrew boys.
3. Mother of Josiah.
4. She saved her nephew Jehoash.
5. Christian of the church in Philippi.
6. Greeted by Paul in Romans 16:12.
7. She was a prophetess.
8. Daughter of Ishmael.
9. Highly regarded by Paul.
10. A deaconess of the early church.
11. Also known as Tabitha.
12. Wife of Nahor.
16. Daughter of Zelophehad.

SUDOKU

MATCH THE HIGHLIGHTED NUMBER SEQUENCE TO THE CHAPTER AND VERSE BELOW.

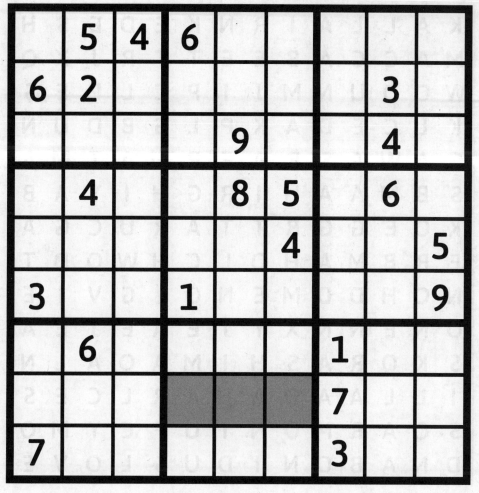

TITUS _ : _ - _

"In the same way, encourage the young men to be self-controlled in everything. Make yourself an example of good works with integrity and dignity in your teaching.

Your message is to be sound beyond reproach, so that any opponent will be ashamed, because he doesn't have anything bad to say about us."

DEFINITION SEARCH

FIND ALL WORDS PLACED HORIZONTALLY, VERTICALLY, OR DIAGONALLY,
AND MATCH THEM TO THE DEFINITIONS BELOW.

```
K A L L A I R N K E D E S H
M A C C A B E E T T R J X Q
W O D U N M J I P C L P E S
K L C E D A K P L G B D U N
G A W A S R A E P M A T M A
S B M A A H I R G H I Y A B
K O E G G R T T A R U C G A
E R B M A H O L C H W O D T
N O H D D M E N Q L G V I E
O N E N N X Y J E A E J E A
S K Q R A S H I M A O A L N
I L L A A D A H A R L C E S
S Q A R M O N I U F C Y M O
D N A B O N I D U S L O V E
```

- Benaiah killed his two sons.
- Hushai's clan.
- Saul and Rizpah's son.
- Worshiped by the habitants of Hamath.
- Greeted by Paul in Romans 16:14.
- —Barnea.
- Head of the priestly family of Sallai.
- Son of Ishmael.
- City conquered by Joshua from a Canaanite king.
- Emptying oneself.
- Father of Mareshah.
- "The man goes out to his work, and to his —until evening."

- Son of Jahath.
- The very nature of God.
- Alkaline substance used for cleansing.
- They revolted against Antiochus Epiphanes.
- Jeremiah prophesied against it.
- Descendant of Esau.
- Land ruled over by Gog.
- Father of four wise sages.
- Son of Caleb.
- Bore Ashhur four sons.
- People ruled by King Aretas.
- Last king of Chaldean Babylonia.

WORD WHEEL

CONNECT EACH LETTER FROM THE WHEEL TO REVEAL THE BIBLICAL WORD.

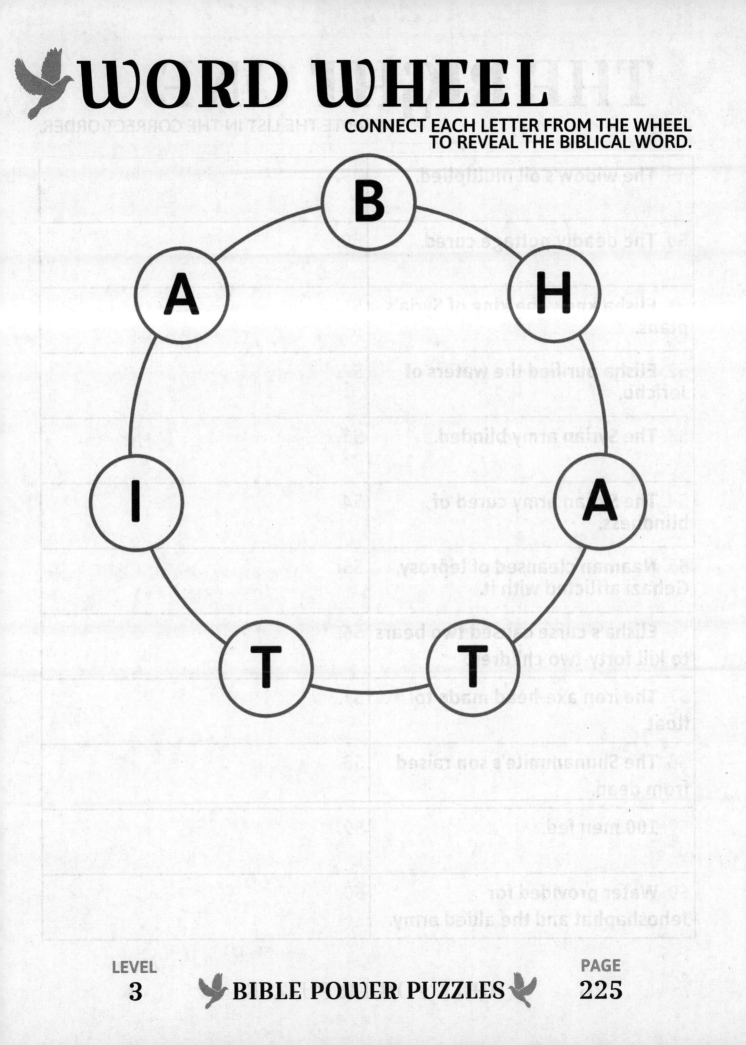

THE RIGHT ONE

REWRITE THE LIST IN THE CORRECT ORDER.

49. The widow's oil multiplied.	49.
50. The deadly pottage cured.	50.
51. Elisha knew the king of Syria's plans.	51.
52. Elisha purified the waters of Jericho.	52.
53. The Syrian army blinded.	53.
54. The Syrian army cured of blindness.	54.
55. Naaman cleansed of leprosy, Gehazi afflicted with it.	55.
56. Elisha's curse caused two bears to kill forty-two children.	56.
57. The iron axe-head made to float.	57.
58. The Shunammite's son raised from dead.	58.
59. 100 men fed.	59.
60. Water provided for Jehoshaphat and the allied army.	60.

PAGE
226   BIBLE POWER PUZZLES   LEVEL 3

CHRISTIAN QUOTES

FROM CHURCH FATHERS TO MODERN CHRISTIAN THINKERS, IDENTIFY THE AUTHOR OF EACH QUOTE.

"If grace is or was best then, it is best now."

AUTHOR:
....
....

AUTHOR:
....
....

"... there is no nation so barbarous, no race so brutish, as not to be imbued with the conviction that there is a God."

"Do not put off till tomorrow the good you can do today. You may not have a tomorrow."

AUTHOR:
....
....

OPPOSITES

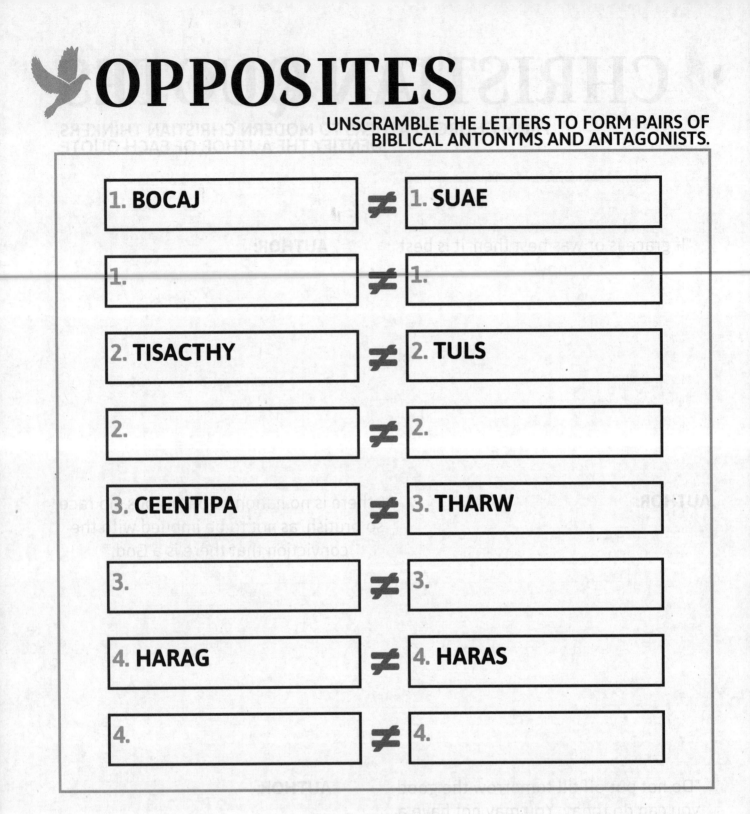

| 1. BOCAJ | ≠ | 1. SUAE |
| 1. | ≠ | 1. |

| 2. TISACTHY | ≠ | 2. TULS |
| 2. | ≠ | 2. |

| 3. CEENTIPA | ≠ | 3. THARW |
| 3. | ≠ | 3. |

| 4. HARAG | ≠ | 4. HARAS |
| 4. | ≠ | 4. |

MATCHMAKER

CONNECT THE SITUATION DESCRIBED TO ITS CORRESPONDING BIBLE BOOK, CHAPTER, AND VERSES.

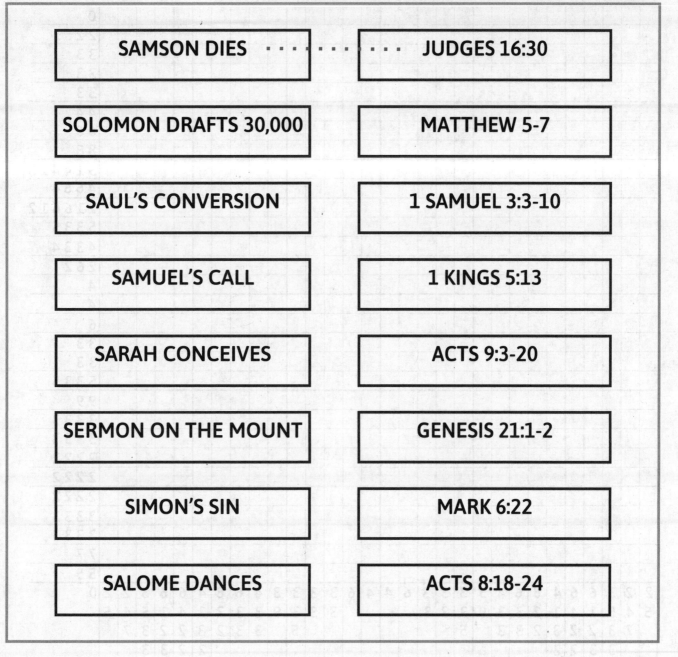

SAMSON DIES	JUDGES 16:30
SOLOMON DRAFTS 30,000	MATTHEW 5-7
SAUL'S CONVERSION	1 SAMUEL 3:3-10
SAMUEL'S CALL	1 KINGS 5:13
SARAH CONCEIVES	ACTS 9:3-20
SERMON ON THE MOUNT	GENESIS 21:1-2
SIMON'S SIN	MARK 6:22
SALOME DANCES	ACTS 8:18-24

PIX-CROSS

SOLVE THE NONOGRAM TO REVEAL THE HIDDEN PICTURE.

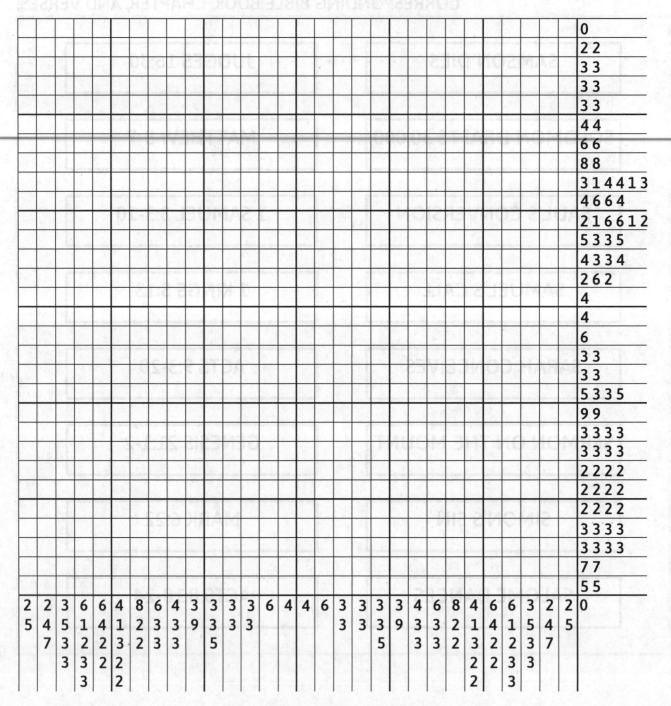

WORD-SEARCH

CONTAINED WITHIN THIS PUZZLE YOU MUST FIND ALL CAPITALIZED WORDS FROM THE VERSES BELOW.

```
P R E P A R E R F I L L E D S
S A A B E A S O S G G W E X T
A O T K M L E U M Z K K B U I
L J A H O O E G C O O Z O Y Z
V M L D S P U H T O A R E M D
A O O W Y E O N R S G L Y O L
T J W V M V A C T Q L N G I O
I Y Q O K E S T R A I G H T R
O V C U E R P N V R I B R V D
N E O D J Y W I L L G N N I H
B T A I S O S O K S G T J T P
K M A I C N V V Q Y T J O U F
O M P M Y E X Y C Q A O I R W
W K I C R Y I N G C M C S H A
U W I L D E R N E S S S U A Y
```

"A **VOICE** of one **CRYING OUT** in the **WILDERNESS**:
PREPARE the **WAY** for the **LORD**; **MAKE** his **PATHS STRAIGHT**!
Every **VALLEY WILL** be **FILLED**, and every **MOUNTAIN** will be **MADE LOW**; the
CROOKED will **BECOME** straight; the **ROUGH** ways **SMOOTH**, and **EVERYONE** will
SEE the **SALVATION** of **GOD**."

CRISS-CROSS

USE THE DEFINITIONS BELOW TO FIND THE WORDS AND GUESS THE THEME.

ACROSS:

2. Mother of Jehoshaphat.
4. Wife of King Ahasuerus.
7. Concubine of Nahor.
8. Egyptian wife of Joseph.
9. Wife of Shaharaim.
11. Grandmother of Mehetabel.
14. Daughter of priest Zadok.
17. Wife of King Hezekiah.
18. With her sisters, she won the right to inherit her father's property.
19. Founded three towns.

DOWN:

1. Second wife of Jerahmeel.
3. Mother of Dan and Naphtali.
5. Saved by Daniel.
6. Jewish prophetess.
10. Mentioned with Euodia.
12. Daughter of Jesse.
13. Another wife of Shaharaim.
14. Wife of Caleb.
15. One of King David's wives.
16. Hittite wife of Esau.

SUDOKU

9		1		2				
2		4		5			3	
8					9			
7	5				1		4	2
4			6	9				
5		9				8		3
		2				4		
						6		

JOB _ : _ - _

"Isn't each person consigned to forced labor on earth? Are not his days like those of a hired worker?

Like a slave he longs for shade; like a hired worker he waits for his pay.

So I have been made to inherit months of futility, and troubled nights have been assigned to me."

DEFINITION SEARCH

FIND ALL WORDS PLACED HORIZONTALLY, VERTICALLY, OR DIAGONALLY,
AND MATCH THEM TO THE DEFINITIONS BELOW.

```
N I M R O D R X R V B E S N R
W Y D E G M J D A H W V N N X
L D L W B R I C K S H D L I A
O Y N A G G A I A E N E U V R
I B Y R D T I L V H I S A R M
L R E M B B O E Q L C N S O A
P S C L H C N R A K O I C B G
A N A A I I Z H R Z D G E E E
N B N N S A H M N E E N D D
O P Q J P N K I E X M R S E D
P O B L A T I O N D U O I D O
L B U R D E N Z I D S O O O N
I U B O Z E Z W A S U K N M I
A Z B I S H O P A U R F F N K
N I S A N O O O B A D I A H B
```

- —of bulrushes.
- Where Sennacherib's sons escaped to.
- Final battleground between good and evil.
- —of Christ.
- Modern day Behramkoy.
- Principal officer of a local church.
- Jonathan climbed it.
- Building block made of dried clay.
- That which is laid upon someone to carry.
- Second son of Nahor.
- Son of Maath.
- Located between Mattanah and Bamoth.
- Son of Vophsi.
- Leading Pharisee who followed Jesus.
- Early deacon of the church originally from Antioch.
- Simeon's surname.
- Son of Cush.
- Jonah was sent to warn its people.
- First month of the Jewish calendar.
- His book is the shortest.
- Eighth son of Joktan.
- Guarded the ark with God's blessing.
- Stone pillar with a pyramidal top.
- Offering.
- Whole armor (Greek).

WORD WHEEL

CONNECT EACH LETTER FROM THE WHEEL TO REVEAL THE BIBLICAL WORD.

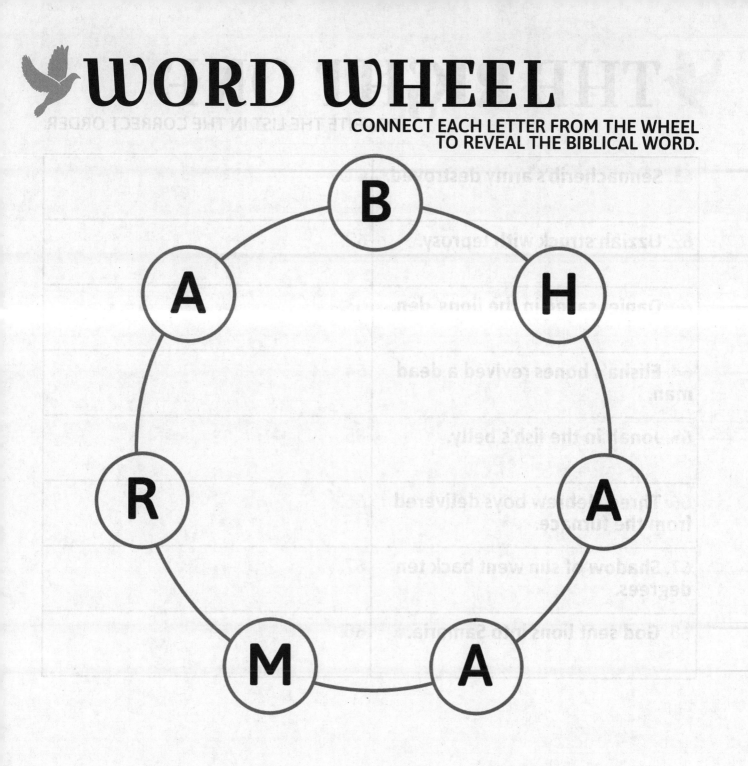

THE RIGHT ONE

REWRITE THE LIST IN THE CORRECT ORDER.

61. Sennacherib's army destroyed.	61.
62. Uzziah struck with leprosy.	62.
63. Daniel saved in the lions' den.	63.
64. Elisha's bones revived a dead man.	64.
65. Jonah in the fish's belly.	65.
66. Three Hebrew boys delivered from the furnace.	66.
67. Shadow of sun went back ten degrees.	67.
68. God sent lions into Samaria.	68.

CHRISTIAN QUOTES

FROM CHURCH FATHERS TO MODERN CHRISTIAN THINKERS, IDENTIFY THE AUTHOR OF EACH QUOTE.

"They are blessed to whom a wonder is not a fable, to whom a mystery is not a mockery, to whom a glory is not an unreality..."

AUTHOR:

....

....

AUTHOR:

....

....

"The greatest glory we can give God is to distrust our own strength utterly, and to commit ourselves wholly to His safe-keeping."

"Free grace will fix those whom free will shook down into a gulf of misery."

AUTHOR:

....

....

OPPOSITES

UNSCRAMBLE THE LETTERS TO FORM PAIRS OF BIBLICAL ANTONYMS AND ANTAGONISTS.

1. NOTIVALAS	≠	1. NOTINAMAD
1.	≠	1.

2. LUSA	≠	2. VIDAD
2.	≠	2.

3. BOJAC	≠	3. BANAL
3.	≠	3.

4. HANAM	≠	4. CAIDEROM
4.	≠	4.

MATCHMAKER

CONNECT THE SITUATION DESCRIBED TO ITS
CORRESPONDING BIBLE BOOK, CHAPTER, AND VERSES.

ABRAHAM'S DEATH	LUKE 19:41-44
PHARAOH EXALTS JOSEPH	NUMBERS 28-29
PRESCRIBED OFFERINGS	ESTHER 7:10
ZIBA HELPS DAVID	REVELATION 14:14
HAMAN'S EXECUTION	GENESIS 25:7-9
JESUS FACES PILATE	GENESIS 41:37-45
JESUS CRIES FOR JERUSALEM	MARK 15:1-5
JESUS ON A CLOUD	2 SAMUEL 16:1-4

PIX-CROSS

SOLVE THE NONOGRAM TO REVEAL THE HIDDEN PICTURE.

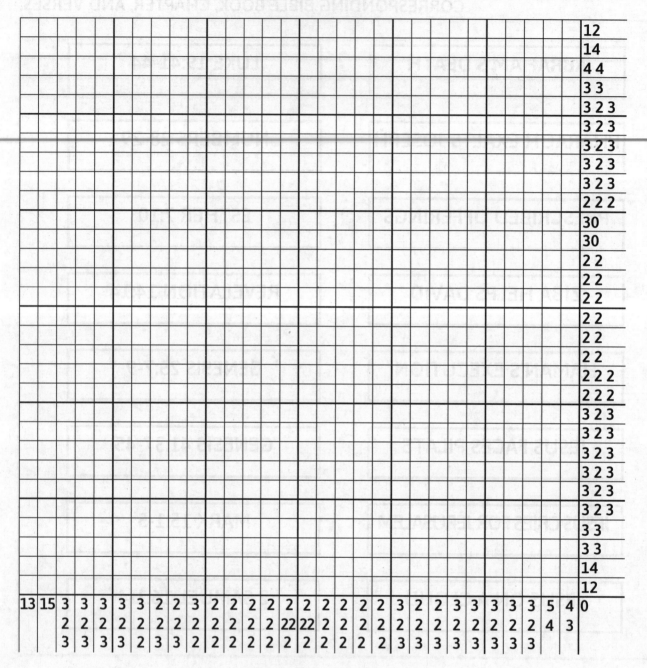

Row clues (top to bottom):

12
14
4 4
3 3
3 2 3
3 2 3
3 2 3
3 2 3
3 2 3
2 2 2
30
30
2 2
2 2
2 2
2 2
2 2
2 2
2 2 2
2 2 2
3 2 3
3 2 3
3 2 3
3 2 3
3 2 3
3 2 3
3 3
3 3
14
12

Column clues (left to right):

13	15	3	3	3	3	3	2	2	3	2	2	2	2	2	2	2	2	2	2	3	2	2	3	3	3	3	3	5	4	0
		2	2	2	2	2	2	2	2	2	2	2	2	22	22	2	2	2	2	2	2	2	2	2	2	2	2	4	3	
		3	3	3	3	2	3	3	2	2	2	2	2	2	2	2	2	2	2	3	3	3	3	3	3	3	3			

WORD-SEARCH

CONTAINED WITHIN THIS PUZZLE YOU MUST FIND ALL CAPITALIZED WORDS FROM THE VERSES BELOW.

```
F A C C O R D I N G R G M I K
O I N C U R A B L E N B H H N
R D E S E R V E H I E N E P L
T M T X N L U H H K O F A A E
U I B P A E E T I D G Q R R H
N D J G O M Y G N M M Y T T D
E D Q N K N I A B S Z I I R E
X L H J A T B N N P M L N I C
R E A C H A K O E V U S R D E
L I Z F F X I X V E T I Q G I
L J C L B T U U M P G V J E T
A I O H C B F O O L N G P Y F
C X F A E R P X T D E L S E U
U N D E R S T A N D T E S T L
C G G H G I V E H A T C H E S
```

"The **HEART** is more **DECEITFUL** than **ANYTHING ELSE**, and **INCURABLE**—who can **UNDERSTAND** it?
I, the Lord, **EXAMINE** the **MIND**, I **TEST** the heart to **GIVE EACH ACCORDING** to his way, according to what his **ACTIONS DESERVE**.
He who makes a **FORTUNE** unjustly is like a **PARTRIDGE** that **HATCHES EGGS** it didn't lay. In the **MIDDLE** of his **LIFE** his **RICHES** will **ABANDO**N him, so in the **END** he will be a **FOOL**."

CRISS-CROSS

USE THE DEFINITIONS BELOW TO FIND THE WORDS AND GUESS THE THEME.

ACROSS:
4. Son of Manoah.
7. Last northern king of Israel.
9. Imprisoned by king Asa.
10. Cruel Judean king.

DOWN:
1. Imprisoned in Babylon.
2. Carried off to an Egyptian prison.
3. Envied by his brothers.
5. Imprisoned by king Ahab.
6. His eyes were gouged out.
8. Held as hostage in Egypt.

SUDOKU

MATCH THE HIGHLIGHTED NUMBER SEQUENCE TO THE CHAPTER AND VERSE BELOW.

ACTS _ : _ - _

"Brothers and sisters, select from among you seven men of good reputation, full of the Spirit and wisdom, whom we can appoint to this duty. But we will devote ourselves to prayer and to the ministry of the word."

LEVEL
3

BIBLE POWER PUZZLES

PAGE
243

DEFINITION SEARCH

FIND ALL WORDS PLACED HORIZONTALLY, VERTICALLY, OR DIAGONALLY,
AND MATCH THEM TO THE DEFINITIONS BELOW.

```
I  T  U  R  E  A  N  I  V  O  R  Y  V  U  P
D  R  L  H  B  N  H  E  C  E  L  A  S  A  H
U  P  E  Q  W  F  O  N  M  D  H  A  V  A  O
S  M  V  K  G  Y  S  U  X  H  R  I  E  Q  R
T  H  D  C  C  N  E  A  W  U  F  Y  N  R  O
H  O  E  C  R  V  A  Z  D  D  S  A  D  W  N
P  S  P  C  R  E  A  T  U  R  E  R  R  H  A
W  H  H  U  C  E  E  H  O  R  N  S  E  D  I
D  A  E  B  N  R  T  D  O  X  V  M  A  U  M
F  M  S  I  W  G  I  E  A  S  Y  T  M  M  M
T  A  I  T  T  R  E  M  Y  L  A  Z  S  A  I
L  P  A  A  Z  E  A  P  S  M  N  N  Y  H  Z
D  L  N  I  S  L  F  S  H  O  P  F  N  W  H
O  B  S  N  N  A  N  I  A  O  N  H  E  A  A
J  D  U  N  G  M  E  Q  X  A  D  D  Q  Q  R
```

- That which is created.
- Authoritative statement of faith.
- Large island SE of the Greek mainland.
- Deep red color.
- Ancient unit of length.
- God used these as a means of communicating with men.
- Sixth son of Ishmael.
- Excrement of man or beast.
- Plain near Babylon.
- Fine, powdery dry earth.
- Grandson of Noah.
- Entrusted with a letter from Jeremiah.
- Ill will towards another's advantages.
- Letter written by Paul while first imprisoned in Rome.
- Father of Hanniel.
- —of the altar.
- "Twin caves" (Hebrew).
- Joyous acclamation to God (Greek).
- Prophet son of Beeri.
- Son of Jeconiah born in exile.
- Small principality in northern Palestine.
- Substance from the tusks of elephants.
- Second month of the Hebrew calendar.
- Son of Kohath.
- Levitical musician.

WORD WHEEL

CONNECT EACH LETTER FROM THE WHEEL TO REVEAL THE BIBLICAL WORD.

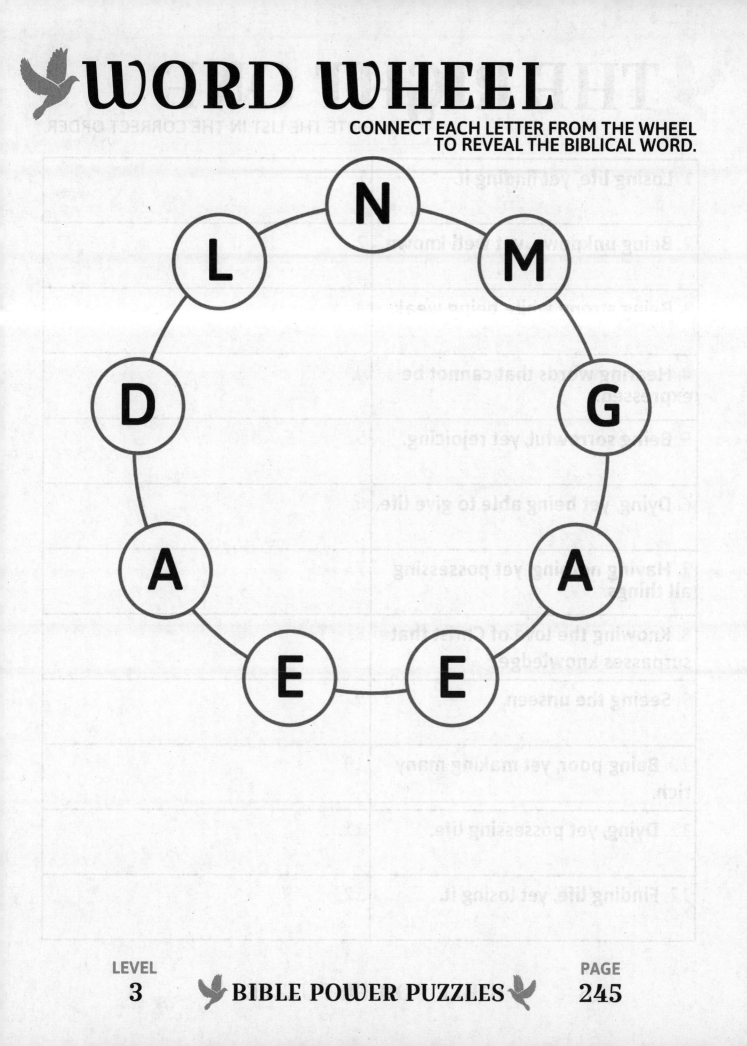

THE RIGHT ONE

REWRITE THE LIST IN THE CORRECT ORDER.

1. Losing life, yet finding it.	1.
2. Being unknown, yet well known.	2.
3. Being strong while being weak.	3.
4. Hearing words that cannot be expressed.	4.
5. Being sorrowful, yet rejoicing.	5.
6. Dying, yet being able to give life.	6.
7. Having nothing, yet possessing all things.	7.
8. Knowing the love of Christ that surpasses knowledge.	8.
9. Seeing the unseen.	9.
10. Being poor, yet making many rich.	10.
11. Dying, yet possessing life.	11.
12. Finding life, yet losing it.	12.

CHRISTIAN QUOTES

FROM CHURCH FATHERS TO MODERN CHRISTIAN THINKERS, IDENTIFY THE AUTHOR OF EACH QUOTE.

"If, however, you seek Jesus in all things, you will surely find Him."

AUTHOR:

....

....

AUTHOR:

....

....

"Those that make their own bosoms their oracle, God is disengaged from being their guide: they need him not; but the snares they run into will soon show them how much they need him."

"To one who has faith, no explanation is necessary. To one without faith, no explanation is possible."

AUTHOR:

....

....

OPPOSITES

UNSCRAMBLE THE LETTERS TO FORM PAIRS OF
BIBLICAL ANTONYMS AND ANTAGONISTS.

1. CEVI ≠ **1. TUEVIR**

1. ≠ 1.

2. PHESOJ ≠ **2. PHARTIPO**

2. ≠ 2.

3. CEGENLIDI ≠ **3. THOLS**

3. ≠ 3.

4. HEGAZI ≠ **4. HASILE**

4. ≠ 4.

MATCHMAKER

CONNECT THE SITUATION DESCRIBED TO ITS
CORRESPONDING BIBLE BOOK, CHAPTER, AND VERSES.

PAUL CHOOSES TIMOTHY	2 KINGS 4:18-36
DARIUS HONORS GOD	1 CHRONICLES 18:1
ELISHA RESURRECTS BOY	PROVERBS 11:2
WISE MEN PRESENT GIFTS	JEREMIAH 1:11-14
ARROGANCE & HUMILITY	DANIEL 6:25-27
JEREMIAH'S TWO VISIONS	MATTHEW 2:11
DAVID TAKES GATH	MARK 6:7-13
JESUS SENDS THE TWELVE	ACTS 16:1-5

PIX-CROSS

SOLVE THE NONOGRAM TO REVEAL THE HIDDEN PICTURE.

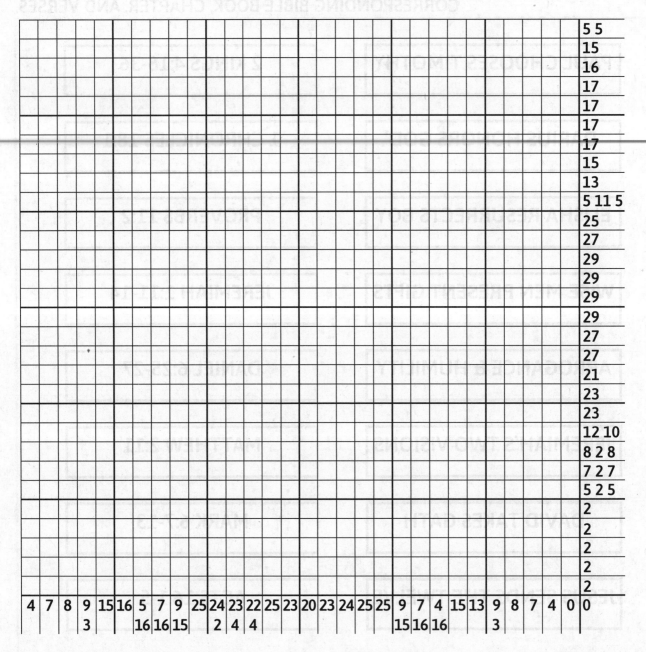

WORD-SEARCH

CONTAINED WITHIN THIS PUZZLE YOU MUST FIND ALL CAPITALIZED WORDS FROM THE VERSES BELOW.

```
L E S T Z B R O U G H T F T E
A C R R K Q R S N E J E S U S
Y F X E S E E I L O O K E D G
I L V E P Y H U C B B L I N D
N A G S E T C A N Y T H I N G
G A J J Y P L A C E D K E V I
M A N R R A E H C Z L J R K N
Q K E J E W A A E A S E O D T
D V C J S M R N W B G O E A E
E H G Y T J L D P A T K A H N
Q G Y W O A Y L L E S I G H T
O W B T R N G L N A O P H N L
L L O E E I I A U W R P Z Z Y
R C D U D V I O I M R G L Q B
S P I T T I N G J N B S K E N
```

"He **TOOK** the **BLIND MAN** by the **HAND** and **BROUGHT** him **OUT** of the **VILLAGE**. **SPITTING** on his **EYES** and **LAYING** his hands on him, he **ASKED** him, 'Do you **SEE ANYTHING**?'
He **LOOKED** up and said, 'I see **PEOPLE**—they look like **TREES WALKING**.'
AGAIN JESUS PLACED his hands on the man's eyes. The man looked **INTENTLY** and his **SIGHT** was **RESTORED** and he saw **EVERYTHING CLEARLY**."

CRISS-CROSS

USE THE DEFINITIONS BELOW TO FIND THE WORDS AND GUESS THE THEME.

ACROSS:
4. Released by an angel.
5. Brother of John.
6. Thrown in the lion's den.
7. Spent a night in prison with Peter.

DOWN:
1. Imprisoned by two kings.
2. Released after an earthquake.
3. Released in Jesus' place.
4. Spent two years under house arrest.
7. —the Baptist.

SUDOKU

MATCH THE HIGHLIGHTED NUMBER SEQUENCE TO THE CHAPTER AND VERSE BELOW.

		3		5				
9		1	2		7			
5	2							
						6		
2							7	9
	7	8					2	
		1	6	4				5
			7		4	9		
1			3				2	

EPHESIANS _ : _ - _

"By reading this you are able to understand my insight into the mystery of Christ. This was not made known to people in other generations as it is now revealed to his holy apostles and prophets by the Spirit: The Gentiles are coheirs, members of the same body, and partners in the promise in Christ Jesus through the gospel."

DEFINITION SEARCH

FIND ALL WORDS PLACED HORIZONTALLY, VERTICALLY, OR DIAGONALLY,
AND MATCH THEM TO THE DEFINITIONS BELOW.

```
F O R N I C A T I O N F Q M
S E Y K M M Q K G R K L L Y
A O Z B Y J U I L W G O E S
I I L R R L P R P M O U N T
H L E B A N O N R T H R W E
I M C S Q S U G S A Z I Z R
R O T O Z W B T K N I Y S Y
A T I H Y N O F O R D N Q S
M E O E E O F H I N N O M S
Q Q N V F M O U R N I N G U
I O A U M N L E T U S H I M
H E R X T O D F Q Z E J H S
L Z Y L E F T H A N D E D D
M U R A T O R I A N C I P X
```

- Pen in which to keep sheep or goats.
- Finely-crushed and sifted grain.
- Ottoman.
- Shallow place in a stream.
- Sexual intercourse between unmarried people.
- Friendly king of Tyre.
- Valley of —.
- To make a sharp sibilant sound.
- Son of Elpaal.
- Land of milk and —.
- Fermentation agent.
- Mountainous region of Phoenicia.
- Benjamin tribe warriors were referred to as such.
- Book of biblical lessons for church service.
- Descendants of Dedan.
- Caananite god of death.
- Small particle.
- Bereavement.
- —of Olives.
- —Canon.
- Pestilence of cattle or sheep.
- Paul changed ships there on his way to Rome.
- Counsel of God unknown to humans except by revelation.

WORD WHEEL

CONNECT EACH LETTER FROM THE WHEEL TO REVEAL THE BIBLICAL WORD.

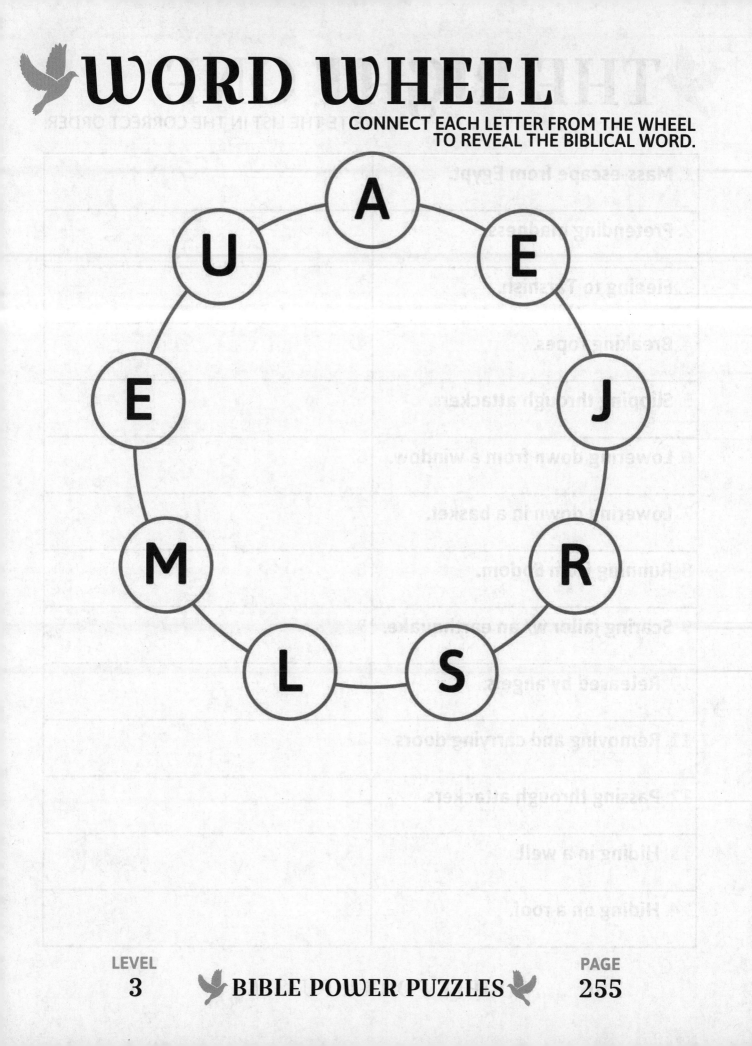

THE RIGHT ONE

REWRITE THE LIST IN THE CORRECT ORDER.

1. **Mass-escape from Egypt.**	1.
2. **Pretending madness.**	2.
3. **Fleeing to Tarshish.**	3.
4. **Breaking ropes.**	4.
5. **Slipping through attackers.**	5.
6. **Lowering down from a window.**	6.
7. **Lowering down in a basket.**	7.
8. **Running from Sodom.**	8.
9. **Scaring jailor w/ an earthquake.**	9.
10. **Released by angels.**	10.
11. **Removing and carrying doors.**	11.
12. **Passing through attackers.**	12.
13. **Hiding in a well.**	13.
14. **Hiding on a roof.**	14.

CHRISTIAN QUOTES

FROM CHURCH FATHERS TO MODERN CHRISTIAN THINKERS, IDENTIFY THE AUTHOR OF EACH QUOTE.

"If you cannot find Christ in the beggar at the church door, you will not find Him in the chalice."

AUTHOR:

....

....

AUTHOR:

....

....

"I cannot fully praise nor love Him, therefore must I die, and cast myself into the divine void till I rise from non-existence to existence."

"Faith abases men, and exalts God; it gives all the glory of redemption to Him alone."

AUTHOR:

....

....

OPPOSITES

1. MODWIS ≠ 1. LYLOF

1. ≠ 1.

2. MOLASBA ≠ 2. BAJO

2. ≠ 2.

3. HEWAY ≠ 3. LABA

3. ≠ 3.

4. PULA ≠ 4. XANDERLEA

4. ≠ 4.

MATCHMAKER

CONNECT THE SITUATION DESCRIBED TO ITS CORRESPONDING BIBLE BOOK, CHAPTER, AND VERSES.

JOSEPH AT POTIPHAR'S	GENESIS 39:1-20
BETTER THAN GOLD	LUKE 1:39-56
MOSES RETURNS	PROVERBS 16:16
MARY VISITS ELIZABETH	JUDGES 1:21
BENJAMINITES FAIL	LUKE 19:45-46
MERCHANTS THROWN OUT	LUKE 23:18-24
MY STRONGHOLD	PSALM 27
BARABBAS FREED	EXODUS 4:19-20

PIX-CROSS

SOLVE THE NONOGRAM TO REVEAL THE HIDDEN PICTURE.

Row clues (top to bottom):

3313
111111
311111
11113
111111
111111
33211
0
2122
11111
21111
11112
11111
11111
1122
0
3313
111111
31113
111111
111111
111111
33211
0
223134133
11111111111111
2131311133
11211111211
1111111111111
221111131111

Column clues (left to right):

3 1	1 4	0	6	1 1	0	6	3 3 1 3 1 2	1 1 1 1 1 1 3 2	1 5 7 1 5	1 1 6	7 7	1 1 7 1 1 6	7 7 1 1	7 3	7 1 1 7	1 5 1 1	6	7 7 1	1 1 1 1 1 1 1 6	7 7 1	7 6	0	6 1 2	3 0 2	6	1 1	6	0

WORD-SEARCH

```
R X C R S T R E T C H E D
D F O U N D A T I O N S A
Q I E S T A B L I S H E D
U U M H M E A S U R I N G
E U S E S D Z H J Y E F H
S S V Y N I N F O R M I K
T Q U G N S Y I E S O X M
I A I P P E I H S H L E D
O N W E P X W O Z H N D B
N S H W T O R E N I M J T
N W E R H C R F L S O A O
A E N H A A U T T K I H N
T R E A D Y T A S Z W U V
```

"Get **READY** to **ANSWER** me like a **MAN**; **WHEN** I **QUESTION** you, you will **INFORM** me.
WHERE were you when I **ESTABLISHED** the **EARTH**?
TELL me, if you have **UNDERSTANDING**.
WHO FIXED its **DIMENSIONS**? Certainly you know!
Who **STRETCHED** a **MEASURING LINE ACROSS** it?
WHAT SUPPORTS its **FOUNDATIONS**?"

CRISS-CROSS

USE THE DEFINITIONS BELOW TO FIND THE WORDS AND GUESS THE THEME.

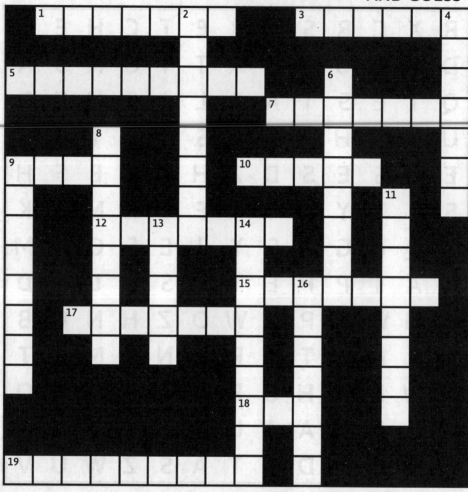

ACROSS:
1. Aaron's grandson.
3. Judah's first high priest after the exile.
5. Struck dumb.
7. Son of Aaron.
9. Ministered during the reconstruction.
10. Officiated at Solomon's coronation.
12. King Jehoshaphat's high priest.
15. Brother of Eleazar.
17. Sent to instruct the people of Judah.
18. Raised Samuel.
19. Managed storehouses.

DOWN:
2. Escaped the bloodbath at Nob.
4. Confronted king Uzziah.
6. Saved young Joash.
8. Assured his king of deliverance.
9. Teaching priest.
11. Mentioned in Nehemiah 12:10.
13. Brother of Moses.
14. Killed by Saul.
16. King Josiah's high priest.

SUDOKU

MATCH THE HIGHLIGHTED NUMBER SEQUENCE TO THE CHAPTER AND VERSE BELOW.

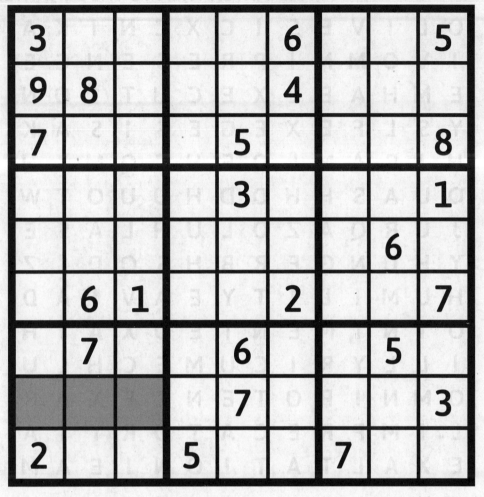

PROVERBS _ : _ - _

"Escape like a gazelle from a hunter, like a bird from a hunter's trap.
Go to the ant, you slacker! Observe its ways and become wise.
Without leader, administrator, or ruler, it prepares its provisions in summer; it
gathers its food during harvest."

DEFINITION SEARCH

FIND ALL WORDS PLACED HORIZONTALLY, VERTICALLY, OR DIAGONALLY, AND MATCH THEM TO THE DEFINITIONS BELOW.

```
O L I V E S I C X C N I K A
I V O M N I P R E S E N C E
E M H A E E X E C U T I O N
Y S L F E X E G E S I S A K
H J R A M L O E H C Q M Y H
O U A S H H D D H U U O T W
J U R Q A Z O L U H L A S E
Y H U N G E R B H S O D L Z
H U M I L I T Y E A V I A D
O I N T M E N T E D X A I H
I L L Y R I C U M E C H L U
O M N I P O T E N C E X A R
L I M P R E C A T O R Y I A
E X A L T A T I O N I E A M
```

- Slain Midianite king.
- From the resurrection to the ascension of Christ.
- Legal deprivation of life.
- Biblical interpretation.
- Deportation of Jews to Babylon.
- Departure from Egypt under Moses.
- Wife of Shallum.
- —nature.
- Freedom from pride.
- Crave.
- Helped Aaron hold Moses' hands aloft.
- Son of Bela.

- "Jesus Christ Conquers" (Greek Christogram).
- Ahohite warrior.
- Roman province N of Greece.
- Father of prophet Micaiah.
- Son of Helem.
- —psalms.
- Solemn promise.
- Father of Shemaiah.
- Balm.
- Mount of —.
- God's attribute of unlimited power.
- God's attribute to be everywhere at once.

WORD WHEEL

CONNECT EACH LETTER FROM THE WHEEL TO REVEAL THE BIBLICAL WORD.

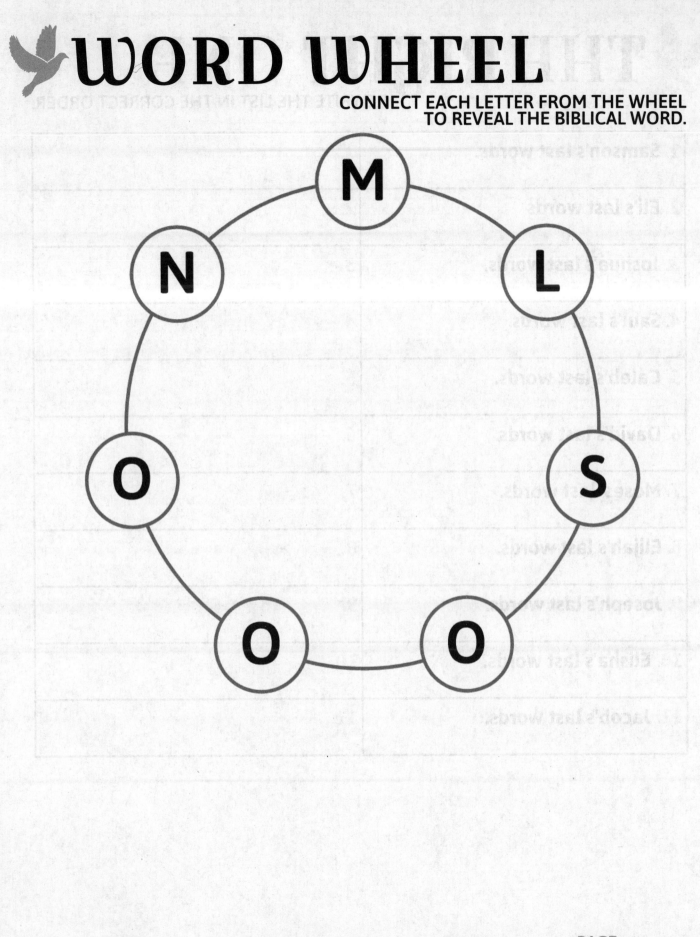

THE RIGHT ONE

1. Samson's last words.	1.
2. Eli's last words	2.
3. Joshua's last words.	3.
4. Saul's last words.	4.
5. Caleb's last words.	5.
6. David's last words.	6.
7. Moses' last words.	7.
8. Elijah's last words.	8.
9. Joseph's last words.	9.
10. Elisha's last words.	10.
11. Jacob's last words.	11.

CHRISTIAN QUOTES

FROM CHURCH FATHERS TO MODERN CHRISTIAN THINKERS, IDENTIFY THE AUTHOR OF EACH QUOTE.

"Christ desires nothing more of us than that we speak of Him."

AUTHOR:

....

....

AUTHOR:

....

....

"Hold on to Christ with your teeth if your hands get crippled."

"Whoever sees me, sees I would be a Christian. Therefore are my ways not like other men's ways."

AUTHOR:

....

....

OPPOSITES

1. RAMPETENCE	≠	1. TONTULGY
1.	≠	1.

2. CELENVONEBE	≠	2. CECENFILEMA
2.	≠	2.

3. ELTYCRU	≠	3. PASCOMSION
3.	≠	3.

4. ACEPE	≠	4. RAW
4.	≠	4.

MATCHMAKER

CONNECT THE SITUATION DESCRIBED TO ITS CORRESPONDING BIBLE BOOK, CHAPTER, AND VERSES.

HEART REFLECTIONS	ECCLESIASTES 8:14
INJUSTICE	ISAIAH 7:14
JAMES EXECUTED	ACTS 18:24-28
MADE A WATCHMAN	ACTS 12:1-2
WALL HANDWRITING	SONG OF SONGS 5:2
APOLLOS ARRIVES	DANIEL 5:5-6
SIGN OF IMMANUEL	EZEKIEL 3:17-21
SLEEPING BUT AWAKE	PROVERBS 16:1

PIX-CROSS

SOLVE THE NONOGRAM TO REVEAL THE HIDDEN PICTURE.

Row clues:

3313
111111
31113
111111
111111
332111
0
333313
111111111
133113
112111111
1111111111
311111111
0
0
0
331113
1111111
3111113
1111111
1111111
33233
0
3113133113
11111111111
133111111
11121131113
11111111111
11111111111
3111113143

Column clues:

7	1	1	0	6	1	1	3	1	1	3	6	1	6	6	6	1	6	6	1	6	0	6	1	6	7	0	4	1	1	0
	1	1		7	1	3	1	1	4	2	6	1	1	4	6	1		1	1	6		3	1	1			1	1	4	
					1	7	3	1	1	3		6	1	1	1	1		6	1	6		1	1	4				1		
							1	6	2	6		1	6		1	1		1	7	1		7	1	1						
							1	1	1			1			1	4							1							
								1	4			7											1							
								1	1																					
								7	2																					

WORD-SEARCH

```
O O Q I O F C U S F I H J A R
R F A X T B E C A U S E X S G
P E F L Q N D Q V K J G D U T
Y D V E T S P E E G J L O F E
O L G E R H D A A L S W X F A
S D J D R E O K R T N E B E R
Y U S A N E D U A N H N Z R S
E Y N R T S N U G P R O N E D
Z B A S V O I C N H P B S D S
H E U D F N W A E D M E G O G
L C U E O N Q B X J I S A N U
N O N S E S R L Y R T L I L E
L Q C X O N E E C T C R I E S
P R A Y E R S H I M U R Y F F
H E A R D F O B E D I E N C E
```

"**DURING** his earthly **LIFE**, he **OFFERED PRAYERS** and **APPEALS** with **LOUD CRIES** and **TEARS** to the **ONE** who was **ABLE** to **SAVE HIM** from **DEATH**, and he was **HEARD BECAUSE** of his **REVERENCE**. **ALTHOUGH** he was the **SON**, he **LEARNED OBEDIENCE** from what he **SUFFERED**."

CRISS-CROSS

USE THE DEFINITIONS BELOW TO FIND THE WORDS AND GUESS THE THEME.

ACROSS:

2. Almost sacrificed by his father.
5. Called to become a prophet.
6. Offered a lamb from his flock.
7. Jacob's fourth son.
10. Caring for his sheep when God spoke to him.
11. Grazed his sheep near Sodom.

DOWN:

1. Insulted David.
3. Owned sheep and oxen.
4. Became the second most powerful man in Egypt.
7. Shepherded his flocks was well as Laban's.
8. Wrote Psalm 23.
9. Moses' father-in-law.

SUDOKU

MATCH THE HIGHLIGHTED NUMBER SEQUENCE TO THE CHAPTER AND VERSE BELOW.

		1			9		
2	6	3			8		4	
8					3			
9					4	5		
3			6		2			9
	6		9					2
			3					5
	5		8			3	1	4
		8						

MARK _ : _ - _

"Since they were not able to bring him to Jesus because of the crowd, they removed the roof above him, and after digging through it, they lowered the mat on which the paralytic was lying. Seeing their faith, Jesus told the paralytic, 'Son, your sins are forgiven.'"

DEFINITION SEARCH

FIND ALL WORDS PLACED HORIZONTALLY, VERTICALLY, OR DIAGONALLY, AND MATCH THEM TO THE DEFINITIONS BELOW.

```
P P P V Q U A R A N T A N I A
X A A E U P A R A H P T O N O
K R R E O R A M O N A N O P M
W T V M H E R S H M F K N A N
P H A G E Q X Q T I W E E R I
A I I Q L X Z H L O K A S A S
R A M U E W Y E T C R D I C C
A W D E T O E Z I T A Q P L I
E Q X E H M N U E P T U H E E
N U E N P P Q E X S V I O T N
E A X Q Q A W Q S M X R R E C
S R O U U A S I G I N I O O E
I R U I A I K E N X M N U N J
S Y D E I O N I A S S U S L N
A G J T L O M R I H T S S Y Z
```

- God's attribute of knowing all things.
- Sixth king of Israel.
- Son of Peleth.
- God killed him directly.
- Philemon's slave.
- Ministered to Paul during his imprisonment.
- Name of three high priests.
- —begotten.
- The Holy Spirit as advocate (Greek).
- Exhortation (Greek).
- Benjaminite town.
- Persian satrapy SE of the Caspian Sea.
- Solomon obtained gold there.
- Father of Joiada.
- Evangelical clergyman.
- Ecclesiastes (Hebrew).
- God provided it to the Hebrews during their Exodus.
- Jesus was tempted there.
- To excavate or remove stone.
- —of Sheba.
- To revive.
- Silent.
- Roman consul.

WORD WHEEL

CONNECT EACH LETTER FROM THE WHEEL TO REVEAL THE BIBLICAL WORD.

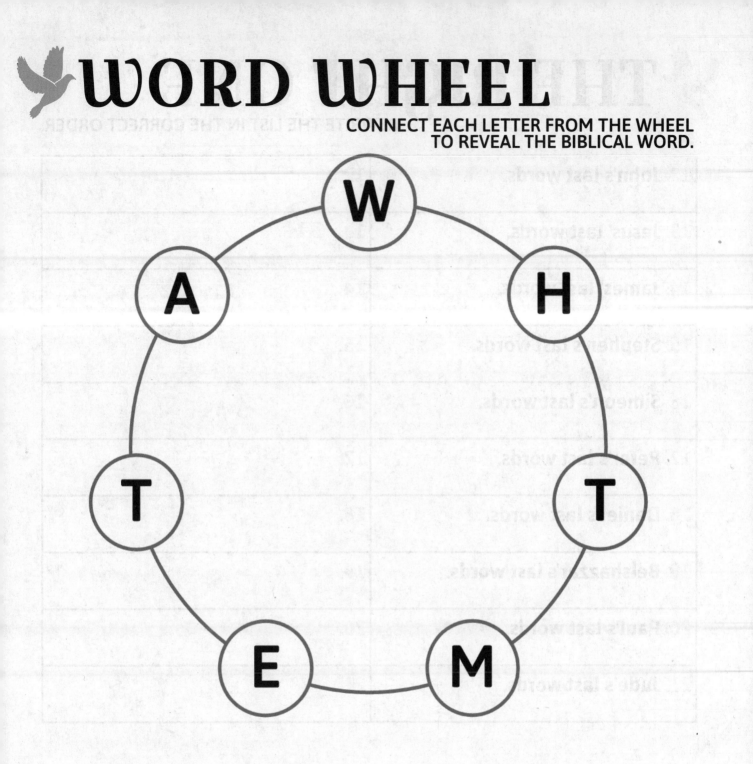

THE RIGHT ONE

12. John's last words.	12.
13. Jesus' last words.	13.
14. James' last words.	14.
15. Stephen's last words.	15.
16. Simeon's last words.	16.
17. Peter's last words.	17.
18. Daniel's last words.	18.
19. Belshazzar's last words.	19.
20. Paul's last words.	20.
21. Jude's last words.	21.

CHRISTIAN QUOTES

FROM CHURCH FATHERS TO MODERN CHRISTIAN THINKERS, IDENTIFY THE AUTHOR OF EACH QUOTE.

"With all your weakness and helplessness, with all your frailties and infirmities, with all your sorrows and cares, He invites you to come to Him."

AUTHOR:
....
....

AUTHOR:
....
....

"Who can describe the tokens of God's goodness that are extended to the human race even in this life?"

"We have no beauty, no goodness to make us desirable in His eyes; all the origins of His love to us as in His own breast."

AUTHOR:
....
....

OPPOSITES

UNSCRAMBLE THE LETTERS TO FORM PAIRS OF BIBLICAL ANTONYMS AND ANTAGONISTS.

1. HAON	≠	1. DOFLO
1.	≠	1.
2. HAROK	≠	2. SEMOS
2.	≠	2.
3. HABITO	≠	3. HAMIHENE
3.	≠	3.
4. SUTRIMEDE	≠	4. LAUP
4.	≠	4.

MATCHMAKER

CONNECT THE SITUATION DESCRIBED TO ITS CORRESPONDING BIBLE BOOK, CHAPTER, AND VERSES.

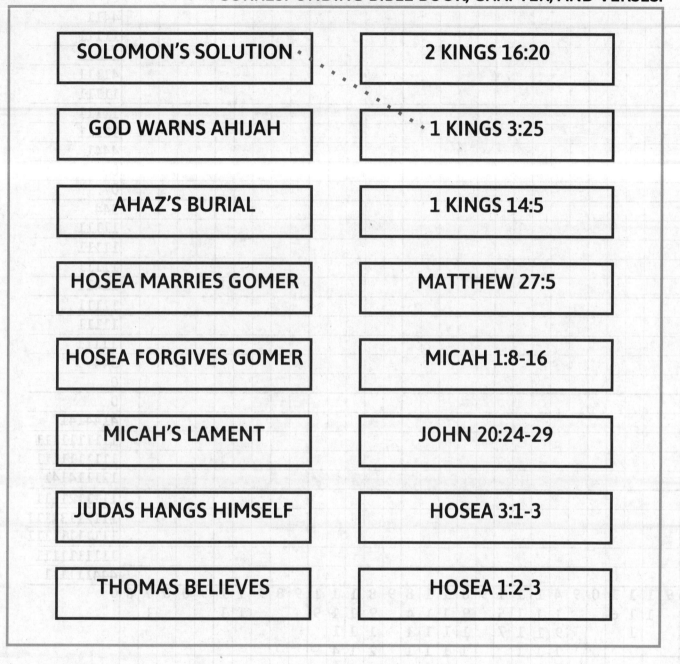

SOLOMON'S SOLUTION	2 KINGS 16:20
GOD WARNS AHIJAH	1 KINGS 3:25
AHAZ'S BURIAL	1 KINGS 14:5
HOSEA MARRIES GOMER	MATTHEW 27:5
HOSEA FORGIVES GOMER	MICAH 1:8-16
MICAH'S LAMENT	JOHN 20:24-29
JUDAS HANGS HIMSELF	HOSEA 3:1-3
THOMAS BELIEVES	HOSEA 1:2-3

PIX-CROSS

SOLVE THE NONOGRAM TO REVEAL THE HIDDEN PICTURE.

Row clues:

4411
11111
11111
41111
11111
11111
11111
4441
0
0
344
11111
11111
11111
11411
11111
11111
11111
344
0
0
4144141
1111111111
1111111111
121114141
1111121111
11121131111
11111111111
1111111111
444111111
0

Column clues:

9
1 1
1 1 1
1 6
0
9
4 1 9 1
1 1 1 1 1 1
1 1 1 1 1 1
1 5 7
9
8 9 1 1
1 1 1 1 1 1 1
1 1 1 1 1 9
8 4 1 1
9
8 9 1 2
1 1 1 1 1 1
1 1 1 4 3
1 9
9
8
9
1 1
1 1
9
0
0
7 1
0

WORD-SEARCH

CONTAINED WITHIN THIS PUZZLE YOU MUST FIND ALL
CAPITALIZED WORDS FROM THE VERSES BELOW.

```
H V I N D I C A T E D S H
E K C H E L I F E L N U R
L U V V L P D H T G O S C
P U S I E O H F Z K V T P
E X K T G Z W H R X J A Y
R U V P R A Y E R S T I Q
A L C I B A U L D D H N V
I G I Z O C N R R T E E K
G N A S Q L O G U V M R E
R U T I T W E O E A H V H
I C I E N E M N N R A I E
S R A D N S N H T S S S A
E F G G E D T M I G H T R
```

"God, **SAVE** me by your **NAME**, and **VINDICATE** me by your **MIGHT**!
God, **HEAR** my **PRAYER**; **LISTEN** to the **WORDS** from my **MOUTH**.
For **STRANGERS RISE** up **AGAINST** me, and **VIOLENT** men **INTEND** to **KILL** me.
They do not let God **GUIDE** them.
GOD is my **HELPER**; the Lord is the **SUSTAINER** of my **LIFE**."

CRISS-CROSS

USE THE DEFINITIONS BELOW TO FIND THE WORDS AND GUESS THE THEME.

ACROSS:
1. Struck down by an angel.
4. Leper commander of Syrian troops.
6. Arrested Jeremiah.
8. Scout of Moses.
9. Baptized by Peter.
11. Betrayed by David.
13. Imprisoned Joseph.
14. Fought against Absalom.
15. Israel's first Commander-in-Chief.
16. Killed 300 enemy soldiers.

DOWN:
2. Led Absalom's troops.
3. Defeated by Barak and Deborah.
5. Served under Nebuchadnezzar.
7. Commander of Saul's troops.
9. Sent Paul to Felix.
10. Treated Paul kindly.
12. Captain under David.
15. Commander of David's troops.

SUDOKU

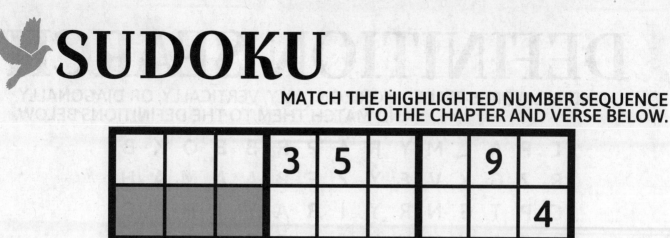

MATCH THE HIGHLIGHTED NUMBER SEQUENCE TO THE CHAPTER AND VERSE BELOW.

			3	5			9	
								4
4					2		7	5
		5					2	1
1	6							7
		4		1				
	9					7	8	6
2	5			8	9			

ZECHARIAH _ : _ - _

"I looked up again and saw a flying scroll. 'What do you see?' he asked me. 'I see a flying scroll,' I replied, 'thirty feet long and fifteen feet wide.'"

DEFINITION SEARCH

FIND ALL WORDS PLACED HORIZONTALLY, VERTICALLY, OR DIAGONALLY, AND MATCH THEM TO THE DEFINITIONS BELOW.

```
L  P  A  L  M  Y  R  A  P  R  B  E  O  K  B
R  Z  G  X  V  F  Y  Z  E  R  A  A  M  A  H
C  P  T  G  N  R  Y  I  R  A  Y  I  H  R  C
A  E  F  X  U  U  H  J  S  B  D  A  S  G  S
H  R  T  J  Q  D  L  Q  E  B  R  O  O  I  G
K  S  R  C  E  E  O  J  V  A  A  Z  V  P  N
S  E  L  E  I  A  R  G  E  H  B  V  E  E  L
P  C  R  N  Q  E  D  B  R  P  M  X  R  R  N
F  U  H  D  Y  B  I  P  A  A  A  M  S  U  L
Q  T  I  O  D  M  N  A  N  L  G  D  E  D  O
O  I  O  H  E  C  A  P  C  T  L  L  E  A  R
R  O  M  Z  P  I  N  Y  E  I  Y  K  R  D  A
A  N  O  N  N  T  C  R  V  E  O  R  E  N  B
C  U  U  K  R  I  E  U  Z  L  C  L  N  F  B
A  P  A  P  H  O  S  S  D  R  A  D  D  A  I
```

- Elderly.
- Decree.
- Son of Jerahmeel.
- Son of Kenaz.
- Heated chamber used to bake.
- Supervisor or manager.
- Older brother of David.
- Son of Gad.
- Tadmor.
- Husband of Michal.
- Capital of Cyprus.
- Paper made from its namesake plant.
- Lying under oath.

- Ill-treatment in the basis of religion or race.
- Persistent determination.
- Servant of Solomon.
- Fourth son of Cush.
- Capital of Ammon.
- Teacher (Hebrew).
- Nergal-Sharezer's title.
- Worthless or stupid (Aramaic).
- Fifth son of Jesse.
- Monster or demonic power.
- —cake.

WORD WHEEL

CONNECT EACH LETTER FROM THE WHEEL TO REVEAL THE BIBLICAL WORD.

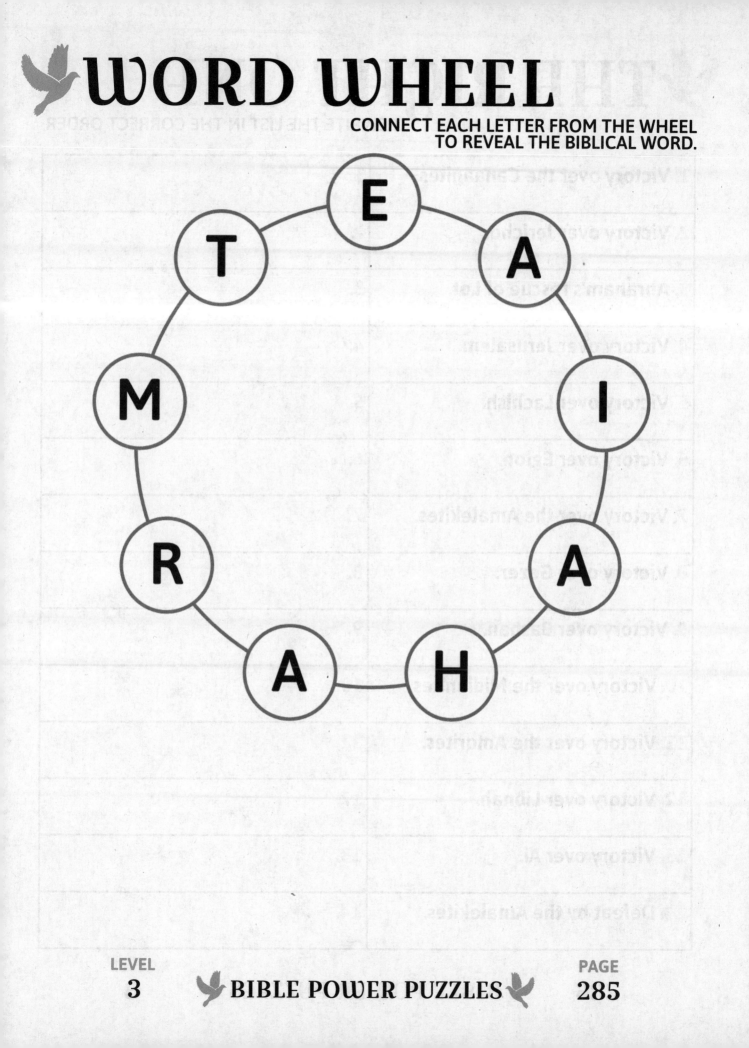

THE RIGHT ONE

REWRITE THE LIST IN THE CORRECT ORDER.

1. **Victory over the Canaanites.**	1.
2. **Victory over Jericho.**	2.
3. **Abraham's rescue of Lot.**	3.
4. **Victory over Jerusalem.**	4.
5. **Victory over Lachish.**	5.
6. **Victory over Eglon.**	6.
7. **Victory over the Amalekites.**	7.
8. **Victory over Gezer.**	8.
9. **Victory over Bashan.**	9.
10. **Victory over the Midianites.**	10.
11. **Victory over the Amorites.**	11.
12. **Victory over Libnah.**	12.
13. **Victory over Ai.**	13.
14. **Defeat by the Amalekites.**	14.

CHRISTIAN QUOTES

FROM CHURCH FATHERS TO MODERN CHRISTIAN THINKERS, IDENTIFY THE AUTHOR OF EACH QUOTE.

"I would have far more fear of being mistaken, and of finding that the Christian religion was true, than of not being mistaken in believing it true."

AUTHOR:

....

....

AUTHOR:

....

....

"...the foe is not the dogmatic infidel who has finally made up his mind that Christianity is a delusion, but anti-Christian thought in the believing man's own heart."

"To be a Christian means to forgive the inexcusable because God has forgiven the inexcusable in you."

AUTHOR:

....

....

OPPOSITES

UNSCRAMBLE THE LETTERS TO FORM PAIRS OF
BIBLICAL ANTONYMS AND ANTAGONISTS.

1. SOMA ≠ **1. HAZIMAA**

1. ≠ 1.

2. JURYPER ≠ **2. THAO**

2. ≠ 2.

3. SEHOA ≠ **3. MERGO**

3. ≠ 3.

4. SAMOTH ≠ **4. NESSES**

4. ≠ 4.

MATCHMAKER

CONNECT THE SITUATION DESCRIBED TO ITS CORRESPONDING BIBLE BOOK, CHAPTER, AND VERSES.

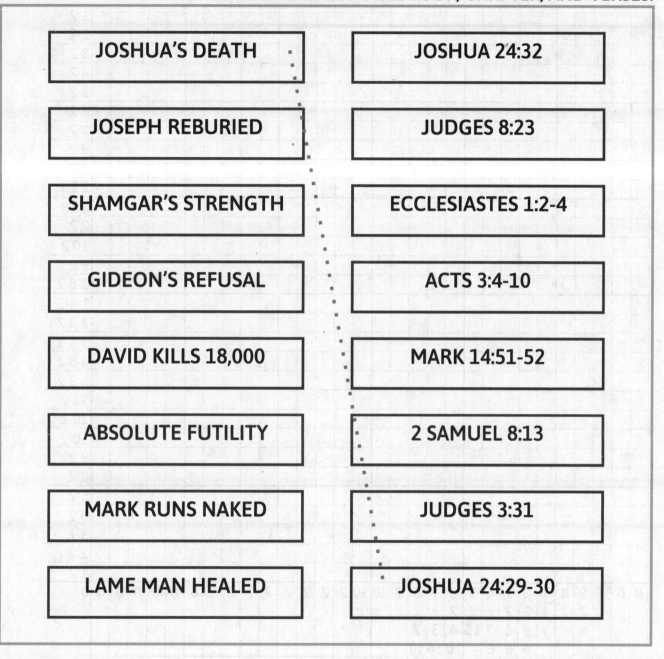

JOSHUA'S DEATH	JOSHUA 24:32
JOSEPH REBURIED	JUDGES 8:23
SHAMGAR'S STRENGTH	ECCLESIASTES 1:2-4
GIDEON'S REFUSAL	ACTS 3:4-10
DAVID KILLS 18,000	MARK 14:51-52
ABSOLUTE FUTILITY	2 SAMUEL 8:13
MARK RUNS NAKED	JUDGES 3:31
LAME MAN HEALED	JOSHUA 24:29-30

PIX-CROSS

SOLVE THE NONOGRAM TO REVEAL THE HIDDEN PICTURE.

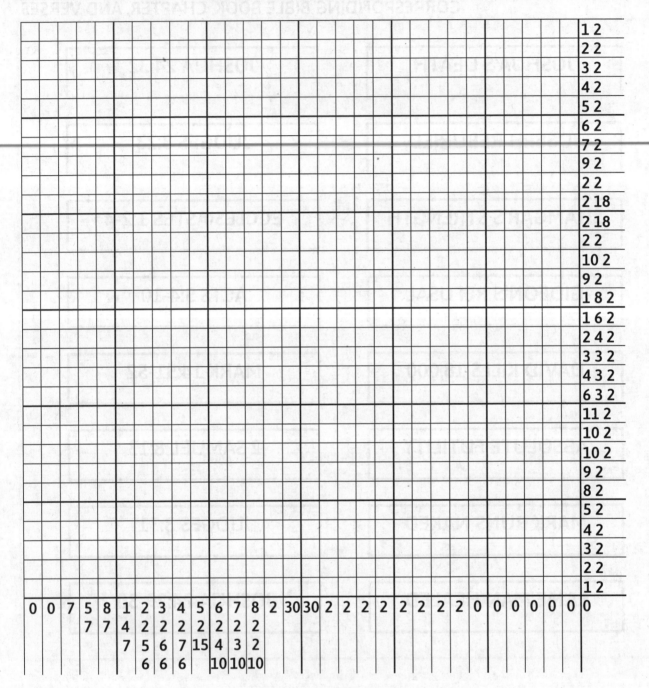

WORD-SEARCH

CONTAINED WITHIN THIS PUZZLE YOU MUST FIND ALL CAPITALIZED WORDS FROM THE VERSES BELOW.

```
N S G E N E R A T I O N G X A
B P A D C V A B S O L U T E R
C A X K V E Z J I S A W E N O
G S T D W R T X O U G O E S G
Z O A Q N Y H Z W Z C A L I Z
E F F O R T S B N V U U I R O
A B Y A I H L Z A X R C E N F
F U T I L I T Y J E N V R G T
R R D L E N X S D O E S N A M
E C I W A G P N U R T I H D U
M O X S S B U E O N T W N Q N
A M E T E R O F R N V V K O L
I E E X E S J R A S E A R T H
N S L P C W C P S A O K Y L T
S R E T U R N S H X C N N Q F
```

"'**ABSOLUTE FUTILITY**... **EVERYTHING** is futile.'
WHAT DOES a **PERSON GAIN** for all his **EFFORTS** that he **LABORS** at **UNDER** the **SUN**?
A **GENERATION GOES** and a generation **COMES**, but the **EARTH REMAINS FOREVER**.
The sun **RISES** and the sun **SETS**; **PANTING**, it **RETURNS** to the place where it rises."

CRISS-CROSS

USE THE DEFINITIONS BELOW TO FIND THE WORDS AND GUESS THE THEME.

ACROSS:
4. Plucked his own hair off.
6. Naturally bald (and touchy about it).
7. Had an abundant mane.
9. Shaved his head in mourning.

DOWN:
1. Wore a camel hair garment (3 words).
2. Purified along with four other men.
3. Refused to shave.
4. Redhead.
5. Cut his hair once a year.
8. Known as "The Tishbite."

SUDOKU

**MATCH THE HIGHLIGHTED NUMBER SEQUENCE
TO THE CHAPTER AND VERSE BELOW.**

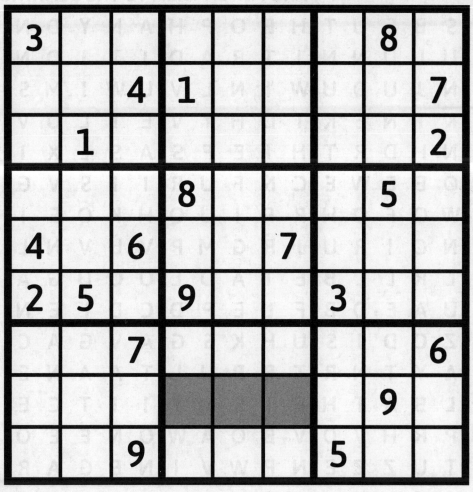

1 JOHN _ : _ - _

"For this is what love for God is: to keep his commands. And his commands are not a burden, because everyone who has been born of God conquers the world..."

DEFINITION SEARCH

FIND ALL WORDS PLACED HORIZONTALLY, VERTICALLY, OR DIAGONALLY,
AND MATCH THEM TO THE DEFINITIONS BELOW.

```
S  B  S  U  T  H  E  O  P  H  A  N  Y  D  N
U  L  U  N  N  I  T  R  A  D  I  T  I  O  N
N  J  U  D  U  W  I  N  L  V  U  W  I  M  S
K  T  N  E  K  T  D  H  Y  V  E  T  L  U  V
N  H  D  R  T  H  I  E  F  S  A  S  L  X  I
O  E  E  W  E  C  N  F  U  R  I  I  S  V  G
W  O  F  O  H  R  F  I  U  Q  H  K  O  E  I
N  C  I  R  U  J  R  G  M  P  V  U  V  N  L
L  R  L  L  B  E  I  A  O  L  O  O  U  G  A
U  A  E  D  B  F  L  E  P  D  C  D  L  E  N
Z  C  D  I  S  U  H  K  S  G  A  V  G  A  C
A  Y  T  N  R  T  B  B  U  L  T  A  A  N  E
L  B  A  T  H  E  I  S  M  Y  I  I  T  C  E
P  R  H  V  D  V  B  Q  A  W  O  N  E  E  O
T  U  Z  Z  E  N  P  W  V  I  N  E  G  A  R
```

- Belief in God's existence.
- Government by divine rule.
- God's manifestation.
- Luke's gospel and Acts were addressed to him.
- The good —.
- Ruled the Roman empire during Christ's ministry.
- Collective customs of a people.
- Change in appearance.
- Descendant of Bani who put away his foreign wife.
- Firstborn of Eshek.
- Not tainted.

- Hades.
- —God.
- Associate of Mattaniah.
- Son of Joktan.
- Village built by Sheerah.
- Futile.
- Retaliation.
- Container of liquid.
- Watchfulness.
- Jesus drank it on the cross.
- Higher calling.
- Latin translation of the Bible.
- Jesus is the—.

WORD WHEEL

CONNECT EACH LETTER FROM THE WHEEL TO REVEAL THE BIBLICAL WORD.

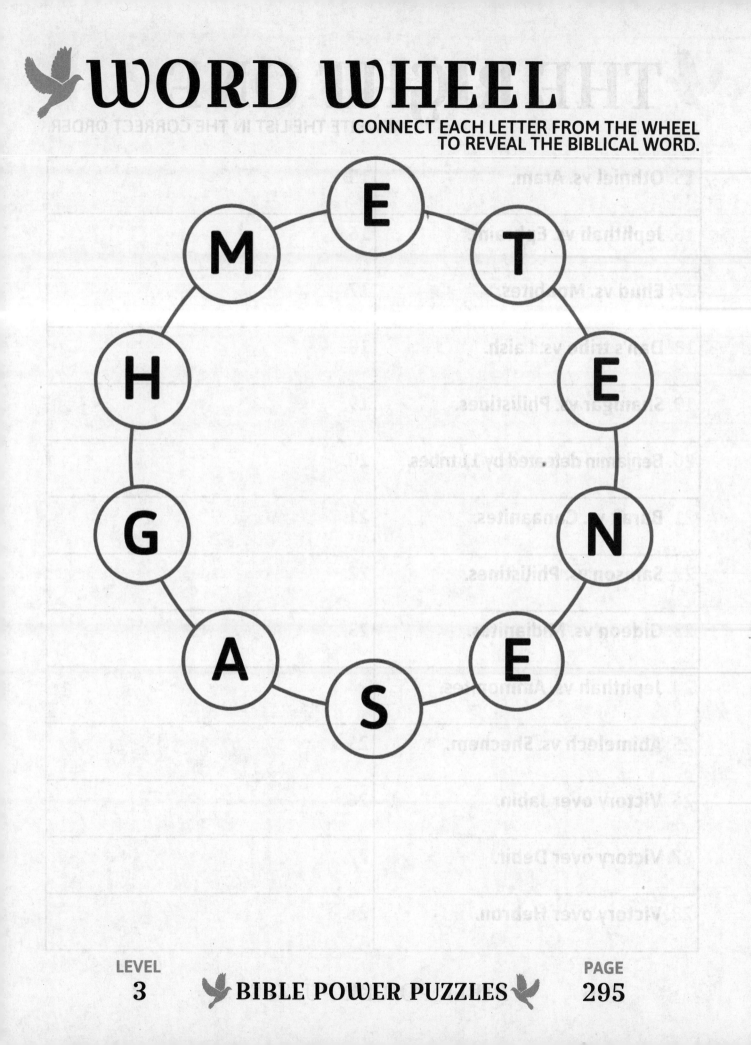

THE RIGHT ONE

15. Othniel vs. Aram.	15.
16. Jephthah vs. Ephraim.	16.
17. Ehud vs. Moabites.	17.
18. Dan's tribe vs. Laish.	18.
19. Shamgar vs. Philistines.	19.
20. Benjamin defeated by 11 tribes.	20.
21. Barak vs. Canaanites.	21.
22. Samson vs. Philistines.	22.
23. Gideon vs. Midianites.	23.
24. Jephthah vs. Ammonites.	24.
25. Abimelech vs. Shechem.	25.
26. Victory over Jabin.	26.
27. Victory over Debir.	27.
28. Victory over Hebron.	28.

CHRISTIAN QUOTES

FROM CHURCH FATHERS TO MODERN CHRISTIAN THINKERS, IDENTIFY THE AUTHOR OF EACH QUOTE.

"When I consider my crosses, tribulations, and temptations, I shame myself almost to death, thinking what are they in comparison of the sufferings of my blessed Savior Christ Jesus."

AUTHOR:

....
....

AUTHOR:

....
....

"Every man must render to God the things that are God's, and that, let it be remembered, is all he is and all he possesses."

"No man is so regenerate, but that continually he has need of the means which Christ Jesus has appointed to be used in his kirk."

AUTHOR:

....
....

OPPOSITES

UNSCRAMBLE THE LETTERS TO FORM PAIRS OF BIBLICAL ANTONYMS AND ANTAGONISTS.

1. HEDU	≠	1. GONLE
1.	≠	1.

2. MOSALBA	≠	2. NOMAN
2.	≠	2.

3. HALE	≠	3. RIMIZ
3.	≠	3.

4. LEJA	≠	4. RASISE
4.	≠	4.

PAGE

298

 BIBLE POWER PUZZLES

LEVEL

3

MATCHMAKER

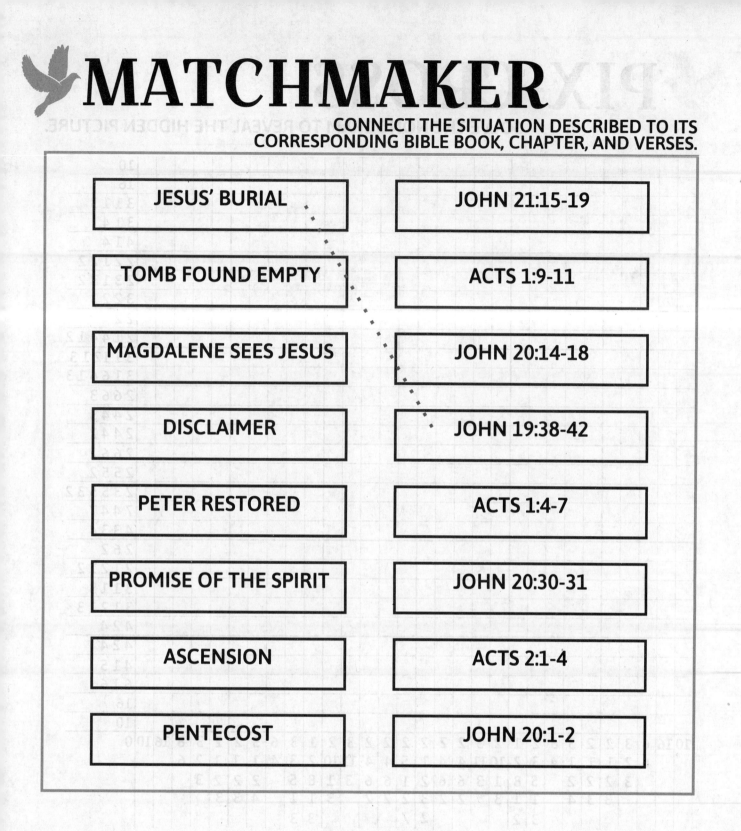

CONNECT THE SITUATION DESCRIBED TO ITS CORRESPONDING BIBLE BOOK, CHAPTER, AND VERSES.

JESUS' BURIAL	JOHN 21:15-19
TOMB FOUND EMPTY	ACTS 1:9-11
MAGDALENE SEES JESUS	JOHN 20:14-18
DISCLAIMER	JOHN 19:38-42
PETER RESTORED	ACTS 1:4-7
PROMISE OF THE SPIRIT	JOHN 20:30-31
ASCENSION	ACTS 2:1-4
PENTECOST	JOHN 20:1-2

PIX-CROSS

SOLVE THE NONOGRAM TO REVEAL THE HIDDEN PICTURE.

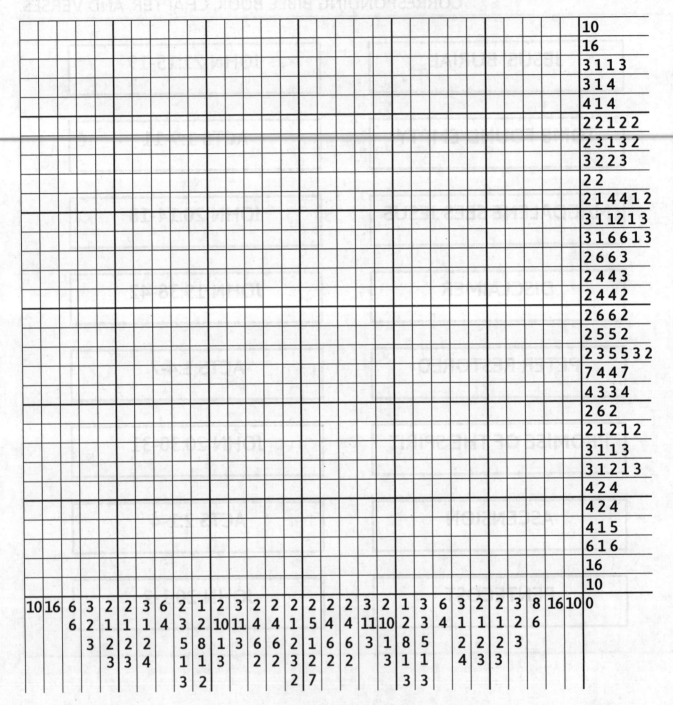

WORD-SEARCH

CONTAINED WITHIN THIS PUZZLE YOU MUST FIND ALL CAPITALIZED WORDS FROM THE VERSES BELOW.

```
E  L  S  T  I  I  I  E  Q  N  T  B  T  V  E  U
C  U  P  P  E  B  G  D  C  D  W  N  G  D  N  E
X  L  D  W  Y  R  E  J  E  L  A  Z  I  B  A  F
I  Q  U  A  T  R  S  T  N  V  Q  R  T  Y  W  R
E  U  L  S  D  U  S  U  R  P  A  I  R  O  I  A
B  C  L  N  T  U  G  E  M  U  M  G  O  U  L  I
W  V  U  I  A  E  S  U  J  M  N  E  Z  N  D  S
K  H  U  H  T  B  R  D  U  I  E  D  E  G  E  I
R  R  X  M  T  H  E  S  K  M  N  R  L  T  R  N
F  E  I  E  S  R  O  Y  D  A  V  I  D  M  N  S
N  L  L  G  E  B  B  S  O  W  I  N  E  X  E  T
B  I  O  W  H  N  R  B  E  N  V  K  H  R  S  H
G  R  S  A  R  T  G  E  F  I  D  Y  Y  O  S  E
C  N  L  C  V  J  L  S  A  D  D  L  E  D  L  R
A  H  O  U  S  E  H  O  L  D  G  A  V  G  Y  E
B  E  C  O  M  E  S  D  O  N  K  E  Y  S  I  Q
```

"When **DAVID** had gone a little **BEYOND** the **SUMMIT**, **ZIBA**, Mephibosheth's **SERVANT**, was **RIGHT THERE** to **MEET** him. He had a **PAIR** of **SADDLED DONKEYS** loaded with two **HUNDRED LOAVES** of **BREAD**, one hundred **CLUSTERS** of **RAISINS**, one hundred bunches of **SUMMER FRUIT**, and a **CLAY** jar of **WINE**. The **KING** said to Ziba, 'Why do you have these?' Ziba **ANSWERED**, 'The donkeys are for the king's **HOUSEHOLD** to **RIDE**, the bread and summer fruit for the **YOUNG** men to eat, and the wine is for **THOSE** to **DRINK** who **BECOME EXHAUSTED** in the **WILDERNESS.'"

CRISS-CROSS

USE THE DEFINITIONS BELOW TO FIND THE WORDS AND GUESS THE THEME.

ACROSS:

1. Wrote Psalm 89.

3. Wrote several letters to early Christian churches.

7. Wrote Proverbs 30.

9. Wrote Jeremiah, and possibly Lamentations and 1-2 Kings.

12. May have written Judges and 1 Samuel.

15. Wrote Joshua.

16. Wrote Psalm 88.

17. Wrote the Song of Songs and Proverbs 1 through 20.

DOWN:

2. Wrote Psalms 50 and 73 through 83.

4. Wrote a gospel and the book of Acts.

5. Wrote two brief letters that bear his name.

6. Wrote a great number of Psalms.

8. Wrote Ezra, and probably 1 and 2 Chronicles.

10. Wrote assorted Psalms from 120 through 136.

11. Wrote Proverbs 31.

13. Wrote Genesis, Exodus, Leviticus, Numbers, and Deuteronomy.

14. Revelation is attributed to him.

15. May have written his own story.

SUDOKU

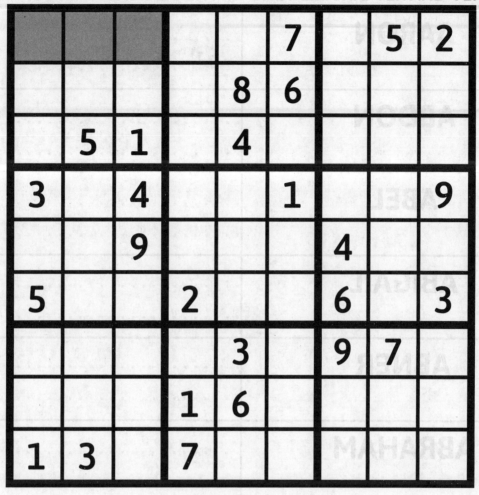

**MATCH THE HIGHLIGHTED NUMBER SEQUENCE
TO THE CHAPTER AND VERSE BELOW.**

					7		5	2
				8	6			
	5	1		4				
3		4			1			9
		9				4		
5			2			6		3
				3		9	7	
			1	6				
1	3		7					

JOHN __ : __

"Who among you can convict me of sin? If I am telling the truth, why don't you believe me?"

LEVEL
4

BIBLE POWER PUZZLES

PAGE
303

THE NAME GAME

DO YOU KNOW THE TRUE
MEANING OF THE BIBLICAL NAMES LISTED BELOW?

AARON	....
	....
ABDON	....
	....
ABEL	....
	....
ABIGAIL	....
	....
ABNER	....
	....
ABRAHAM	....
	....
ADAM	....
	....
ANNA	....
	....

WORD WHEEL

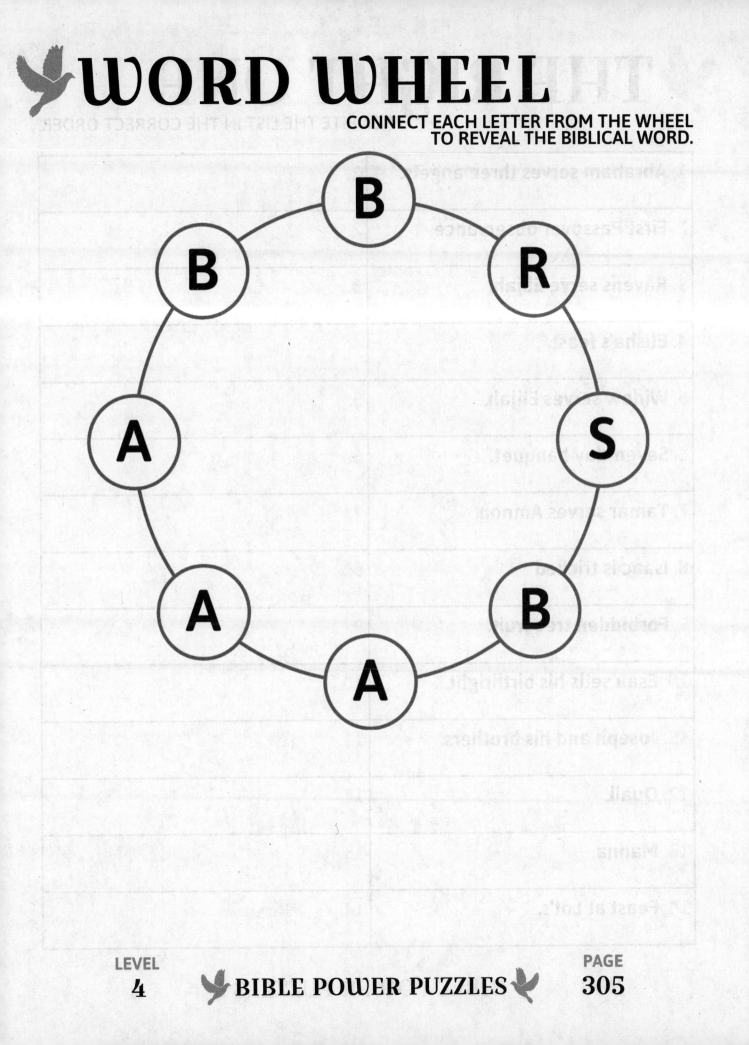

THE RIGHT ONE

1. Abraham serves three angels.	1.
2. First Passover observance	2.
3. Ravens serve Elijah.	3.
4. Elisha's feast.	4.
5. Widow serves Elijah.	5.
6. Seven-day banquet.	6.
7. Tamar serves Amnon.	7.
8. Isaac is tricked	8.
9. Forbidden tree fruit.	9.
10. Esau sells his birthright.	10.
11. Joseph and his brothers.	11.
12. Quail.	12.
13. Manna.	13.
14. Feast at Lot's.	14.

CHRISTIAN QUOTES

"The Bible is absolutely honest in its presentation. The Bible is not a Book that man could write if he would, or would write if he could."

AUTHOR:

....

....

AUTHOR:

....

....

"Let your door stand open to receive Him, unlock your soul to Him, offer Him a welcome in your mind, and then you will see the riches of simplicity, the treasures of peace, the joy of grace. Throw wide the gate of your heart, stand before the sun of the everlasting light."

"We should ask ourselves three questions before we speak: Is it true? Is it kind? Does it glorify Christ?"

AUTHOR:

....

....

FRIENDS

1. DIVAD	=	**1. HANTANJO**
1.	=	1.
2. RAONA	=	**2. SEMOS**
2.	=	2.
3. HAJILE	=	**3. HASILE**
3.	=	3.
4. MINAO	=	**4. THUR**
4.	=	4.

PROMISEMAKER

CONNECT EACH BIBLICAL ASSURANCE TO ITS CORRESPONDING BOOK, CHAPTER, AND VERSES.

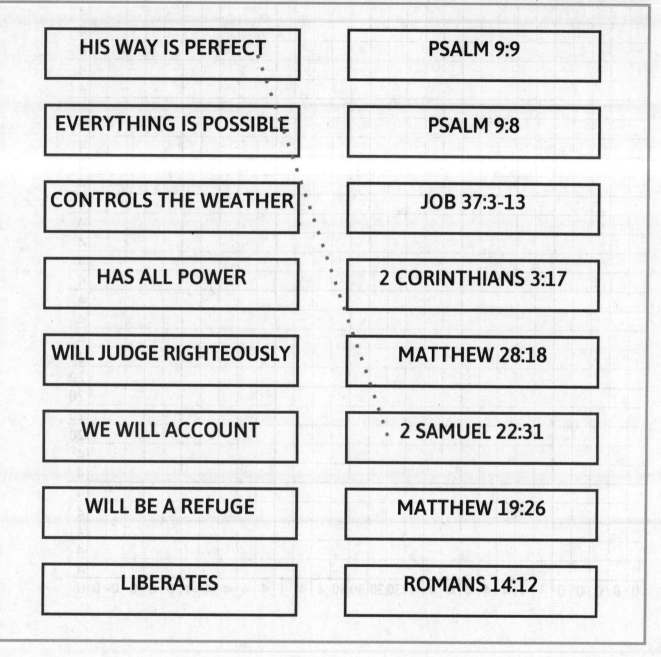

HIS WAY IS PERFECT	PSALM 9:9
EVERYTHING IS POSSIBLE	PSALM 9:8
CONTROLS THE WEATHER	JOB 37:3-13
HAS ALL POWER	2 CORINTHIANS 3:17
WILL JUDGE RIGHTEOUSLY	MATTHEW 28:18
WE WILL ACCOUNT	2 SAMUEL 22:31
WILL BE A REFUGE	MATTHEW 19:26
LIBERATES	ROMANS 14:12

PIX-CROSS

SOLVE THE NONOGRAM TO REVEAL THE HIDDEN PICTURE.

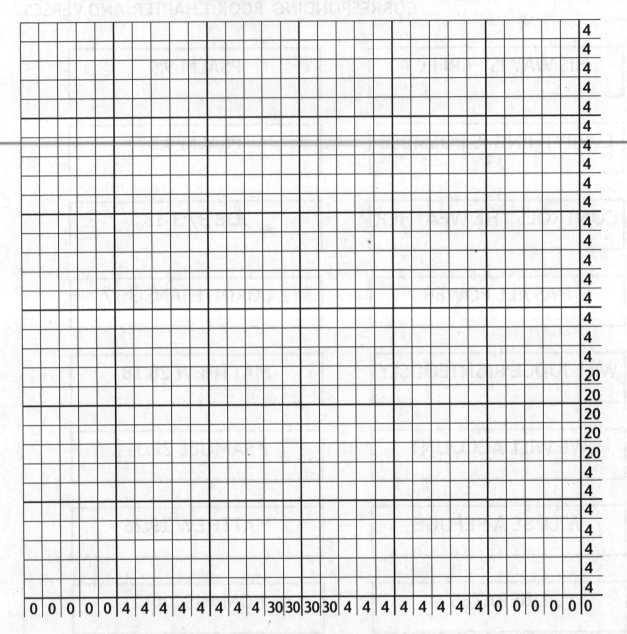

Row clues (top to bottom): 4, 4, 4, 4, 4, 4, 4, 4, 4, 4, 4, 4, 4, 4, 4, 4, 4, 4, 4, 20, 20, 20, 20, 20, 4, 4, 4, 4, 4, 4, 4, 4

Column clues (left to right): 0, 0, 0, 0, 0, 4, 4, 4, 4, 4, 4, 4, 4, 30, 30, 30, 30, 4, 4, 4, 4, 4, 4, 4, 4, 0, 0, 0, 0, 0, 0, 0

WORD-SEARCH

CONTAINED WITHIN THIS PUZZLE YOU MUST FIND ALL CAPITALIZED WORDS FROM THE VERSES BELOW.

```
T D B A F O U R S C T R S I P
M U C B L O X Z A W H K W N I
T O J H K G U E E C O X R S D
H B L O O R R E A W S C T E R
E D Q R S A A O A I E J Y C J
S R P R W S B U U T A A R T O
E Q D E G S A E D N M L D S I
T W Z N L H V H F D D P L N N
O Q I T L O K O L X D E L I T
Q B E N B P A P O G G H P E E
N Y D A G P T P C N V D K M D
L E G S F E Y I U U S C I O C
I G T Z E R D N S Y I T N J C
W I N G E D I G T R H Q D C T
W A L K T G D D C U C Q S V R
```

"**ALL WINGED INSECTS** that **WALK** on all **FOURS** are to be **ABHORRENT** to you. But you **MAY EAT** these **KINDS** of all the **WINGED** insects that walk on all fours: **THOSE** that have **JOINTED LEGS ABOVE** their **FEET** for **HOPPING** on the **GROUND**. You may eat **THESE**: any kind of **LOCUST**, **KATYDID**, **CRICKET**, and **GRASSHOPPER**."

CRISS-CROSS

USE THE DEFINITIONS BELOW TO FIND THE WORDS AND GUESS THE THEME.

ACROSS:

1. His father was murdered when when he was 8 years old.

4. Rachel died giving birth to him.

6. Lost his father as a young child.

7. His father was murdered when he was 16 years old.

8. His father, Azahiah, was slain.

9. Orphaned as a young girl and raised by her cousin.

DOWN:

1. His mother died giving birth to his younger brother.

2. The Philistines killed his father and uncle.

3. Together with his friends Hananiah, Mishael, and Azariah, he was probably an orphan.

5. His father died when he was 18 years old.

6. His father died when he was 12 years old.

# SUDOKU

MATCH THE HIGHLIGHTED NUMBER SEQUENCE TO THE CHAPTER AND VERSE BELOW.

	7			5	8			
8		2				7		
	6		7			4		
1		7						
	9						5	
						3		2
		3			6		4	
		6	2		9	5		1
			1	7			3	

GENESIS __ : __

"Then God said to Noah, 'I have decided to put an end to every creature, for this earth is filled with wickedness because of them; therefore I am going to destroy them along with the earth.'"

THE NAME GAME

DO YOU KNOW THE TRUE
MEANING OF THE BIBLICAL NAMES LISTED BELOW?

AENEAS	
AGRIPPA	
AHAB	
ALPHAEUS	
ALIAH	
AMOS	
ANDRONICUS	
AQUILA	

WORD WHEEL

CONNECT EACH LETTER FROM THE WHEEL TO REVEAL THE BIBLICAL WORD.

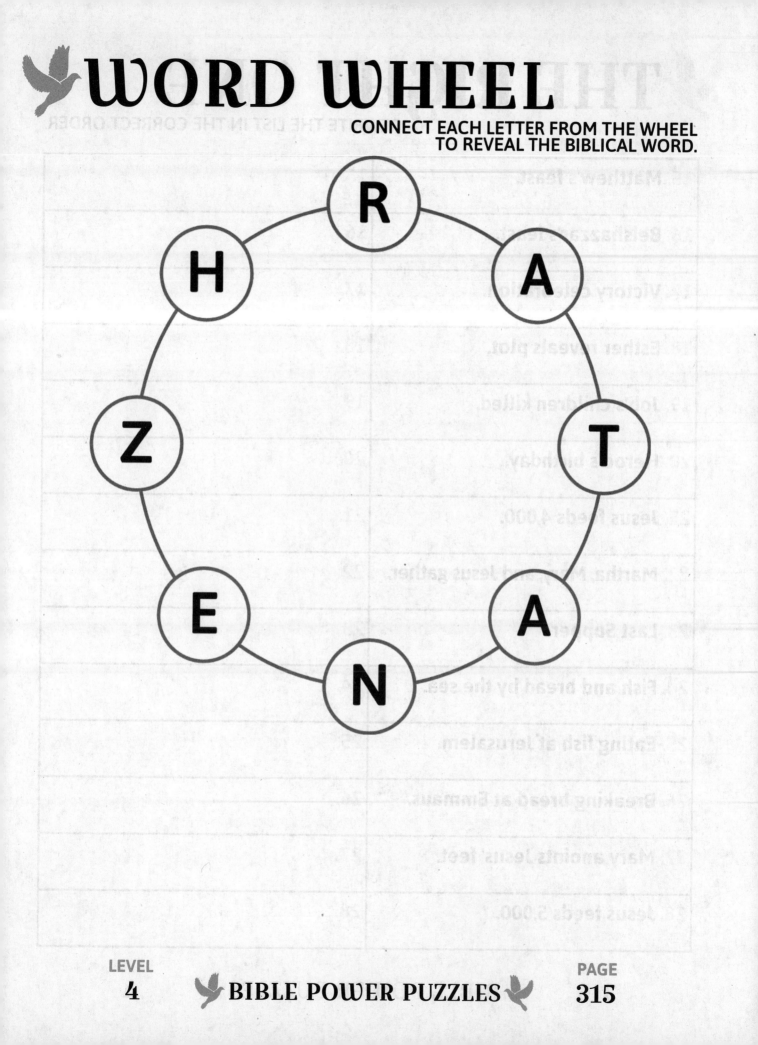

THE RIGHT ONE

REWRITE THE LIST IN THE CORRECT ORDER.

15. Matthew's feast.	15.
16. Belshazzar's feast.	16.
17. Victory celebration.	17.
18. Esther reveals plot.	18.
19. Job's children killed.	19.
20. Herod's birthday.	20.
21. Jesus feeds 4,000.	21.
22. Martha, Mary, and Jesus gather.	22.
23. Last Supper.	23.
24. Fish and bread by the sea.	24.
25. Eating fish at Jerusalem.	25.
26. Breaking bread at Emmaus.	26.
27. Mary anoints Jesus' feet.	27.
28. Jesus feeds 5,000.	28.

CHRISTIAN QUOTES

"When you begin to read or listen to the Holy Scriptures, pray to God thus: 'Lord Jesus Christ, open the ears and eyes of my heart so that I may hear Thy words and understand them, and may fulfill Thy will.' Always pray to God like this, that He might illumine your mind and open to you the power of His words. Many, having trusted in their own reason, have turned away into deception."

AUTHOR:

....

....

AUTHOR:

....

....

"Love works the likeness of God into the soul."

"We must remember that the shortest distance between our problems and their solutions is the distance between our knees and the floor."

AUTHOR:

....

....

FRIENDS

UNSCRAMBLE THE LETTERS TO FORM PAIRS OF BIBLICAL ALLIES.

1. HAMABRA	=	**1. TOL**
1.	=	1.
2. SUJES	=	**2. SUZARLA**
2.	=	2.
3. HILPPI	=	**3. WEMOLOTHARB**
3.	=	3.
4. WERNAD	=	**4. TERPE**
4.	=	4.

PROMISEMAKER

CONNECT EACH BIBLICAL ASSURANCE TO ITS
CORRESPONDING BOOK, CHAPTER, AND VERSES.

GODLY REPENTANCE SAVES	PSALM 19:1
FOREVER KING	2 TIMOTHY 2:19
NO DIFFERENCES	PSALM 11:7
THRONE IN HEAVEN	2 TIMOTHY 2:13
REMAINS FAITHFUL	PSALM 11:4
UPRIGHT WILL SEE	COLOSSIANS 3:11
KNOWS YOU ARE HIS	PSALM 10:16
HEAVENS DECLARE	2 CORINTHIANS 7:10

PIX-CROSS

SOLVE THE NONOGRAM TO REVEAL THE HIDDEN PICTURE.

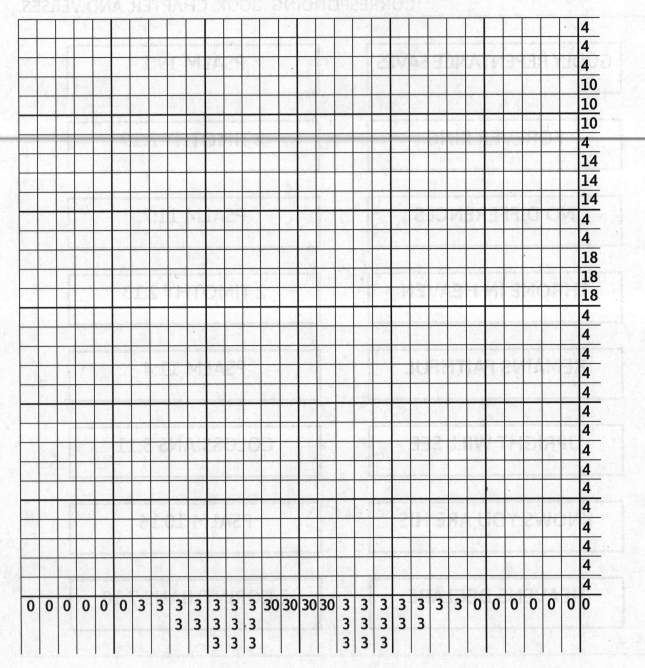

WORD-SEARCH

CONTAINED WITHIN THIS PUZZLE YOU MUST FIND ALL CAPITALIZED WORDS FROM THE VERSES BELOW.

```
S M S Q W I T N E S S E D T C
P O L S W L O H G Q W W D L W
E U L U X B Z N U W I I O B Q
A N P D Q T I X O N B G O D P
K T U R X N G Q V L D R D L E
D A E R T M I O M U D E P R O
L I X H M O S E S K D D R L P
K N G M Z S K J U N N N S I L
D I S T A N C E U U A L L S E
L E Q B D N G O O T S V S T H
G D V O K X R S E Q A K Q E W
S M O K E R D H M O I N P N H
W T A R U S A W R H D I E N E
S Q O S T R U M P E T H B O N
T R E M B L E D B A K T H E Y
```

"**ALL** the **PEOPLE WITNESSED** the **THUNDER** and **LIGHTNING**, the **SOUND** of the **TRUMPET**, and the **MOUNTAIN SURROUNDED** by **SMOKE**. **WHEN** the people **SAW** it **THEY TREMBLED** and **STOOD** at a **DISTANCE**. 'You **SPEAK** to us, and we will **LISTEN**,' they **SAID** to **MOSES**, 'but don't let **GOD** speak to us or we will **DIE**.'"

CRISS-CROSS

USE THE DEFINITIONS BELOW TO FIND THE WORDS AND GUESS THE THEME.

ACROSS:

2. Son of Elizabeth (3 words).

5. God promised to give him rest from his enemies.

6. Wrestled with an angel.

8. His pride doomed mankind.

9. Originally called Sarai.

11. Son of Isaiah.

12. Son of Hagar.

DOWN:

1. Gabriel told his adoptive father how to name him.

3. Formerly known as Pashur.

4. Daughter of Gomer.

6. Son of Hosea.

7. Formerly known as Simon.

8. Called to leave the house of his father.

10. Son of Gomer.

SUDOKU

9		4					7	
8		7			2	4	3	9
1				9				
			3	1			9	
		3				8		
	6			8	5			
			2					4
3	4	8	6			7		2
	7					9		3

MATTHEW __ : __

"'Leave,' he said, 'because the girl is not dead but asleep.' And they laughed at him."

THE NAME GAME

DO YOU KNOW THE TRUE
MEANING OF THE BIBLICAL NAMES LISTED BELOW?

ANTIPAS	....
APOLLOS	....
ARIEL	....
AUGUSTUS	....
BATHSHEBA	....
BERNICE	....
BILHAH	....
CANDACE	....

WORD WHEEL

CONNECT EACH LETTER FROM THE WHEEL TO REVEAL THE BIBLICAL WORD.

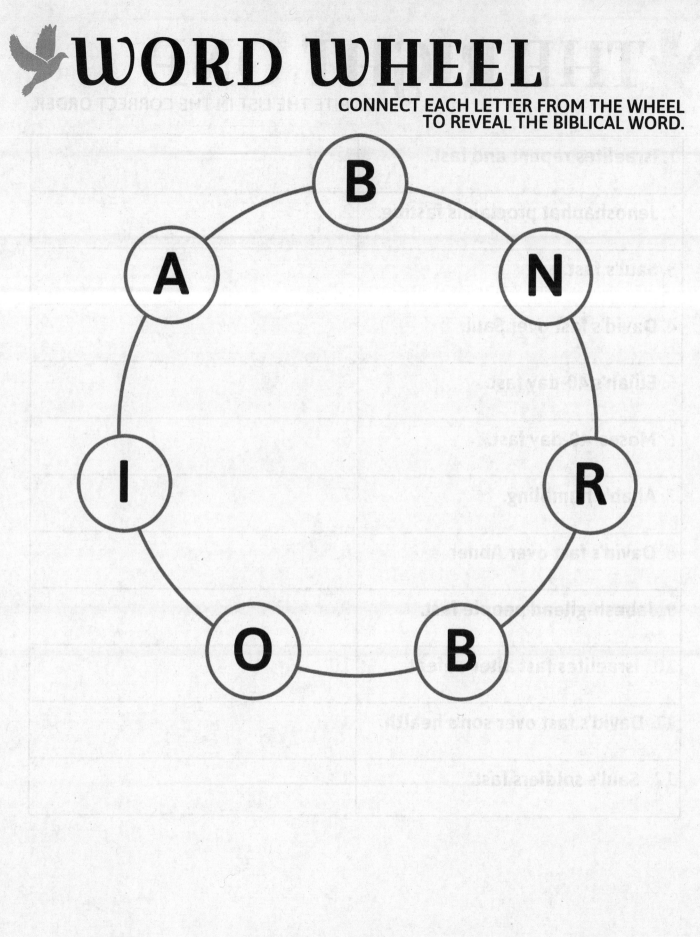

THE RIGHT ONE

REWRITE THE LIST IN THE CORRECT ORDER.

1. Israelites repent and fast.	1.
2. Jehoshaphat proclaims fasting.	2.
3. Saul's fast.	3.
4. David's fast over Saul.	4.
5. Elijah's 40-day fast.	5.
6. Moses' 40-day fast.	6.
7. Ahab's humbling.	7.
8. David's fast over Abner	8.
9. Jabesh-gilead people fast.	9.
10. Israelites fast after defeat.	10.
11. David's fast over son's health.	12.
12. Saul's soldiers fast.	13.

CHRISTIAN QUOTES

FROM CHURCH FATHERS TO MODERN CHRISTIAN THINKERS, IDENTIFY THE AUTHOR OF EACH QUOTE.

"While you are proclaiming peace with your lips, be careful to have it even more fully in your heart."

AUTHOR:

....

....

AUTHOR:

....

....

"Social justice cannot be attained by violence. Violence kills what it intends to create."

"There will be no peace in any soul until it is willing to obey the voice of God."

AUTHOR:

....

....

FRIENDS

UNSCRAMBLE THE LETTERS TO FORM PAIRS OF BIBLICAL ALLIES.

1. DIVAD	= 1. THARABIA
1.	= 1.
2. SHAHAN	= 2. DIVAD
2.	= 2.
3. DIVAD	= 3. TAITI
3.	= 3.
4. HARIM	= 4. DIVAD
4.	= 4.

PROMISEMAKER

CONNECT EACH BIBLICAL ASSURANCE TO ITS CORRESPONDING BOOK, CHAPTER, AND VERSES.

WORLDWIDE WORSHIP	1 PETER 3:22
FOREVER THE SAME	PSALM 22:27
BLESS WITH PEACE	PSALM 56:9
DOES NOT TEMPT	HEBREWS 13:8
MAKES WARS CEASE	JAMES 1:17
EVERY GOOD GIFT	PSALM 29:11
FOR ME	PSALM 46:9
AT THE RIGHT HAND	JAMES 1:13

PIX-CROSS

SOLVE THE NONOGRAM TO REVEAL THE HIDDEN PICTURE.

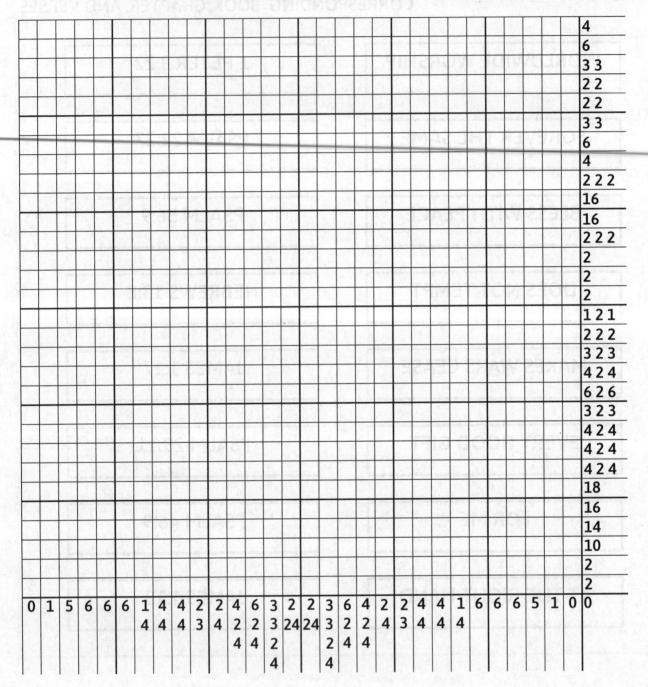

WORD-SEARCH

CONTAINED WITHIN THIS PUZZLE YOU MUST FIND ALL CAPITALIZED WORDS FROM THE VERSES BELOW.

```
F O R E I G N D B O P U Q F F
Y H X X A U I P H R V N D E C
T S A I D R O D V M O A Z L E
Y O U R S E L V E S Z T W Y W
D X T K B P U R I F Y D H L H
C J R T L F R T U B E I E E O
L T H E R E S B R S H X Q R
O M G C O G G E A R T W J A T
T M E F G N L E A E Y E S A U
H J M D O T P T B L J P U P G
E D E M T P L K I C H A N G E
S L A E A A U M T W W W C L J
F O S L P B A A W I G H K O I
B U I L D F M R X T S O E I B
P U N Y Q G O D X H F O U N C
```

"**GOD SAID** to **JACOB**, '**GET** up! **GO** to **BETHEL** and **SETTLE THERE. BUILD** an **ALTAR** there to the God who **APPEARED** to you **WHEN** you **FLED** from your **BROTHER ESAU**.'

So Jacob said to his **FAMILY** and all **WHO** were **WITH** him, 'Get **RID** of the **FOREIGN** gods that are **AMONG** you. **PURIFY YOURSELVES** and **CHANGE** your **CLOTHES**.'"

CRISS-CROSS

USE THE DEFINITIONS BELOW TO FIND THE WORDS AND GUESS THE THEME.

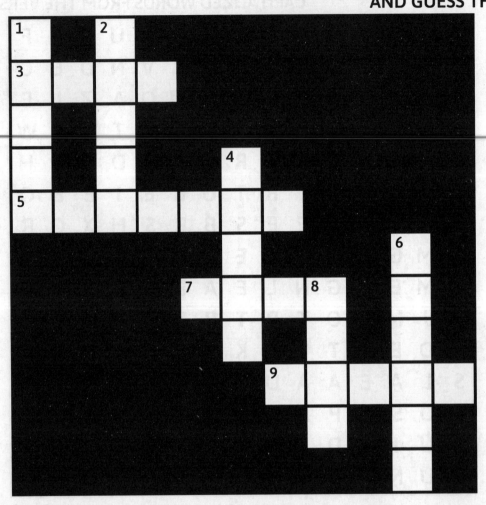

ACROSS:

3. An arrow found him despite his disguise.

5. Disguised her younger son as her firstborn.

7. Went to see a medium in disguise.

9. Pretended to be a madman to avoid capture.

DOWN:

1. Mother of twins (Perez and Zerah).

2. Pretended to be his elder brother.

4. Posed as her husband's sister.

6. Disguised himself to fight King Necho.

8. Posed as her sister Rachel.

SUDOKU

2		7	9					3
	1	9						8
4	8			1				
3	2		4	7			9	5
5	9			2	6		7	4
				4			3	7
7						2	8	
					2	9		6

EXODUS _ : __

"The LORD did as Moses had said: He removed the swarms of flies from Pharaoh, his officials, and his people; not one was left."

THE NAME GAME

DO YOU KNOW THE TRUE
MEANING OF THE BIBLICAL NAMES LISTED BELOW?

BARAK	
BARNABAS	
BARTHOLOMEW	
BARUCH	
BELA	
BENJAMIN	
CHLOE	
CLAUDIA	

WORD WHEEL

CONNECT EACH LETTER FROM THE WHEEL TO REVEAL THE BIBLICAL WORD.

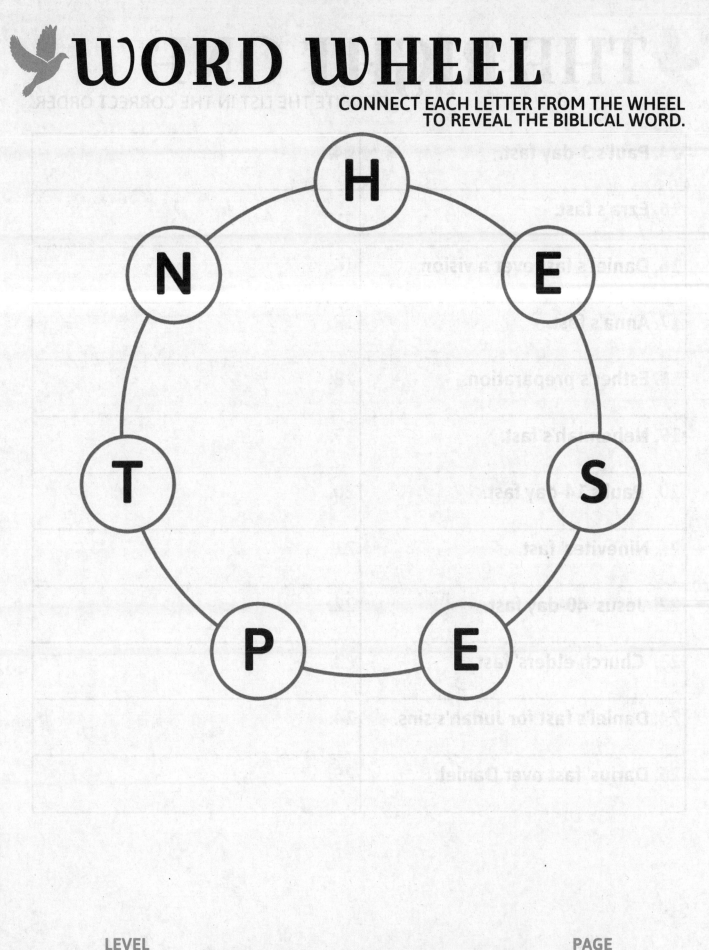

THE RIGHT ONE

REWRITE THE LIST IN THE CORRECT ORDER.

14. Paul's 3-day fast.	14.
15. Ezra's fast.	15.
16. Daniel's fast over a vision.	16.
17. Anna's fast.	17.
18. Esther's preparation.	18.
19. Nehemiah's fast.	19.
20. Paul's 14-day fast.	20.
21. Ninevites' fast.	21.
22. Jesus' 40-day fast.	22.
23. Church elders' fast.	23.
24. Daniel's fast for Judah's sins.	24.
25. Darius' fast over Daniel.	25.

CHRISTIAN QUOTES

"I find daily that men would rather suffer any measure of bondage in the things of religion than dwell in individual responsibility before God for every action, thought, and affection."

AUTHOR:

....

....

AUTHOR:

....

....

"Another scheme of Satan is to eliminate from the church all the humble, self-denying ordinances that are offensive to unsanctified tastes and unregenerate hearts. He seeks to reduce the church to a mere human institution—popular, natural, fleshly, and pleasing."

"Let us, therefore, forsake the vanity of the crowd and their false teachings, and turn back to the word delivered to us from the beginning."

AUTHOR:

....

....

FRIENDS

UNSCRAMBLE THE LETTERS TO FORM PAIRS OF BIBLICAL ALLIES.

1. BOJ	**=**	**1. ZAPHILE**
1.	**=**	**1.**
2. DADBIL	**=**	**2. BOJ**
2.	**=**	**2.**
3. BOJ	**=**	**3. PHARZO**
3.	**=**	**3.**
4. LENIDA	**=**	**4. CHARDASH**
4.	**=**	**4.**

PROMISEMAKER

CONNECT EACH BIBLICAL ASSURANCE TO ITS CORRESPONDING BOOK, CHAPTER, AND VERSES.

DOES NOT DELAY	REVELATION 1:7
KNOWS MY SINS	REVELATION 20:1-3
COMING WITH CLOUDS	2 PETER 3:9
WON'T VIOLATE	PSALM 89:34
KING OF KINGS	PSALM 94:11
ENEMIES SHALL PERISH	PSALM 69:5
SATAN BOUND	REVELATION 17:14
KNOWS MY THOUGHTS	PSALM 92:9

PIX-CROSS

SOLVE THE NONOGRAM TO REVEAL THE HIDDEN PICTURE.

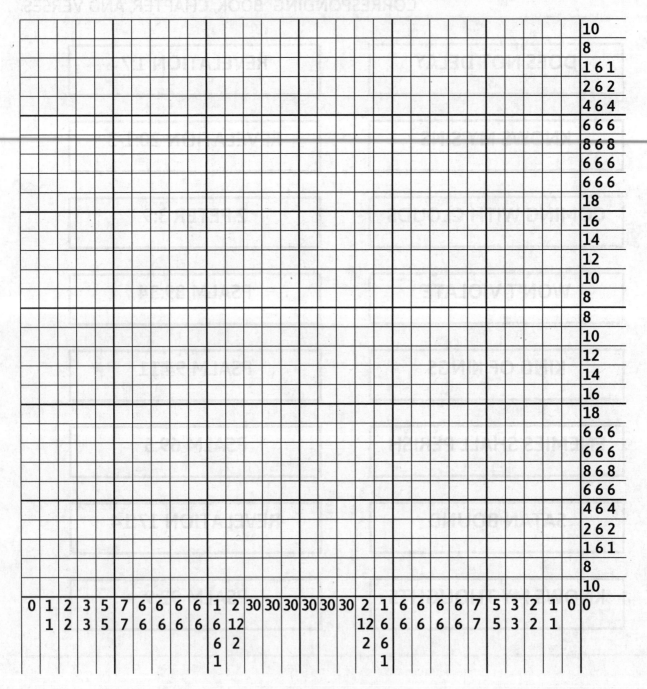

WORD-SEARCH

```
S R R E C O V E R T L W H E N
P A G A I N S T K M O U N T G
E Y I G I N V S I N N E D O C
A O M D Y H S Q D M O U X E A
K M N I N T E R C E D E K W M
I A O X M T S L O R D A M I E
N W U S Z A S X C X T D Y L I
G A X P E K V C E W X C T L M
L Y U Z N S T N B J B Y O U A
O P J B E R O T W N X Z C W G
O H E K I Y K O A T Q E O U E
K J A O N T N Y W Z H U C M M
S N R A P X T Z W V A E G A W
S R L C P L C E R U Y L N K E
D Z R I K B E M N Q P O L E O
```

"The **PEOPLE** then **CAME** to **MOSES** and **SAID**, 'We have **SINNED** by **SPEAKING** **AGAINST** the **LORD** and against **YOU**. **INTERCEDE** with the Lord so that he **WILL** **TAKE** the **SNAKES** **AWAY** from us.' **AND** Moses interceded for the people. **THEN** the Lord said to Moses, '**MAKE** a snake **IMAGE** and **MOUNT** it on a **POLE**. **WHEN** **ANYONE** who is **BITTEN** **LOOKS** at it, he will **RECOVER**.'"

CRISS-CROSS

USE THE DEFINITIONS BELOW TO FIND THE WORDS AND GUESS THE THEME.

ACROSS:
1. Son of Hiel.
5. Son of Jehoram.
7. Had seven brothers.
8. The youngest of seventy.
10. Three years younger than Aaron.

DOWN:
2. The youngest of twelve.
3. Caleb's brother.
4. Youngest son of Joseph.
6. Stole his brother's birthright.
9. Son of Noah.

SUDOKU

MATCH THE HIGHLIGHTED NUMBER SEQUENCE TO THE CHAPTER AND VERSE BELOW.

		7				4	9	
	8			4	6		5	
							8	
8					2	5		
	2	9	8		3	1	7	
	5	7						8
	1							
	5		3	7			1	
	3	4				9		

LUKE __ : __

"At that very moment, she came up and began to thank God and to speak about him to all who were looking forward to the redemption of Jerusalem."

THE NAME GAME

BILDAD	....
BUNNI	....
BUZ	....
CAESAR	....
CAIAPHAS	....
CAIN	....
CALEB	....
CEPHAS	....

WORD WHEEL

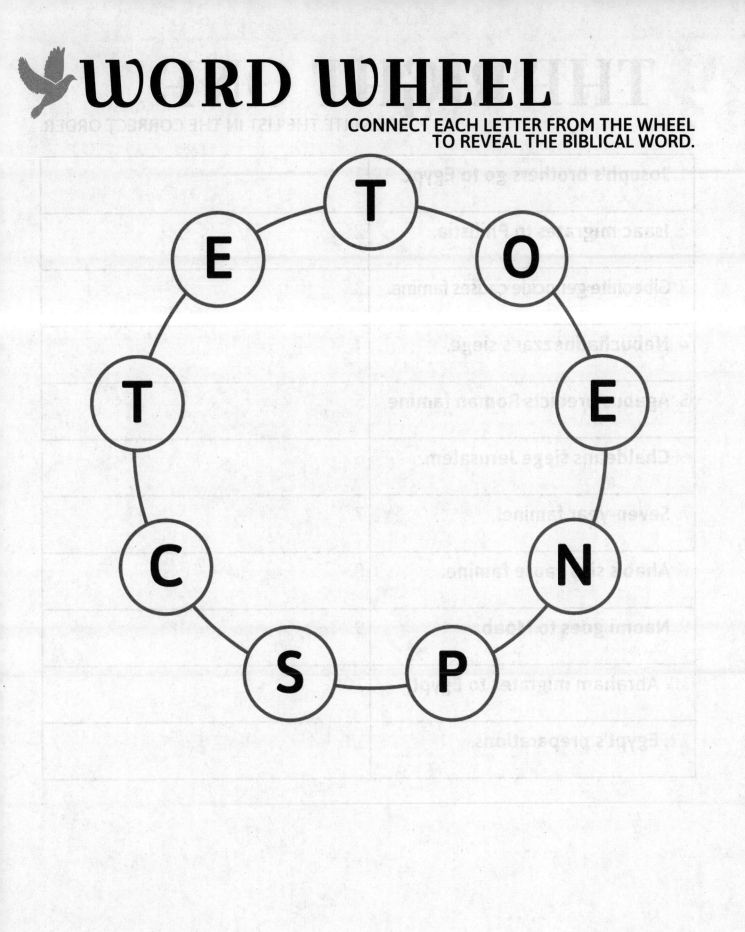

THE RIGHT ONE

1. Joseph's brothers go to Egypt.	1.
2. Isaac migrates to Philistia.	2.
3. Gibeonite genocide causes famine.	3.
4. Nebuchadnezzar's siege.	4.
5. Agabus predicts Roman famine.	5.
6. Chaldeans siege Jerusalem.	6.
7. Seven-year famine.	7.
8. Ahab's sins cause famine.	8.
9. Naomi goes to Moab.	9.
10. Abraham migrates to Egypt.	10.
11. Egypt's preparations.	11.

CHRISTIAN QUOTES

**FROM CHURCH FATHERS TO MODERN CHRISTIAN THINKERS,
IDENTIFY THE AUTHOR OF EACH QUOTE.**

"During my solitude, conflicting thoughts
increased; but much exercise of soul had
the effect of causing the scriptures to
gain complete ascendancy over me."

AUTHOR:

....

....

AUTHOR:

....

....

"Christ the Lord is risen. Our joy that hath
no end."

"Retire at various times into the solitude
of your own heart, even while outwardly
engaged in discussions or transactions
with others, and talk to God."

AUTHOR:

....

....

FRIENDS

1. LENIDA	=	1. CHAMESH
1.	=	1.

2. GONEDEBA	=	2. LENIDA
2.	=	2.

3. HERTES	=	3. CAIDEROM
3.	=	3.

4. SUJES	=	4. RYMA
4.	=	4.

PROMISEMAKER

CONNECT EACH BIBLICAL ASSURANCE TO ITS CORRESPONDING BOOK, CHAPTER, AND VERSES.

HIS LOVE ENDURES	PSALM 100:5
CAST INTO FIRE	PSALM 103:8
COMPASSIONATE	PSALM 103:8
INHERIT THE EARTH	REVELATION 20:7-10
GRACIOUS	MATTHEW 24:14
GREAT REWARD	MATTHEW 5:11-12
SLOW TO ANGER	PSALM 103:8
THE END SHALL COME	MATTHEW 5:5

PIX-CROSS

SOLVE THE NONOGRAM TO REVEAL THE HIDDEN PICTURE.

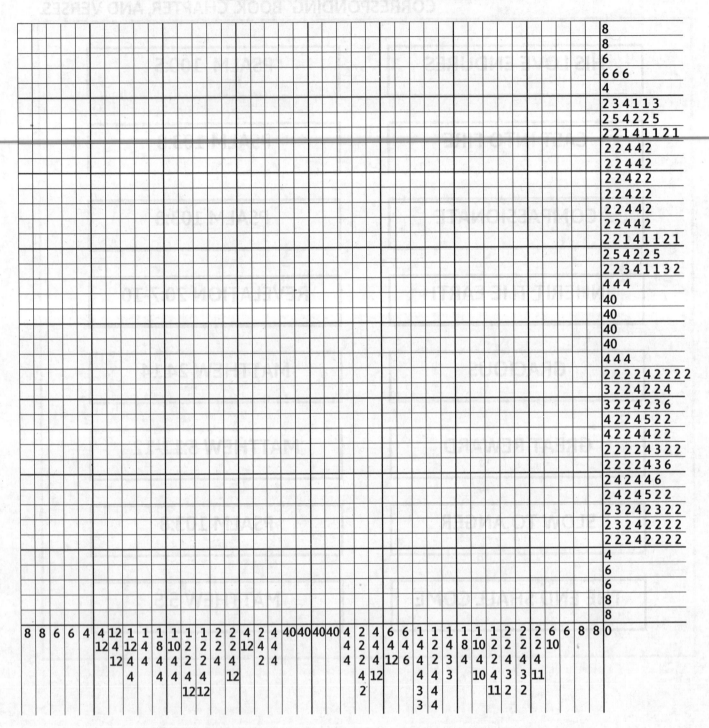

WORD-SEARCH

CONTAINED WITHIN THIS PUZZLE YOU MUST FIND ALL CAPITALIZED WORDS FROM THE VERSES BELOW.

```
W O R S H I P E D R Y I X E S
E J P L E A S E S C K H W E B
T E E W N O G A R T E J E J M
S H C G B Y Q D I H H U M R N
U D I O C P O P S D H O S A E
R X G S L N R S T Y M L M S M
E I Q I S R Y A N N O O W C P
L Q C Y W S H H H W N V C E
Y L X X E W T Q W I V G C V S
V R A V G B P O R F N V A L J
Y Z I I R R H W O H S G V T F
N L N V X V Y B T D H I M H D
J F L G I V E N R F X Y M E B
A S K E D V X O I G I V E R O
B E S I D E L S I N C E Z E Y
```

"'**PLEASE** my lord,' **SHE SAID**, 'as **SURELY** as you **LIVE**, my lord, I am the **WOMAN WHO STOOD HERE BESIDE** you **PRAYING** to the **LORD**. I prayed for **THIS BOY**, and **SINCE** the Lord **GAVE** me **WHAT** I **ASKED HIM** for, I now **GIVE** the boy to the Lord. For as **LONG** as he lives, he is **GIVEN** to the Lord.' Then he **WORSHIPED** the Lord **THERE**."

CRISS-CROSS

USE THE DEFINITIONS BELOW TO FIND THE WORDS AND GUESS THE THEME.

ACROSS:

1. Dreamed of a ladder to heaven.

4. An angel sent him to Peter.

7. Dreamed of fat and malnourished cattle.

9. Saw the Almighty in a trance.

12. Was warned against taking Abraham's wife.

13. Requested discernment.

DOWN:

1. Saw his family bowing down to him.

2. Was promised infinite descendants.

3. Traveled to Chaldea.

5. Saw Ananias praying for the restoration of his sight.

6. God asked him to write down his dreams.

8. Told to pray for Saul.

10. God clarified the matter of what's unclean for him.

11. Warned about Eli's sons.

SUDOKU

MATCH THE HIGHLIGHTED NUMBER SEQUENCE TO THE CHAPTER AND VERSE BELOW.

		9			1	8		
6		8	7					3
				5				6
	5		1	2				
	9	4				2	6	
			4	7		5		
2			3					
9						6		8
		3	9			7		

NUMBERS __ : __

"They are to take all the serving utensils they use in the sanctuary, place them in a blue cloth, cover them with a covering made of fine leather, and put them on a carrying frame."

THE NAME GAME

DO YOU KNOW THE TRUE MEANING OF THE BIBLICAL NAMES LISTED BELOW?

CORNELIUS	....
CRISPUS	....
CYRUS	....
DAMARIS	....
DANIEL	....
DARIUS	....
DAVID	....
DEBORAH	....

WORD WHEEL

CONNECT EACH LETTER FROM THE WHEEL
TO REVEAL THE BIBLICAL WORD.

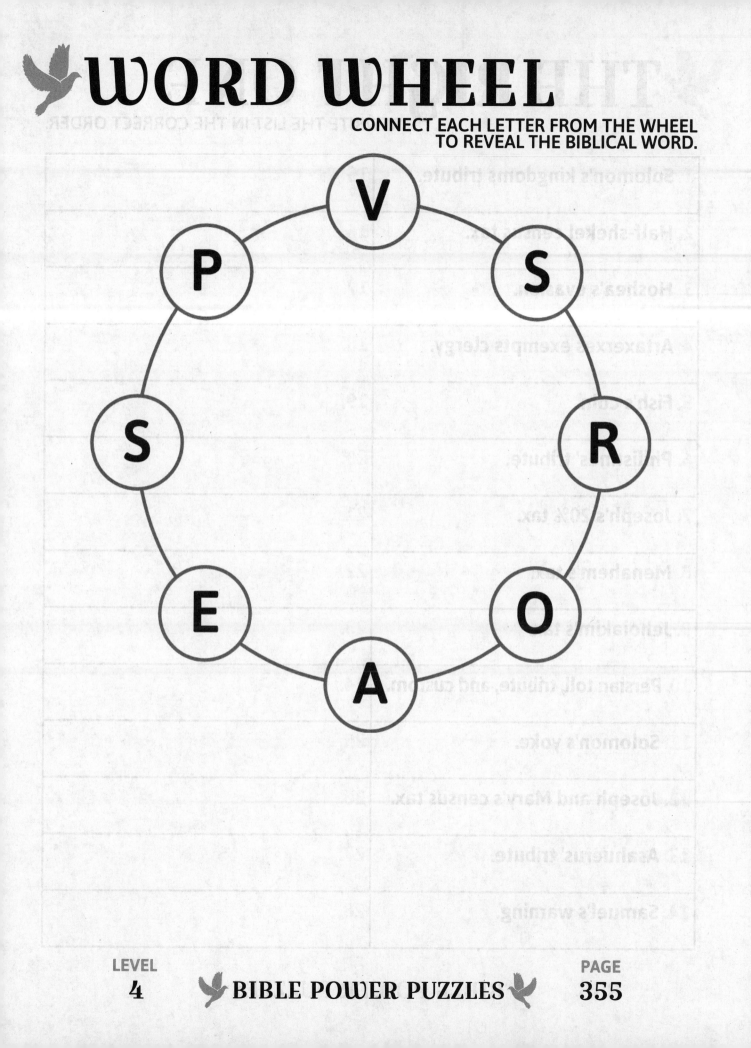

THE RIGHT ONE

REWRITE THE LIST IN THE CORRECT ORDER.

1. Solomon's kingdoms tribute.	15.
2. Half-shekel census tax.	16.
3. Hoshea's evasion.	17.
4. Artaxerxes exempts clergy.	18.
5. Fish's coin.	19.
6. Philistines' tribute.	20.
7. Joseph's 20% tax.	21.
8. Menahem's tax.	22.
9. Jehoiakim's tax.	23.
10. Persian toll, tribute, and custom.	24.
11. Solomon's yoke.	25.
12. Joseph and Mary's census tax.	26.
13. Asahuerus' tribute.	27.
14. Samuel's warning.	28.

CHRISTIAN QUOTES

FROM CHURCH FATHERS TO MODERN CHRISTIAN THINKERS, IDENTIFY THE AUTHOR OF EACH QUOTE.

"I saw also that there was an ocean of darkness and death, but an infinite ocean of light and love, which flowed over the ocean of darkness."

AUTHOR:

....

....

AUTHOR:

....

....

"The truly wise man is he who believes the Bible against the opinions of any man. If the Bible says one thing, and any body of men says another, the wise man will decide, 'This book is the Word of Him who cannot lie.'"

"Shun the praise of men and love the one who, in the fear of the Lord, reprimands you."

AUTHOR:

....

....

FRIENDS

UNSCRAMBLE THE LETTERS TO FORM PAIRS OF BIBLICAL ALLIES.

1. THAMAR = 1. SUJES

1. = 1.

2. SEMAJ = 2. HOJN

2. = 2.

3. THEBAZILE = 3. RYMA

3. = 3.

4. PHESOJ = 4. HORAPHA

4. = 4.

PROMISEMAKER

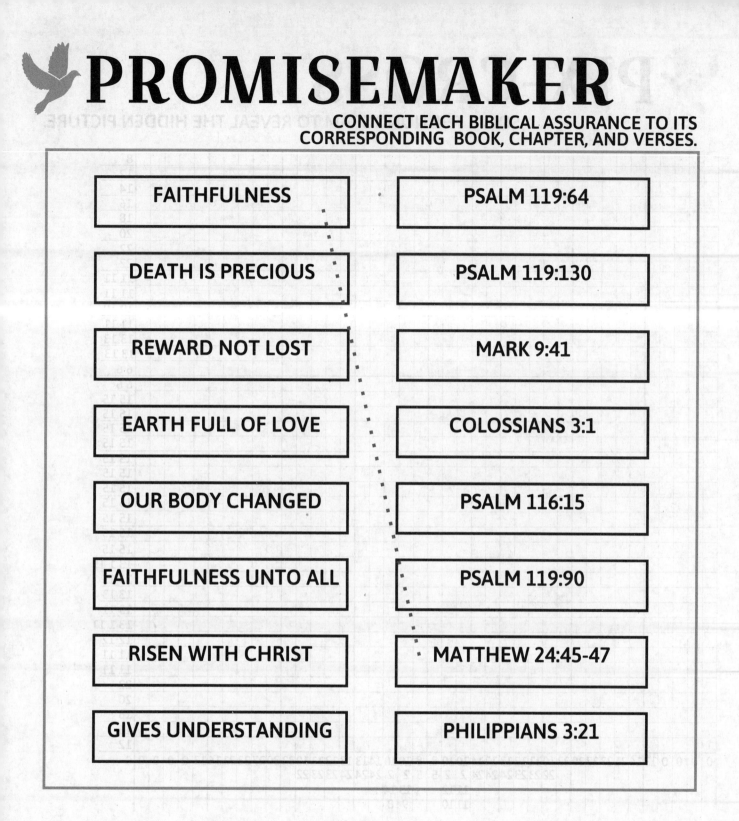

FAITHFULNESS	PSALM 119:64
DEATH IS PRECIOUS	PSALM 119:130
REWARD NOT LOST	MARK 9:41
EARTH FULL OF LOVE	COLOSSIANS 3:1
OUR BODY CHANGED	PSALM 116:15
FAITHFULNESS UNTO ALL	PSALM 119:90
RISEN WITH CHRIST	MATTHEW 24:45-47
GIVES UNDERSTANDING	PHILIPPIANS 3:21

PIX-CROSS

SOLVE THE NONOGRAM TO REVEAL THE HIDDEN PICTURE.

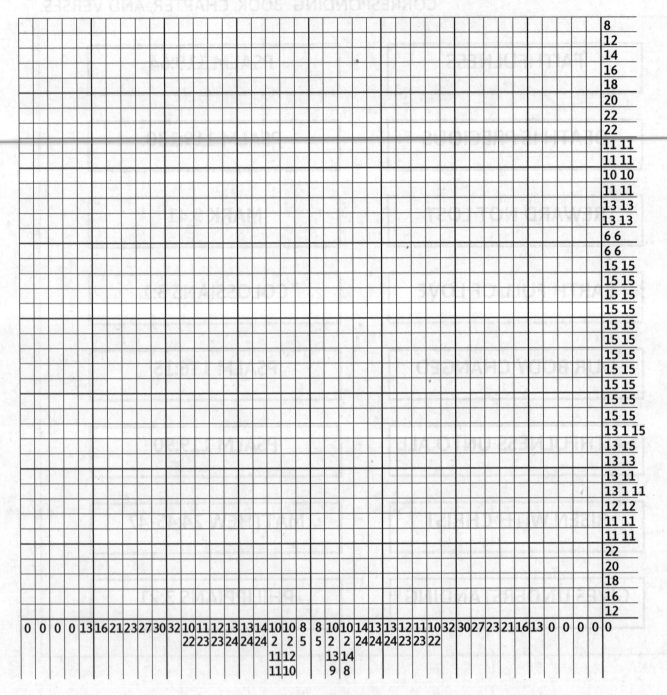

WORD-SEARCH

CONTAINED WITHIN THIS PUZZLE YOU MUST FIND ALL CAPITALIZED WORDS FROM THE VERSES BELOW.

```
F G X Z L R A B A N D O N E D
T O O K I N G S S O L E R I W
V G J D W I D R W T V Z E T H
P S L A V E R Y A I P X L D S
R H Z F R O N H G C V S I A E
E J M S C K T F Y R E E E G X
S Q U W Y F S J X E U E F C T
E C M D P K L T G B S D I Z E
N E F G A W A L L U Q E G L N
C J K I U H V X O I R U A C D
E O Z X O W E H O L U K R J E
M G Q I Y Z S D Z D I N E N D
O C O P P E R S I A N M A M Z
I L U G T H O U G H S C L R X
J E R U S A L E M R E P A I R
```

"**THOUGH** we **ARE SLAVES**, our **GOD** has **NOT ABANDONED** us in **OUR SLAVERY**. He has **EXTENDED GRACE** to us in the **PRESENCE** of the **PERSIAN KINGS**, giving us **RELIEF**, so **THAT** we **CAN REBUILD** the **HOUSE** of our God and **REPAIR** its **RUINS**, to **GIVE** us a **WALL** in **JUDAH** and **JERUSALEM**."

CRISS-CROSS

USE THE DEFINITIONS BELOW TO FIND THE WORDS
AND GUESS THE THEME.

ACROSS:

2. Lived in central Asia Minor.
4. Lived in Palestine and S Syria.
7. Assimilated into Babylonia.
9. Lived in ancient Mesopotamia.
10. Lived N of the Arabian Peninsula.
11. Lived S of the Dead Sea.

DOWN:

1. Lived S of Egypt.
3. Also called Horites or Hivites.
4. Called the Kue people in the OT.
5. Formed the first Mesopotamian empire.
6. Lived in central Sinai.
8. Lived in central Mesopotamia.

SUDOKU

4				2	8		7	
	7	5			9			
	8		5	6				
5						7		4
6								3
	4	7						6
				1	3		6	
			2			1	8	
	9		7	4				2

MARK __ : __

"He ordered them to tell no one, but the more he ordered them, the more they proclaimed it."

THE NAME GAME

DO YOU KNOW THE TRUE
MEANING OF THE BIBLICAL NAMES LISTED BELOW?

DELILAH	....
DEMAS	....
DEMETRIUS	....
DIDYMUS	....
DINAH	....
DIONYSIUS	....
DODO	....
DORCAS	....

WORD WHEEL

CONNECT EACH LETTER FROM THE WHEEL TO REVEAL THE BIBLICAL WORD.

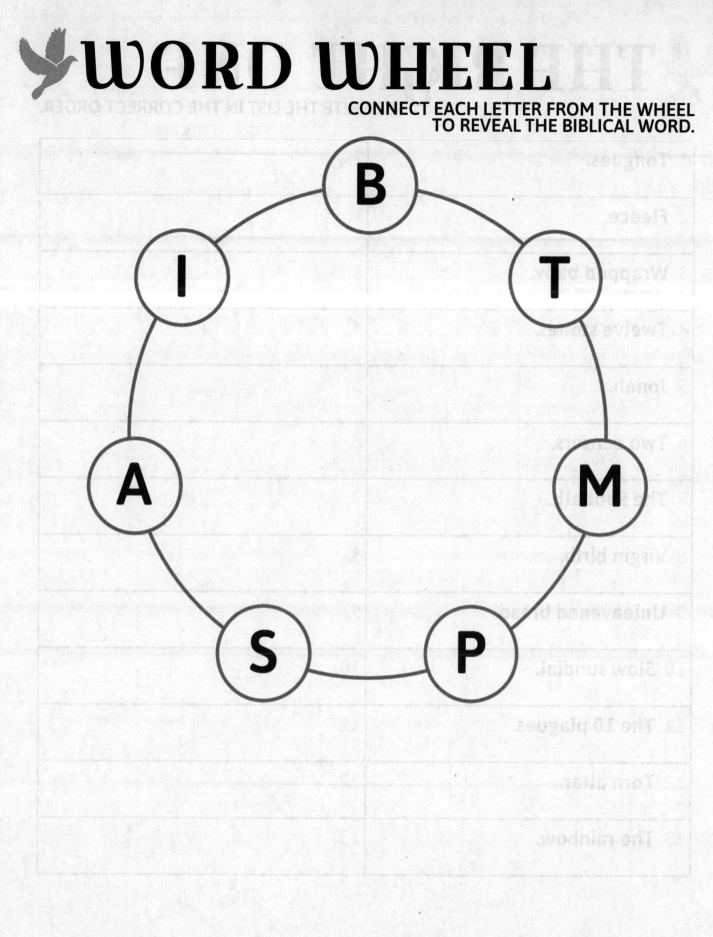

THE RIGHT ONE

1. Tongues.	1.
2. Fleece.	2.
3. Wrapped baby.	3.
4. Twelve stones.	4.
5. Jonah.	5.
6. Two censers.	6.
7. The Sabbath.	7.
8. Virgin birth.	8.
9. Unleavened bread.	9.
10. Slow sundial.	10.
11. The 10 plagues.	11.
12. Torn altar.	12.
13. The rainbow.	13.

CHRISTIAN QUOTES

"Art thou in the darkness? Mind it not, for if thou dost it will feed thee more. But stand still, and act not, and wait in patience, till light arises out of darkness and leads thee."

AUTHOR:

....

....

AUTHOR:

....

....

"We are all thieves; we are all thieves; we have taken the scriptures in words, and know nothing of them in ourselves."

"It is in the low valley, it is in the humiliation of the pride of man, that we are to expect effectual instruction."

AUTHOR:

....

....

FRIENDS

UNSCRAMBLE THE LETTERS TO FORM PAIRS OF BIBLICAL ALLIES.

1. HABORDE	**=**	**1. KABAR**
1.	**=**	**1.**
2. LUPA	**=**	**2. LACILPRIS**
2.	**=**	**2.**
3. ALIQUA	**=**	**3. LUPA**
3.	**=**	**3.**
4. LUPA	**=**	**4. KELU**
4.	**=**	**4.**

PROMISEMAKER

DOESN'T SLEEP	HEBREWS 12:28
SHALL RISE FIRST	2 TIMOTHY 4:8
GOOD	1 THESSALONIANS 4:14-17
CROWN OF RIGHTEOUSNESS	PSALM 121:3-4
HE IS EVERYWHERE	PSALM 135:3
KINGDOM NOT SHAKEN	PSALM 139:7-8
UNDERSTANDING	PSALM 147:5
COVERS ALL SINS	PROVERBS 10:12

PIX-CROSS

SOLVE THE NONOGRAM TO REVEAL THE HIDDEN PICTURE.

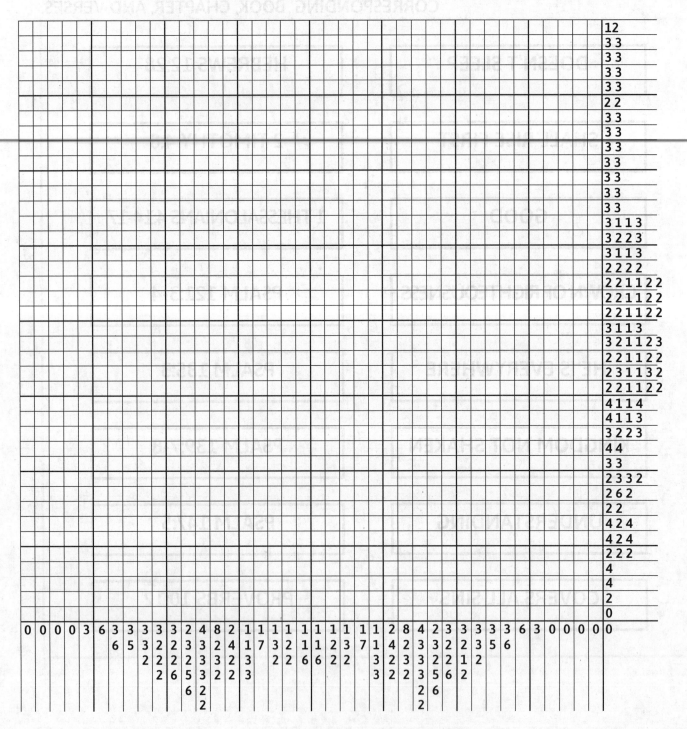

WORD-SEARCH

CONTAINED WITHIN THIS PUZZLE YOU MUST FIND ALL CAPITALIZED WORDS FROM THE VERSES BELOW.

```
P R O M I S E D Y T F Y Y D A
C S Y P N K B F B O G S O X H
O O Q E R E O E A N K U F U B
M R A R J E C Y I T W N Q N R
M D I V T P S H M A H H B R Q
A I E V B O T R N E V E R V Q
N N S U V Y V F D T E S R R Y
D A N Q R S M A N E T T Y Y Z
E N I E H A V E M A H A V W H
D C V S X M T L T R R B R I B
B E F O R E X I Y I O L O L D
I S U Z W A L K O F N I Y L O
S T A T U T E S U A E S A P I
W Z Z T X E B L P I Z H L S N
D A V I D C F R U L I N G X G
```

"As for **YOU**, if you **WALK BEFORE ME** as **YOUR FATHER DAVID** walked, **DOING EVERYTHING I HAVE COMMANDED** you, and if you **KEEP** my **STATUTES** and **ORDINANCES, I WILL ESTABLISH** your **ROYAL THRONE**, as I **PROMISED** your father David: You will **NEVER FAIL** to have a **MAN RULING** in **ISRAEL**."

CRISS-CROSS

USE THE DEFINITIONS BELOW TO FIND THE WORDS AND GUESS THE THEME.

ACROSS:

4. From the third largest Mediterranean island.
7. Also called Ludim.
8. Lived in S Mesopotamia.
10. From the largest Greek island.
11. Theirs was the cradle of Western civilization.
12. Lived E of the Sea of Galilee.

DOWN:

1. Ancient Iranians.
2. Lived E of Babylon.
3. Famous sea merchants.
5. Lived in S Palestine.
6. Lived E of the Dead Sea.
9. Lived in NW Persia.

SUDOKU

MATCH THE HIGHLIGHTED NUMBER SEQUENCE TO THE CHAPTER AND VERSE BELOW.

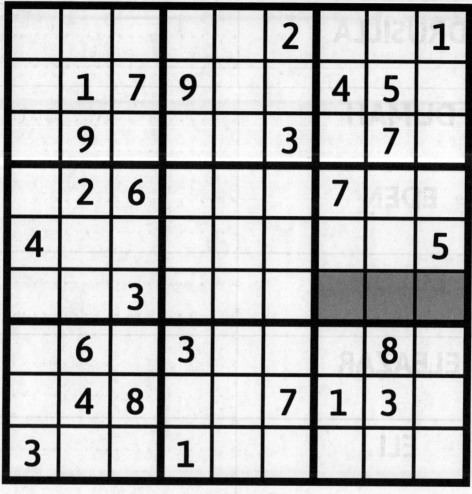

					2			1
	1	7	9			4	5	
	9				3		7	
	2	6				7		
4								5
		3				░	░	░
	6		3				8	
	4	8			7	1	3	
3			1					

ACTS __ : __

"Every day they devoted themselves to meeting together in the temple, and broke bread from house to house. They ate their food with joyful and sincere hearts..."

THE NAME GAME

DO YOU KNOW THE TRUE
MEANING OF THE BIBLICAL NAMES LISTED BELOW?

DRUSILLA	....
DUMAH	....
EDEN	....
EGLON	....
ELEAZAR	....
ELI	....
ELIJAH	....
ELISHA	....

WORD WHEEL

CONNECT EACH LETTER FROM THE WHEEL TO REVEAL THE BIBLICAL WORD.

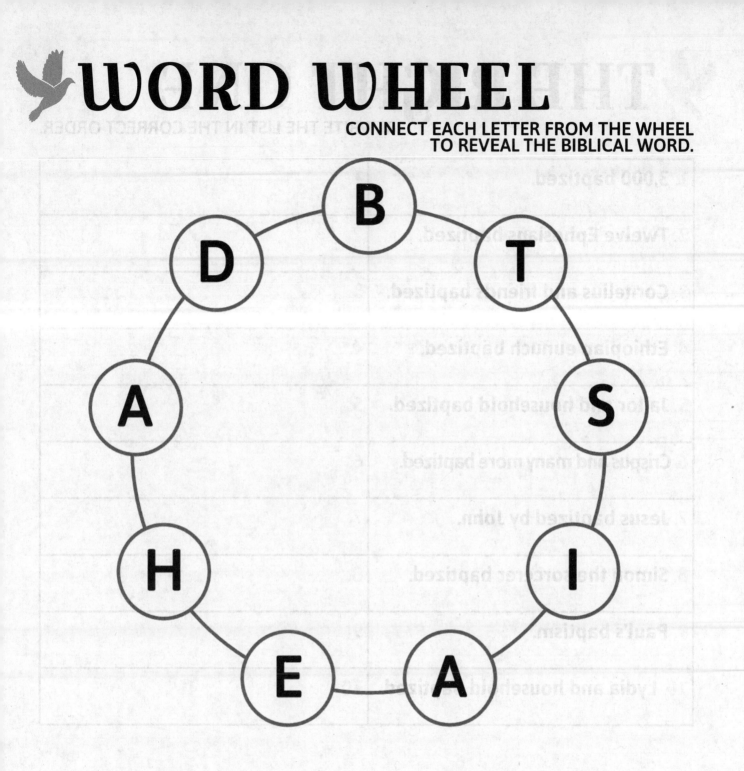

THE RIGHT ONE

REWRITE THE LIST IN THE CORRECT ORDER.

1. 3,000 baptized.	1.
2. Twelve Ephesians baptized.	2.
3. Cornelius and friends baptized.	3.
4. Ethiopian eunuch baptized.	4.
5. Jailor and household baptized.	5.
6. Crispus and many more baptized.	6.
7. Jesus baptized by John.	7.
8. Simon the sorcerer baptized.	8.
9. Paul's baptism.	9.
10. Lydia and household baptized.	10.

CHRISTIAN QUOTES

"A soul which gives itself to prayer, either much or little, should on no account be kept within narrow bounds."

AUTHOR:

....

....

AUTHOR:

....

....

"Faithless is he that says farewell when the road darkens."

"If fate clips your wings and casts you on the humbler plains of life, be a hero there."

AUTHOR:

....

....

FRIENDS

UNSCRAMBLE THE LETTERS TO FORM PAIRS OF BIBLICAL ALLIES.

1. THOMTIY	=	1. LUPA
1.	=	1.
2. LUPA	=	2. TUSDIORPAEPH
2.	=	2.
3. HATPAHHOSJE	=	3. HABA
3.	=	3.
4. MUELAS	=	4. DIVAD
4.	=	4.

PROMISEMAKER

CONNECT EACH BIBLICAL ASSURANCE TO ITS
CORRESPONDING BOOK, CHAPTER, AND VERSES.

CROWN OF LIFE	ISAIAH 51:6
CROWN OF GLORY	ISAIAH 46:10-11
BECOME LIKE HIM	ISAIAH 40:8
FULL REWARD	ISAIAH 31:5
DEFEND JERUSALEM	2 JOHN 7-8
WORD STANDS FOREVER	1 JOHN 3:2
PLANS STAND	1 PETER 5:1-4
SALVATION FOREVER	JAMES 1:12

PIX-CROSS

SOLVE THE NONOGRAM TO REVEAL THE HIDDEN PICTURE.

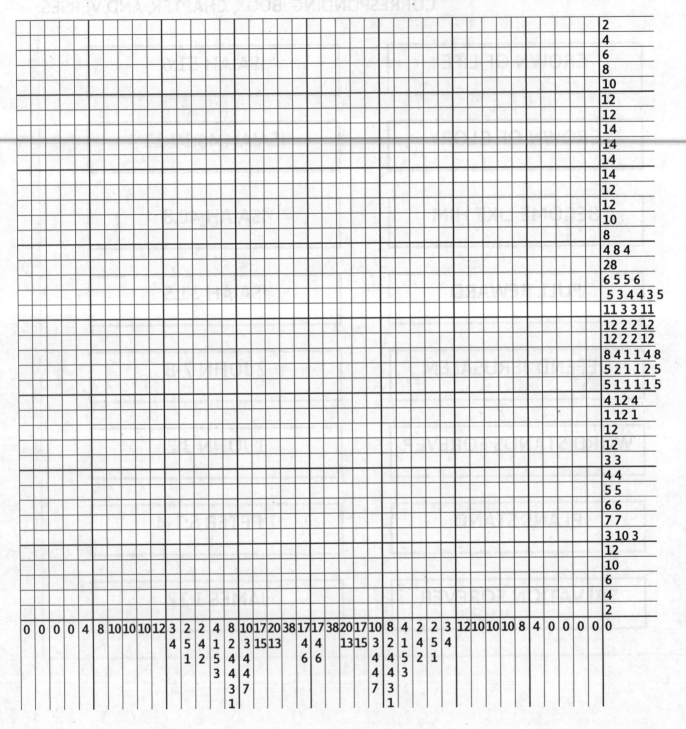

WORD-SEARCH

CONTAINED WITHIN THIS PUZZLE YOU MUST FIND ALL CAPITALIZED WORDS FROM THE VERSES BELOW.

```
B Y B I S T R E A T E D T J V
E O Q K H H E X D H O I V R Y
C U U N I H A N R Y M C G O B
A R V F M T W K M C F B C T M
U B I O L E I D E R T Q C R H
S F R E O P B X S N R K E U R
E E A S R E U V V S I N G S E
H T F I D O T G L P U D I T J
B P S P T E U R A X M V B E O
L N O C H H Q Y Y B P O S D I
W L Y T T E F M X A H V M V C
I B O R H X E U Z U E E Z Z E
L S A V S N P K L M D R Z Y H
L E A G E N E R O U S L Y B E
H U Y Y D E L I V E R A N C E
```

"**MY ENEMY WILL SAY**, 'I have **TRIUMPHED OVER HIM**,' and my **FOES** will **REJOICE BECAUSE** I am **SHAKEN**.
BUT I have **TRUSTED** in **YOUR FAITHFUL LOVE**; my **HEART** will rejoice in your **DELIVERANCE**.
I will **SING** to **THE LORD** because **HE** has **TREATED** me **GENEROUSLY**."

CRISS-CROSS

USE THE DEFINITIONS BELOW TO FIND THE WORDS AND GUESS THE THEME.

ACROSS:

3. Played the trumpet regularly.
4. Son of Lamech and Adah.
5. Composed half the songs of the Psalms.
6. Has three songs recorded in the bible.
10. Samuel's grandson.
11. Levite musical leader.

DOWN:

1. Trumpeter and priest.
2. Played the tambourine.
4. One of the chief musicians appointed by David.
7. King and composer.
8. Probably composed Psalms 73-83.
9. Composed Psalm 89.

SUDOKU

**MATCH THE HIGHLIGHTED NUMBER SEQUENCE
TO THE CHAPTER AND VERSE BELOW.**

	3	6		1				8
	8		9		4		6	
				7		2		
5						6		
	6	4						
		1						4
		3		6				
	9		7		3		2	
6				2		9	4	

LEVITICUS _ : __

"It is a guilt offering; he is indeed guilty before the LORD."

LEVEL
4

 BIBLE POWER PUZZLES

PAGE
383

THE NAME GAME

ELIZABETH	....
ELON	....
ENOCH	....
ENOS	....
EPHRAIM	....
ESTHER	....
EUNICE	....
EVE	....

WORD WHEEL

CONNECT EACH LETTER FROM THE WHEEL TO REVEAL THE BIBLICAL WORD.

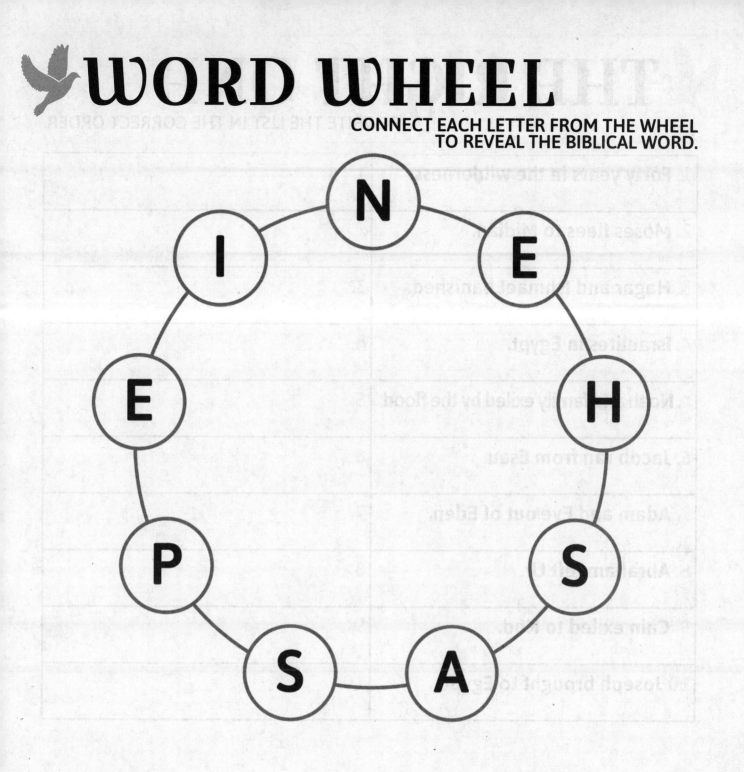

THE RIGHT ONE

REWRITE THE LIST IN THE CORRECT ORDER.

1. Forty years in the wilderness.	1.
2. Moses flees to Midian.	2.
3. Hagar and Ishmael banished.	3.
4. Israelites in Egypt.	4.
4. Noah and family exiled by the flood.	5.
6. Jacob ran from Esau.	6.
7. Adam and Eve out of Eden.	7.
8. Abraham left Ur.	8.
9. Cain exiled to Nod.	9.
10 Joseph brought to Egypt.	10.

CHRISTIAN QUOTES

FROM CHURCH FATHERS TO MODERN CHRISTIAN THINKERS, IDENTIFY THE AUTHOR OF EACH QUOTE.

"A day is coming upon us all when the value of everything will be altered."

AUTHOR:

....

AUTHOR:

....

....

"To become Christ-like is the only thing in the whole world worth caring for, the thing before which every ambition of man is folly and all lower achievement vain."

"I wish not merely to be called Christian, but also to be Christian."

AUTHOR:

....

....

FRIENDS

UNSCRAMBLE THE LETTERS TO FORM PAIRS OF BIBLICAL ALLIES.

1. HAMABRA	=	1. REMAM
1.	=	1.
2. COLESH	=	2. HAMABRA
2.	=	2.
3. HAMABRA	=	3. RENA
3.	=	3.
4. DEKEZLEMICH	=	4. HAMABRA
4.	=	4.

PROMISEMAKER

CONNECT EACH BIBLICAL ASSURANCE TO ITS CORRESPONDING BOOK, CHAPTER, AND VERSES.

WOUNDED FOR US	MALACHI 3:6
TREE OF LIFE	REVELATION 2:11
PROMISED GOOD	MALACHI 1:11
CROWN OF LIFE	ZEPHANIAH 3:17
WARRIOR SAVIOR	REVELATION 2:7
UNCHANGEABLE	ISAIAH 53:5
NO SECOND DEATH	REVELATION 2:10
GREAT AMONG GENTILES	JEREMIAH 32:42

PIX-CROSS

SOLVE THE NONOGRAM TO REVEAL THE HIDDEN PICTURE.

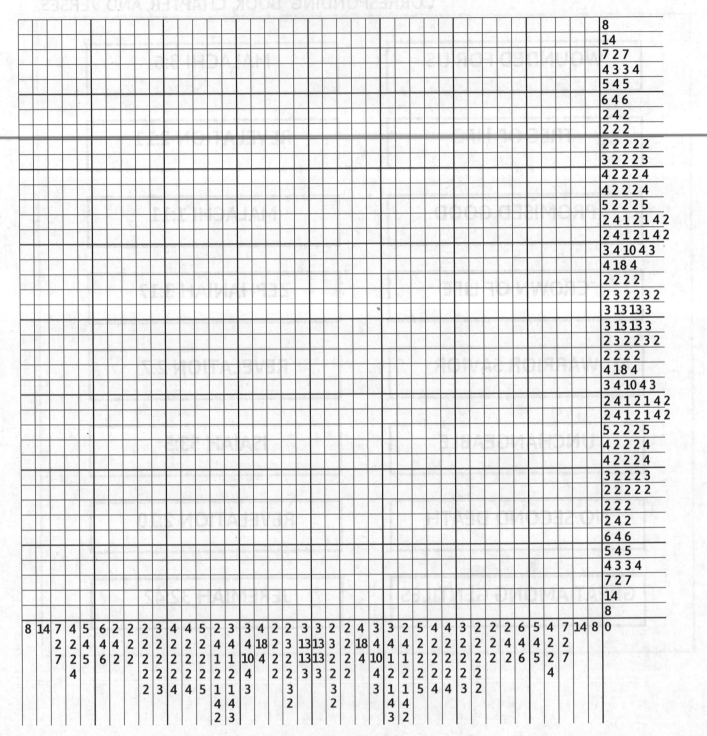

WORD-SEARCH

CONTAINED WITHIN THIS PUZZLE YOU MUST FIND ALL
CAPITALIZED WORDS FROM THE VERSES BELOW.

```
I P P I L E S D A S H A M E D
D L O Q S S E K K Y H M G Q D
I A W R L T C R U S H E D O Y
S N E I S A M R O O F T O P S
M T R A N F O R T I F I E D A
A S L Z D D R O W H L U E C P
Y B E T N W D O S T N O C L S
E C S G C I T I E S D P N S D
D A S K O N H E A R D A A G B
E B D V I N N F E S E R Y R R
B E C O M E E V F C G V W S O
N C S I N H A B I T A N T S U
O J J X R H D E S I G N E D G
T P L A N N E D F P N O W S H
U D T E N D E R U B B L E R T
```

"**HAVE** you **NOT HEARD**?
I **DESIGNED** it **LONG AGO**; I **PLANNED** it in **DAYS GONE** by.
I have **NOW BROUGHT** it to pass, and you have **CRUSHED FORTIFIED CITIES INTO**
PILES of **RUBBLE**.
Their **INHABITANTS** have **BECOME POWERLESS**, **DISMAYED**, and **ASHAMED**.
They are **PLANTS** of the **FIELD**, **TENDER GRASS**, grass on the **ROOFTOPS**, **BLASTED**
by the **EAST WIND**."

CRISS-CROSS

USE THE DEFINITIONS BELOW TO FIND THE WORDS
AND GUESS THE THEME.

ACROSS:
2. Curved horn.
4. Two brass plates clanged together.
6. Triangular string instrument.
9. From the Zither family.
10. Made from silver in one occasion.

DOWN:
1. Portable harplike instrument.
3. Wooden hoop w/ skin pulled across.
4. Two hollow chestnuts clicking together.
5. Five-string harp.
7. First instrument mentioned in the Bible.
8. Straight pipe with holes.

SUDOKU

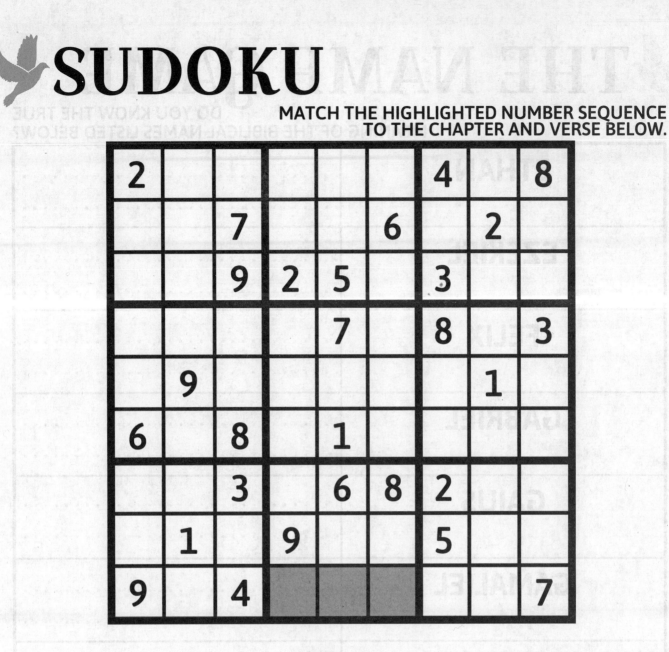

MATCH THE HIGHLIGHTED NUMBER SEQUENCE TO THE CHAPTER AND VERSE BELOW.

2						4		8
		7			6		2	
		9	2	5		3		
				7		8		3
	9						1	
6		8		1				
		3		6	8	2		
	1		9			5		
9		4						7

LUKE __ : __

"The angel replied to her: 'The Holy Spirit will come upon you, and the power of the Most High will overshadow you. Therefore, the holy one to be born will be called the Son of God.'"

THE NAME GAME

ETHAN	....
EZEKIEL	....
FELIX	....
GABRIEL	....
GAIUS	....
GAMALIEL	....
GEHAZI	....
GOMER	....

WORD WHEEL

CONNECT EACH LETTER FROM THE WHEEL TO REVEAL THE BIBLICAL WORD.

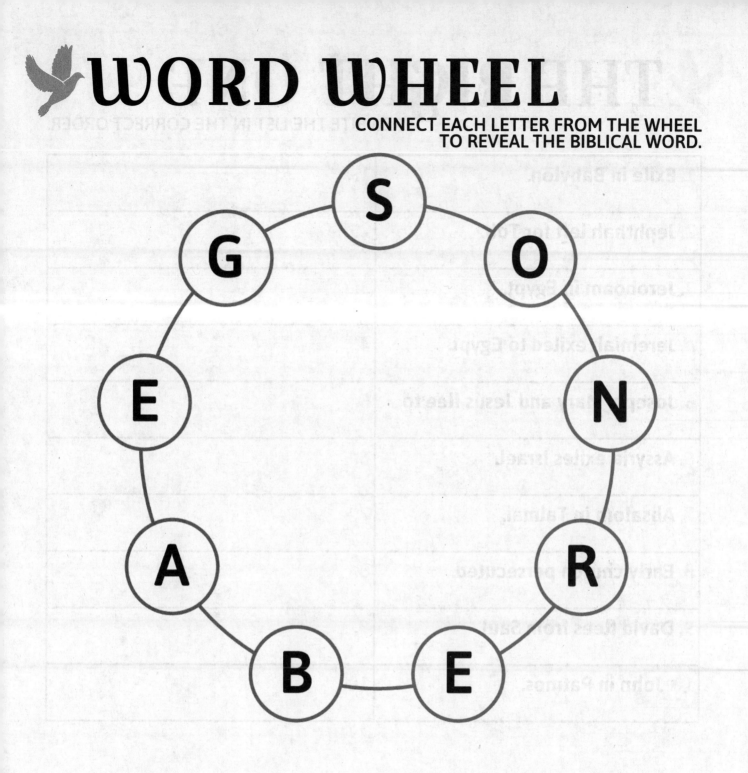

THE RIGHT ONE

REWRITE THE LIST IN THE CORRECT ORDER.

1. Exile in Babylon.	1.
2. Jephthah left for Tob.	2.
3. Jeroboam in Egypt.	3.
4. Jeremiah exiled to Egypt.	4.
5. Joseph, Mary and Jesus flee to	5.
6. Assyria exiles Israel.	6.
7. Absalom in Talmai.	7.
8. Early church persecuted.	8.
9. David flees from Saul.	9.
10. John in Patmos.	10.

CHRISTIAN QUOTES

"To love and to be loved, one must do good to others. The inevitable condition whereby to become blessed, is to bless others."

AUTHOR:

....
....

AUTHOR:

....
....

"God had one son on earth without sin, but never one without suffering."

"There is one Physician, of flesh and of spirit, originate and unoriginate, God in man, true Life in death, son of Mary and son of God, first passible and then impassible: Jesus Christ our Lord."

AUTHOR:

....
....

FRIENDS

UNSCRAMBLE THE LETTERS TO FORM PAIRS OF BIBLICAL ALLIES.

1. ILE	=	1. MUELSA
1.	=	1.

2. BAMO	=	2. HAJDU
2.	=	2.

3. MODE	=	3. BAMO
3.	=	3.

4. TEGYP	=	4. SHUC
4.	=	4.

PROMISEMAKER

NEW MANNA	DEUTERONOMY 28:2-6
ACCORDING TO WORKS	REVELATION 2:23
POWER OVER NATIONS	PSALM 128
NAME ACKNOWLEDGED	REVELATION 2:17
BLESSED FRUIT	PSALM 146:9
RIGHTEOUSNESS	REVELATION 2:26-28
BLESSED LIFE	PSALM 103:17
RELIEF FOR WIDOWS	REVELATION 3:5

PIX-CROSS

SOLVE THE NONOGRAM TO REVEAL THE HIDDEN PICTURE.

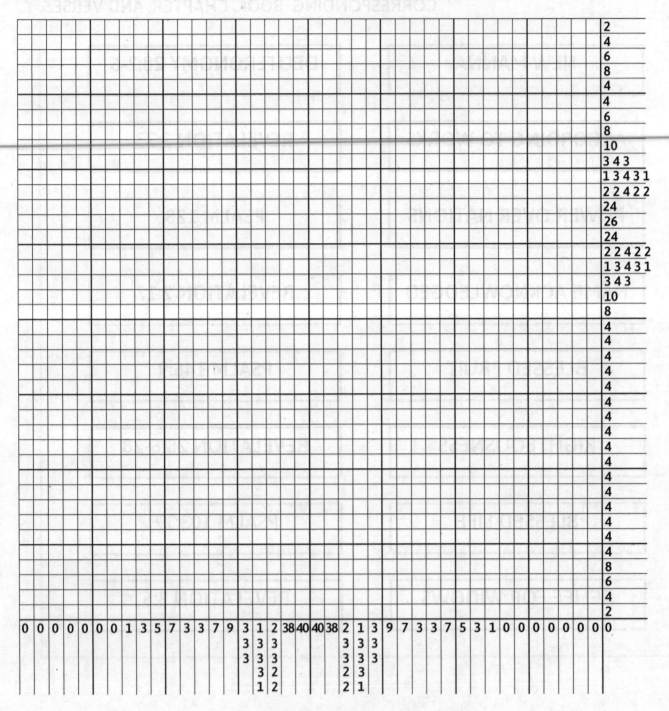

WORD-SEARCH

CONTAINED WITHIN THIS PUZZLE YOU MUST FIND ALL CAPITALIZED WORDS FROM THE VERSES BELOW.

```
F X T H E R E F O R E P O U P
H S V L C S M A S S E M B L E
K P L C W E B Y R U C L I N Z
J E A L O U S Y Q T S C O D W
N E K I N G D O M S H I I E B
U C O N S U M E D S T D Q C U
U H R R I S E S N A W J Z I R
L A C E C I E O N T H I M S N
O N V S S R I G Z T O C F I I
R G L Y U T I L G T L Y S O N
D E S P A D O R T A E Q E N G
M R J N N L B R Z Z T R R X H
B W A I T S Z K E M U H V X R
D E C L A R A T I O N T E K O
P L U N D E R C P F I R E R Z
```

"**THEREFORE**, **WAIT** for me—this is the **LORD**'s **DECLARATION**—until the way I **RISE** up for **PLUNDER**.
For my **DECISION** is to **GATHER NATIONS**, to **ASSEMBLE KINGDOMS**, in order to **POUR** out my **INDIGNATION** on them, all my **BURNING ANGER**; for the **WHOLE EARTH** will be **CONSUMED** by the **FIRE** of my **JEALOUSY**.
For I will then **RESTORE PURE SPEECH** to my peoples so that all of them may call on the name of the Lord and **SERVE HIM**..."

CRISS-CROSS

USE THE DEFINITIONS BELOW TO FIND THE WORDS AND GUESS THE THEME.

ACROSS:
2. One of the sons of Anak.
4. King of Bashan.
5. Father of Anak.
7. Brother of Sheshai.
8. Brother of Goliath.

DOWN:
1. Killed by David in a duel.
2. Slain by Sibbechai the Hushathite
3. Killed by Abishai (2 words).
6. Brother of Ahiman.
7. Patriarch of a race of giants.

SUDOKU

MATCH THE HIGHLIGHTED NUMBER SEQUENCE TO THE CHAPTER AND VERSE BELOW.

2	6	4		3		7		
5		9						
░	░	░	5					
1		5		4	7		2	
	7		3					
	2		6		5	4		
9							4	1
						6		
			9		4			8

DEUTERONOMY _ : __

"The Arabah and Jordan are also borders from Chinnereth as far as the Sea of the Arabah, the Dead Sea, under the slopes of Pisgah on the east."

THE NAME GAME

GIDEON	....
GILEAD	....
GOLIATH	....
HADAD	....
HAGAR	....
HAMAN	....
HANNAH	....
HERODIAS	....

WORD WHEEL

CONNECT EACH LETTER FROM THE WHEEL TO REVEAL THE BIBLICAL WORD.

THE RIGHT ONE

REWRITE THE LIST IN THE CORRECT ORDER.

1. Esau and Jacob reunite.	1.
2. Laban kisses Jacob.	2.
3. Jacob kisses Rachel on sight.	3.
4. Jacob kisses his dead father.	4.
5. Aaron greets Moses.	5.
6. Joseph and his brothers reunite.	6.
7. Isaac kisses Jacob by mistake.	7.
8. Israel blesses Joseph's sons.	8.
9. Laban kisses Jacob's kids.	9.

CHRISTIAN QUOTES

FROM CHURCH FATHERS TO MODERN CHRISTIAN THINKERS, IDENTIFY THE AUTHOR OF EACH QUOTE.

"Christ did not die for the good and beautiful. It is easy enough to die for the good and beautiful; the hard thing is to die for the miserable and corrupt."

AUTHOR:

....

....

AUTHOR:

....

....

"It is impossible to find a saint who did not take the 'two P's' seriously: prayer and penance."

"Be on your constant guard against the least confidence and trust in yourselves."

AUTHOR:

....

....

FRIENDS

UNSCRAMBLE THE LETTERS TO FORM PAIRS OF BIBLICAL ALLIES.

1. YABIL	=	**1. TUP**
1.	=	1.
2. CHEMELABI	=	**2. HAMABRA**
2.	=	2.
3. CASAI	=	**3. CHEMELABI**
3.	=	3.
4. NABAL	=	**4. BOCAJ**
4.	=	4.

PROMISEMAKER

CONNECT EACH BIBLICAL ASSURANCE TO ITS
CORRESPONDING BOOK, CHAPTER, AND VERSES.

WICKED PUNISHED	REVELATION 3:21
MADE A PILLAR	PROVERBS 11:21
INHERITANCE	PROVERBS 13:22
PLACE BY THE THRONE	REVELATION 3:12
WILL BE BLESSED	GENESIS 12:3
HUNGER NO MORE	REVELATION 20:4
BLESSED IN ABRAHAM	GENESIS 18:18
1,000 YEAR REIGN	REVELATION 7:15-17

PIX-CROSS

SOLVE THE NONOGRAM TO REVEAL THE HIDDEN PICTURE.

Row clues:

3 4 3
3 4 3
3 2 3
4 2 4
4 2 4
4 2 4
3 2 3
3 4 3
3 4 3
3 4 3
3 4 3
10
8
2
4 5
2 2
11 6 11
7 6 7
2
14 2 14
14 14
15 15
8
6
12 4 12
12 4 12
12 4 12
3 4 3
3 4 3
2 3 4 3 2
2 3 4 3 2
2 3 4 3 2
3 3 4 3 3
3 3 4 3 3
3 3 4 3 3
4 3 4 3 4
4 3 4 3 4
1 4 3 4 3 4 1
2 4 3 4 3 4 2
2 5 3 4 3 5 2
2 4 3 4 3 4 2
3 4 3 4 3 4 3
3 3 3 4 3 3 3
4 3 3 4 3 3 4
4 3 3 4 3 3 4
4 2 3 4 3 2 4
4 2 3 4 3 2 4
6 14 6
5 14 5
3 14 3

Column clues:

0
0
0
0
0
0
0
5
9
2 3 3 3 8
2 3 3 7
2 3 3 7 5
2 3 3 10 3
2 3 3 18
3 3 3 3 13
3 3 3 2 6
2 3 3 1
2 3 3
1 3 3 26
11 3 3 26
12 2 3 26
12 2 4 3
3 2 4 5 3
2 6 3 29
14 5 28
14 5 28
2 6 3 29
3 2 4 5 3
12 2 4 3
12 2 3 26
11 3 3 26
1 3 3 26
2 3 3
2 3 3 1
3 3 3 2 6
3 3 3 3 13
2 3 3 18
2 3 3 10 3
2 3 3 7 5
2 3 3 7
2 3 3 3 8
9
5
0
0
0
0
0
0
0
0

WORD-SEARCH

CONTAINED WITHIN THIS PUZZLE YOU MUST FIND ALL CAPITALIZED WORDS FROM THE VERSES BELOW.

```
L I G H T S U W S I J H K
T S N Q H Q K V Q G A T Y
K O G N U L H M Z I M F O
O U D L M Z N L E A R N U
L L Q I B B U R D E N E D
T S D P L U P O Z D C Y Z
A S M H E W G P N F L Z S
K Q P P E E L I I W S P S
E Y O K E A F R O M O L C
C Y Q G W R R L G C K Y A
X O V I H Y P T R E S T L
C G M V O N B K S A E F L
M X B E C A U S E G W X F
```

"**COME** to me, **ALL** of you **WHO** are **WEARY** and **BURDENED**, and I will **GIVE YOU REST. TAKE** up my **YOKE** and **LEARN FROM** me, **BECAUSE** I am **LOWLY** and **HUMBLE** in **HEAR**T, and you will **FIND** rest for your **SOULS**. For my yoke is **EASY** and my burden is **LIGHT**."

CRISS-CROSS

USE THE DEFINITIONS BELOW TO FIND THE WORDS AND GUESS THE THEME.

ACROSS:

4. Killed for disobeying God.
6. Killed for elevating himself above man (2 words).
9. Killed for lying to the Holy Spirit.
10. Killed for offering unauthorized fire.
12. Killed for apostasy.

DOWN:

1. Killed for revolting against Moses.
2. Stricken by fatal disease.
3. Killed for misleading the people.
4. Killed alongside her husband.
5. Killed for being careless w/ the ark.
7. Killed for being wicked.
8. Killed for refusing to impregnate Tamar.
10. Killed for his arrogance.
11. Killed alongside Nadab.

SUDOKU

MATCH THE HIGHLIGHTED NUMBER SEQUENCE TO THE CHAPTER AND VERSE BELOW.

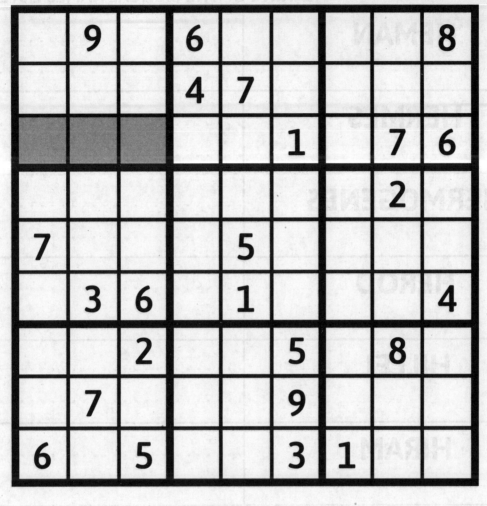

JOHN _ : __

"You yourselves can testify that I said, 'I am not the Messiah, but I've been sent ahead of him.'"

THE NAME GAME

HEMAN	....
HERMES	....
HERMOGENES	....
HEROD	....
HILLEL	....
HIRAM	....
HORAM	....
HUR	....

WORD WHEEL

CONNECT EACH LETTER FROM THE WHEEL TO REVEAL THE BIBLICAL WORD.

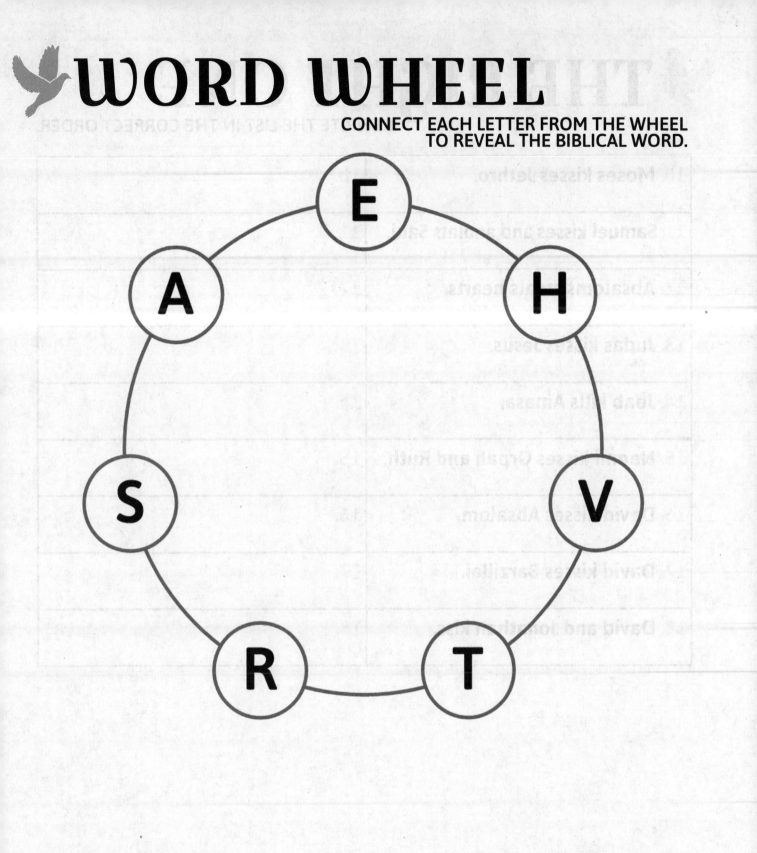

THE RIGHT ONE

REWRITE THE LIST IN THE CORRECT ORDER.

10. Moses kisses Jethro.	10.
11. Samuel kisses and anoints Saul.	11.
12. Absaloms steals hearts.	12.
13. Judas kisses Jesus.	13.
14. Joab kills Amasa.	14.
15. Naomi kisses Orpah and Ruth.	15.
16. David kisses Absalom.	16.
17. David kisses Barzillai.	17.
18. David and Jonathan kiss.	18.

CHRISTIAN QUOTES

"Anticipate your battles; fight them on your knees before temptation comes, and you will always have victory."

AUTHOR:

....

....

AUTHOR:

....

....

"We must learn to regard people less in light of what they do or omit to do, and more in the light of what they suffer."

"Let your religion be less of a theory and more of a love affair."

AUTHOR:

....

....

FRIENDS

UNSCRAMBLE THE LETTERS TO FORM PAIRS OF BIBLICAL ALLIES.

1. DIVAD	=	1. HISCHA
1.	=	1.
2. NERBA	=	2. DIVAD
2.	=	2.
3. DIVAD	=	3. MARIH
3.	=	3.
4. OTI	=	4. DIVAD
4.	=	4.

PROMISEMAKER

CONNECT EACH BIBLICAL ASSURANCE TO ITS
CORRESPONDING BOOK, CHAPTER, AND VERSES.

INHERIT ALL	2 CHRONICLES 7:14
SECRET REWARD	PSALM 1:1-3
HOLY JERUSALEM	MATTHEW 6:3-6
HEAR AND FORGIVE	PSALM 4:3
COMFORTED	REVELATION 21:10-27
PROSPERITY	MATTHEW 5:7
OBTAIN MERCY	MATTHEW 5:4
SET APART	REVELATION 21:7

PIX-CROSS

SOLVE THE NONOGRAM TO REVEAL THE HIDDEN PICTURE.

Row clues (top to bottom):
0
0
0
0
0
0
0
0
0
3
6
63
834
10 3 2 1
12 3 3 1
15 6 11 1
9 11 8 1
6 3 11 1 2 1
1 3 3 19 2 1
1 3 3 8 7 1
2 1 3 8 11 2
3 1 10 8 1 1
25 6 6 1
20 6 11 1
27 8 2 2
21 7 6 1
3 8 11 1 1
25 9 2 4
5 8 3 4
25 9 2
2 7 2 1
26 2 2
3 2 2
37
32
0
0
0
0
0
0
0
0
0
0
0
0
0

WORD-SEARCH

CONTAINED WITHIN THIS PUZZLE YOU MUST FIND ALL CAPITALIZED WORDS FROM THE VERSES BELOW.

```
M S U C S H V S W S G R O W S
P M C O M P A R E H E P S K Y
G A T M P D R D S T A E P S C
L L U E B H A L A E B T D T Q
A L Z S T H I H Y H R I S D T
R E L S S O T R V M A E L E A
G S M I S Q T P L A N T S S L
E T F G K P R O D U C E S C L
G L L A A E F P G P H N M R E
U P A R A B L E R O E L W I R
B I R D S O W N O N S Q H B X
A B G E G N Z C U G G W E E Q
F K I N G D O M N E D I N Q Z
I M U S T A R D D O T T W P F
P B Q B B K Y O G Z S H U S E
```

"...**WITH WHAT** can we **COMPARE** the **KINGDOM** of **GOD**, or what **PARABLE** can we **USE** to **DESCRIBE** it? It's **LIKE** a **MUSTARD SEED THAT, WHEN SOWN UPON** the **SOIL**, is the **SMALLEST** of all seeds on the **GROUND**. And when sown, it **COMES** up and **GROWS TALLER** than all the **GARDEN PLANTS**, and **PRODUCES LARGE BRANCHES**, so that the **BIRDS** of the **SKY** can **NEST** in its **SHADE**."

CRISS-CROSS

USE THE DEFINITIONS BELOW TO FIND THE WORDS AND GUESS THE THEME.

ACROSS:
3. 34 chapters.
5. 50 chapters.
6. 48 chapters.
7. 36 chapters (preceded by number).
9. 36 chapters.

DOWN:
1. 24 chapters.
2. 52 chapters.
4. 150 chapters.
6. 40 chapters.
8. 66 chapters.

SUDOKU

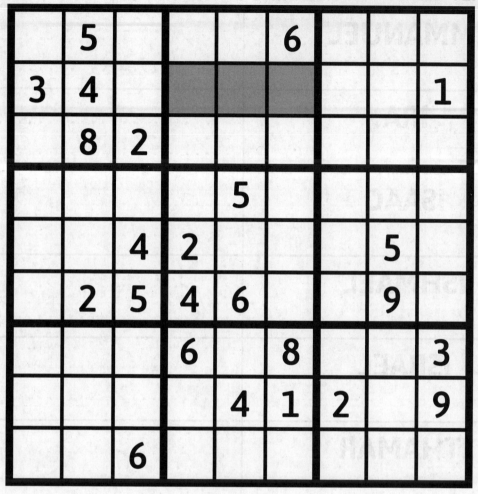

HEBREWS _ : __

"Therefore, he is able to save completely those who come to God through him, since he always lives to intercede for them."

THE NAME GAME

DO YOU KNOW THE TRUE MEANING OF THE BIBLICAL NAMES LISTED BELOW?

IMMANUEL	....
	....
IRA	....
	....
ISAAC	....
	....
ISHMAEL	....
	....
ISRAEL	....
	....
ITHAMAR	....
	....
IZRI	....
	....
ISCAH	....
	....

WORD WHEEL

CONNECT EACH LETTER FROM THE WHEEL TO REVEAL THE BIBLICAL WORD.

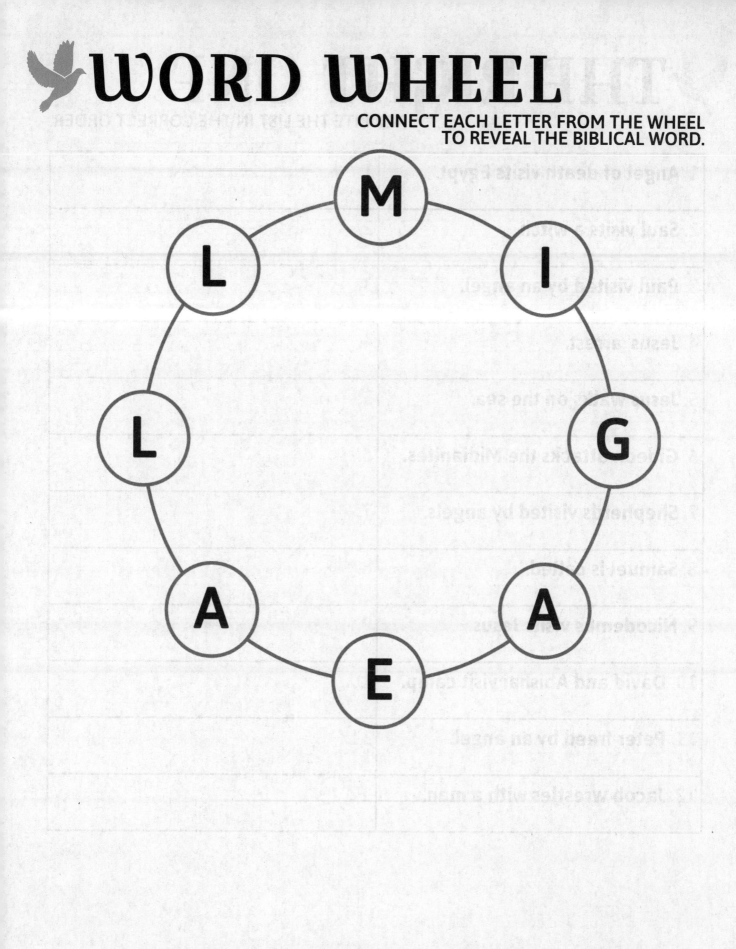

THE RIGHT ONE

REWRITE THE LIST IN THE CORRECT ORDER.

1. Angel of death visits Egypt.	1.
2. Saul visits a witch.	2.
3. Paul visited by an angel.	3.
4. Jesus' arrest.	4.
5. Jesus walks on the sea.	5.
6. Gideon attacks the Midianites.	6.
7. Shepherds visited by angels.	7.
8. Samuel is called.	8.
9. Nicodemus visits Jesus.	9.
10. David and Abishai visit camp.	10.
11. Peter freed by an angel.	11.
12. Jacob wrestles with a man.	12.

CHRISTIAN QUOTES

FROM CHURCH FATHERS TO MODERN CHRISTIAN THINKERS, IDENTIFY THE AUTHOR OF EACH QUOTE.

"The beginning of anxiety is the end of faith, and the beginning of true faith is the end of anxiety."

AUTHOR:

....

....

AUTHOR:

....

....

"Expect great things from God; attempt great things for God."

"Why should I fear? I am on a Royal Mission. I am in the service of the King of kings."

AUTHOR:

....

....

FRIENDS

UNSCRAMBLE THE LETTERS TO FORM PAIRS OF BIBLICAL ALLIES.

1. **SUMISENO** = 1. **LUPA**

1. _____ = 1. _____

2. **LUPA** = 2. **CUSCHITY**

2. _____ = 2. _____

3. **HUSCARTRISA** = 3. **LUPA**

3. _____ = 3. _____

4. **LUPA** = 4. **NOHJ**

4. _____ = 4. _____

PROMISEMAKER

CONNECT EACH BIBLICAL ASSURANCE TO ITS CORRESPONDING BOOK, CHAPTER, AND VERSES.

SWEET SLEEP	JAMES 4:6
JOINT-HEIRS	ISAIAH 40:31
SINS CLEANSED	ROMANS 8:17
CONFESS AND BE SAVED	ROMANS 10:9
WALK AND NOT FAINT	ISAIAH 1:18
JUSTIFIED	PROVERBS 3:21-24
NOT LABOR IN VAIN	ISAIAH 65:23
GRACE	GALATIANS 2:16

PIX-CROSS

SOLVE THE NONOGRAM TO REVEAL THE HIDDEN PICTURE.

Row clues (top to bottom):

0
0
0
1
1
2
3
4
4
4
4 1
4 2
4 3
4 4
4 4
4 4
4 4 1
4 4 2 2
3 4 2 2
3 4 3 2
2 4 3 3
2 4 3 3
1 4 3 4
4 3 4
4 3 4 1
4 3 4 2
3 3 4 3
2 3 3 3
1 3 3 3
3 3 3 1
4 2 3 2
3 1 3 3
2 3 3
2 3 4
1 3 4
1 2 4
1 4
4
13 2 6
16 1 10
14 14
15 15
19 1 17
20 18
21 20
13 3 3 13
8 2 2 8
4 1 1 4
0
0

Column clues (left to right):

1
2
3
4
4
5
6
7
8
7
7
8
8
2 4 8
3 4 2 8
4 4 5 7
4 4 7 7
4 4 4 1 7
4 4 3 7
4 4 3 7
4 4 3 7
4 4 3 2 4
4 4 3 2 5
4 4 3 2 6
4 4 3
4 4 3
4 4 3 3 3 1 1 3
4 4 3 3 3 1 3
5 4 2 4 3 2 4
4 3 2 5
4 3 3 5
4 3 4 5
1 4 3 4 6
8 3 4 7
6 3 4 7
3 3 4 8
3 3 8
8
8
7
7
8
7
6
5
4
4
3
2
1
0

WORD-SEARCH

CONTAINED WITHIN THIS PUZZLE YOU MUST FIND ALL
CAPITALIZED WORDS FROM THE VERSES BELOW.

```
M J T H R O W T W I Y Z G
A U J U D G E J H R U N W
K D W M H B S H A E I P A
E G K D O W E S T O N R Y
S E T T L E R F G O I I B
M Q N N Q E F U O V R S A
M I W H V D C F L R T O I
H A N D J R A T O E E N L
X Q A J I A D D V R R N I
W Y X W N G R X E T T H F
R I G H T L I P N R E L F
R Z H Y O U R S E L V E S
A P O N G P V B B D U V E
```

"**WHY** don't you **JUDGE** for **YOURSELVES WHAT** is **RIGHT**? As you are **GOING** with
your **ADVERSARY** to the **RULER**, **MAKE** an **EFFORT** to **SETTLE** with him on the **WAY**.
THEN he won't **DRAG** you **BEFORE** the **JUDGE**, the judge **HAND** you over to the
BAILIFF, and the bailiff **THROW** you **INTO PRISON**."

CRISS-CROSS

USE THE DEFINITIONS BELOW TO FIND THE WORDS AND GUESS THE THEME.

ACROSS:

3. 1 chapter, 15 verses (preceded by number).

6. 1 chapter, 25 verses, 445 words.

7. 3 chapters, 47 verses (preceded by number).

10. 1 chapter, 13 verses (preceded by number).

DOWN:

1. 1 chapter, 21 verses.

2. 1 chapter, 25 verses, 613 words.

4. 2 chapters.

5. 4 chapters.

8. 3 chapters, 46 verses.

9. 3 chapters, 47 verses.

SUDOKU

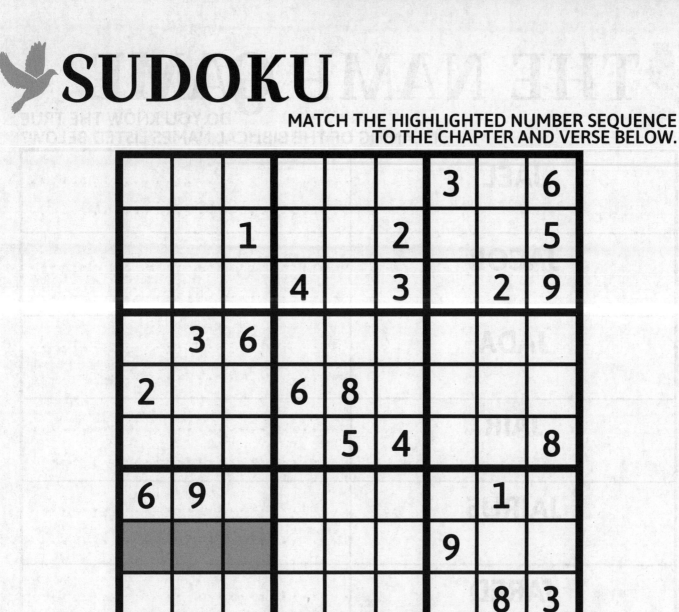

PROVERBS _ : __

"If you respond to my warning, then I will pour out my spirit on you and teach you my words."

THE NAME GAME

DO YOU KNOW THE TRUE MEANING OF THE BIBLICAL NAMES LISTED BELOW?

JAEL	....
JACOB	....
JADA	....
JAIR	....
JAIRUS	....
JARED	....
JASON	....
JEDIDAH	....

WORD WHEEL

CONNECT EACH LETTER FROM THE WHEEL TO REVEAL THE BIBLICAL WORD.

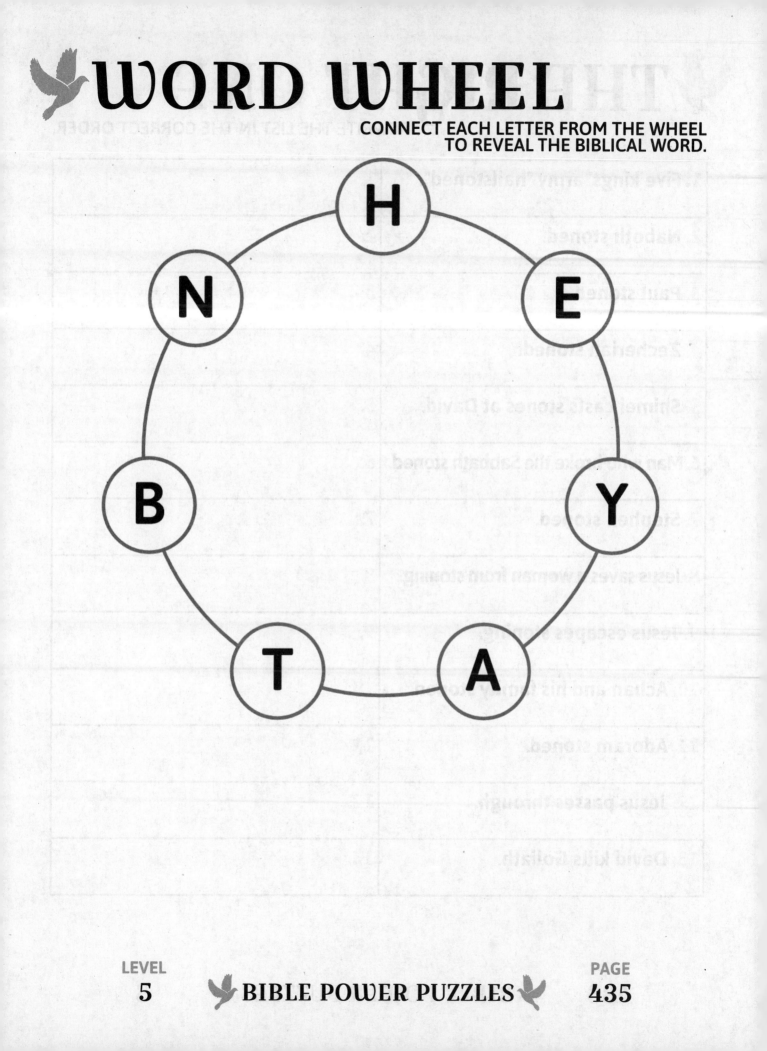

THE RIGHT ONE

REWRITE THE LIST IN THE CORRECT ORDER.

1. Five kings' army "hailstoned".	1.
2. Naboth stoned.	2.
3. Paul stoned.	3.
4. Zecheriah stoned.	4.
5. Shimei casts stones at David.	5.
6. Man who broke the Sabbath stoned.	6.
7. Stephen stoned.	7.
8. Jesus saves a woman from stoning.	8.
9. Jesus escapes stoning.	9.
10. Achan and his family stoned.	10.
11. Adoram stoned.	11.
12. Jesus passes through.	12.
13. David kills Goliath.	13.

CHRISTIAN QUOTES

FROM CHURCH FATHERS TO MODERN CHRISTIAN THINKERS, IDENTIFY THE AUTHOR OF EACH QUOTE.

"There are three great truths: first, that there is a God; second, that He has spoken to us in the Bible; third, that He means what He says."

AUTHOR:

....

....

AUTHOR:

....

....

"Oh God, here's my Bible, here's my money. Here's me. Use me, God."

"Seek each day to do or say something to further Christianity among the heathen."

AUTHOR:

....

....

FRIENDS

UNSCRAMBLE THE LETTERS TO FORM PAIRS OF BIBLICAL ALLIES.

1. LUPA	=	1. NOMELIPH
1.	=	1.

2. HIAPAP	=	2. LUPA
2.	=	2.

3. LUPA	=	3. HASPYMN
3.	=	3.

4. SUTIT	=	4. LUPA
4.	=	4.

PROMISEMAKER

CONNECT EACH BIBLICAL ASSURANCE TO ITS CORRESPONDING BOOK, CHAPTER, AND VERSES.

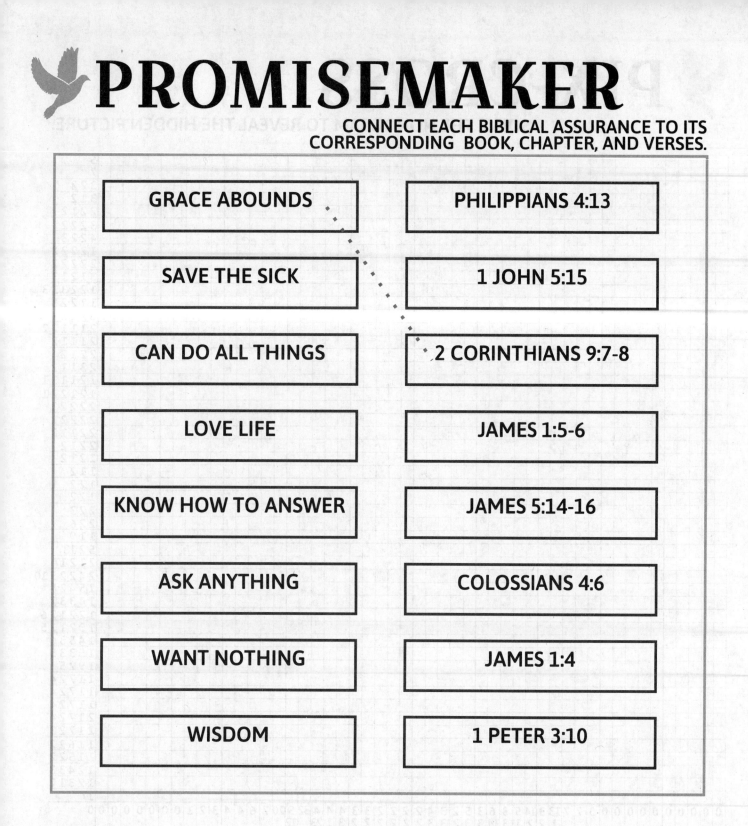

GRACE ABOUNDS	PHILIPPIANS 4:13
SAVE THE SICK	1 JOHN 5:15
CAN DO ALL THINGS	2 CORINTHIANS 9:7-8
LOVE LIFE	JAMES 1:5-6
KNOW HOW TO ANSWER	JAMES 5:14-16
ASK ANYTHING	COLOSSIANS 4:6
WANT NOTHING	JAMES 1:4
WISDOM	1 PETER 3:10

PIX-CROSS

SOLVE THE NONOGRAM TO REVEAL THE HIDDEN PICTURE.

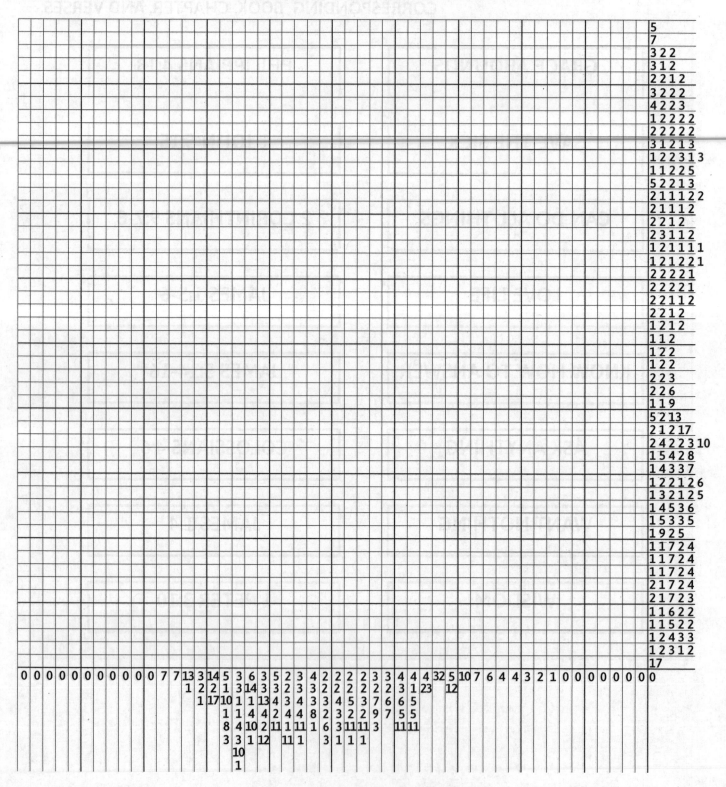

WORD-SEARCH

CONTAINED WITHIN THIS PUZZLE YOU MUST FIND ALL CAPITALIZED WORDS FROM THE VERSES BELOW.

```
E N T E R H B L A Q U G O H D
H K X N A R R O W G N Q U N F
T X D C B A A M E I Y U T S D
J E K A L N A G Y O N C S T A
S Z N T E S I A X L N N I A J
A M O T H W S F B T Z C D N Y
U K W N B E C A U S E M E D M
W H E R E R N M A S A Q Z L A
T H R O U G H E P K F H L Z K
X F T W P U G F B Q N I S S E
T E R Y K E I F D S W O O S V
R F N O J D N O O H N M C O E
Y A V O W N E R O U O A X K R
M X V L W A R T R T Q P C W Y
G U V C F R O M P S L O R D X
```

"...**MAKE EVERY EFFORT** to **ENTER THROUGH** the **NARROW DOOR, BECAUSE** I tell you, **MANY WILL TRY** to enter and won't be **ABLE ONCE** the **OWNER** gets up and **SHUTS** the door. **THEN** you will **STAND OUTSIDE** and **KNOCK** on the door, **SAYING**, 'LORD, OPEN** up for us!' He will **ANSWER** you, 'I don't **KNOW** you or **WHERE** you are **FROM.**'"

CRISS-CROSS

USE THE DEFINITIONS BELOW TO FIND THE WORDS AND GUESS THE THEME.

ACROSS:

2. Mentioned in Joshua 10:13.

4. King's historical record mentioned in Esther 2:23.

5. Mentioned in Malachi 3:16.

7. King's historical record mentioned in 1 Chronicles 27:24.

9. Mentioned in 1 Chronicles 29:29.

10. Mentioned in 1 Kings 11:41.

DOWN:

1. Mentioned in 2 Chronicles 20:34.

3. Mentioned in 2 Chronicles 12:15.

6. Mentioned in Numbers 21:14.

8. Mentioned in 2 Chronicles 13:22.

SUDOKU

						3	4	
				4		9	2	
		8						3
	1							
8								
	5			6		1	8	2
5			2	1				
	3	2			4		9	1
		9		5			4	

ROMANS _ : __

"They exchanged the truth of God for a lie, and worshiped and served what has been created instead of the Creator, who is praised forever. Amen."

THE NAME GAME

JEREMIAH	....
JESSE	....
JETHRO	....
JEMIMA	....
JEZEBEL	....
JOANNA	....
JOB	....
JOEL	....

WORD WHEEL

CONNECT EACH LETTER FROM THE WHEEL TO REVEAL THE BIBLICAL WORD.

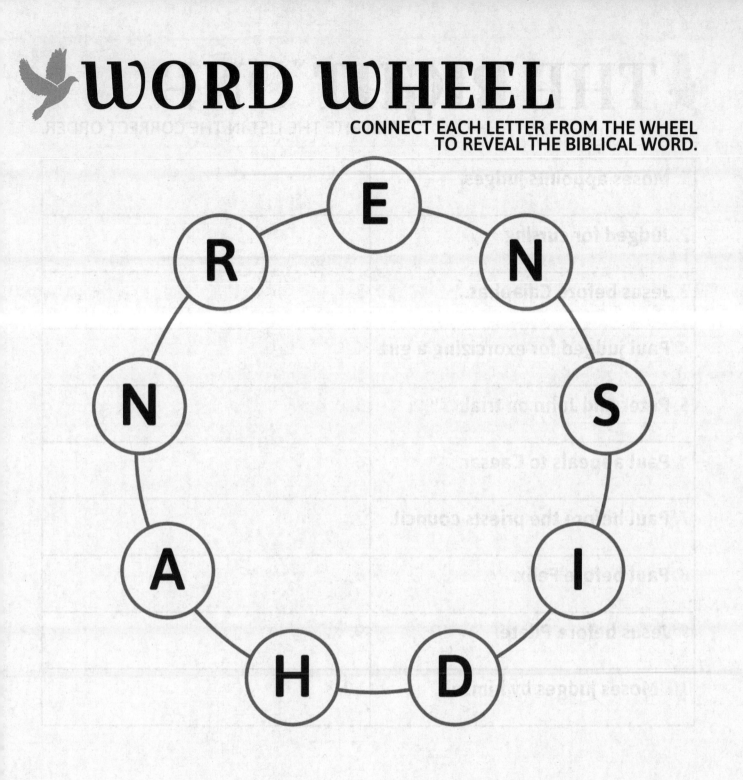

THE RIGHT ONE

REWRITE THE LIST IN THE CORRECT ORDER.

1. Moses appoints judges.	1.
2. Judged for cursing.	2.
3. Jesus before Caiaphas.	3.
4. Paul judged for exorcizing a girl.	4.
5. Peter and John on trial.	5.
6. Paul appeals to Caesar.	6.
7. Paul before the priests council.	7.
8. Paul before Felix.	8.
9. Jesus before Pilate.	9.
10. Moses judges by himself.	10.

CHRISTIAN QUOTES

FROM CHURCH FATHERS TO MODERN CHRISTIAN THINKERS, IDENTIFY THE AUTHOR OF EACH QUOTE.

"The chief reason we doubt, is that we don't appreciate the God we're dealing with."

AUTHOR:

....

....

AUTHOR:

....

....

"For the Christian, the truth is a living being, the most alive of all those who were or will ever be; it bears a name, that of Christ."

"As much wrong as I did in life and as many people as I hurt, I can say that God never stopped talking to me. I just stopped listening."

AUTHOR:

....

....

FRIENDS

UNSCRAMBLE THE LETTERS TO FORM PAIRS OF BIBLICAL ALLIES.

| 1. HAVAL | = | 1. USAE |
| 1. | = | 1. |

| 2. USAE | = | 2. NAMIT |
| 2. | = | 2. |

| 3. THETHEJ | = | 3. USAE |
| 3. | = | 3. |

| 4. USAE | = | 4. HAMBAOLIHO |
| 4. | = | 4. |

PROMISEMAKER

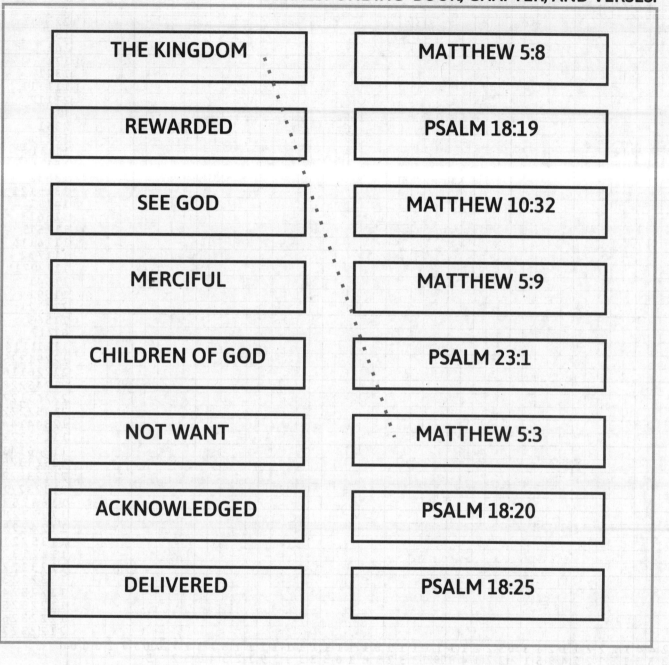

THE KINGDOM	MATTHEW 5:8
REWARDED	PSALM 18:19
SEE GOD	MATTHEW 10:32
MERCIFUL	MATTHEW 5:9
CHILDREN OF GOD	PSALM 23:1
NOT WANT	MATTHEW 5:3
ACKNOWLEDGED	PSALM 18:20
DELIVERED	PSALM 18:25

PIX-CROSS

SOLVE THE NONOGRAM TO REVEAL THE HIDDEN PICTURE.

Row clues (top to bottom):
0
3
22
131
161
171
1321
111111
21112
10 5
2361
19211
11031
15121
13832
1315121
14191
315613
111515
1116112
111732
1111071
11641
11591
214321
11563
61212
11111114
12291225
21226118
21245228
22263127
214522223
12344144
1114332223
112461433
425233252
21223222342
2132321023
11632824
1122328322
11242954
11352210331
11121322832
122332247 11
11323233431
1122324441
1122325121
1222326732
2122327632

WORD-SEARCH

CONTAINED WITHIN THIS PUZZLE YOU MUST FIND ALL CAPITALIZED WORDS FROM THE VERSES BELOW.

```
R E S U R R E C T I O N R
G U B Q S Z D H D T Y N C
L N B E O P V L D W Y J K
H I M A N G O D W D K W I
D O F O C T N X I Y S O E
C L M E O U S A L E R R V
W I V E O U S Y V S S L E
L V G Y S D S E E T N D R
W E D E O S I V M G E B Y
I F J T U L I H K D V N O
L Y N J E D N A R F E L N
L I Q B D I E O H V R L E
H E R K Q A L I E Y S H E
```

"**JESUS SAID** to **HER**, 'I am the **RESURRECTION** and the **LIFE**. The one who **BELIEVES** in me, **EVEN** if he **DIES**, **WILL LIVE**. **EVERYONE** who lives and believes in me will **NEVER DIE**. Do **YOU** believe this?' '**YES, LORD**,' **SHE TOLD HIM**, 'I believe you are the **MESSIAH**, the **SON** of **GOD**, who **COMES INTO** the **WORLD**.'"

CRISS-CROSS

ACROSS:
1. Shortest man.
5. Strongest man.
6. Fattest man.
7. Most mentioned man (OT).
10. Cruelest man.
11. Oldest man.

DOWN:
2. First man.
3. Wisest and richest man.
4. Tallest man.
8. Fastest man.
9. Meekest man.

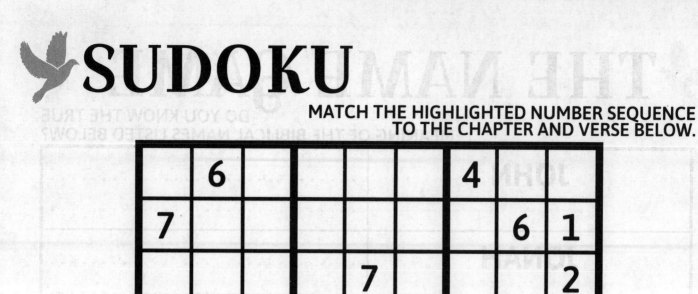

SUDOKU

	6					4		
7							6	1
				7				2
	1							6
6				1		3		9
2		5						
				4	1			
9	3		7					
5				3	2			7

2 CORINTHIANS __ : __

"Don't become partners with those who do not believe. For what partnership is there between righteousness and lawlessness? Or what fellowship does light have with darkness?"

THE NAME GAME

DO YOU KNOW THE TRUE
MEANING OF THE BIBLICAL NAMES LISTED BELOW?

JOHN	....
	....
JONAH	....
	....
JONATHAN	....
	....
JOSEPH	....
	....
JUDITH	....
	....
JULIA	....
	....
JUNIA	....
	....
JUDE	....
	....

WORD WHEEL

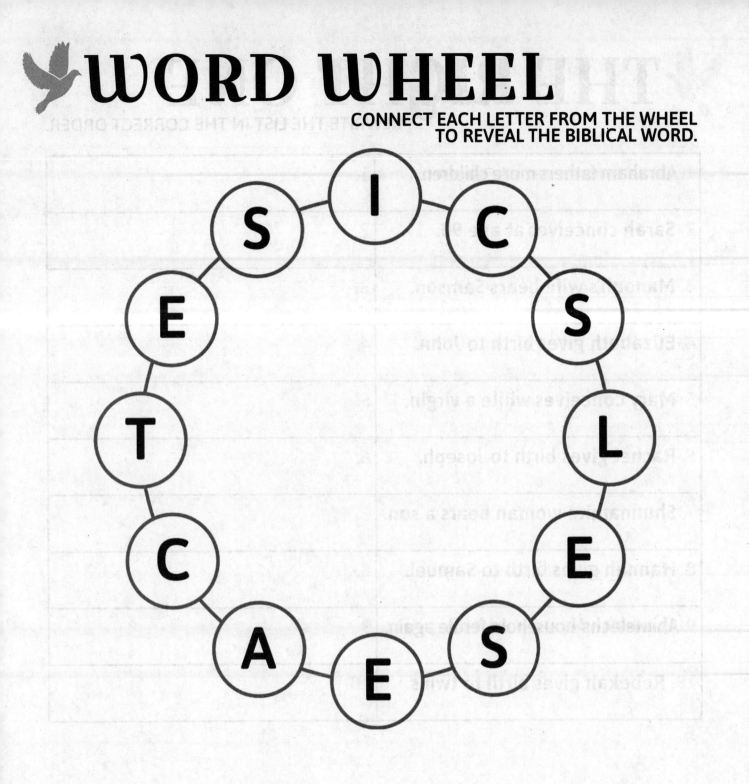

THE RIGHT ONE

REWRITE THE LIST IN THE CORRECT ORDER.

1. **Abraham fathers more children.**	1.
2. **Sarah conceives at age 90.**	2.
3. **Manoah's wife bears Samson.**	3.
4. **Elizabeth gives birth to John.**	4.
5. **Mary conceives while a virgin.**	5.
6. **Rachel gives birth to Joseph.**	6.
7. **Shunnamite woman bears a son.**	7.
8. **Hannah gives birth to Samuel.**	8.
9. **Abimelechs' household fertile again.**	9.
10. **Rebekah gives birth to twins.**	10.

CHRISTIAN QUOTES

FROM CHURCH FATHERS TO MODERN CHRISTIAN THINKERS, IDENTIFY THE AUTHOR OF EACH QUOTE.

"You might say, 'Can't we have a more human Christianity, without the cross, without Jesus, without stripping ourselves?' In this way we'd become pastry-shop Christians, like a pretty cake and nice sweet things. Pretty, but not true Christians."

AUTHOR:

....

....

AUTHOR:

....

....

"You were made by God and for God, and until you understand that, life will never make sense."

"It costs something to be a real Christian, according to the standard of the Bible. There are enemies to be overcome, battles to be fought, sacrifices to be made, an Egypt to be forsaken, a wilderness to be passed through, a cross to be carried, a race to be run. Conversion is not putting a person in an arm-chair and taking them easily to heaven. It is the beginning of a mighty conflict, in which it costs much to win the victory."

AUTHOR:

....

....

FRIENDS

UNSCRAMBLE THE LETTERS TO FORM PAIRS OF BIBLICAL ALLIES.

1. USAE	=	1. HALE
1.	=	1.

2. NOPIN	=	2. USAE
2.	=	2.

3. USAE	=	3. ZANEK
3.	=	3.

4. NAMET	=	4. USAE
4.	=	4.

PROMISEMAKER

CONNECT EACH BIBLICAL ASSURANCE TO ITS CORRESPONDING BOOK, CHAPTER, AND VERSES.

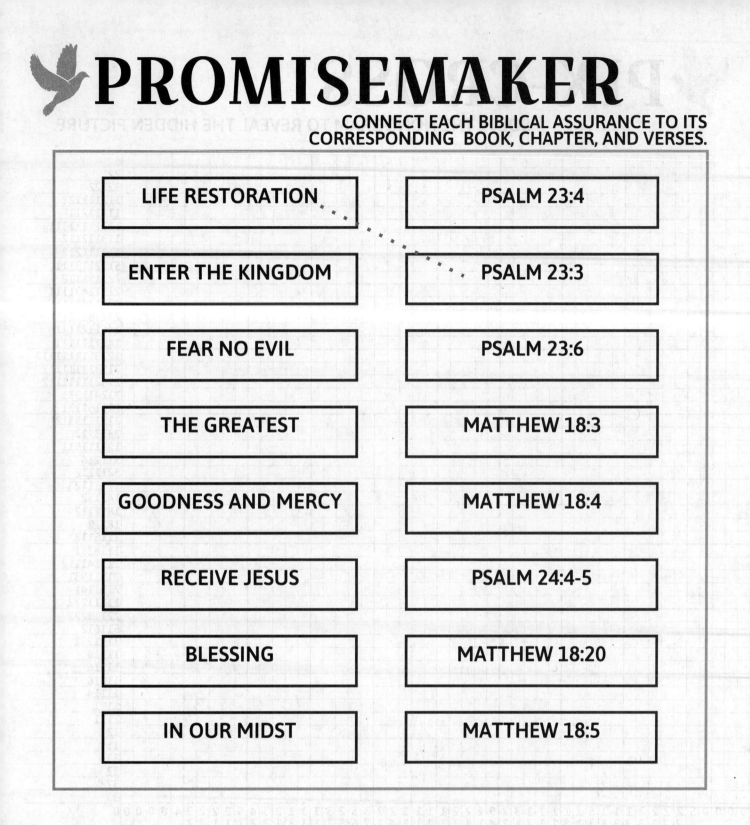

LIFE RESTORATION	PSALM 23:4
ENTER THE KINGDOM	PSALM 23:3
FEAR NO EVIL	PSALM 23:6
THE GREATEST	MATTHEW 18:3
GOODNESS AND MERCY	MATTHEW 18:4
RECEIVE JESUS	PSALM 24:4-5
BLESSING	MATTHEW 18:20
IN OUR MIDST	MATTHEW 18:5

PIX-CROSS

SOLVE THE NONOGRAM TO REVEAL THE HIDDEN PICTURE.

Row clues (top to bottom):

- 6
- 22
- 32322
- 11211112
- 11111211
- 11111111311
- 113112112
- 112111212
- 5112113111
- 221151112
- 21112431111
- 2221441111
- 2323611211
- 1461121111
- 1451111111
- 1223111111112
- 211311111112
- 213211111112
- 212411331
- 211151131
- 2111115312
- 2313212
- 121111511
- 311116
- 3211112
- 17111123
- 141132
- 1811112
- 18112
- 1115112
- 1116231
- 111141112
- 21111531
- 2111141
- 11111222
- 22113222
- 511612
- 3111231
- 11116
- 11116
- 11116
- 11114
- 1111
- 1111
- 12
- 11
- 33
- 12
- 323
- 33

WORD-SEARCH

CONTAINED WITHIN THIS PUZZLE YOU MUST FIND ALL
CAPITALIZED WORDS FROM THE VERSES BELOW.

```
T  T  H  K  M  M  A  S  R  Z  P  B  F
H  Z  H  W  R  M  A  O  N  U  W  R  K
E  U  A  E  B  J  O  S  R  T  T  Z  R
S  V  N  L  Y  Z  A  K  E  N  H  E  V
E  U  A  K  S  W  Z  X  L  O  H  E  M
S  W  T  H  R  O  U  G  H  T  Y  E  M
Q  E  O  T  H  O  S  E  A  A  N  I  E
P  J  N  R  V  Y  E  F  M  O  E  V  W
U  R  Q  T  L  T  H  D  Y  J  A  O  O
P  B  A  N  E  D  S  T  L  H  V  J  R
F  G  O  Y  F  B  E  L  I  E  V  E  D
V  G  I  V  E  N  A  E  Z  Y  O  U  U
N  O  S  G  L  O  R  Y  E  J  I  X  S
```

"'I **PRAY NOT ONLY** for **THESE**, but **ALSO** for **THOSE** who **BELIEVE** in me **THROUGH** their **WORD. MAY THEY ALL** be **ONE**, as **YOU, FATHER**, are in me and I am in you. May they also be in **US**, so that the **WORLD** may believe you **SENT** me. I **HAVE GIVEN THEM** the **GLORY** you have given me, so that they may be one as we are one.'"

CRISS-CROSS

USE THE DEFINITIONS BELOW TO FIND THE WORDS AND GUESS THE THEME.

ACROSS:
2. Most mentioned man (NT).
4. Proudest man.
5. Most doubtful man.
9. Most imprudent man.
10. Most frightened man.

DOWN:
1. Most persecuted man.
2. Most treasonous man.
3. Most sorrowful man.
6. Most beautiful woman.
7. Most lovestruck man.
8. Most traveled man.

SUDOKU

	7	8			3	2		
	3		5		9		4	
					8			
			6	3				
						5		2
1			7		2	6		
		2			5	1		
	6	4	1				9	

DANIEL _ : __

"Therefore, may my advice seem good to you my king. Separate yourself from your sins by doing what is right, and from your injustices by showing mercy to the needy. Perhaps there will be an extension of your prosperity."

THE NAME GAME

KENAN	....
KETURAH	....
LAMECH	....
LAZARUS	....
LEAH	....
LEVI	....
LOIS	....
LUKE	....

WORD WHEEL

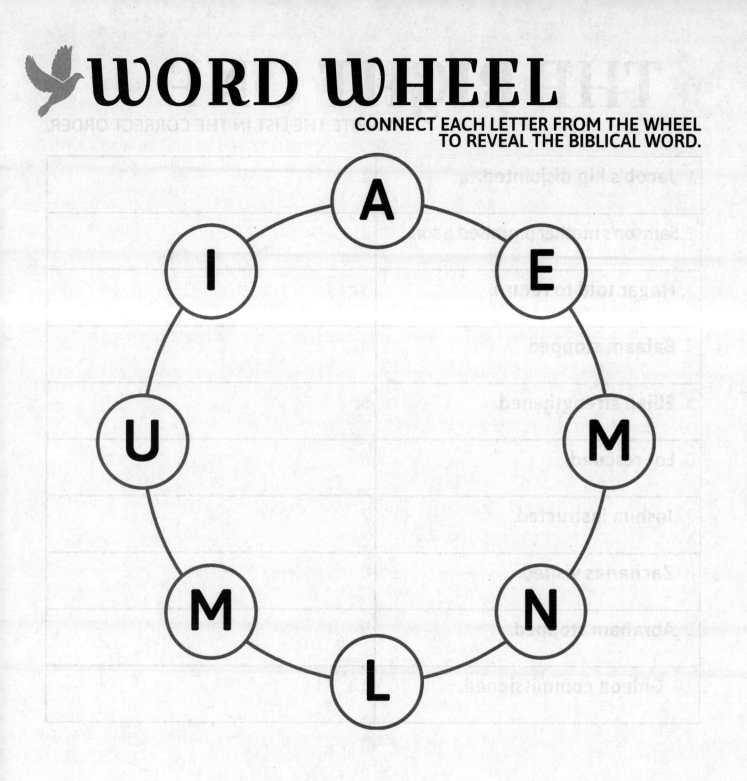

CONNECT EACH LETTER FROM THE WHEEL TO REVEAL THE BIBLICAL WORD.

A
E
I
M
U
N
M
L

THE RIGHT ONE

1. Jacob's hip disjointed.	1.
2. Samson's mother promised a son.	2.
3. Hagar told to return.	3.
4. Balaam stopped.	4.
5. Elijah strengthened.	5.
6. Lot rescued.	6.
7. Joshua instructed.	7.
8. Zacharias visited.	8.
9. Abraham stopped.	9.
10. Gideon commissioned.	10.

CHRISTIAN QUOTES

FROM CHURCH FATHERS TO MODERN CHRISTIAN THINKERS, IDENTIFY THE AUTHOR OF EACH QUOTE.

"Once you become aware that the main business that you are here for is to know God, most of life's problems fall into place of their own accord."

AUTHOR:

....

....

AUTHOR:

....

....

"The Bible says that all things work together for the good of those who love the Lord and are called according to his purpose. I believe that. Because I've seen it all work."

"Be humble, talk little, think and pray much."

AUTHOR:

....

....

FRIENDS

UNSCRAMBLE THE LETTERS TO FORM PAIRS OF BIBLICAL ALLIES.

1. HEPJOS = **1. MINAJNEB**

1. = 1.

2. NEBURE = **2. HEPJOS**

2. = 2.

3. SEMOS = **3. ROTHJE**

3. = 3.

4. MARIMI = **4. NOARA**

4. = 4.

PROMISEMAKER

CONNECT EACH BIBLICAL ASSURANCE TO ITS
CORRESPONDING BOOK, CHAPTER, AND VERSES.

SAVED	JOHN 3:16
EVERLASTING LIFE	MATTHEW 28:19-20
WHATEVER YOU DID	JOHN 8:31-32
ETERNAL LIFE	LUKE 11:13
ALWAYS WITH US	JOHN 8:12
NO DARKNESS	JOHN 6:54
HOLY SPIRIT GIFT	MATTHEW 24:13
SET FREE	MATTHEW 25:40

PIX-CROSS

SOLVE THE NONOGRAM TO REVEAL THE HIDDEN PICTURE.

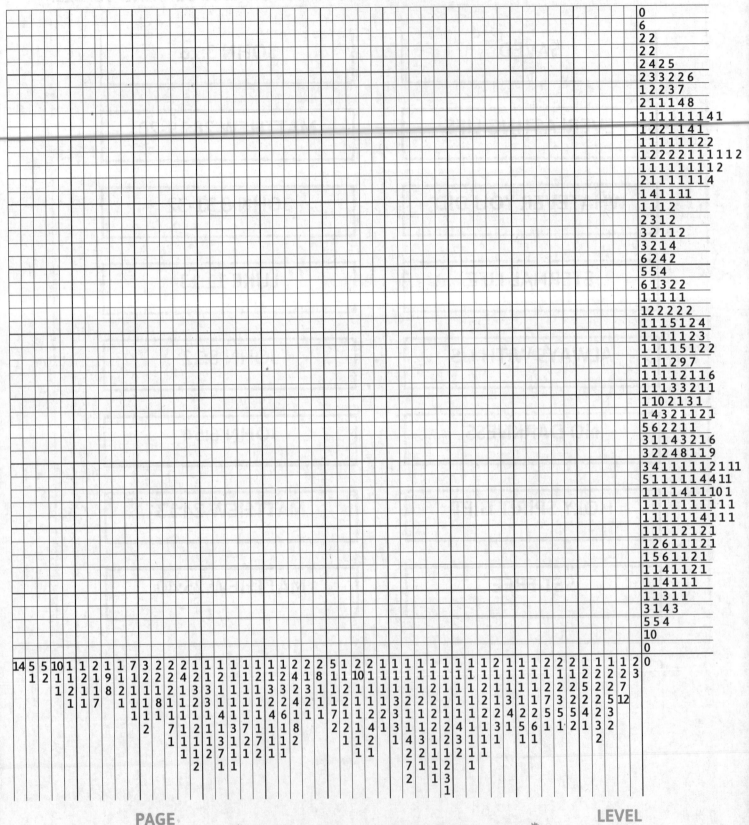

WORD-SEARCH

```
U U E B E F H O U S E M K P D
K D W P O C H A E D S B N H L
V H N A M E D F V R E W L U A
T P K T S Z M G E E A A C T S
M L D A J T L O D G I N G P Z
F D C V O D Q H K Y S I T E F
I T U Z P B E F O R E A C T F
W K U A P M R S N T N S H E B
J J R Z A E E K E N D C A R J
E Y O U R M S N H F H E R A O
A K A Y V O A I U O I N I W C
P R A Y E R S Z M G W D T H W
O F F E R I N G Q O Y E Y O Z
A L S O E A S L E D N D N S J
C A L L M L T A N N E R L E J
```

"...'**YOUR PRAYERS** and your **ACTS** of **CHARITY HAVE ASCENDED** as a **MEMORIAL OFFERING BEFORE GOD. NOW SEND MEN** to **JOPPA** and **CALL** for **SIMON**, who is **ALSO NAMED PETER**. He is **LODGING** with Simon, a **TANNER**, **WHOSE HOUSE** is by the **SEA**.'"

CRISS-CROSS

USE THE DEFINITIONS BELOW TO FIND THE WORDS AND GUESS THE THEME.

ACROSS:
3. Spoke to Balaam.
4. Fed Elijah (plural).
6. Sent to feed the Hebrews.
8. Crowed three times for Peter.
9. Third plague of Egypt.
11. A big one swallowed Jonah.
13. Sent to punish the Hebrews (plural).
14. Ate Jezebel (plural).
15. Provided to be sacrificed instead of Isaac.

DOWN:
1. Two females killed forty-two children (plural).
2. Fourth plague of Egypt (plural).
5. Jesus sent unclean spirits into a herd.
7. Eighth plague of Egypt (plural).
9. Killed a disobedient prophet.
10. Two of them towed the ark (plural).
11. Second plague of Egypt (plural).
12. Paul was bitten by one, but was unharmed.

SUDOKU

MATCH THE HIGHLIGHTED NUMBER SEQUENCE TO THE CHAPTER AND VERSE BELOW.

6	4						8	
	9	7			3			
	5							
8								
		2	4	3				
		3	8	1			7	
5	3					4		
					6	9		
				9			3	2

ROMANS __ : __

"The Spirit himself testifies together with our spirit that we are God's children..."

THE NAME GAME

LYDIA	....
MARK	....
MATTHEW	....
MARA	....
MARTHA	....
MICHAL	....
MOSES	....
NAOMI	....

WORD WHEEL

CONNECT EACH LETTER FROM THE WHEEL TO REVEAL THE BIBLICAL WORD.

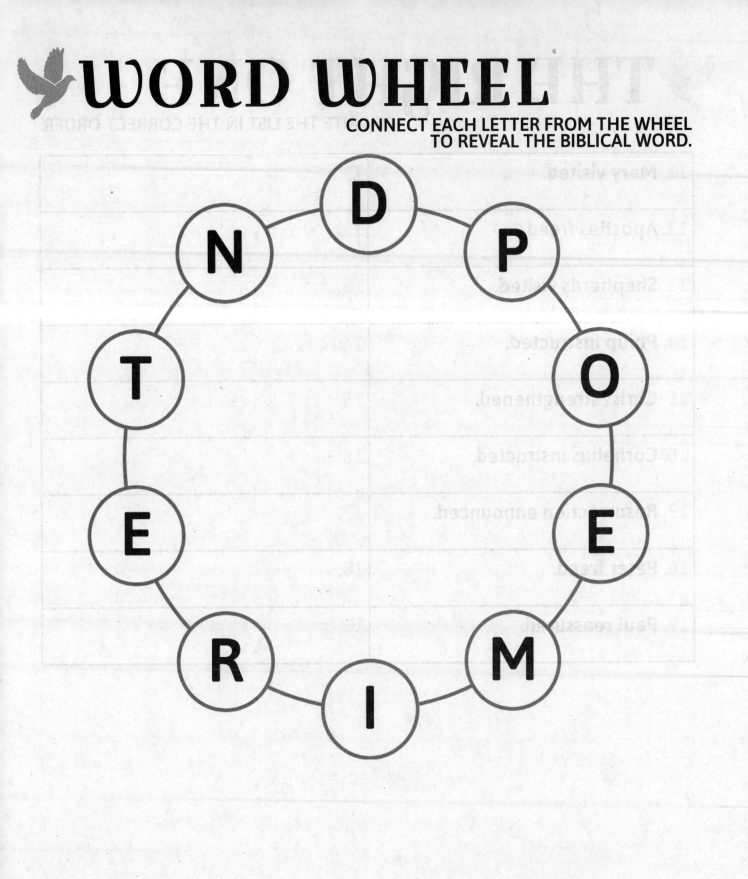

THE RIGHT ONE

REWRITE THE LIST IN THE CORRECT ORDER.

11. Mary visited.	11.
12. Apostles freed.	12.
13. Shepherds visited.	13.
14. Philip instructed.	14.
15. Christ strengthened.	15.
16. Cornelius instructed.	16.
17. Resurrection announced.	17.
18. Peter freed.	18.
19. Paul reassured.	19.

CHRISTIAN QUOTES

"Christians should live in the world, but not be filled with it. A ship lives in the water; but if the water gets into the ship, she goes to the bottom. So Christians may live in the world; but if the world gets into them, they sink."

AUTHOR:
....
....

AUTHOR:
....
....

"What good does it do me if Christ was born in Bethlehem once if he is not born again in my heart through faith?"

"Christians seem to act as if they thought God did not see what they do in politics. But I tell you He does see it—and He will bless or curse this nation according to the course they take."

AUTHOR:
....
....

FRIENDS

UNSCRAMBLE THE LETTERS TO FORM PAIRS OF BIBLICAL ALLIES.

1. BAHAR	=	1. HUASOJ
1.	=	1.
2. NIBAJ	=	2. BAJOB
2.	=	2.
3. HURT	=	3. ZABO
3.	=	3.
4. MABOROJE	=	4. HAJIHA
4.	=	4.

PROMISEMAKER

CONNECT EACH BIBLICAL ASSURANCE TO ITS CORRESPONDING BOOK, CHAPTER, AND VERSES.

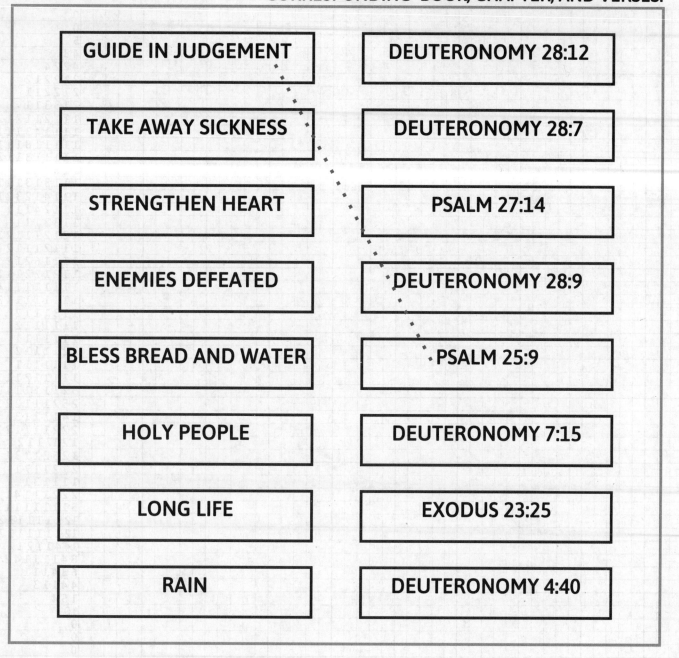

GUIDE IN JUDGEMENT	DEUTERONOMY 28:12
TAKE AWAY SICKNESS	DEUTERONOMY 28:7
STRENGTHEN HEART	PSALM 27:14
ENEMIES DEFEATED	DEUTERONOMY 28:9
BLESS BREAD AND WATER	PSALM 25:9
HOLY PEOPLE	DEUTERONOMY 7:15
LONG LIFE	EXODUS 23:25
RAIN	DEUTERONOMY 4:40

PIX-CROSS

SOLVE THE NONOGRAM TO REVEAL THE HIDDEN PICTURE.

Row clues (top to bottom):
- 0
- 0
- 5
- 4 3
- 4 2 2 4
- 2 1 2 2 1 2
- 2 1 2 2 1 1
- 2 1 3 3 1 1
- 1 1 1 2 1 1 2 1 2
- 1 1 1 1 4 3 1 1 1
- 1 1 1 1 1 8 1 1 1
- 1 1 1 1 3 1 1 2
- 1 1 6 7 1 1
- 1 1 1 3 1 3 1 1 1
- 1 1 1 4 1 2 3 2 1 1
- 1 1 1 2 4 1 1 1
- 1 1 3 2 1 1 1
- 1 2 1 2 1 1 1 2 1 2
- 1 1 1 2 1 1 1 2
- 1 1 1 1 6 2 1 2
- 1 1 2 1 2 2 1 1 2
- 1 1 1 1 1 1 1 1 4
- 1 1 1 1 1 1 1 1 3
- 1 1 3 1 1 1 2
- 1 1 1 1 1 1 2
- 1 1 1 1 1 1 1
- 2 2 1 1 1 1 2
- 1 1 1 1 1 1 1
- 1 1 1 1 1 2 1 1 1 2
- 5 2 1 1 1 1 1 1 3
- 2 5 2 1 1 1 2 2 1 2 1
- 1 4 1 1 1 1 3 1
- 2 2 2 1 1 1 1 2 2
- 1 2 1 7 1 1 2 2
- 1 2 5 2 1 1 3 1
- 2 1 2 1 1 7 1
- 1 1 1 1 3 1
- 2 2 2 1 1 1 4 1
- 5 1 1 1 1 1 1 1 1 1
- 1 2 1 1 1 1 1 3 2
- 1 2 1 1 1 1 1 1 1 2
- 1 4 4 1 1 2 1 2
- 8 4 1 1 1 1 4 2
- 6 3 4 1 1 1
- 4 4 1 1 3
- 1 5 4
- 1 0
- 0
- 0
- 0

Column clues (left to right):
- 0
- 4 7
- 7 4 4
- 4 3 3 5
- 20 2 6
- 2 2 4 6
- 2 2 2 5 1 6
- 2 1 1 2 10 1 7
- 1 1 5 8
- 1 1 4 1 4 1 4 5
- 2 6 4 2 4
- 2 2 8 2 5
- 7 8 3 3 1
- 3 7 1 2 1
- 2 4 1 2 1
- 2 2 1 2 2 1
- 2 4 1 2 2 1
- 2 1 1 1 2 2 1
- 1 2 2 1 2
- 2 2 2 3 7 2
- 1 1 1 2 2 1 1 1
- 1 1 1 2 1 1 1
- 1 2 3 1 1 1 1 2
- 1 3 1 1 1 1 1
- 1 7 1 1 1 1 1 1
- 1 7 1 1 1 1 1 2
- 2 4 5 1 2 1 1
- 2 2 1 3 1 1 1 1
- 2 4 3 1 1 1 1 1
- 3 3 2 4 7 1 1 1 2
- 7 2 2 1
- 2 1 9 1
- 2 4 8 1 7 1
- 1 7 1 6 1 1 1
- 1 6 2 1 1 1 1
- 2 1 1 2 1
- 4 1 7 1 1 2 1
- 4 6 1 2 2 1
- 20 1 1 2
- 5 2 1 6 1
- 2 2 1 1 1 1
- 2 1 1 1 1 1
- 2 2 5 1 1 1
- 2 1 1 1
- 3 2 1
- 5 1
- 2 1
- 5 2
- 5 2
- 3 0

WORD-SEARCH

CONTAINED WITHIN THIS PUZZLE YOU MUST FIND ALL
CAPITALIZED WORDS FROM THE VERSES BELOW.

```
C O M M A N D E R I C O L K Q
S O N R O M A N H R M E J H K
Y D M E L A C S A U I W H A T
Q G O P E N E Q C B G N E U I
V N C O G C N J R N M C Y N B
D T Q R A S T A N D I N G C T
S J E T L N U B U L T G H O U
C C H E S T R E T C H E D N H
O H I D S Y I H D K E E C D E
U S I T I P O V U E Y K N E A
R A R M I L N J D T S G A M R
G I K Q P Z A Q L S H B V N D
E D C L E A E S Z D V I T E N
R D X O U T U N H L O X S D O
N X G Q P W P L W H E N Q W H
```

"As **THEY STRETCHED HIM OUT** for the **LASH**, **PAUL SAID** to the **CENTURION**
STANDING by, 'Is it **LEGAL** for you to **SCOURGE** a man who is a **ROMAN CITIZEN**
and is **UNCONDEMNED**?'
WHEN the centurion **HEARD THIS**, he **WENT** and **REPORTED** to the **COMMANDER**,
saying, '**WHAT** are you going to do? For this **MAN** is a Roman citizen.'"

CRISS-CROSS

USE THE DEFINITIONS BELOW TO FIND THE WORDS AND GUESS THE THEME.

ACROSS:

2. Lazarus' home.

4. Paul preached his Mars Hill sermon there.

5. Jeremiah's home.

8. Daniel and Ezekiel lived there in exile.

11. Aquila and Priscilla's home.

12. Home of Cornelius.

13. Where Matthew lived and worked.

DOWN:

1. Rachel's burial place.

3. Birthplace of Herod the Great.

5. Apollos' home.

6. Where Paul preached his first sermon.

7. Where Jesus performed his first miracle.

8. Home of Philip, Andrew, and Peter.

9. Birthplace of Jesus.

10. Joseph's home.

SUDOKU

								1
			6	4				
		4						2
3	6			2				
			9					
		9				8	4	7
6	5	2						9
		3			2		7	
				8			5	

JOB __ : __

"Though I am blameless, I no longer care about myself; I renounce my life."

THE NAME GAME

DO YOU KNOW THE TRUE
MEANING OF THE BIBLICAL NAMES LISTED BELOW?

NOAH	....
	....
OG	....
	....
OMAR	....
	....
OREN	....
	....
PAUL	....
	....
PEREZ	....
	....
PHOEBE	....
	....
PRISCILLA	....
	....

WORD WHEEL

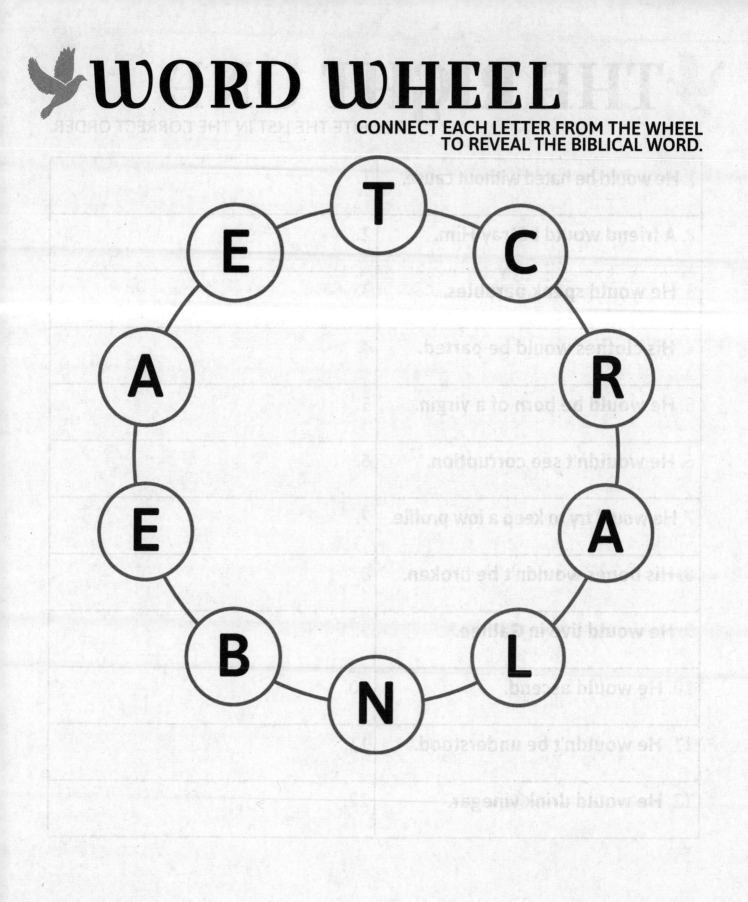

THE RIGHT ONE

REWRITE THE LIST IN THE CORRECT ORDER.

1. He would be hated without cause.	1.
2. A friend would betray Him.	2.
3. He would speak parables.	3.
4. His clothes would be parted.	4.
5. He would be born of a virgin.	5.
6. He wouldn't see corruption.	6.
7. He would try to keep a low profile.	7.
8. His bones wouldn't be broken.	8.
9. He would live in Galilee.	9.
10. He would ascend.	10.
11. He wouldn't be understood.	11.
12. He would drink vinegar.	12.

CHRISTIAN QUOTES

FROM CHURCH FATHERS TO MODERN CHRISTIAN THINKERS, IDENTIFY THE AUTHOR OF EACH QUOTE.

"Let me remind you that this is God's universe, and He is doing things His way. You may think you have a better way, but you don't have a universe to rule."

AUTHOR:
....
....

AUTHOR:
....
....

"You can't undo anything you've already done, but you can face up to it. You can tell the truth. You can seek forgiveness. And then let God do the rest."

"When a certain shameless fellow mockingly asked a pious old man what God had done before the creation of the world, the latter aptly countered that he had been building hell for the curious."

AUTHOR:
....
....

FRIENDS

UNSCRAMBLE THE LETTERS TO FORM PAIRS OF BIBLICAL ALLIES.

1. NOMOLOS	=	1. MAHIR
1.	=	1.

2. MABOHORE	=	2. HAJIBA
2.	=	2.

3. SAA	=	3. NEB-DADAH
3.	=	3.

4. HAMIHENE	=	4. RAZE
4.	=	4.

PROMISEMAKER

CONNECT EACH BIBLICAL ASSURANCE TO ITS CORRESPONDING BOOK, CHAPTER, AND VERSES.

SHALL BE LOVED	JOHN 15:5
STRONGER	ACTS 1:8
MUCH FRUIT	PROVERBS 2:7
PROSPEROUS	JOHN 14:21
POWER	JOB 36:11
SUCCESS	PROVERBS 3:5-6
REMISSION OF SINS	ACTS 10:43
DIRECT PATHS	JOB 17:9

PIX-CROSS

SOLVE THE NONOGRAM TO REVEAL THE HIDDEN PICTURE.

Row clues (top to bottom):

- 0
- 0
- 7
- 33
- 22
- 22
- 6227
- 2224232
- 2322111
- 22141342
- 11112212111
- 1111111111
- 111131111
- 11112211111111
- 11111111111112
- 11111111121111
- 11111111211111
- 11111211111111
- 111115411111
- 211113211111
- 21111211111111
- 221111111111111
- 21111111115
- 111121111115
- 1111171115
- 116101131
- 11341172
- 1421111112
- 1211111211
- 311141111
- 2111111121
- 211411111
- 24111
- 1102
- 16103
- 142212
- 23331112
- 1622322112
- 37272412
- 10151211
- 261111211
- 232222111
- 227325
- 22443
- 3222
- 2661
- 166
- 121121
- 0
- 0

Column clues (left to right):

0 · 5/9/3/3 · 9/3/1/4 · 5/2/1/6 · 2/4/2/2/1/3 · 2/1/4/1/2/4 · 1/1/4/1/2/1/2 · 1/1/3/1/1/7 · 1/2/3/1/1/2/6 · 1/3/1/3/3/6 · 2/2/1/3/2/5 · 6/2/1/1/1/2 · 2/3/1/2/1/2/1 · 3/2/1/3/1/1/1/3 · 2/4/2/1/2/4/2 · 2/2/1/2/3/4/2/3 · 2/1/1/4/1/2/2/3 · 1/1/3/1/6/3/5 · 2/1/7/1/1/1/2/2/6 · 1/1/1/1/1/1/1/2/2 · 1/1/1/1/1/1/6/1/5 · 4/1/1/1/1/2/2/2 · 1/1/1/1/6/2/2/5 · 2/1/2/1/1/2/2/2 · 1/1/4/1/1/2/1/5 · 2/1/4/2/3/2/4 · 2/2/4/3/2/4 · 2/3/2/6/5/2/3 · 7/2/1/3/1/5/2 · 2/1/1/1/1/3 · 3/4/1/1/1 · 1/1/3/2/2 · 2/1/2/1/4 · 1/1/4/2/1/2 · 1/1/1/7/1/1 · 1/1/1/1/1/8 · 1/1/4/1/9 · 2/1/1/1/1/4 · 3/1/10/10/4 · 6/2/4 · 12/2 · 5/1 · 4/2 · 4/8 · 6 · 0

WORD-SEARCH

CONTAINED WITHIN THIS PUZZLE YOU MUST FIND ALL CAPITALIZED WORDS FROM THE VERSES BELOW.

```
B M P E I Y R R A A H A O M W
L O M O V E C X P G I V E W O
I U A F F A H A R N T C O T V
I N I S H A V E N C P A R X N
J T O E T B I A L L W Z D L P
P A B I U U L T R S P T E I G
Q I O L O V E O H B M N R Z A
P N V W F H N J V L V Y D C I
R S E M Y S T E R I E S Y N N
O X R T B Z T H O S X D J O J
P S O F U A W A Y O O D Q T G
H F N V V A X D H B B Y A H I
E K N O W L E D G E P D J I F
C P P O S S E S S I O N S N T
Y U N D E R S T A N D I U G X
```

"If I **HAVE** the **GIFT** of **PROPHECY** and **UNDERSTAND ALL MYSTERIES** and all **KNOWLEDGE**, and if I have all **FAITH** so that I **CAN MOVE MOUNTAINS** but do not have **LOVE**, I am **NOTHING**. And if I **GIVE AWAY** all my **POSSESSIONS**, and if I give **OVER MY BODY** in **ORDER** to **BOAST** but do not have love, I **GAIN** nothing."

CRISS-CROSS

ACROSS:

3. Home of Esau.

4. Rebekah's home.

5. Where Elisha cured a pot of poisoned stew.

8. Goliath's home.

10. Sisera's HQ.

11. Visited by Paul on his second missionary journey.

12. Where Joseph was sold into slavery.

13. Jesus appeared to two disciples on the way.

DOWN:

1. Birthplace of Judas Iscariot.

2. Where Samson was imprisoned.

5. Saul's home.

6. Wicked city destroyed alongside Sodom.

7. Paul was struck blind on the way.

8. Where God appeared to Solomon.

9. Home of Timothy.

SUDOKU

MATCH THE HIGHLIGHTED NUMBER SEQUENCE TO THE CHAPTER AND VERSE BELOW.

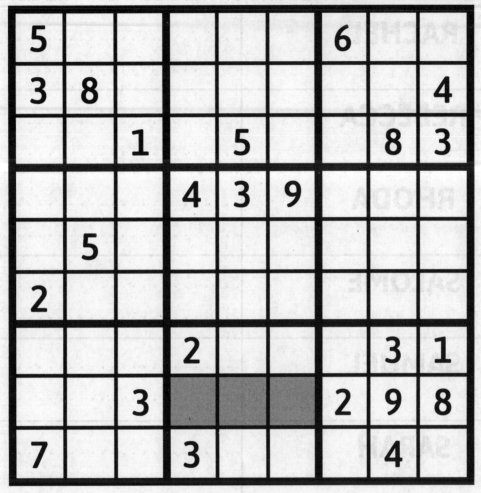

5						6		
3	8							4
		1		5			8	3
			4	3	9			
	5							
2								
			2				3	1
		3				2	9	8
7			3				4	

MATTHEW _ : __

"Don't think I have come to abolish the Law or the Prophets. I did not come to abolish but to fulfill."

THE NAME GAME

RACHEL	. . . .
REBECCA	. . . .
RHODA	. . . .
SALOME	. . . .
SAMUEL	. . . .
SARAH	. . . .
SETH	. . . .
STEPHEN	. . . .

WORD WHEEL

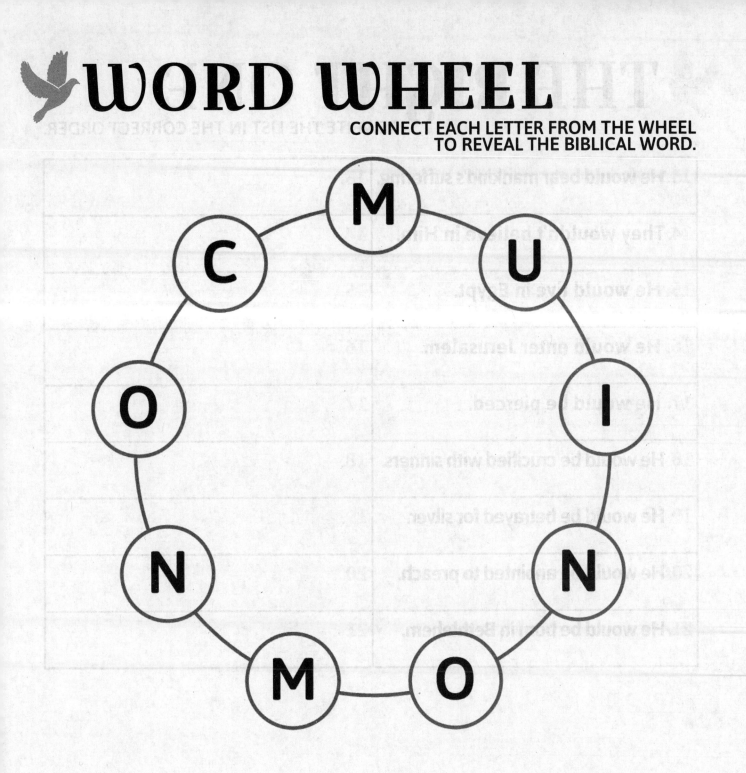

CONNECT EACH LETTER FROM THE WHEEL TO REVEAL THE BIBLICAL WORD.

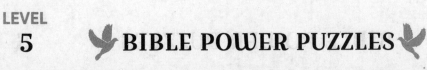

THE RIGHT ONE

REWRITE THE LIST IN THE CORRECT ORDER.

13. He would bear mankind's suffering.	13.
14. They wouldn't believe in Him.	14.
15. He would live in Egypt.	15.
16. He would enter Jerusalem.	16.
17. He would be pierced.	17.
18. He would be crucified with sinners.	18.
19. He would be betrayed for silver.	19.
20. He would be anointed to preach.	20.
21. He would be born in Bethlehem.	21.

CHRISTIAN QUOTES

FROM CHURCH FATHERS TO MODERN CHRISTIAN THINKERS, IDENTIFY THE AUTHOR OF EACH QUOTE.

"Between us and heaven or hell there is only life, which is the frailest thing in the world."

AUTHOR:

....

....

AUTHOR:

....

....

"When one man dies, one chapter is not torn out of the book, but translated into a better language."

"All our life is like a day of celebration for us; we are convinced, in fact, that God is always everywhere. We work while singing, we sail while reciting hymns, we accomplish all other occupations of life while praying."

AUTHOR:

....

....

FRIENDS

UNSCRAMBLE THE LETTERS TO FORM PAIRS OF BIBLICAL ALLIES.

1. NILEDA	=	**1. SURIDA**
1.	=	1.
2. SUJES	=	**2. SUMEDCONI**
2.	=	2.
3. PHESOJ FO HETAMARIA	=	**3. SUJES**
3.	=	3.
4. SUJES	=	**4. OYU**
4.	=	4.

PROMISEMAKER

CONNECT EACH BIBLICAL ASSURANCE TO ITS
CORRESPONDING BOOK, CHAPTER, AND VERSES.

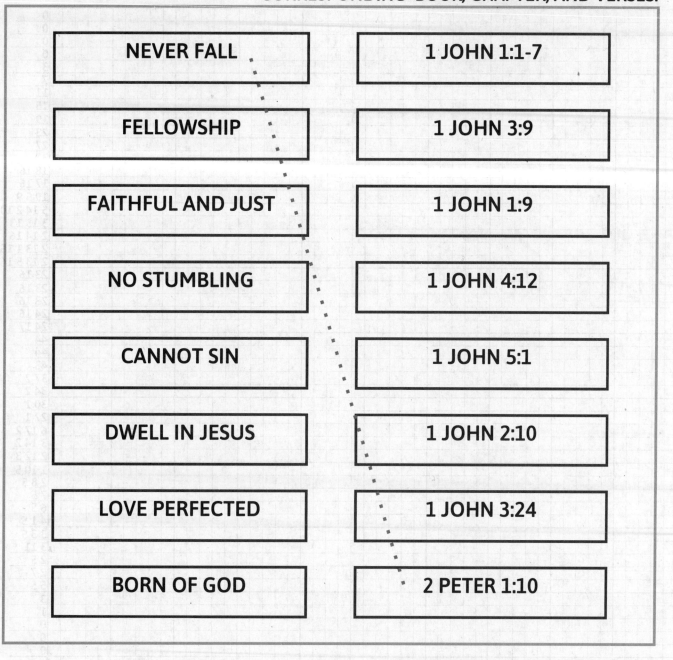

NEVER FALL	1 JOHN 1:1-7
FELLOWSHIP	1 JOHN 3:9
FAITHFUL AND JUST	1 JOHN 1:9
NO STUMBLING	1 JOHN 4:12
CANNOT SIN	1 JOHN 5:1
DWELL IN JESUS	1 JOHN 2:10
LOVE PERFECTED	1 JOHN 3:24
BORN OF GOD	2 PETER 1:10

PIX-CROSS

SOLVE THE NONOGRAM TO REVEAL THE HIDDEN PICTURE.

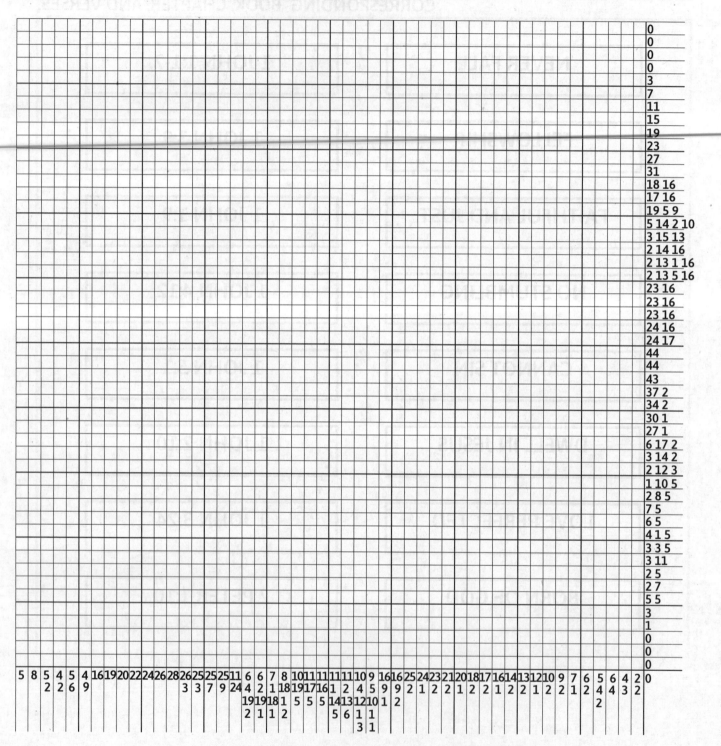

Row clues (top to bottom):

0
0
0
0
3
7
11
15
19
23
27
31
18 16
17 16
19 5 9
5 14 2 10
3 15 13
2 14 16
2 13 1 16
2 13 5 16
23 16
23 16
23 16
24 16
24 17
44
44
43
37 2
34 2
30 1
27 1
6 17 2
3 14 2
2 12 3
1 10 5
2 8 5
7 5
6 5
4 1 5
3 3 5
3 11
2 5
2 7
5 5
3
1
0
0
0

Column clues (left to right):

5
8
5 2
4 2
5 6
4 9
16
19
20
22
24
26
28
26 3
25 3
25 7
25 9
11 24
6 4 19 2
6 2 19 1
7 1 18 1
8 18 1 2
10 19 5
11 17 5
11 16 5
11 1 14 5
11 2 13 6
10 4 12 1 3
9 5 10 1 1
16 9 1
16 9 2
25 2
24 1
23 2
21 2
20 1
18 2
17 2
16 1
14 2
13 2
12 1
10 2
9 2
7 1
6 2
5 4 2
6 4
4 3
2 2
0

SOLUTIONS

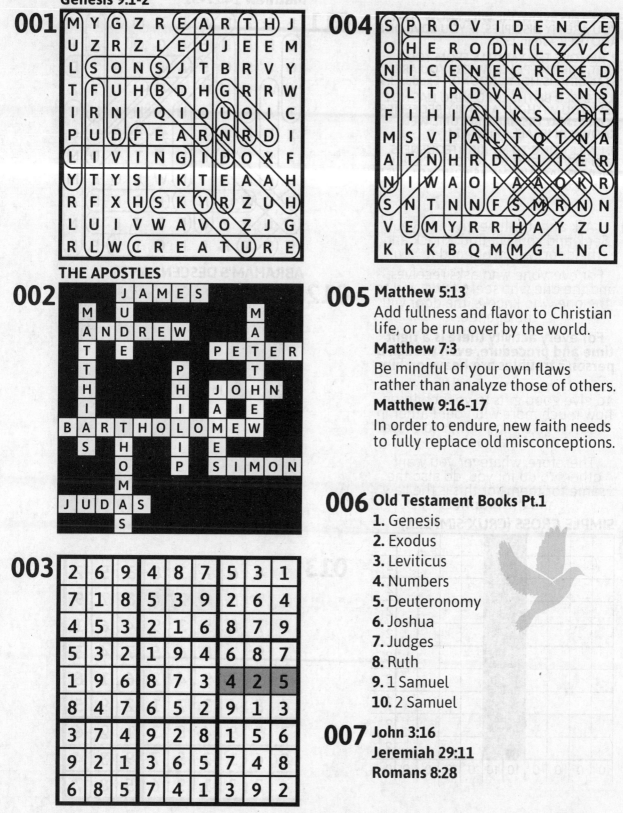

001 Genesis 9:1-2

```
M Y G Z R E A R T H J
U Z R Z L E U J E E M Y
L S O N S J T B R V Y M
T F U H B D H G R R W C
I R N I Q I O U O I I L
P U D F E A R N R D V F
L I V I N G I D O X I F
Y T Y S I K T E A A H
R F X H S K Y R Z U H
L U I V W A V O Z J G
R L W C R E A T U R E
```

002 THE APOSTLES

```
            J A M E S
      M     U
      A N D R E W           M
      T     E         P E T E R
      T           P H   A     T
      H           I   J O H N
      I           L   A   E
      B A R T H O L O M E W
      A     H     I   E
      S     O     P   S I M O N
            M
            A
            S
  J U D A S
            S
```

003

```
2 6 9 4 8 7 5 3 1
7 1 8 5 3 9 2 6 4
4 5 3 2 1 6 8 7 9
5 3 2 1 9 4 6 8 7
1 9 6 8 7 3 4 2 5
8 4 7 6 5 2 9 1 3
3 7 4 9 2 8 1 5 6
9 2 1 3 6 5 7 4 8
6 8 5 7 4 1 3 9 2
```

004

```
S P R O V I D E N C E E
O H E R O D N L Z V C
N I C E N E C R E E D
O L T P D V A J E N S
F M S H I A I K S L H T
M A S T V P A L T O T N A
A N I W A O H R D T I E R
N S N T N O L A A O K R
S V E M Y R R H A Y Z U
K K K B Q M M G L N C
```

005 **Matthew 5:13**
Add fullness and flavor to Christian life, or be run over by the world.

Matthew 7:3
Be mindful of your own flaws rather than analyze those of others.

Matthew 9:16-17
In order to endure, new faith needs to fully replace old misconceptions.

006 **Old Testament Books Pt.1**
1. Genesis
2. Exodus
3. Leviticus
4. Numbers
5. Deuteronomy
6. Joshua
7. Judges
8. Ruth
9. 1 Samuel
10. 2 Samuel

007 **John 3:16**
Jeremiah 29:11
Romans 8:28

SOLUTIONS

008
1. BY THIS EVERYONE WILL KNOW THAT YOU ARE MY DISCIPLES, IF YOU LOVE ONE ANOTHER. –John 13:35

2. REMOVE THE SANDALS FROM YOUR FEET, FOR THE PLACE WHERE YOU ARE STANDING IS HOLY GROUND. –Exodus 3:5

3. BLESSED BE THE LORD, WHO HAS NOT LEFT YOU WITHOUT A FAMILY REDEEMER TODAY. MAY HIS NAME BECOME WELL KNOWN IN ISRAEL. –Ruth 4:14

4. I WILL CLING TO MY RIGHTEOUSNESS AND NEVER LET IT GO. MY CONSCIENCE WILL NOT ACCUSE ME AS LONG AS I LIVE! –Job 27:6

009
"'Ask and it will be given to you. Seek and you will find. Knock and the door will be opened to you.

For everyone who asks receives, and the one who seeks finds, and to the one who knocks, the door will be opened.

For every activity there is a right time and procedure, even though a person's troubles are heavy on him.

If you then, who are evil, know how to give good gifts to your children, how much more will your Father in heaven give good things to those who ask Him.

Therefore, whatever you want others to do for you, do also the same for them, for this is the Law and the Prophets.'"

SIMPLE CROSS (*CRUX SIMPLEX*)

010

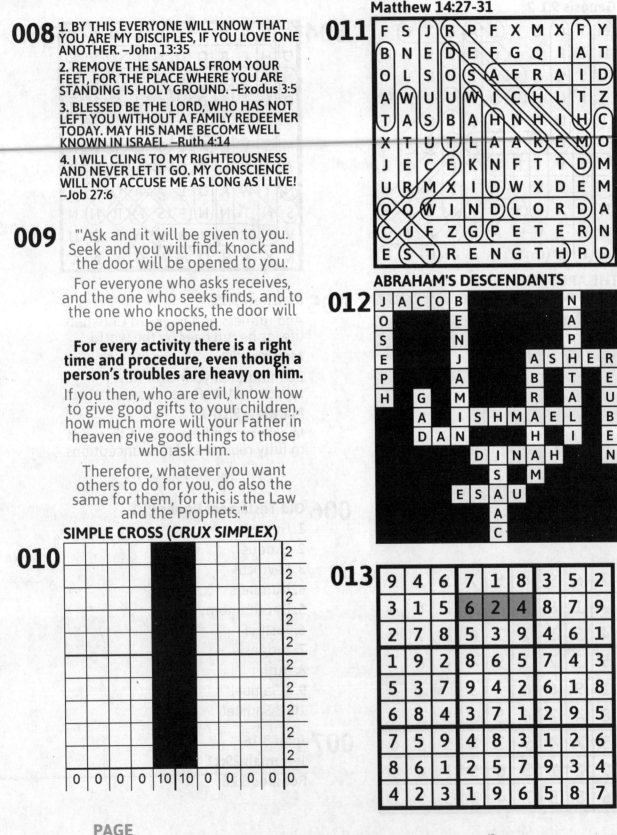

011 Matthew 14:27-31

ABRAHAM'S DESCENDANTS

012

013

SOLUTIONS

014

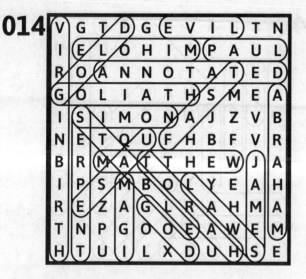

V	G	T	D	G	E	V	I	L	T	N
I	E	L	O	H	I	M	P	A	U	L
R	O	A	N	N	O	T	A	T	E	D
G	O	L	I	A	T	H	S	M	E	A
I	S	I	M	O	N	A	J	Z	V	B
N	E	T	O	U	F	H	B	F	V	R
B	R	M	A	T	T	H	E	W	J	A
I	P	S	M	B	O	L	Y	E	A	H
R	E	Z	A	G	L	R	A	H	M	A
T	N	P	G	O	O	E	A	W	E	M
H	T	U	I	L	X	D	U	H	S	E

015 Matthew 5:14-15

Faith must be put in the forefront of our life and be shared with all.

Matthew 9:37-38

Many souls need to hear God's Word, but few answer the call to spread it.

Matthew 13:31-32

Faith grows large from humble beginnings.

016 Old Testament Books Pt.2

11. 1 Kings
12. 2 Kings
13. 1 Chronicles
14. 2 Chronicles
15. Ezra
16. Nehemiah
17. Esther
18. Job
19. Psalms
20. Proverbs

017 Philippians 4:13

Genesis 1:1

Proverbs 3:5

018

1. HE TRULY IS AN ISRAELITE IN WHOM THERE IS NO DECEIT. –John 1:47

2. IF YOUR BROTHER SINS AGAINST YOU, GO AND REBUKE HIM IN PRIVATE. IF HE LISTENS TO YOU, YOU HAVE WON YOUR BROTHER. –Matthew 18:15

3. WITH GREAT POWER THE APOSTLES WERE GIVING TESTIMONY TO THE RESURRECTION OF THE LORD JESUS... –Acts 4:33

4. HOW LONG WILL YOU WAVER BETWEEN TWO OPINIONS? IF THE LORD IS GOD, FOLLOW HIM. –1 Kings 18:20

019

"In the beginning was the Word, and the Word was with God.

He was with God in the beginning.

All things were created through him, and apart from him not one thing was created that has been created. In him was life, and that light was the light of men.

God saw that the light was good, and God separated the light from the darkness.

That light shines in the darkness, and yet the darkness did not overcome it."

020

ANTHONY'S CROSS (*CRUX COMMISSA*)

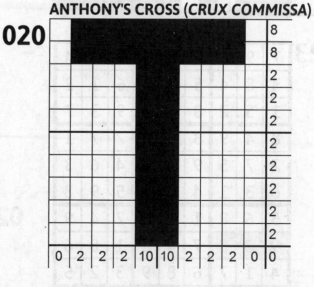

											8
											8
											2
											2
											2
											2
											2
											2
											2
											2
0	2	2	2	10	10	2	2	2	0	0	

SOLUTIONS

Job 1:20-22

021

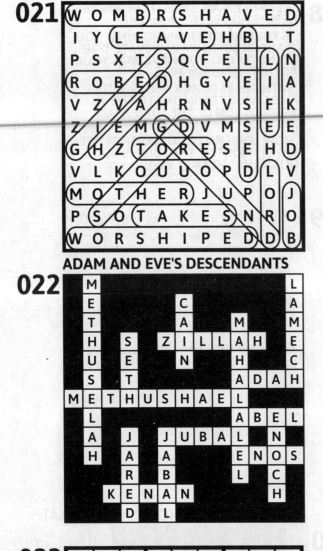

W	O	M	B	R	S	H	A	V	E	D
I	Y	L	E	A	V	E	H	B	L	T
P	S	X	T	S	Q	F	E	L	L	N
R	O	B	E	D	H	G	Y	E	I	A
V	Z	V	A	H	R	N	V	S	F	K
Z	I	E	M	G	D	V	M	S	E	E
G	H	Z	T	O	R	E	S	E	H	D
V	L	K	O	U	U	O	P	D	L	V
M	O	T	H	E	R	J	U	P	O	J
P	S	O	T	A	K	E	S	N	R	O
W	O	R	S	H	I	P	E	D	D	B

ADAM AND EVE'S DESCENDANTS

022

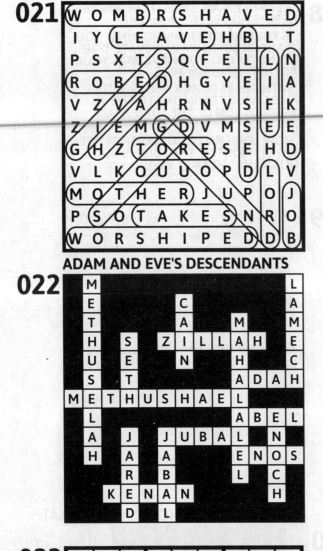

023

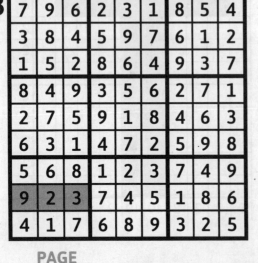

7	9	6	2	3	1	8	5	4
3	8	4	5	9	7	6	1	2
1	5	2	8	6	4	9	3	7
8	4	9	3	5	6	2	7	1
2	7	5	9	1	8	4	6	3
6	3	1	4	7	2	5	9	8
5	6	8	1	2	3	7	4	9
9	2	3	7	4	5	1	8	6
4	1	7	6	8	9	3	2	5

024

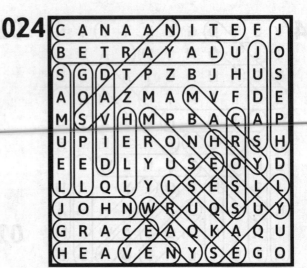

C	A	N	A	A	N	I	T	E	F	J
B	E	T	R	A	Y	A	L	U	J	O
S	G	D	T	P	Z	B	J	H	U	S
A	O	A	Z	M	A	M	V	F	D	E
M	S	V	H	M	P	B	A	C	A	P
U	P	I	E	R	O	N	H	R	S	H
E	E	D	L	Y	U	S	E	O	Y	D
L	L	Q	L	Y	L	S	E	S	L	L
J	O	H	N	W	R	U	Q	S	U	Y
G	R	A	C	E	A	Q	K	A	Q	U
H	E	A	V	E	N	Y	S	E	G	O

025 Matthew 7:24-28

Solid faith must be founded on equally firm action to endure.

Matthew 11:16-17

Mankind if too immature to accept heavenly truths, always making excuses to deny them.

Matthew 13:28-29

Be alert to the signs of Christ's second coming.

026 Old Testament Books Pt.3

21. Ecclesiastes
22. Song of Songs
23. Isaiah
24. Jeremiah
25. Lamentations
26. Ezekiel
27. Daniel
28. Hosea
29. Joel
30. Amos

027 Genesis 32:28
Judges 16:28
Acts 7:60

SOLUTIONS

028
1. THIS IS MY SERVANT; I STRENGTHEN HIM, THIS IS MY CHOSEN ONE; I DELIGHT IN HIM. –Isaiah 42:1

2. WHO MAY ASCEND TO THE MOUNTAIN OF THE LORD? WHO MAY STAND IN HIS HOLY PLACE? –Psalms 24:3

3. THE LORD APPOINTED A GREAT FISH TO SWALLOW JONAH, AND JONAH WAS IN THE BELLY OF THE FISH THREE DAYS AND THREE NIGHTS. –Jonah 1:17

4. BUT WOE TO YOU WHO ARE RICH, FOR YOU HAVE RECEIVED YOUR COMFORT. –Luke 6:24

029
"They came to Jerusalem, and he went into the temple and began to throw out those buying and selling. He overturned the tables of money changers and the chairs of those selling doves, and would not permit anyone to carry goods through the temple.

He found a fresh jawbone of a donkey, reached out his hand, took it, and killed a thousand men with it.

He was teaching them: 'Is it not written, *My house will be called a house of prayer for all nations?* But you have made it a *den of thieves!*'"

GREEK CROSS (CRUX QUADRATA)

030

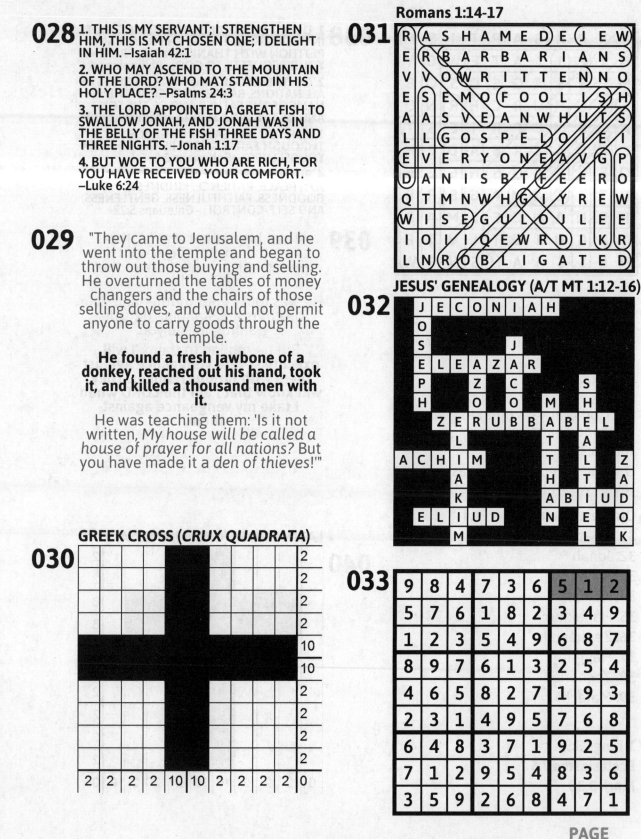

Romans 1:14-17

031

JESUS' GENEALOGY (A/T MT 1:12-16)

032

033

SOLUTIONS

034

```
F X R R B A P T I S M
O I P I L A T E W C Y
M E S S A G E Q S O B
J P C H U R C H R N Q
A U S M E P R I E S T
C P D A B R E A D E H
O E K E L Q S N E C E
B T I L A M A G E R B
P E N A N C E E M A R
T R G U I L T L V T E
M E S S I A H S V E W
```

035 **Mark 4:26-29**

Only after growing in the faith and being fruitful we'll be ready for heaven.

Luke 13:6-9

Unless we repent, we'll be damned; but God is always open to giving us a second chance.

John 6:35

Only by accepting Christ as our savior we will have eternal life.

036 **Old Testament Books Pt.4**

31. Obadiah
32. Jonah
33. Micah
34. Nahum
35. Habakkuk
36. Zephaniah
37. Haggai
38. Zechariah
39. Malachi

037 **1 Kings 3:9**
Ecclesiastes 7:5
Mark 3:35

038
1. DON'T WORRY ABOUT ANYTHING, BUT IN EVERYTHING THROUGH PRAYER AND PETITION WITH THANKSGIVING, PRESENT YOUR REQUESTS TO GOD. –Philippians 4:6

2. GO, THEREFORE, AND MAKE DISCIPLES OF ALL NATIONS, BAPTIZING THEM IN THE NAME OF THE FATHER AND OF THE SON AND OF THE HOLY SPIRIT... –Matthew 28:19

3. FOR YOU ARE SAVED BY GRACE THROUGH FAITH, AND THIS IS NOT FROM YOURSELVES... –Ephesians 2:8

4. BUT THE FRUIT OF THE SPIRIT IS LOVE, JOY, PEACE, PATIENCE, KINDNESS, GOODNESS, FAITHFULNESS, GENTLENESS, AND SELF-CONTROL. –Galatians 5:22

039

"Then his mother and brothers came to him, but they could not meet with him because of the crowd.

He was told, ' your mother and your brothers are standing outside, wanting to see you.'

But he replied to them, **'I will execute severe vengeance against them with furious rebukes. They will know that I am the LORD when I take my vengeance against them.'**"

040 LATIN CROSS (*CRUX IMMISSA*)

										2
										2
										8
										8
										2
										2
										2
										2
										2
										2
0	2	2	2	10	10	2	2	2	0	0

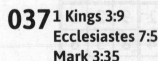 BIBLE POWER PUZZLES

SOLUTIONS

Ecclesiastes 3:1-8

041

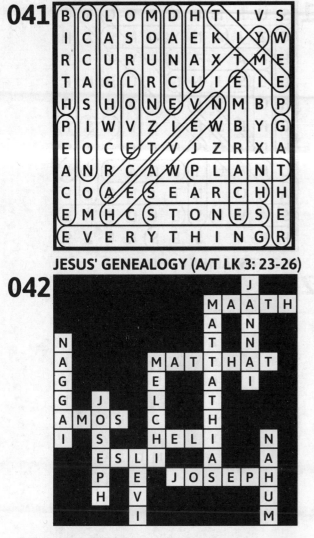

JESUS' GENEALOGY (A/T LK 3: 23-26)

042

043

3	4	6	5	1	7	8	9	2
7	1	2	9	8	4	6	3	5
5	9	8	6	2	3	4	7	1
4	6	1	2	3	5	7	8	9
2	5	7	8	4	9	3	1	6
8	3	9	1	7	6	5	2	4
6	8	5	3	9	2	1	4	7
9	7	3	4	6	1	2	5	8
1	2	4	7	5	8	9	6	3

044

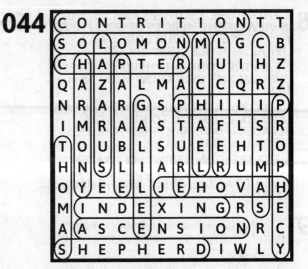

045 **Matthew 12:25-26**
Christ's words and deeds are one.

Luke 14:12-14
Do good onto others without expecting a reward in this life.

Luke 11:11-13
God will provide Grace to those who ask for it.

046 **New Testament Books Pt.1**
1. Matthew
2. Mark
3. Luke
4. John
5. Acts
6. Romans
7. 1 Corinthians
8. 2 Corinthians
9. Galatians
10. Ephesians

047 **Exodus 14:16**
2 Samuel 22:2-3
Jeremiah 1:5

SOLUTIONS

048
1. THEREFORE, BROTHERS AND SISTERS, IN VIEW OF THE MERCIES OF GOD, I URGE YOU TO PRESENT YOUR BODIES AS A LIVING SACRIFICE... –Romans 12:1

2. I AM THE GOOD SHEPHERD. I KNOW MY OWN, AND MY OWN KNOW ME... – John 10:14

3. FOR I AM WITH YOU, AND NO ONE WILL LAY A HAND ON YOU TO HURT YOU, BECAUSE I HAVE MANY PEOPLE IN THIS CITY. –Acts 18:10

4. FOR FREEDOM, CHRIST SET US FREE. STAND FIRM THEN AND DON'T SUBMIT AGAIN TO A YOKE OF SLAVERY. –Galatians 5:1

049
"Now Israel loved Joseph more than his other sons because Joseph was a son born to him in his old age, and he made a robe of many colors for him.

There was an opening in the center of the robe like that of body armor with a collar around the opening so that it would not tear.

When his brothers saw that their father loved him more than all his brothers, they hated him, and could not bring themselves to speak peaceably to him."

PATRIARCHAL CROSS (CRUX GEMINA)

050

051 James 5:13-15

OLD TESTAMENT PROPHETS

052

053

6	5	2	4	1	8	9	3	7
1	3	8	5	9	7	6	2	4
9	4	7	2	3	6	8	5	1
5	8	4	6	2	3	7	1	9
3	1	9	7	8	4	5	6	2
2	7	6	1	5	9	4	8	3
8	6	3	9	4	1	2	7	5
4	2	1	8	7	5	3	9	6
7	9	5	3	6	2	1	4	8

054

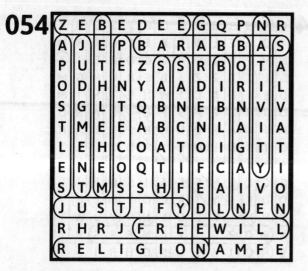

```
Z E B E D E E G Q P N R
A J E P B A R A B B A S
P U D E Z S R B O T A
O D G E Z S A R B T I V
S L M H N Y A D I R A L
T E E N T A N E B N A V
L N H E C Q B C N L A A
E T O O B A T I I G T
S M E M S S H F C A I I
J U S T I F Y D L N O
R H R J F R E E W I L L
R E L I G I O N A M F E
```

055 Luke 10:30-36

It is our Christian duty to regard every man as a brother, and to lend him a helping hand to the utmost of our power, unhindered by any consideration of situation or circumstance, be it our own or his.

Mark 2:17

Christ came to this world not to save the arrogant, but those who recognize themselves as sinners.

056 New Testament Books Pt.2

11. Philippians
12. Colossians
13. 1 Thessalonians
14. 2 Thessalonians
15. 1 Timothy
16. 2 Timothy
17. Titus
18. Philemon
19. Hebrews
20. James

057 Exodus 33:16
1 Peter 4:8
Acts 18:9

058
1. I HAVE BEEN CRUCIFIED WITH CHRIST, AND I NO LONGER LIVE, BUT CHRIST LIVES IN ME. –Galatians 2:20

2. IF WE CONFESS OUR SINS, HE IS FAITHFUL AND RIGHTEOUS TO FORGIVE US OUR SINS AND TO CLEANSE US FROM ALL UNRIGHTEOUSNESS. –1 John 1:9

3. I AM THE WAY, THE TRUTH, AND THE LIFE. NO ONE COMES TO THE FATHER EXCEPT THROUGH ME. –John 14:6

4. BUT GOD PROVES HIS OWN LOVE FOR US IN THAT WHILE WE WERE STILL SINNERS, CHRIST DIED FOR US. –Romans 5:8

059

"As soon as Martha heard that Jesus was coming, she went to meet him, but Mary remained seated in the house. Then Martha said to Jesus, **'Lord, hear my prayer; let my cry for help come before you. Do not hide your face from me in my day of trouble. Listen closely to me; answer me quickly when I call.'** 'Your brother will rise again,' Jesus told her. Martha said to him, 'I know that he will rise again in the resurrection at the last day.' Jesus said to her, 'I am the resurrection and the life. The one who believes in me, even if he dies, will live. Everyone who lives and believes in me will never die. Do you believe this?' 'Yes, Lord,' she told him, 'I believe you are the Messiah, the Son of God, who comes into the world.'"

060

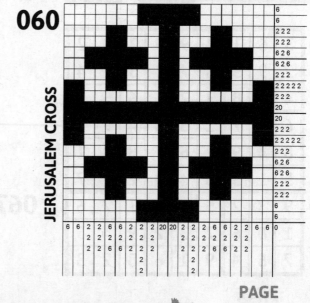

JERUSALEM CROSS

SOLUTIONS

Song of Songs 2:10-12

061

KINGS OF ISRAEL AND JUDAH Pt.1

062

063

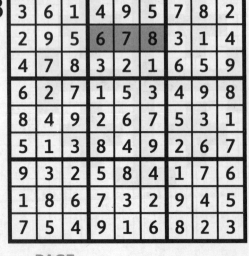

064

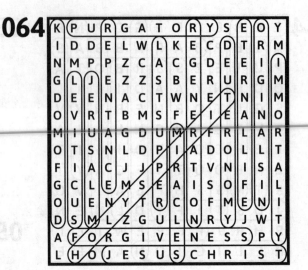

065 **John 10:1-3**
Only through God's Grace do we enter His Kingdom.
John 10:7-9
Only by accepting Christ we are saved.
John 10:14-16
Jesus gives his life for us, as he does for all mankind.

066 **New Testament Books Pt.3**
21. 1 Peter
22. 2 Peter
23. 1 John
24. 2 John
25. 3 John
26. Jude
27. Revelation

067 **Genesis 4:9**
2 Samuel 24:17
Luke 17:1

SOLUTIONS

068 1. AND THE PEACE OF GOD, WHICH SURPASSES ALL UNDERSTANDING, WILL GUARD YOUR HEARTS AND MINDS IN CHRIST JESUS. –Philippians 4:7

2. DO NOT BE AFRAID OR DISCOURAGED, FOR THE LORD YOUR GOD IS WITH YOU WHEREVER YOU GO. –Joshua 1:9

3. ...THOSE WHO TRUST THE LORD WILL RENEW THEIR STRENGTH; THEY WILL SOAR ON WINGS LIKE EAGLES... –Isaiah 40:31

4. ALL SCRIPTURE IS INSPIRED BY GOD AND IS PROFITABLE FOR TEACHING, FOR REBUKING, FOR CORRECTING, FOR TRAINING IN RIGHTEOUSNESS... –2 Timothy 3:16

069 "When Joshua was near Jericho, he looked up and saw a man standing in front of him with a drawn sword in his hand. Joshua approached him and asked, 'Are you for us or for our enemies?'

'Neither', he replied. **'Don't let your heart be troubled. Believe in God; believe also in me.'**

The Joshua bowed with his face to the ground in worship and asked him, 'What does my lord want to say to his servant?'"

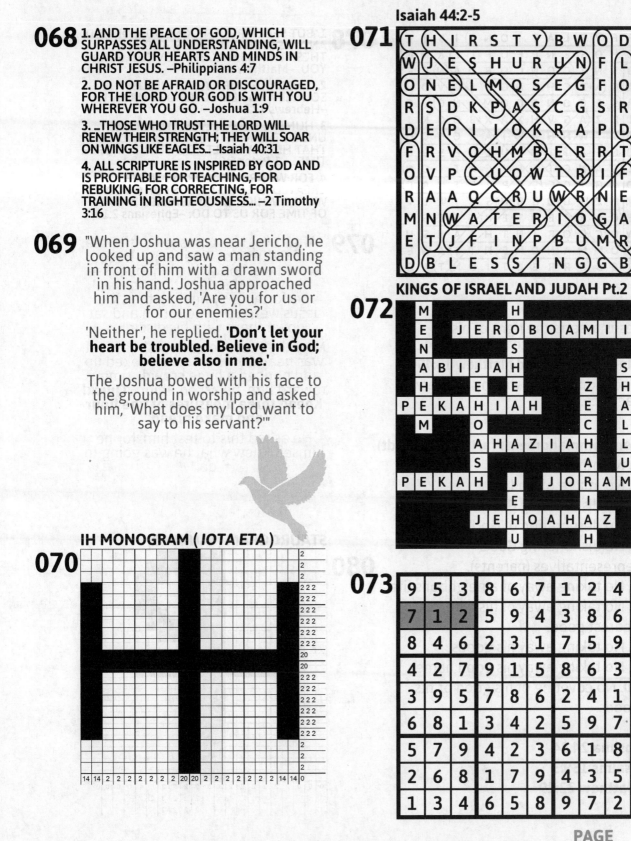

071 Isaiah 44:2-5

KINGS OF ISRAEL AND JUDAH Pt.2

072

070 IH MONOGRAM (*IOTA ETA*)

073

SOLUTIONS

074

```
R E V E L A T I O N S I S I L
C H O S E N P E O P L E K M N
B S N T C O N C O R D A N C E
A G A R C H A N G E L O V O M
R S E C O N D C O M I N G T C
T D Z A G V H X A X B D G K J
H T T W N H R P I A K C N C U
O G F A I T H F U L N E S S E
L S A N C T I F I C A T I O N
O J G J C C S C R I P T U R E
M M Z W U U G B H S A I W L V
E C A R P E N T E R C K Z S B
W O C C O R I N T H I A N S H
C O M M A N D M E N T S A W E
R E S U R R E C T I O N T W C
```

075 Luke 5:34-35
Jesus asserts the right of his disciples to rejoice in his presence.
Matthew 13:44 and Matthew 13:45-46
God's kingdom is worthy of every sacrifice.

076 **Ten Commandments (a/t C.E. Luthardt)**
1. No other gods.
2. No image of God.
3. No dishonoring God's name.
4. No desecration of God's day.
5. No dishonoring God's representatives (parents).
6. No taking away of a neighbor's life.
7. No taking away of his wife, his dearest good.
8. No taking away his goods.
9. No taking away his good name.
10. No coveting of his good or his goods.

077 **Joshua 24:24**
Psalms 139:3
Matthew 22:29

078 1. BUT SEEK FIRST THE KINGDOM OF GOD AND HIS RIGHTEOUSNESS, AND ALL THESE THINGS WILL BE PROVIDED FOR YOU. –Matthew 6:33

2. ... KEEPING OUR EYES ON JESUS, THE SOURCE AND PERFECTER OF OUR FAITH. –Hebrews 12:2

3. HUMBLE YOURSELVES, THEREFORE, UNDER THE MIGHTY HAND OF GOD, SO THAT HE MAY EXALT YOU AT THE PROPER TIME... –1 Peter 5:6

4. FOR WE ARE HIS WORKMANSHIP, CREATED IN CHRIST JESUS FOR GOOD WORKS, WHICH GOD PREPARED AHEAD OF TIME FOR US TO DO. –Ephesians 2:10

079 "After this, Jesus crossed to the sea of Galilee (or Tiberias). A huge crowd was following him because they saw the signs that he was performing by healing the sick. Jesus went up a mountain and sat down there with his disciples.

Now the Passover, a Jewish festival, was near. So when Jesus looked up and noticed a huge crowd coming toward him, he asked Philip, **'Quick! Knead three measures of fine flour and make bread.'**

He asked this to test him, for he himself knew what he was going to do."

080 **STAUROGRAM (TAU-RHO)**

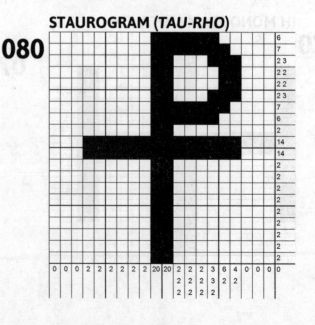

SOLUTIONS

Philippians 3:4-6

081
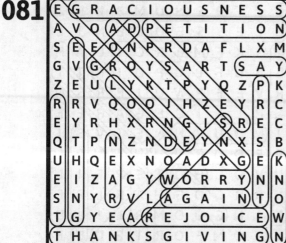

KINGS OF JUDAH

082
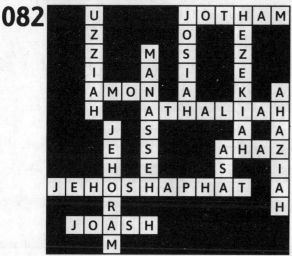

083

084

085 **Luke 14:7-10**

"For everyone who exalts himself will be humbled, and the one who humbles himself will be exalted."

Matthew 13:52

Doubly rich is the learned man who is willing to humble himself to learn God's Word.

086 **Bible resurrections**

1. Widow of Zarephath's son, by Elijah (1 Kings 17:22).

2. Shunammite woman's son, by Elisha (2 Kings 4:34-35).

3. Man raised after touching Elisha's bones (2 Kings 13:20-21).

4. Widow of Nain's son, by Jesus (Luke 7:14-15).

5. Jairus' daughter, by Jesus (Luke 8:52-56).

6. Lazarus after three days, by Jesus (John 11:43-44).

7. Jesus Himself (all four Gospels).

8. Many holy people after Jesus died on the cross (Matthew 27:52).

9. Dorcas, by Peter (Acts 9:40).

10. Eutychus, by Paul (Acts 20:9-12).

087 **Genesis 37:35**

Exodus 15:18

Psalms 68:1

SOLUTIONS

088   1. NO TEMPTATION HAS COME UPON YOU EXCEPT WHAT IS COMMON TO HUMANITY. –1 Corinthians 10:13

2. COME TO ME, ALL OF YOU WHO ARE WEARY AND BURDENED, AND I WILL GIVE YOU REST. –Matthew 11:28

3. NOW FAITH IS THE REALITY OF WHAT IS HOPED FOR, THE PROOF OF WHAT IS NOT SEEN. –Hebrews 11:1

4. THEREFORE, IF ANYONE IS IN CHRIST, HE IS A NEW CREATION; THE OLD HAS PASSED AWAY, AND SEE, THE NEW HAS COME! –2 Corinthians 5:17

089   "When they had crossed over, Elijah said to Elisha, 'Tell me what I can do for you before I am taken from you.' So Elisha answered, 'Please, let me inherit two shares of your spirit.' Elijah replied, 'You have asked for something difficult. **If anyone wants to follow me, let him deny himself, take up his cross daily, and follow me.'** As they continued walking and talking, a chariot of fire with horses of fire suddenly appeared and separated the two of them. Then Elijah went up into heaven in the whirlwind. As Elisha watched, he kept crying out, 'My father, my father, the chariots and horsemen of Israel!'"

"JESUS FISH" (ICHTHYS OR ICHTHUS)

090

091 Matthew 5:3-8

092 JUDGES OF ISRAEL

093

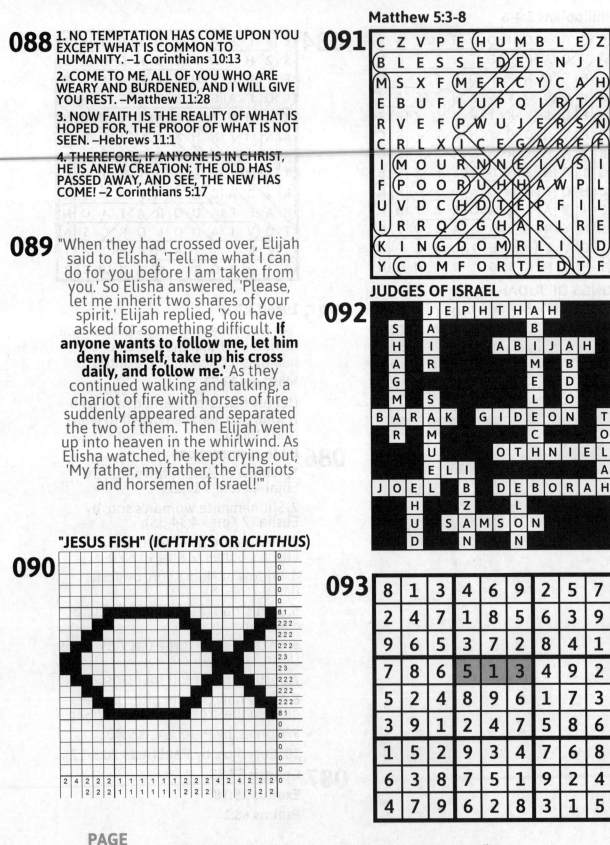

SOLUTIONS

094

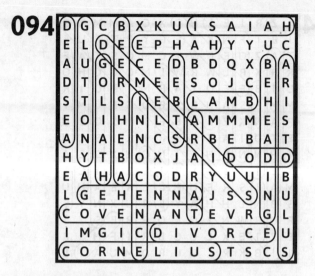

095 Matthew 20:1-16

No Christian is above another, as the reward for those who believe is the same.

Matthew 13:57

Men of God are least recognized as such by those closest to them.

096 What Jesus said on the cross

1. "Father, forgive them, because they do not know what they are doing." (Luke 23:34)

2. "Truly I tell you, today you will be with me in paradise." (Luke 23:43)

3. "Woman, here is your son." "Here is your mother." (John 19:26-27)

4. "Eli, Eli, lema sabachthani?" (Matthew 27:46)

5. "I'm thirsty." (John 19:28)

6. "It is finished." (John 19:30)

7. "Father, into your hands I entrust my spirit." (Luke 23:46)

097 Ecclesiastes 5:10
Mark 1:25
Luke 23:18

098
1. KEEP YOUR LIFE FREE FROM THE LOVE OF MONEY. –Hebrews 13:5

2. MY GRACE IS SUFFICIENT FOR YOU, FOR MY POWER IS PERFECTED IN WEAKNESS. –2 Corinthians 12:9

3. IF YOU CONFESS WITH YOUR MOUTH, "JESUS IS LORD", AND BELIEVE IN YOUR HEART THAT GOD RAISED HIM FROM THE DEAD, YOU WILL BE SAVED. –Romans 10:9

4. DO NOT FEAR, FOR I AM WITH YOU; DO NOT BE AFRAID, FOR I AM YOUR GOD. –Isaiah 41:10

099
"When Herod was about to bring him out for trial, that very night Peter, bound with two chains, was sleeping between two soldiers, while the sentries in front of the door guarded the prison. Suddenly an angel of the Lord appeared, and a light shone in the cell. Striking Peter on the side, he woke him up and said, 'Quick, get up!' And the chains fell off his wrists. 'Get dressed,' the angel told him, 'and put on your sandals.' And he did. **'The LORD is with you, valiant warrior'** he told him. So he went out and followed, and he did not know that what the angel did was really happening, but thought he was seeing a vision."

100 IHS CHRISTOGRAM (*IOTA ETA SIGMA*)

SOLUTIONS

Psalms 25:4-7

101

N	B	O	J	A	O	C	F	A	I	T	H	F	U	L
A	Y	Q	F	V	P	Q	K	P	A	T	H	S	D	T
N	V	I	N	M	S	X	N	A	U	F	E	Z	I	F
C	O	M	P	A	S	S	I	O	N	R	V	A	G	Y
F	U	T	D	K	G	R	Y	K	N	O	W	N	C	X
C	L	V	R	M	L	I	C	O	E	L	Z	A	S	H
X	R	E	B	E	L	L	I	O	N	E	S	R	Y	Q
F	Q	S	U	T	M	T	O	N	O	T	P	T	P	S
X	C	Y	C	M	A	E	C	R	W	J	I	I	S	V
R	J	T	W	V	P	B	M	M	B	U	O	E	N	W
A	P	A	L	O	V	E	P	B	O	O	N	A	R	G
B	A	A	O	V	Y	I	Q	I	E	D	U	K	K	N
C	S	H	R	T	R	U	T	H	O	R	S	S	H	O
H	E	E	D	O	A	N	S	O	L	N	Z	H	S	H
G	A	W	G	C	A	C	G	U	I	D	E	J	B	Z

104

A	Z	R	I	E	L	H	D	X	C	A	M	M	Y	S
J	B	T	F	N	X	A	E	G	Y	P	T	F	U	F
T	A	Z	O	E	D	W	Y	C	M	O	S	T	A	F
R	U	I	X	R	L	W	R	W	L	M	Q	C	H	O
M	M	R	B	E	E	Q	T	A	R	M	I	P	I	R
P	A	M	E	S	A	U	B	I	B	D	G	E	M	T
A	N	K	Z	E	S	B	E	J	M	S	O	L	U	N
E	T	O	I	A	X	O	N	R	T	C	I	S	O	A
T	H	N	N	R	H	E	I	N	O	H	X	S	C	T
X	E	I	I	T	B	X	R	I	E	E	M	E	H	U
M	A	I	S	R	E	U	H	C	L	C	R	E	Y	S
S	B	N	L	H	H	A	Y	E	U	X	N	T	I
R	U	R	W	N	Y	G	K	Q	G	B	E	S	T
E	Z	I	E	X	L	U	Q	B	R	I	F	H	S	R
J	B	K	P	L	U	U	R	Q	M	U	A	I	L

OLDEST PEOPLE

102

K	E	N	A	N					
	N			O					
	O			A	D	A	M		L
S	E	T	H		A				A
					H				M
			E		A	J	A	R	E	D
			N		L				C
			O		A				H
			C		L				
M	E	T	H	U	S	E	L	A	H

103

1	2	8	3	9	5	7	4	6
7	4	3	6	8	1	5	9	2
5	9	6	2	4	7	8	1	3
9	1	7	8	2	3	6	5	4
2	6	5	1	7	4	3	8	9
3	8	4	9	5	6	1	2	7
4	5	1	7	3	2	9	6	8
6	7	9	4	1	8	2	3	5
8	3	2	5	6	9	4	7	1

105 **Mark 12:1-12**

Evil and the rejection of God's truth brings upon itself its own destruction.

Luke 14:31-33

Unless we humble ourselves before God and detach ourselves from possessions, we won't be able follow His Son.

106 **Seven Sacraments of the Catholic Church**

1. Baptism
2. Confirmation
3. Holy Communion
4. Confession
5. Marriage
6. Holy Orders
7. Anointing of the Sick

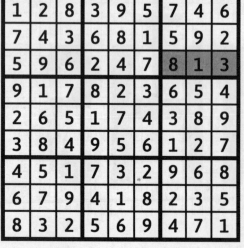

107 **Judges 4:9**
Job 13:3
Acts 9:40

SOLUTIONS

108
1. LET US MAKE MAN IN OUR IMAGE, ACCORDING TO OUR LIKENESS. –Genesis 1:26

2. TAKE UP MY YOKE AND LEARN FROM ME, BECAUSE I AM LOWLY AND HUMBLE IN HEART, AND YOU WILL FIND REST FOR YOUR SOULS. –Matthew 11:29

3. I HAVE TOLD YOU THESE THINGS SO THAT IN ME YOU MAY HAVE PEACE. –John 16:33

4. IT IS NOT FOR YOU TO KNOW TIMES OR PERIODS THAT THE FATHER HAS SET BY HIS OWN AUTHORITY. –Acts 1:7

109
"At dawn he went to the temple again, and all the people were coming to him. He sat down and began to teach them.

Then the scribes and the Pharisees brought a woman caught in adultery, making her stand in the center. 'Teacher,' they said to Him, 'this woman was caught in the act of committing adultery. In the law Moses commanded us to stone such women. So what do you say?' They asked this to trap him, in order that they might have evidence to accuse Him.

Jesus stooped down and started writing on the ground with his finger. When they persisted in questioning him, he stood up and said to them, 'The one without sin among you should be the first to throw a stone at her.'

Then he stooped down again and continued writing on the ground. When they heard this, they left one by one, starting with the older men. Only he was left, with the woman in the center. When Jesus stood up, he said to her, **'Rise, plead your case before the mountains, and let the hills hear your complaint.'"**

110 *(IESVS NAZARENVS REX IVDÆORVM)*

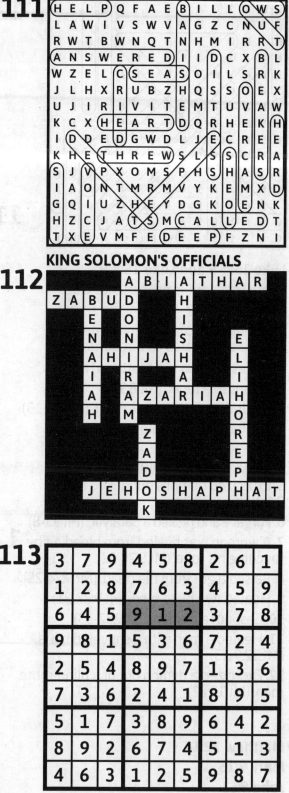

111 Jonah 2:2-4

KING SOLOMON'S OFFICIALS

112

113

BIBLE POWER PUZZLES

SOLUTIONS

114

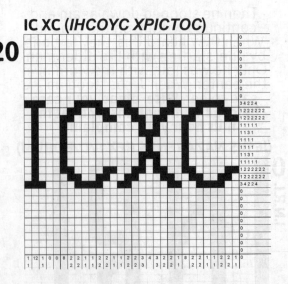

115 **Luke 15:4-6 and Luke 15:8-9**

Every lost soul is precious to God.

Matthew 13:47-48

The kingdom of heaven is open to all, but also holds us accountable.

116 **Miracles of Jesus (a/t Matthew) Pt.1**

1. Cleansed a leper. (Mt 8:3)

2. Healed a centurion's servant. (Mt 8:5-13)

3. Healed many people and cast out demons. (Mt 8:14-17)

4. Calmed the windstorm. (Mt 8:23-27)

5. Exorcized demons out of two men. (Matthew 8:28-34)

6. Forgave and healed a paralytic. (Mt 9:1-8)

7. A woman was healed from bleeding by touching his robe. (Mt 9:20-22)

8. Raised a girl from the dead. (Mt 9:24-25)

9. Healed two blind men. (Mt 9:27-31)

10. Cast out a demon. (Mt 9:32-33)

11. Healed a man with a shriveled hand. (Mt 12:9-13)

12. Exorcized a demon out of a blind-mute man. (Mt 12:22)

117 **Matthew 22:14**

Mark 7:15

John 8:51

118 1. FOR GOD HAS NOT GIVEN US A SPIRIT OF FEAR, BUT ONE OF POWER, LOVE, AND SOUND JUDGEMENT. –2 Timothy 1:7

2. YET HE HIMSELF BORE OUR SICKNESS, AND HE CARRIED OUR PAINS... –Isaiah 53:4

3. HE MADE THE ONE WHO DID NOT KNOW SIN TO BE SIN FOR US, SO THAT IN HIM WE MIGHT BECOME THE RIGHTEOUSNESS OF GOD. –2 Corinthians 5:21

4. NOW MAY THE GOD OF HOPE FILL YOU WITH ALL JOY AND PEACE AS YOU BELIEVE SO THAT YOU MAY OVERFLOW WITH HOPE... –Romans 15:13

119 "She placed the child in it and set it among the reeds by the bank of the Nile. Then his sister stood at a distance in order to see what would happen to him.

Pharaoh's daughter went down to bathe at the Nile while her servant girls walked along the riverbank. She saw the basket among the reeds, sent her slave girl, took it, opened it, and saw him, the child— and there he was, a little boy, crying.

The child grew up and became spiritually strong, and he was in the wilderness until the day of his public appearance to Israel."

120 **IC XC (*IHCOYC XPICTOC*)**

SOLUTIONS

Psalms 38:1-4

121

KING SOLOMON'S DEPUTIES

122
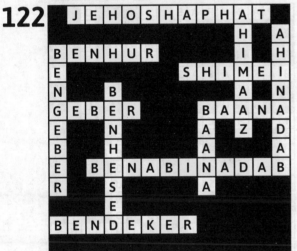

123

9	2	7	8	6	1	3	4	5
3	5	6	4	7	9	2	1	8
4	1	8	5	3	2	9	7	6
2	7	5	3	1	8	4	6	9
1	8	9	2	4	6	7	5	3
6	4	3	9	5	7	8	2	1
7	3	4	1	9	5	6	8	2
5	9	2	6	8	4	1	3	7
8	6	1	7	2	3	5	9	4

124
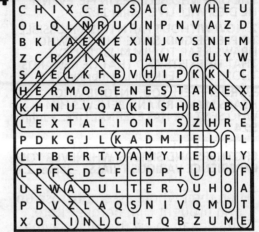

125 Matthew 22:2-14

Since the arrogant won't accept God's Truth, He has opened an invitation to everyone else; but in order to be accepted, we must also live the faith.

Luke 18:10-13

"... everyone who exalts himself will be humbled, but the one who humbles himself will be exalted." –Luke 18:14

126 Miracles of Jesus (a/t Matthew) Pt.2

13. Fed 5,000. (Mt 14:13-21)

14. Walked on water. (Mt 14:22-32)

15. Many healed by touching the end of his robe. (Mt 14:34-36)

16. Cast a demon out of a Canaanite woman's daughter. (Mt 15:21-28)

17. Healed crowds. (Mt 15:29-31)

18. Fed 4,000. (Mt 15:32-39)

19. Transfigured in front of Peter, James, and John. (Mt 17:1-9)

20. Cast a demon out of an epileptic boy. (Mt 17:14-18)

21. Healed two blind men (Mt 20:29-34)

22. Withered a fig tree. (Mt 21:18-22)

23. Resurrected! (Mt 28:1-10)

127 Deuteronomy 11:26-28
1 Samuel 12:2
John 18:38

SOLUTIONS

128 1. I AM THE RESURRECTION AND THE LIFE. THE ONE WHO BELIEVES IN ME, EVEN IF HE DIES, WILL LIVE. –John 11:25

2. NOW WITHOUT FAITH IT IS IMPOSSIBLE TO PLEASE GOD, SINCE THE ONE WHO DRAWS NEAR TO HIM MUST BELIEVE THAT HE EXISTS AND THAT HE REWARDS THOSE WHO SEEK HIM. –Hebrews 11:6

3. TRULY I TELL YOU, ANYONE WHO HEARS MY WORD AND BELIEVES HIM WHO SENT ME HAS ETERNAL LIFE... –John 5:24

4. CONSIDER IT A GREAT JOY, MY BROTHERS AND SISTERS, WHENEVER YOU EXPERIENCE VARIOUS TRIALS... –James 1:2

129 "Then their whole assembly rose up and brought Him before Pilate. They began to accuse Him, saying, 'We found this man misleading our nation, opposing payment of taxes to Caesar, and saying that He Himself is the Messiah, a king.'

So Pilate asked Him, 'Are You the King of the Jews?' He answered him, 'You say so.'

Pilate then told the chief priests and the crowds, **'No one will be executed this day, for today the LORD has provided deliverance in Israel.'**

But they kept insisting, 'He stirs up the people, teaching throughout all Judea, from Galilee where He started even to here.'"

130

STAR OF DAVID

Luke 5:34-36

131

PAUL'S MISSIONARY COMPANIONS

132

133

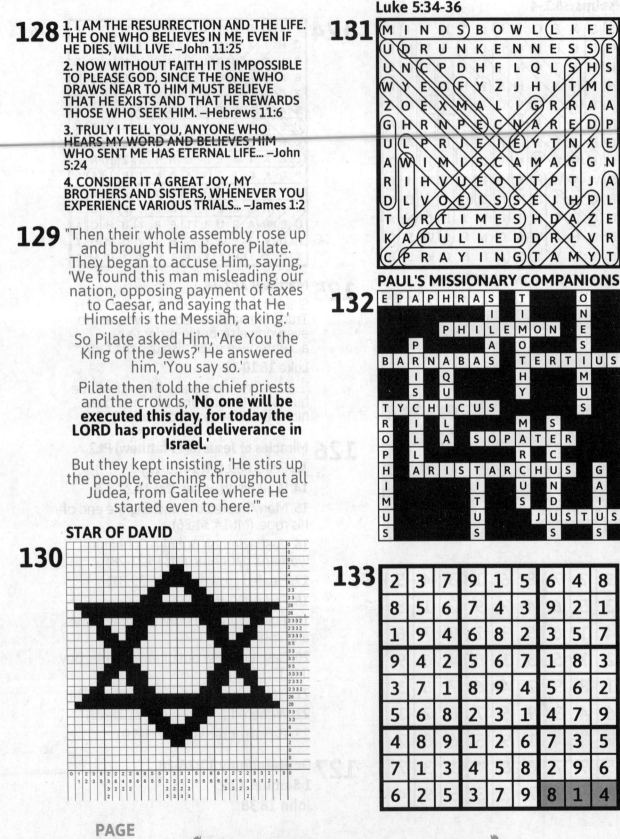

SOLUTIONS

134

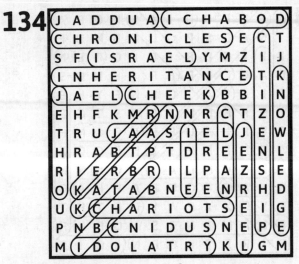

```
J A D D U A  I C H A B O D   E  C  T
C H R O N I C L E S   E     I  J
S F I S R A E L Y M Z     T  J
I N H E R I T A N C E     I  K
J A E L  C H E E K  B B   Z  N
E H F K M R N N R C T     E  O
T R U J A A S I E L J     N  W
H R A B T P T D R E A     S  L
R I E R B R I L P A Z     H  E
O K A T A B N E E N R     I  D
U K C H A R I O T S E     P  G
P N B C N I D U S N E        E
M I D O L A T R Y K L G    M
```

135 Luke 15:11-32

God's mercy towards those who sincerely regret and learn from their mistakes knows no bounds; yet those who have remained close to Him have no need to envy the Father's love for those who repent.

136 Miracles of Jesus (a/t Mark) Pt.1

1. Cast out a demon. (Mk 1:23-26)

2. Healed Simon's mother-in-law. (Mk 1:30-31)

3. Healed many people and cast out demons. (Mk 1:32-34)

4. Cleansed a leper. (Mk 1:40-42)

5. Forgave and healed a paralytic. (Mk 2:1-12)

6. Healed a man with a shriveled hand. (Mk 3:1-5)

7. Calmed the windstorm. (Mk 4:35-40)

8. Cast many demons ("Legion") out of one man. (Mk 5:1-15)

9. A woman was healed from bleeding by touching his robe. (Mk 5:25-34)

10. Raised Jairus' daughter from the dead. (Mk 5:35-42)

11. Fed 5,000. (Mk 6:30-44)

137 1 Samuel 3:10

Ezra 9:5

Luke 3:11

138 1. SO GOD CREATED MAN IN HIS OWN IMAGE... –Genesis 1:27

2. THEREFORE, AS GOD'S CHOSEN ONES, HOLUY AND DEARLY LOVED, PUT ON COMPASSION, KINDNESS, HUMILITY, GENTLENESS, AND PATIENCE... –Colossians 3:12

3. LET US RUN WITH ENDURANCE THE RACE THAT LIES BEFORE US, KEEPING OUR EYES ON JESUS... –Hebrews 12:1

4. THEREFORE CONFESS YOUR SINS TO ONE ANOTHER AND PRAY FOR ONE ANOTHER, SO THAT YOU MAY BE HEALED. –James 5:16

139 "The Lord hates six things; in fact, seven are detestable to him: arrogant eyes, a lying tongue, hands that shed innocent blood, a heart that plots wicked schemes, feet eager to run to evil, a lying witness who gives false testimony, and one who stirs up trouble among brothers.

Let no one deceive you with empty arguments, for God's wrath is coming to the disobedient because of these things.

Therefore, do not become their partners. For you were once darkness, but now you are light in the Lord."

THE TORAH

140

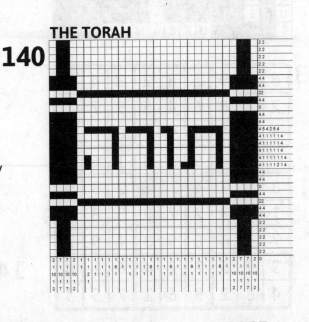

SOLUTIONS

Joshua 23:14-15

141

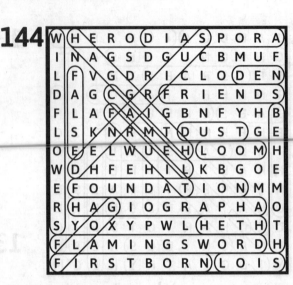

```
R G F U L F I L L E D S E
S I N C E U W R Z Z E L E
Y K E W U T A T H D O F H
M F P T H I N G A H S A A
R I Z L W A N M W E O I X
N Y P R O M I S E X R L G
E V E R Y T H I N G P E O
T M Q W P V I O Z K H D I
T T Q A Y G L D R G O D N
P N N N Y O O A B O U T Z G
F B O I U O T S O U L I W
Y K N O W D E E A R T H J
A H E A R T D J S G O B N
```

PAUL'S SUPPORTERS

142

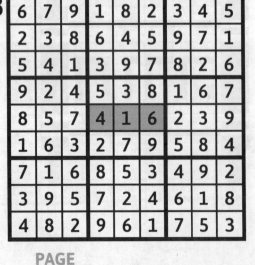

```
E R A S T U S           O
      Y       J   A     N
  E   R       U   R     E
  P   A N D R O N I C U S
J A S O N   E   I   H   I
  P       N Y M P H A   P
  H       U   A     I   H
  R       S   S     P   O
  O               P   R
  D                   U
L Y D I A       C A R P U S
U       T       P     S
C       I     P H O E B E
I       U     H
U       S     I
S       U R B A N U S
```

Luke 16:19-31

145

Beware the dangers stemming from the attachment to riches and the lifestyle they buy.

Luke 17:7-10

Let us fulfill our duties in the most humble way, for we are nothing without Christ.

144

```
W H E R O D I A S P O R A
I N A G S D G U C B M U F
L F V G D R I C L O D E N
D A G C G R F R I E N D S
F L A F A I G B N F Y H B
L S K N R M T D U S T G E
O E E L W U E H L O O M H
W D H F E H I K B G O E
E F O U N D A T I O N M M
R H A G I O G R A P H A O
S Y O X Y P W L H E T H T
F L A M I N G S W O R D H
F I R S T B O R N L O I S
```

146 Miracles of Jesus (a/t Mark) Pt.2

12. Walked on water. (Mk 6:45-52)

13. Many healed by touching the end of his robe. (Mk 6:53-56)

14. Cast a demon out of a Gentile woman's daughter. (Mk 7:24-30)

15. Healed a deaf, speech-impaired man. (Mk 7:32-37)

16. Fed 4,000. (Mk 8:1-9)

17. Healed a blind man. (Mk 8:22-26)

18. Transfigured in front of Peter, James, and John. (Mk 9:2-10)

19. Cast a demon out of an epileptic boy. (Mk 9:17-29)

20. Healed a blind beggar. (Mk 10:46-52)

21. Withered a fig tree. (Mk 11:12-14)

22. Resurrected! (Mk 16:1-13)

143

6	7	9	1	8	2	3	4	5
2	3	8	6	4	5	9	7	1
5	4	1	3	9	7	8	2	6
9	2	4	5	3	8	1	6	7
8	5	7	4	1	6	2	3	9
1	6	3	2	7	9	5	8	4
7	1	6	8	5	3	4	9	2
3	9	5	7	2	4	6	1	8
4	8	2	9	6	1	7	5	3

147 Luke 17:19
John 2:5
Acts 10:15

SOLUTIONS

148 1. WE ALL WENT ASTRAY LIKE SHEEP; WE ALL HAVE TURNED TO OUR OWN WAY; AND THE LORD HAS PUNISHED HIM FOR THE INIQUITY OF US ALL. –Isaiah 53:6

2. REPENT AND BE BAPTIZED, EACH OF YOU, IN THE NAME OF JESUS CHRIST FOR THE FORGIVENESS OF OUR SINS... –Acts 2:38

3. HE EXERCISED HIS POWER IN CHRIST BY RAISING HIM FROM THE DEAD AND SEATING HIM AT HIS RIGHT IN THE HEAVENS... –Ephesians 3:20

4. FOR MY YOKE IS EASY AND MY BURDEN IS LIGHT. –Matthew 11:30

149 "On the third day a wedding took place in Cana of Galilee. Jesus' mother was there, and Jesus and his disciples were invited to the wedding as well. When the wine ran out, Jesus' mother told Him, 'They don't have any wine.' 'What has this concern of yours to do with you and me, woman?' Jesus asked. 'My hour has not yet come.'

'How long are you going to be drunk? Get rid of your wine!' his mother told the servants.

Now six stone water jars had been set there for Jewish purification. Each contained twenty or thirty gallons.

'Fill the jars with water,' Jesus told them. So they filled them to the brim."

YAHWEH

150

Revelation 22:14-15

151

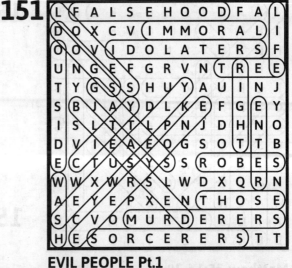

EVIL PEOPLE Pt.1

152

153

SOLUTIONS

154

```
I E A R T H Q U A K E Q S
Z B R B D F I C O N I U M
P D L E V A N G E L I S T
J P U E F E R R Y B O A T
F U R N A C E S G G K K B
G E H G L M L T R A T E C
G A M A L I E L E A F L G
C S L L O F C J E L G O O
W T G L W K G R K N O A S
W A L O I X G J O Y H M H
A T C S F R E E D M A N N
D E C C L E S I A S T E S
```

155 Matthew 25:14-30

God will hold us accountable over the gifts He bestowed upon us, regardless how many, by the use we give them and the fruit we bear.

156 Miracles of Jesus (a/t Luke) Pt.1

1. Cast out a demon. (Lk 4:33-35)

2. Healed Simon's mother-in-law. (Lk 4:38-39)

3. Healed many people and cast out demons. (Lk 4:40-41)

4. Made Simon Peter catch a large number of fish. (Lk 5:4-7)

5. Cleaned a leper. (Lk 5:12-14)

6. Forgave and healed a paralytic. (Lk 5:17-26)

7. Healed a man with a shriveled hand. (Lk 6:6-10)

8. Healed many people and cast out demons. (Lk 6:17-19)

9. Healed a centurion's servant. (Lk 7:1-10)

10. Raised a widow's son from the dead. (Lk 7:11-15)

11. Calmed the windstorm. (Lk 8:22-25)

12. Cast many demons ("Legion") out of one man. (Lk 8:26-33)

157 Acts 9:4

Acts 9:34

Acts 13:10

158 1. ...SINCE THEY RECEIVED THE WORD WITH EAGERNESS AND EXAMINED THE SCRIPTURES DAILY TO SEE IF THESE THINGS WERE SO. –Acts 17:11

2. AND MY GOD WILL SUPPLY ALL YOUR NEEDS ACCORDING TO HIS RICHES IN GLORY IN CHRIST JESUS. –Philippians 4:19

3. IN THE BEGINNING WAS THE WORD, AND THE WORD WAS WITH GOD, AND THE WORD WAS GOD. –John 1:1

4. DO YOU NOT KNOW THAT YOUR BODY IS A TEMPLE OF THE HOLY SPIRIT, WHO IS IN YOU, WHOM YOU HAVE RECEIVED FROM GOD? –1 Corinthians 6:19

159 "Absalom was riding on his mule when he happened to meet David's soldiers. When the mule went under the tangled branches of a large oak tree, Absalom's head was caught fast in the tree. The mule under him kept going, so he was suspended in midair. One of the men saw him and informed Joab.

He said, 'I just saw Absalom hanging in an oak tree!' 'You just saw him!' Joab exclaimed. 'Why didn't you strike him to the ground right there? I would have given you ten silver pieces and a belt!' The man replied to Joab, 'Even if I had te weight of a thousand pieces of silver in my hand, I would not raise my hand against the king's son.' **So he threw the silver into the temple and departed.**"

MENORAH

160

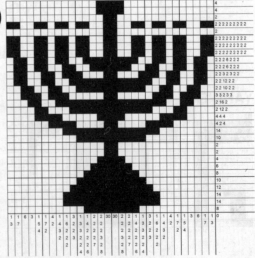

BIBLE POWER PUZZLES

SOLUTIONS

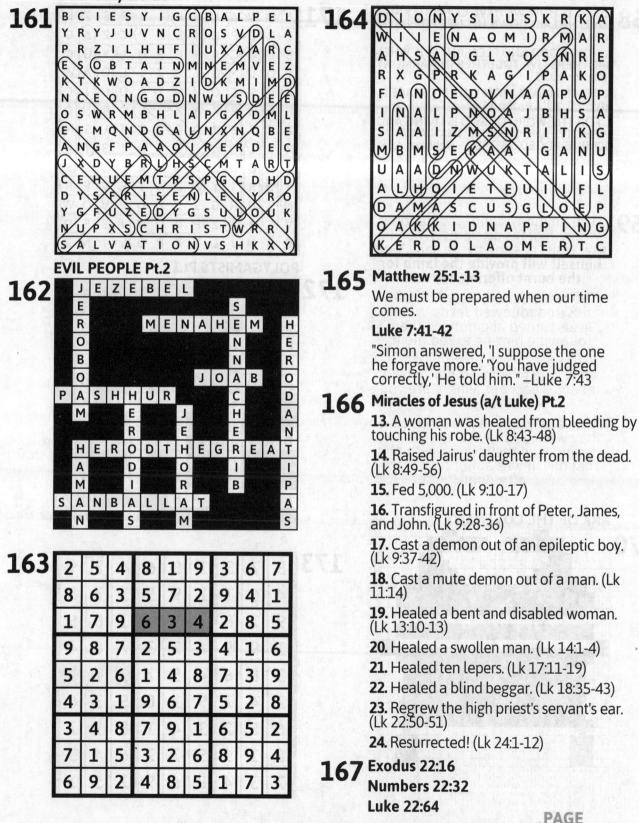

2 Timothy 2:8-10

161

EVIL PEOPLE Pt.2

162

163

164

165 **Matthew 25:1-13**

We must be prepared when our time comes.

Luke 7:41-42

"Simon answered, 'I suppose the one he forgave more.' 'You have judged correctly,' He told him." –Luke 7:43

166 **Miracles of Jesus (a/t Luke) Pt.2**

13. A woman was healed from bleeding by touching his robe. (Lk 8:43-48)

14. Raised Jairus' daughter from the dead. (Lk 8:49-56)

15. Fed 5,000. (Lk 9:10-17)

16. Transfigured in front of Peter, James, and John. (Lk 9:28-36)

17. Cast a demon out of an epileptic boy. (Lk 9:37-42)

18. Cast a mute demon out of a man. (Lk 11:14)

19. Healed a bent and disabled woman. (Lk 13:10-13)

20. Healed a swollen man. (Lk 14:1-4)

21. Healed ten lepers. (Lk 17:11-19)

22. Healed a blind beggar. (Lk 18:35-43)

23. Regrew the high priest's servant's ear. (Lk 22:50-51)

24. Resurrected! (Lk 24:1-12)

167 **Exodus 22:16**
Numbers 22:32
Luke 22:64

SOLUTIONS

168
1. THIS IS HOW WE HAVE COME TO KNOW LOVE: HE LAID DOWN HIS LIFE FOR US. –1 John 3:16

2. HOW GOOD AND PLEASANT IT IS WHEN BROTHERS LIVE TOGETHER IN HARMONY! –Psalms 133:1

3. PEACE I LEAVE WITH YOU. MY PEACE I GIVE TO YOU. –John 14:27

4. FOR THE WORD OF GOD IS LIVING AND EFFECTIVE AND SHARPER THAN ANY DOUBLE-EDGED SWORD... –Hebrews 4:12

169
"The next day, John was standing with two of his disciples. When he saw Jesus passing by, he said, **'God himself will provide the lamb for the burnt offering, my son.'**

The two disciples heard him say this and followed Jesus. When Jesus turned and noticed them following him, he asked them, 'What are you looking for?'

They said to Him, 'Rabbi' (which means 'Teacher'), 'where are you staying?'

'Come and you'll see,' he replied. So they went and saw where he was staying, and they stayed with him that day. It was about four in the afternoon."

ARK OF THE COVENANT

170

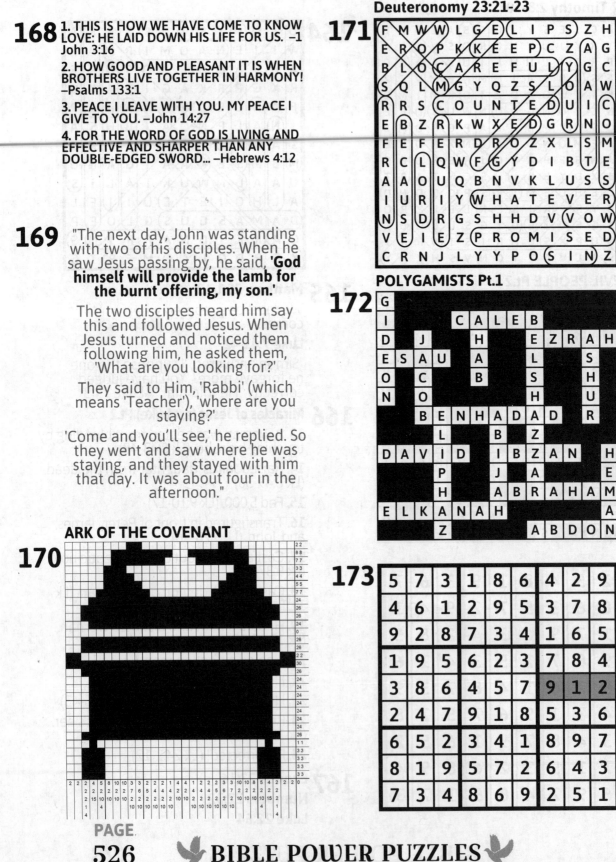

Deuteronomy 23:21-23

171

POLYGAMISTS Pt.1

172

173

SOLUTIONS

174

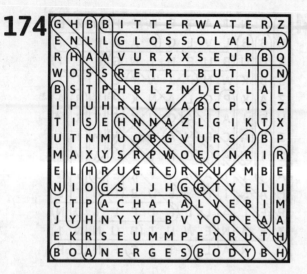

175 **Mark 4: 3-8** explained in **Mark 4: 13-20**

Matthew 21: 28-31 explained in **Matthew 21: 31-32**

Luke 12: 35-36 explained in **Luke 12: 40.**

176 **Miracles of Jesus (a/t John)**

1. Turned water into wine at a wedding. (Jn 2:1-11)

2. Showed knowledge of a woman's sinful life. (Jn 4:16-19)

3. Healed an official's son. (Jn 4:46-54)

4. Healed a disabled man. (Jn 5:1-9)

5. Fed 5,000. (Jn 6:1-14)

6. Walked on water. (Jn 6:16-21)

7. Healed a man born blind. (Jn 9:1-11)

8. Raised Lazarus from the dead. (Jn 11:38-44)

9. Judas and the soldiers fall back. (Jn 18:5-6)

10. Resurrected! (Jn 20:1-18)

11. Gave the apostles a large catch of fish. (Jn 21:1-12)

177 Jeremiah 49:12

Romans 6:15

Philippians 1:21

178 **1.** NO ONE HAS GREATER LOVE THAN THIS: TO LAY DOWN HIS LIFE FOR HIS FRIENDS. –John 15:13

2. MANKIND, HE HAS TOLD EACH OF YOU WHAT IS GOOD AND WHAT IT IS THE LORD REQUIRES OF YOU... –Micah 6:8

3. SO FAITH COMES FROM WHAT IS HEARD, AND WHAT IS HEARD COMES THROUGH THE MESSAGE ABOUT CHRIST. –Romans 10:17

4. BUT TO ALL WHO DID RECEIVE HIM, HE GAVE THEM THE RIGHT TO BE CHILDREN OF GOD... –John 1:12

179 "Just one thing: **With one act of vengeance, let me pay back the Philistines for my two eyes.** Then, whether I come and see you or I am absent, I will hear about you that you are standing firm in one spirit, in one accord, contending together for the faith of the gospel, not being frightened in any way by your opponents. This is a sing of destruction for them, but of your salvation—and this is from God."

DOVE W/ OLIVE BRANCH

180

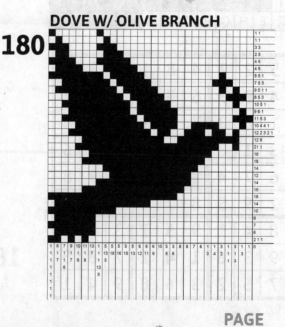

SOLUTIONS

James 4:7-10

181

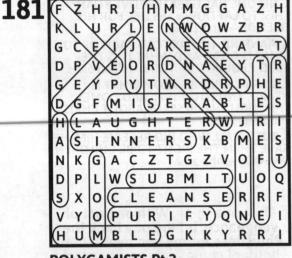

184

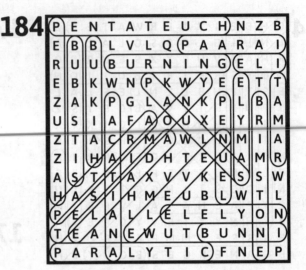

POLYGAMISTS Pt.2

182

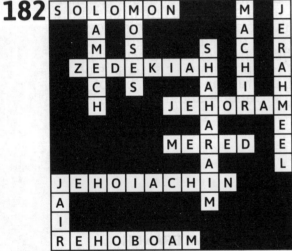

183

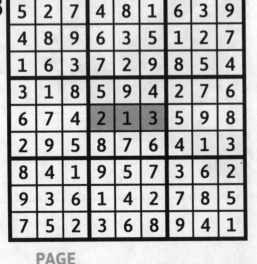

185
Luke 16:1-8 explained in **Luke 16:9-13**
Luke 18:2-5 explained in **Luke 2:6-8**

186 Miracles in the Old Testament Pt.1
1. Creation. (Genesis 1-2).
2. The Flood. (Genesis 7-8)
3. The confusion of tongues. (Genesis 11:1-9)
4. Destruction of Sodom and Gomorrah. (Genesis 19:1-29)
5. Lot's wife turned into a pillar of salt. (Genesis 19:26)
6. Birth of Isaac. (Genesis 21:1-3)
7. The burning bush. (Exodus 3:2-3)
8. Aaron's rod changed into a serpent. (Exodus 7:10-12)
9. The ten plagues of Egypt (Exodus 7: 14-12:32)
10. The Red Sea parted. (Exodus 14:21-22)
11. Waters of Marah sweetened. (Exodus 15:23-25)
12. Manna from heaven. (Exodus 16:14-35)

187 2 Kings 2:21
Isaiah 56:1
Luke 7:50

SOLUTIONS

188
1. BLESSED IS THE ONE WHO ENDURES TRIALS, BECAUSE WHEN HE HAS STOOD THE TEST HE WILL RECEIVE THE CROWN OF LIFE... –James 1:12

2. ... LET US DRAW NEAR WITH A TRUE HEART IN FULL ASSURANCE OF FAITH, WITH OUR HEARTS SPRINKLED CLEAN... –Hebrews 10:22

3. FOR THIS VERY REASON, MAKE EVERY EFFORT TO SUPPLEMENT YOUR FAITH WITH GOODNESS, GOODNESS WITH KNOWLEDGE... –2 Peter 1:5

4. I AM SURE OF THIS, THAT HE WHO STARTED THE GOOD WORK IN YOU WILL CARRY IT ON TO COMPLETION UNTIL THE DAY OF CHRIST JESUS. –Philippians 1:6

189
"Suddenly, a hand touched me and set me shaking to my hands and knees. He said to me, 'Daniel, you are a man treasured by God. Understand the words that I'm saying to you. Stand on your feet, for I have now been sent to you.' After he said this to me, I stood trembling. 'Don't be afraid, Daniel,' he said to me, **'I know your works, your labor, and your endurance, and that you cannot tolerate evil people.** I have come because of your prayers. But the prince of the kingdom of Persia opposed me for twenty-one days. Then Michael, one of the chief princes, came to help me after I had been left there with the kings of Persia. Now I have come to help you understand what will happen to your people in the last days, for the vision refers to those days.'

While he was saying these words to me, I turned my face toward the ground and was speechless."

MACCABEE

190

1 Kings 8:44-45

191

CRAFTSMEN

192

193

8	7	5	6	3	1	9	2	4
4	6	2	5	9	8	1	7	3
1	9	3	7	2	4	6	8	5
9	8	6	3	7	2	5	4	1
2	3	1	8	4	5	7	6	9
5	4	7	1	6	9	2	3	8
3	5	8	2	1	6	4	9	7
6	1	9	4	8	7	3	5	2
7	2	4	9	5	3	8	1	6

SOLUTIONS

194

A	A	P	W	Y	F	U	R	R	O	W	Y	U	S	
F	O	R	K	S	O	R	O	Y	U	O	T	D	D	
Z	Z	T	S	U	R	D	A	U	G	H	T	E	R	
J	A	M	I	N	E	Q	L	H	B	W	N	A	C	
C	O	N	F	E	S	S	I	O	N	O	S	E	I	
J	E	B	U	S	A	C	G	V	K	U	C	S	S	
C	L	A	U	D	I	U	S	R	I	A	I	N	T	
D	X	Y	N	C	L	J	A	R	N	M	O	J	E	
P	A	H	Y	B	S	D	A	R	A	H	N	O	R	
K	R	T	A	Z	N	D	U	M	P	H	E	E	N	
B	K	B	H	M	S	F	L	L	X	S	L	U	U	
U	O	B	Z	A	M	X	A	U	E	E	A	O	M	
J	B	Q	L	N	N	D	C	I	L	I	C	I	A	
C	I	R	C	U	M	C	I	S	I	O	N	H	W	

195 **Matthew 18:23-34** explained in **Matthew 18:35**

196 **Miracles in the Old Testament Pt.2**

13. Water sprouted from a rock. (Exodus 17:5-6)

14. Fire devoured Nadab and Abihu. (Leviticus 10:1-2)

15. People consumed by fire. (Numbers 11:1-3)

16. Miriam contracted leprosy (Numbers 12:10)

17. Korah and company swallowed by the earth. (Numbers 16:31-33)

18. Fire consumed 250. (Numbers 16:35)

19. 14,700 slain by a plague. (Numbers 16:46-50)

20. Aaron's rod budded at Kadesh (Numbers 17:8)

21. Water sprouted from the rock in Zin. (Numbers 20:7-11)

22. The bronze serpent healed the people. (Numbers 21:8-9)

23. Balaam's donkey spoke. (Numbers 22:28-31)

24. Jordan river parted. (Joshua 3:14-17)

197 **Leviticus 12:3**
Daniel 8:24
Revelation 11:15

198 **1.** FOR THE LORD HAS APPOINTED THE BLESSING—LIFE FOREVERMORE. –Psalms 133:3

2. THEREFORE, LET US APPROACH THE THRONE OF GRACE WITH BOLDNESS, SO THAT WE MAY RECEIVE MERCY AND FIND GRACE... –Hebrews 4:16

3. TAKE DELIGHT IN THE LORD AND HE WILL GIVE YOU YOUR HEART'S DESIRES. –Psalms 37:4

4. FOR GOD DID NOT SEND HIS SON INTO THE WORLD TO CONDEMN THE WORLD, BUT TO SAVE THE WORLD THROUGH HIM. –John 3:17

199 "When those around him saw what was going to happen, they asked, 'Lord, should we strike with the sword?' Then one of them struck the high priest's slave and cut off his right ear.

But Jesus responded, 'No more of this!' And touching his ear, He healed him. Then Jesus said to the chief priests, temple police, and the elders who had come for Him, **'You come against me with sword, spear, and javelin, but I come against you in the name of the Lord of Armies, the God of the ranks of Israel—you have defied him.'**"

TABLETS OF THE COVENANT (*LUCHOT HABRIT*)

200

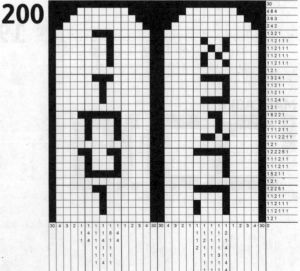

 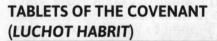

SOLUTIONS

James 5:1-4

201

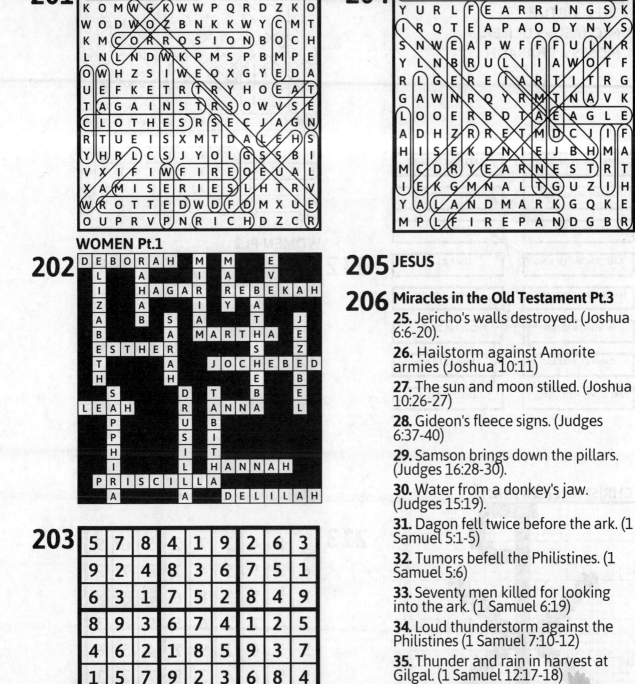

```
W I T H H E L D  P E O P L E  M
K O M W G K W W P Q R D Z K O
W O D W O Z B N K K W Y C M T
K M C O R R O S I O N O O H
L N D W K P M S P B W M P E E
O W H Z S I W E O X G Y E D A
U E F K E T R T R Y H O E A T
T A G A I N S T R S O W V S E
C L O T H E S R S E C J A G N
R T U E I S X M T D A L E H
Y H R L C S J Y O L G S S I
V X I F I W F I R E O E U A L
X A M I S E R I E S L H T R V
W R O T T E D W D F D M X U E
O U P R V P N R I C H D Z C R
```

WOMEN Pt.1

202

```
D E B O R A H    M    M      E
  L          A    I    A      V
  I        H A G A R    R E B E K A H
  Z          B    S    A    T    J
  A          B    A R    T    E
  B          S A R A    M A R T H A    E
  E S T H E R    A    S      Z
  T          A    J O C H E B E D
  H          H    E      B
    S        D    E      E
  L E A H    R    B      L
    A        U    T
    P        S    I
    P        I    L
    H        L    L    H A N N A H
    I        L    A
  P R I S C I L L A
    A          A    D E L I L A H
```

203

5	7	8	4	1	9	2	6	3
9	2	4	8	3	6	7	5	1
6	3	1	7	5	2	8	4	9
8	9	3	6	7	4	1	2	5
4	6	2	1	8	5	9	3	7
1	5	7	9	2	3	6	8	4
3	1	6	5	9	8	4	7	2
2	4	9	3	6	7	5	1	8
7	8	5	2	4	1	3	9	6

204

```
I N T E R P R E T A T I O N
Y U R L F E A R R I N G S K
I R Q T E A P A O D Y N Y S
S N W E A P W F F U I N R
Y L N B R U L I I A W O T F
R L G E R E I A R T I T R G
L A W N R Q Y R M T N A V K
L O O E R R E T M D C I F
A D H Z R R E T M D C I F
H I S E K D N I E J B H M A
M C D R Y E A R N E S T R T
I E K G M N A L T G U Z I H
Y A L A N D M A R K G Q K E
M P L F I R E P A N D G B R
```

205 JESUS

206 Miracles in the Old Testament Pt.3

25. Jericho's walls destroyed. (Joshua 6:6-20).

26. Hailstorm against Amorite armies (Joshua 10:11)

27. The sun and moon stilled. (Joshua 10:26-27)

28. Gideon's fleece signs. (Judges 6:37-40)

29. Samson brings down the pillars. (Judges 16:28-30).

30. Water from a donkey's jaw. (Judges 15:19).

31. Dagon fell twice before the ark. (1 Samuel 5:1-5)

32. Tumors befell the Philistines. (1 Samuel 5:6)

33. Seventy men killed for looking into the ark. (1 Samuel 6:19)

34. Loud thunderstorm against the Philistines (1 Samuel 7:10-12)

35. Thunder and rain in harvest at Gilgal. (1 Samuel 12:17-18)

36. Sound in the balsam trees at Rephaim. (2 Samuel 5:23-25)

207 Saint Augustine
John Calvin
Pope John Paul II

208
1. GOOD ≠ EVIL
2. SIN ≠ VIRTUE
3. MICHAEL ≠ LUCIFER
4. MOSES ≠ PHARAOH

209

TEMPTATION OF JESUS	MATTHEW 20:29-34
TAMAR IN DISGUISE	DEUTERONOMY 20
RULES OF WAR	1 SAMUEL 10:1
SAUL ANOINTED KING	LUKE 4:1-13
JEHOIADA'S COVENANT	DANIEL 6:19-24
A WORD SPOKEN	PROVERBS 25:11
DANIEL'S RELEASE	2 KINGS 11:17-20
TWO BLIND MEN HEALED	GENESIS 38:12-19

210 CHRISMON (*CHI RHO*)

211 Psalms 64:1-4

212 WOMEN Pt.2

213

1	8	4	3	7	2	5	6	9
6	3	9	5	4	1	8	7	2
2	5	7	9	8	6	1	3	4
7	4	1	2	6	5	9	8	3
3	2	8	1	9	7	4	5	6
5	9	6	4	3	8	7	2	1
8	1	2	6	5	9	3	4	7
9	7	3	8	2	4	6	1	5
4	6	5	7	1	3	2	9	8

SOLUTIONS

214

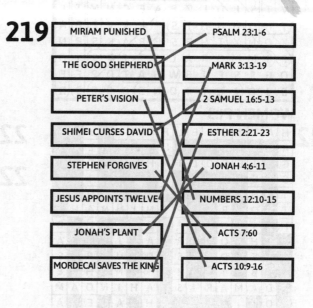

215 MOSES

216 Miracles in the Old Testament Pt.4

37. Uzzah killed for touching the ark. (2 Samuel 6:6-7)

38. Jeroboam's hand withered. (1 Kings 13:4)

39. Jeroboam's altar destroyed. (1 Kings 13:5)

40. Elijah fed by ravens (1 Kings 17:6)

41. Widow's meal and oil increased. (1Kings 17:14-16)

42. Drought at Elijah's prayers. (1 Kings 17-18)

43. Widow's son raised from the dead. (1Kings 17:17-24)

44. Fire at Elijah's prayers. (1 Kings 18:19-39)

45. Rain at Elijah's prayers (1 Kings 18:41-45)

46. Ahaziah's captains consumed by fire. (2 Kings 1:10-12)

47. The Jordan divided by Elijah and then by Elisha. (2 Kings 2:8-14)

48. Elijah carried up into heaven. (2

217 Martin Luther
Maximilian Kolbe
C. S. Lewis

218 1. HERODIAS ≠ JOHN THE BAPTIST
2. GENEROSITY ≠ GREED
3. ABEL ≠ CAIN
4. ARROGANCE ≠ HUMILITY

219

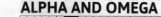

MIRIAM PUNISHED	PSALM 23:1-6
THE GOOD SHEPHERD	MARK 3:13-19
PETER'S VISION	2 SAMUEL 16:5-13
SHIMEI CURSES DAVID	ESTHER 2:21-23
STEPHEN FORGIVES	JONAH 4:6-11
JESUS APPOINTS TWELVE	NUMBERS 12:10-15
JONAH'S PLANT	ACTS 7:60
MORDECAI SAVES THE KING	ACTS 10:9-16

ALPHA AND OMEGA

220

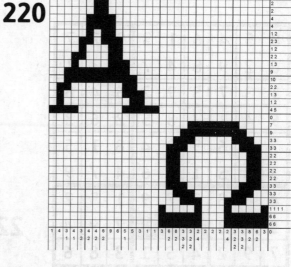

SOLUTIONS

221 — Mark 7:20-23

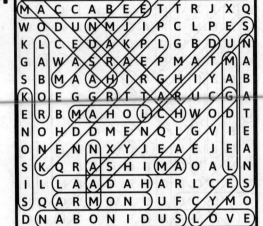

Word search grid solution.

222 — WOMEN Pt.3

Crossword solution containing: HAZZELELPONI, JECOLIAH, PENINNAH, DAMARIS, AHINOAM, LYDIA, EUNICE, ADAH, BITHIAH, HAGGITH, HOSHEB, JEDIDIAH, BASEMATH

223

Sudoku solution:

8	5	4	6	1	3	9	2	7
6	2	9	8	4	7	5	3	1
1	3	7	5	9	2	6	4	8
9	4	1	7	8	5	2	6	3
2	7	6	9	3	4	8	1	5
3	8	5	1	2	6	4	7	9
4	6	8	3	7	9	1	5	2
5	1	3	2	6	8	7	9	4
7	9	2	4	5	1	3	8	6

224

Word search grid solution.

225 TABITHA

226 — Miracles in the Old Testament Pt.5

49. Elisha purified the waters of Jericho. (2 Kings 2:21-22)

50. Elisha's curse caused two bears to kill forty-two children. (2 Kings 2:24)

51. Water provided for Jehoshaphat and the allied army. (2 Kings 3:16-20)

52. The widow's oil multiplied. (2 Kings 4:2-7)

53. The Shunammite's son raised from dead. (2 Kings 4:32-37)

54. The deadly pottage cured. (2 Kings 4:38-41)

55. 100 men fed. (2 Kings 4:42-44)

56. Naaman cleansed of leprosy, Gehazi afflicted with it. (2 Kings 5)

57. The iron axe-head made to float. (2 Kings 6:5-7)

58. Elisha knew the king of Syria's plans. (2 Kings 6:8-12)

59. The Syrian army blinded. (2 Kings 6:18)

60. The Syrian army cured of blindness. (2 Kings 6:20)

227

Richard Sibbes

John Calvin

Don Bosco

SOLUTIONS

228
1. JACOB ≠ ESAU
2. CHASTITY ≠ LUST
3. PATIENCE ≠ WRATH
4. HAGAR ≠ SARAH

229

SAMSON DIES	JUDGES 16:30
SOLOMON DRAFTS 30,000	MATTHEW 5-7
SAUL'S CONVERSION	1 SAMUEL 3:3-10
SAMUEL'S CALL	1 KINGS 5:13
SARAH CONCEIVES	ACTS 9:3-20
SERMON ON THE MOUNT	GENESIS 21:1-2
SIMON'S SIN	MARK 6:22
SALOME DANCES	ACTS 8:18-24

230

THE KEYS OF THE KINGDOM

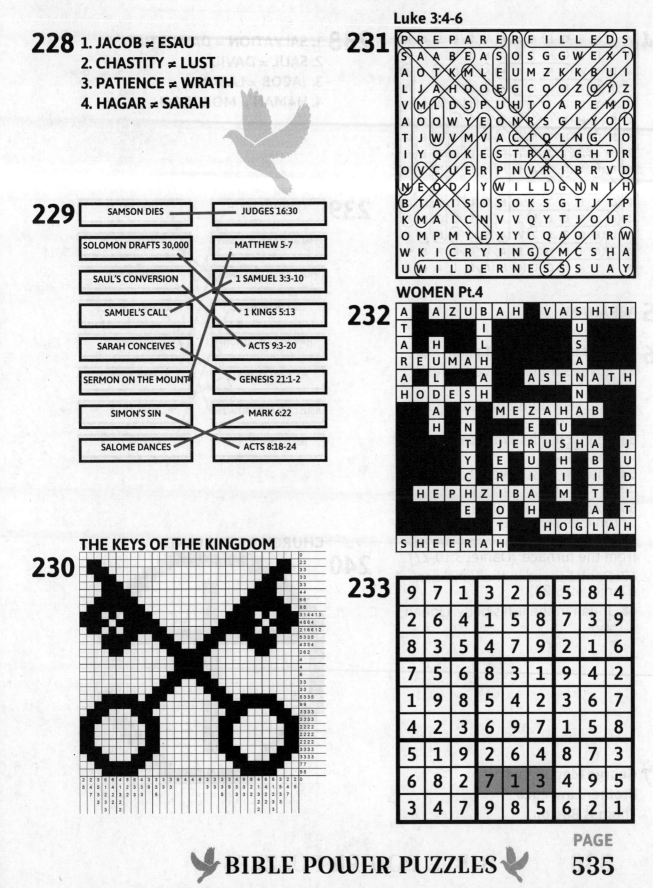

231 Luke 3:4-6

232 WOMEN Pt.4

233

9	7	1	3	2	6	5	8	4
2	6	4	1	5	8	7	3	9
8	3	5	4	7	9	2	1	6
7	5	6	8	3	1	9	4	2
1	9	8	5	4	2	3	6	7
4	2	3	6	9	7	1	5	8
5	1	9	2	6	4	8	7	3
6	8	2	7	1	3	4	9	5
3	4	7	9	8	5	6	2	1

234

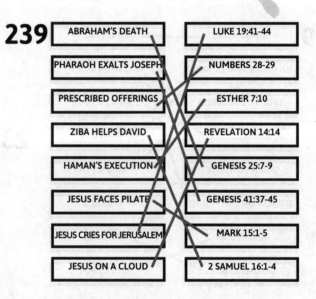

```
N I M R O D R X R V B E S N R
W Y D E G M J D A H W V N N X
L D L W B R I C K S H D L I A
O Y N A G G A I A E N E U V R
I B Y R D T I L V H I S A R M
L R E M B B O E Q L C N S O A
P S C L H C N R A K O I C B G
A N A A I Z H R Z D G E N E E
N B N N N S A H M N E E N D D
O P Q J P N K I E X M R S E O
P O B L A T I O N D U O I D N
L B U R D E N Z I D S O O N I
I U B O Z E Z W A S U K N M I
A Z B I S H O P A U R F N K
N I S A N O O O B A D I A H B
```

235 **ABRAHAM**

236 **Miracles in the Old Testament Pt.5**

61. Elisha's bones revived a dead man. (2 Kings 13:21)

62. God sent lions into Samaria. (2 Kings 17:25)

63. Sennacherib's army destroyed. (2 Kings 19:35)

64. Shadow of sun went back ten degrees. (2 Kings 20:9-11)

65. Uzziah struck with leprosy. (2 Chronicles 26:16-21)

66. Three Hebrew boys delivered from the furnace. (Daniel 3:10-27)

67. Daniel saved in the lions' den. (Daniel 6:16-23)

68. Jonah in the fish's belly. (Jonah 2:1-10)

237 George MacDonald
Brother Lawrence
Thomas Boston

238
1. SALVATION ≠ DAMNATION
2. SAUL ≠ DAVID
3. JACOB ≠ LABAN
4. HAMAN ≠ MORDECAI

239

ABRAHAM'S DEATH	LUKE 19:41-44
PHARAOH EXALTS JOSEPH	NUMBERS 28-29
PRESCRIBED OFFERINGS	ESTHER 7:10
ZIBA HELPS DAVID	REVELATION 14:14
HAMAN'S EXECUTION	GENESIS 25:7-9
JESUS FACES PILATE	GENESIS 41:37-45
JESUS CRIES FOR JERUSALEM	MARK 15:1-5
JESUS ON A CLOUD	2 SAMUEL 16:1-4

CHURCH OF ENGLAND

240

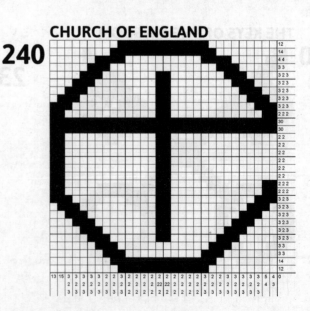

SOLUTIONS

Jeremiah 17:9-11

241

```
F A C C O R D I N G R G M I K
O I N C U R A B L E N B H H N
R D E S E R V E H I E N E P A
T M T X N L U H H K O F A R L
U I B P A E E T I D G Q R R E
N D J G O M Y G N M M Y T R D
E D Q N X I A B S Z I I R E E
X L H J A T B N N P M L N I C
R E A C H A K O E V U S R D E
L I Z F F X I X V E T I Q G I
L J C L B T U U M P G V J E T
A I O H C B F O O L N G P Y F
C X F A E R P X T D E L S E U
U N D E R S T A N D T E S T L
C G G H G I V E H A T C H E S
```

PRISONERS Pt.1

242

```
              J
J       J     E
E       O     H
H     S A M S O N
O       E   I     Z
A       P   C     E
H O S H E A   H   D
A       I   I     E
Z       M   A     K
        E   H     I
        O   H A N A N I
                  A
M A N A S S E H   H
```

243

7	5	8	1	6	3	4	9	2
9	1	6	4	2	5	7	8	3
3	2	4	9	8	7	1	5	6
1	4	2	8	5	9	6	3	7
5	7	9	6	3	4	2	1	8
6	8	3	2	7	1	5	4	9
8	9	7	5	4	6	3	2	1
2	6	5	3	1	8	9	7	4
4	3	1	7	9	2	8	6	5

244

```
I T U R E A N I V O R Y V U P
D R L H B N H E C E L A S A H
U P E Q W F O N M D H A V A O
S M V K G Y S U X H R I E Q R
T H D C C N E A W U F Y N R O
H O S P H U C R V A Z D D S A D W N A
P W H A M P H U C E E H O R N S R E D U M
W D F A E B N R T D O X V M A M
F M S I I W G I E A S Y T M M I
T A I T R E M Y L A Z S Z H
L P A A Z E A P S M N N Y H I
D L N I S L F S H O P F N W
O B S N N A N I A O N H E A
J D U N G M E Q X A D D Q Q R
```

245 MAGDALENE

246 Paradoxes of Christian life.

1. Finding life, yet losing it. (Matthew 10:39)

2. Losing life, yet finding it. (Matthew 10:39)

3. Dying, yet being able to give life. (John 12:24)

4. Seeing the unseen (2 Corinthians 4:18)

5. Being unknown, yet well known. (2 Corinthians 6:9)

6. Dying, yet possessing life. (2 Corinthians 6:9)

7. Being sorrowful, yet rejoicing. (2 Corinthians 6:10)

8. Being poor, yet making many rich. (2 Corinthians 6:10)

9. Having nothing, yet possessing all things. (2 Corinthians 6:10)

10. Hearing words that cannot be expressed. (2 Corinthians 12:4)

11. Being strong while being weak. (2 Corinthians 12:10)

12. Knowing the love of Christ that surpasses knowledge. (Ephesians 3:19)

247 **Thomas à Kempis**
Thomas Manton
Thomas Aquinas

SOLUTIONS

248
1. VICE ≠ VIRTUE
2. JOSEPH ≠ POTIPHAR
3. DILIGENCE ≠ SLOTH
4. GEHAZI ≠ ELISHA

249

PAUL CHOOSES TIMOTHY	2 KINGS 4:18-36
DARIUS HONORS GOD	1 CHRONICLES 18:1
ELISHA RESURRECTS BOY	PROVERBS 11:2
WISE MEN PRESENT GIFTS	JEREMIAH 1:11-14
ARROGANCE & HUMILITY	DANIEL 6:25-27
JEREMIAH'S TWO VISIONS	MATTHEW 2:11
DAVID TAKES GATH	MARK 6:7-13
JESUS SENDS THE TWELVE	ACTS 16:1-5

250 SHAMROCK

251 Mark 8:23-25

252 PRISONERS Pt.2

253

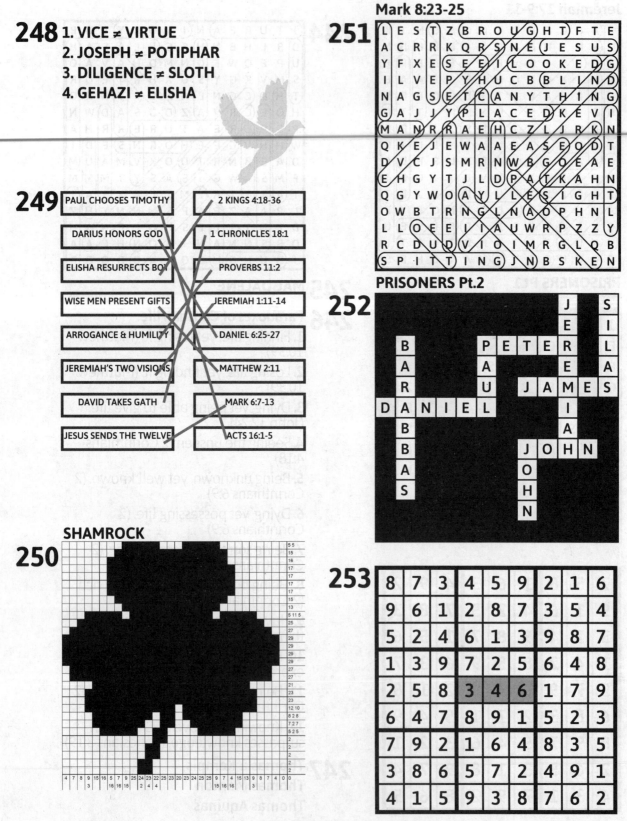

PAGE
538
  BIBLE POWER PUZZLES

SOLUTIONS

254

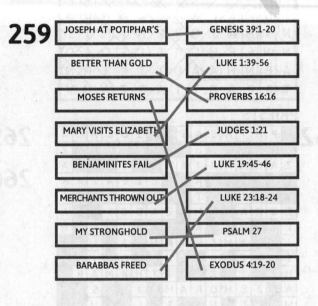

```
F O R N I C A T I O N F Q M
S E Y K M M Q K G R K L L Y
A O Z B Y J U I L W G O E S
I L R R L P R P M O U N T T
H L E B A N O N R T H R W E
I M C S Q S U G S A Z I Z R
R O T O Z W B T K N I Y S S
A T I H Y N O F O R D N Q S
M E O E E O F H I N N O M S
Q O N V F M O U R N I N G U
I O A U M N L E T U S H I M
H E R X T O D F Q Z E J H S
L Z Y L E F T H A N D E D D
M U R A T O R I A N C I P X
```

255 JERUSALEM

256 Great Escapes

1. Running from Sodom. (Genesis 19:15-26)

2. Mass-escape from Egypt. (Exodus 12:37-38)

3. Hiding on a roof. (Joshua 2:1-22)

4. Breaking ropes. (Judges 15:11-15)

5. Removing and carrying doors. (Judges 16:1-3)

6. Lowering down from a window. (1 Samuel 19:12-16)

7. Pretending madness. (1 Samuel 21:10-22:1)

8. Hiding in a well. (2 Samuel 17:15-21)

9. Unsuccessfully fleeing to Tarshish. (Jonah 1:3)

10. Passing through attackers. (Luke 4:29-30)

11. Slipping through attackers. (John 10:39).

12. Released by angels. (Acts 5:17-25)

13. Lowering down in a basket. (Acts 9:23-25)

14. Scaring jailor w/ an earthquake. (Acts 16:25-33)

257 John Chrysostom

Meister Eckhart

Jonathan Edwards

258
1. WISDOM ≠ FOLLY
2. ABSALOM ≠ JOAB
3. YAWEH ≠ BAAL
4. PAUL ≠ ALEXANDER

259

JOSEPH AT POTIPHAR'S	GENESIS 39:1-20
BETTER THAN GOLD	LUKE 1:39-56
MOSES RETURNS	PROVERBS 16:16
MARY VISITS ELIZABETH	JUDGES 1:21
BENJAMINITES FAIL	LUKE 19:45-46
MERCHANTS THROWN OUT	LUKE 23:18-24
MY STRONGHOLD	PSALM 27
BARABBAS FREED	EXODUS 4:19-20

SOLA FIDE | SOLA SCRIPTURA

260

SOLUTIONS

Job 38:3-6

261

```
R X C R S T R E T C H E D A
D F O U N D A T I O N S A
Q I E S T A B L I S H E D
U U M H M E A S U R I N G
E U S E S D Z H J Y E F H
S S V Y N I N F O R M I K
T Q U G N S Y I E S O X M
A I P P E I H S H L E D
N W E P X W O Z H N D B
S H W T O R E N I M J T
W E R C R F L S O A O
A E N H A A U T T K I H N
T R E A D Y T A S Z W U V
```

PRIESTS

262

```
    PHINEAS       JOSHUA
           B            Z
ZACHARIAH        J      A
           A  ELEAZAR   R
      J    T     H      I
  EZRA     H  ZADOK     A
  L    H   A     I   E  H
  I  AMARIAH     A   L
  S    Z    R    H   I
  H    I    R  ITHAMAR
  A   JEHORAM   M    S
  M    L    N   E    H
  A            L  K  I
              E  L  B
              C  I
SHELEMIAH     H  AH
```

263

3	1	4	8	2	6	9	7	5
9	8	5	7	1	4	6	3	2
7	2	6	3	5	9	1	4	8
8	9	7	6	3	5	4	2	1
4	3	2	1	8	7	5	6	9
5	6	1	9	4	2	3	8	7
1	7	9	2	6	3	8	5	4
6	5	8	4	7	1	2	9	3
2	4	3	5	9	8	7	1	6

264

```
O L I V E S I C X C N I K A
I V O M N I P R E S E N C E
E M H A E E X E C U T I O N
Y S L F E X E G E S I S A K
H J R A M L O E H C O M Y H
O U A S H H D D H U U O T W
J U R O A Z O L U H L A S E
Y H U N G E R B H S O D L Z
H U M I L I T Y E A V I A D
O I N T M E N T E D X A I H
I L L Y R I C U M E C H L U
O M N I P O T E N C E X A R
L I M P R E C A T O R Y I A
E X A L T A T I O N I E A M
```

265 SOLOMON

266 Last Words Pt.1

1. Jacob's last words. (Genesis 49:29-32)

2. Joseph's last words. (Genesis 50:24)

3. Moses' last words. (Deuteronomy 33:2-29)

4. Caleb's last words. (Joshua 14:6-12)

5. Joshua's last words. (Joshua 24:27)

6. Samson's last words. (Judges 16:30)

7. Eli's last words. (1 Samuel 4:15-18)

8. Saul's last words. (1 Samuel 31:4)

9. David's last words. (1 Kings 2:1-9)

10. Elijah's last words. (2 Kings 2:9-11)

11. Elisha's last words. (2 Kings 13:15-19)

267 Martin Luther
Elizabeth Prentiss
John Wesley

SOLUTIONS

268
1. TEMPERANCE ≠ GLUTTONY
2. BENEVOLENCE ≠ MALEFICENCE
3. CRUELTY ≠ COMPASSION
4. PEACE ≠ WAR

269

HEART REFLECTIONS	ECCLESIASTES 8:14
INJUSTICE	ISAIAH 7:14
JAMES EXECUTED	ACTS 18:24-28
MADE A WATCHMAN	ACTS 12:1-2
WALL HANDWRITING	SONG OF SONGS 5:2
APOLLOS ARRIVES	DANIEL 5:5-6
SIGN OF IMMANUEL	EZEKIEL 3:17-21
SLEEPING BUT AWAKE	PROVERBS 16:1

270

SOLA GRATIA | SOLUS CHRISTUS

271 Hebrews 5:7-8

```
O O Q I O F C U S F I H J A R
R F A X T B E C A U S E X S G
P E F L O N D Q V K J G D U F
Y D V E T S P E E G J L O F E
O L G E R H D A A L S W X F R
S D J D R E O K R T N E B E S
Y U S A N E D U A N H N Z R D
E Y N R T S N U G P R O N E D
Z B A S V O I C N H P B S D
H E U D F N W A E D M E G O G
L C U E O N Q B X J I S A N U
N O N S E S R L Y R T L I L E
L Q C X O N E E C T C R I E S
P R A Y E R S H I M U R Y F F
H E A R D F O B E D I E N C E
```

272 SHEPHERDS

```
            N
I S A A C   A           J
        B   B           O
        R   A M O S      S
        A B E L          E
J U D A H   A           P
A   A   A   R           H
C   V   M O S E S
O   I       U
B   D       E
            L O T
```

273

4	7	5	1	2	6	9	3	8
2	6	3	5	9	8	7	4	1
8	1	9	4	7	3	2	5	6
9	2	1	7	8	4	5	6	3
3	4	7	6	5	2	1	8	9
5	8	6	9	3	1	4	7	2
6	9	4	3	1	7	8	2	5
7	5	2	8	6	9	3	1	4
1	3	8	2	4	5	6	9	7

SOLUTIONS

274

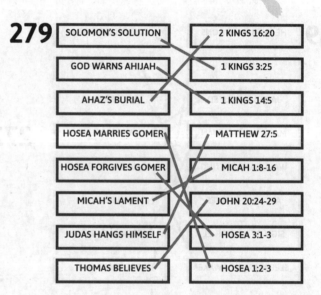

278
1. NOAH ≠ FLOOD
2. KORAH ≠ MOSES
3. TOBIAH ≠ NEHEMIAH
4. DEMETRIUS ≠ PAUL

275 MATTHEW

279

SOLOMON'S SOLUTION	2 KINGS 16:20
GOD WARNS AHIJAH	1 KINGS 3:25
AHAZ'S BURIAL	1 KINGS 14:5
HOSEA MARRIES GOMER	MATTHEW 27:5
HOSEA FORGIVES GOMER	MICAH 1:8-16
MICAH'S LAMENT	JOHN 20:24-29
JUDAS HANGS HIMSELF	HOSEA 3:1-3
THOMAS BELIEVES	HOSEA 1:2-3

276 Last Words Pt.2
12. Belshazzar's last words. (Daniel 5:13-16)
13. Daniel's last words. (Daniel 12:8)
14. Simeon's last words. (Luke 2:34-35)
15. Jesus' last words. (Acts 1:7-8)
16. Stephen's last words. (Acts 7:59-60)
17. Paul's last words. (2 Timothy 4:22)
18. James' last words. (James 5:19-20)
19. Peter's last words. (2 Peter 3:17-18)
20. Jude's last words. (Jude 24-25)
21. John's last words. (Revelation 22:18-21)

280 SOLI DEO GLORIA!

277 John Dawson
Saint Augustine
John Flavel

 BIBLE POWER PUZZLES

SOLUTIONS

Psalms 54:1-4

281

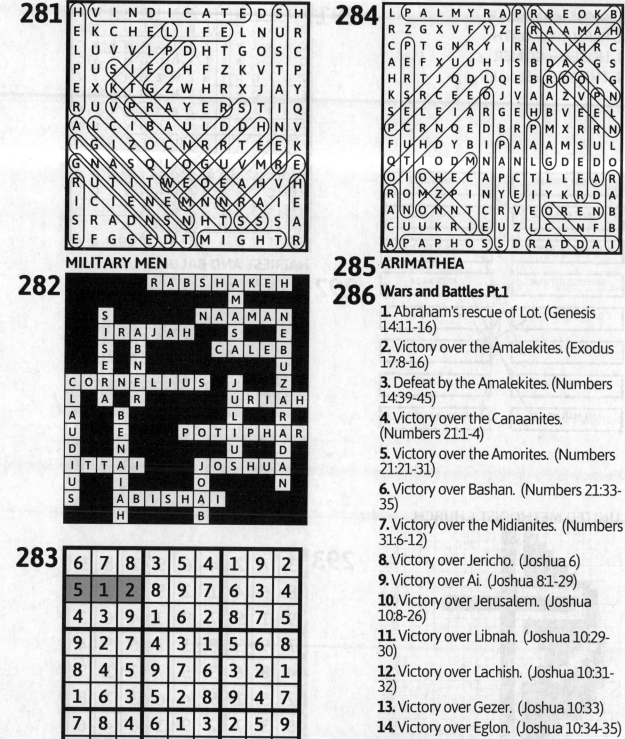

MILITARY MEN

282

283

284

285 ARIMATHEA

286 Wars and Battles Pt.1

1. Abraham's rescue of Lot. (Genesis 14:11-16)

2. Victory over the Amalekites. (Exodus 17:8-16)

3. Defeat by the Amalekites. (Numbers 14:39-45)

4. Victory over the Canaanites. (Numbers 21:1-4)

5. Victory over the Amorites. (Numbers 21:21-31)

6. Victory over Bashan. (Numbers 21:33-35)

7. Victory over the Midianites. (Numbers 31:6-12)

8. Victory over Jericho. (Joshua 6)

9. Victory over Ai. (Joshua 8:1-29)

10. Victory over Jerusalem. (Joshua 10:8-26)

11. Victory over Libnah. (Joshua 10:29-30)

12. Victory over Lachish. (Joshua 10:31-32)

13. Victory over Gezer. (Joshua 10:33)

14. Victory over Eglon. (Joshua 10:34-35)

287 Blaise Pascal

Alexander Balmain Bruce

C. S. Lewis

SOLUTIONS

288
1. AMOS ≠ AMAZIAH
2. PERJURY ≠ OATH
3. HOSEA ≠ GOMER
4. THOMAS ≠ SENSES

289

JOSHUA'S DEATH	JOSHUA 24:32
JOSEPH REBURIED	JUDGES 8:23
SHAMGAR'S STRENGTH	ECCLESIASTES 1:2-4
GIDEON'S REFUSAL	ACTS 3:4-10
DAVID KILLS 18,000	MARK 14:51-52
ABSOLUTE FUTILITY	2 SAMUEL 8:13
MARK RUNS NAKED	JUDGES 3:31
LAME MAN HEALED	JOSHUA 24:29-30

UNITED METHODIST CHURCH

290

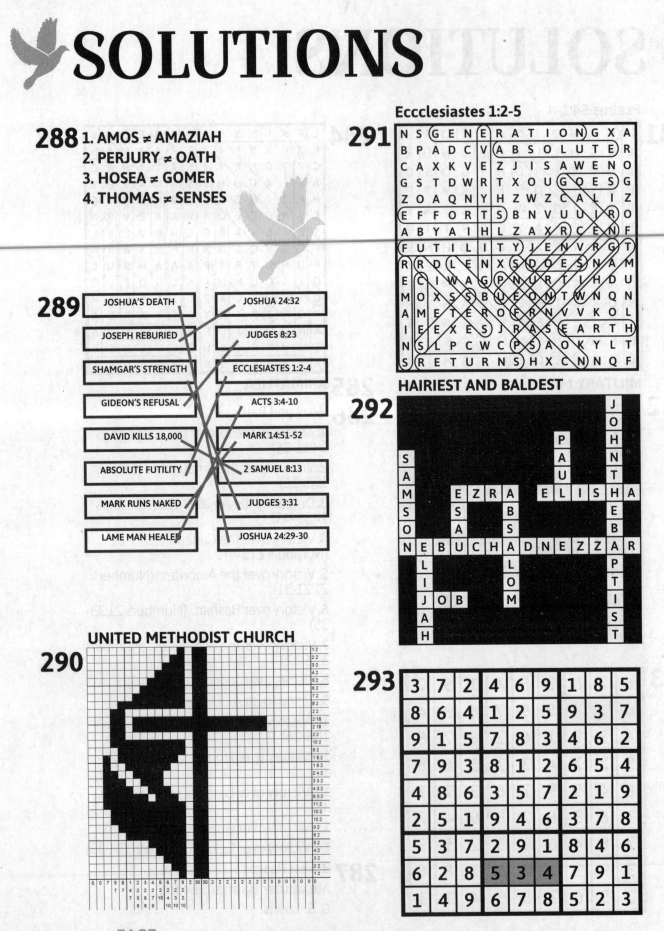

Eccclesiastes 1:2-5

291

HAIRIEST AND BALDEST

292

293

3	7	2	4	6	9	1	8	5
8	6	4	1	2	5	9	3	7
9	1	5	7	8	3	4	6	2
7	9	3	8	1	2	6	5	4
4	8	6	3	5	7	2	1	9
2	5	1	9	4	6	3	7	8
5	3	7	2	9	1	8	4	6
6	2	8	5	3	4	7	9	1
1	4	9	6	7	8	5	2	3

BIBLE POWER PUZZLES

SOLUTIONS

294

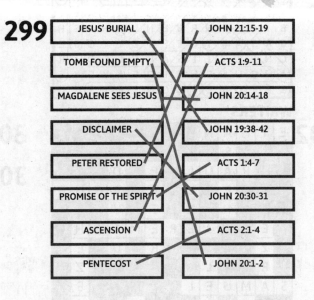

```
S B S U T H E O P H A N Y D N
U L U N N I T R A D I T I O N
N J J U D U W I N L V U W I M S
K T N E K T D H Y V E T L U V
N H D U R T H I E F A S L X I
O E W E C N F U R I I S V G
W O R H R F I U Q H K O E I
N C R U J R G M P V U V N L
L R L B E I A O L O O U A A
U A D I S U H K S G A D G N
Z C Y T N R T B B U L T A G C
A Y L B A T H E I S M Y I O E
L P R H V D V B O Q A W O N E
T U Z Z E N P W V I N E G A R
```

295 GETHSEMANE

296 Wars and Battles Pt.2

15. Victory over Hebron. (Joshua 10:36-37)

16. Victory over Debir. (Joshua 10:38-39)

17. Victory over Jabin. (Joshua 11:1-15)

18. Othniel vs. Aram. (Judges 3:10)

19. Ehud vs. Moabites. (Judges 3:26-29)

20. Shamgar vs. Philistines. (Judges 3:31)

21. Barak vs. Canaanites. (Judges 4:1-16)

22. Gideon vs. Midianites. (Judges 7:9-25)

23. Abimelech vs. Shechem. (Judges 9:42-57)

24. Jephthah vs. Ammonites. (Judges 11:32-33)

25. Jephthah vs. Ephraim. (Judges 12:1-6)

26. Samson vs. Philistines. (Judges 15:9-15)

27. Dan's tribe vs. Laish. (Judges 18:27-29)

28. Benjamin defeated by 11 tribes. (Judges 20:18-48)

297 Martin Luther
Richard Baxter
John Knox

298
1. EHUD ≠ EGLON
2. ABSALOM ≠ AMNON
3. ELAH ≠ ZIMRI
4. JAEL ≠ SISERA

299

JESUS' BURIAL	JOHN 21:15-19
TOMB FOUND EMPTY	ACTS 1:9-11
MAGDALENE SEES JESUS	JOHN 20:14-18
DISCLAIMER	JOHN 19:38-42
PETER RESTORED	ACTS 1:4-7
PROMISE OF THE SPIRIT	JOHN 20:30-31
ASCENSION	ACTS 2:1-4
PENTECOST	JOHN 20:1-2

LUTHER'S ROSE

300

SOLUTIONS

2 Samuel 16:1-2

301

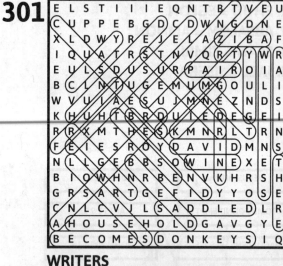

WRITERS

302

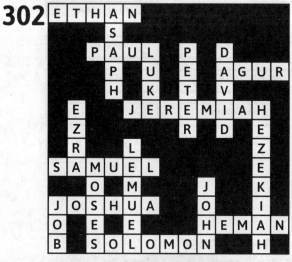

303

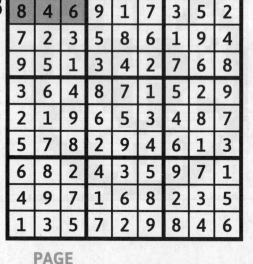

304
AARON = ENLIGHTENED
ABDON = CLOUD OF JUDGMENT
ABEL = MEADOW
ABIGAIL = CAUSE OF JOY
ABNER = FATHER OF LIGHT
ABRAHAM = FATHER OF A MULTITUDE
ADAM = TAKEN FROM THE RED EARTH
ANNA = GRACE

305 BARABBAS

306 Meals Pt.1

1. Forbidden tree fruit. (Genesis 3:6)
2. Abraham serves three angels. (Genesis 18:1-8)
3. Feast at Lot's. (Genesis 19:1-3)
4. Esau sells his birthright. (Genesis 25:29-34)
5. Isaac is tricked. (Genesis 27:1-29)
6. Joseph and his brothers. (Genesis 43:16-34)
7. First Passover observance. (Exodus 12:1-20)
8. Manna. (Exodus 16)
9. Quail. (Exodus 16:1-13)
10. Tamar serves Amnon. (2 Samuel 13:1-14)
11. Ravens serve Elijah. (1 Kings 17:3-6)
12. Widow serves Elijah. (1 Kings 17:8-16)
13. Elisha's feast. (1 Kings 19:19-21)
14. Seven-day banquet. (Esther 1:5-12)

307 Harold L. Willmington
Saint Ambrose of Milan
Billy Graham

SOLUTIONS

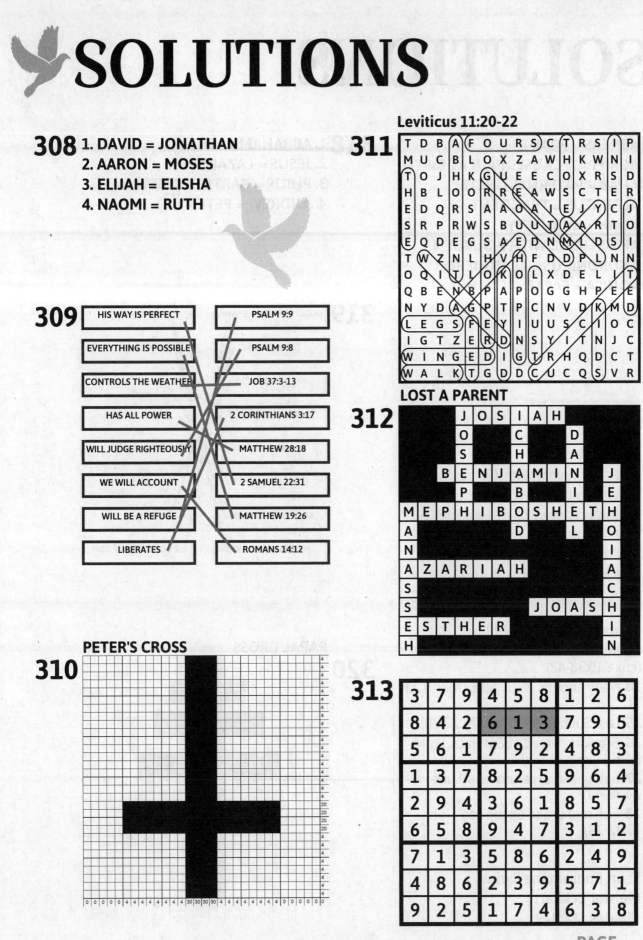

308
1. DAVID = JONATHAN
2. AARON = MOSES
3. ELIJAH = ELISHA
4. NAOMI = RUTH

311 Leviticus 11:20-22

309

HIS WAY IS PERFECT	PSALM 9:9
EVERYTHING IS POSSIBLE	PSALM 9:8
CONTROLS THE WEATHER	JOB 37:3-13
HAS ALL POWER	2 CORINTHIANS 3:17
WILL JUDGE RIGHTEOUSLY	MATTHEW 28:18
WE WILL ACCOUNT	2 SAMUEL 22:31
WILL BE A REFUGE	MATTHEW 19:26
LIBERATES	ROMANS 14:12

312 LOST A PARENT

310 PETER'S CROSS

313

SOLUTIONS

314 AENEAS = PRAISE
AGRIPPA = CAUSES PAIN AT BIRTH
AHAB = PATERNAL UNCLE
ALPHAEUS = TRANSIENT
ALIAH = SUBLIMITY
AMOS = ONE WITH A BURDEN
ANDRONICUS = CONQUEROR
AQUILA = EAGLE

315 NAZARETH

316 Meals Pt.2
15. Esther reveals plot. (Esther 7)
16. Victory celebration. (Esther 9:17-32)
17. Job's children killed. (Job 1:18-19)
18. Belshazzar's feast. (Daniel 5)
19. Herod's birthday. (Mark 6:21-28)
20. Matthew's feast. (Luke 5:29-32)
21. Jesus feeds 4,000. (Matthew 15:32-38)
22. Jesus feeds 5,000. (John 6:5-14)
23. Martha, Mary, and Jesus gather. (Luke 10:38-42)
24. Mary anoints Jesus' feet. (John 12:1-3)
25. Last Supper. (Matthew 26:17-30)
26. Breaking bread at Emmaus. (Luke 24:30)
27. Eating fish at Jerusalem. (Luke 24:38-43)
28. Fish and bread by the sea. (John 21:12-14)

317 Saint Ephrem the Syrian
Meister Eckhart
Charles Stanley

318 1. ABRAHAM = LOT
2. JESUS = LAZARUS
3. PHILIP = BARTHOLOMEW
4. ANDREW = PETER

319

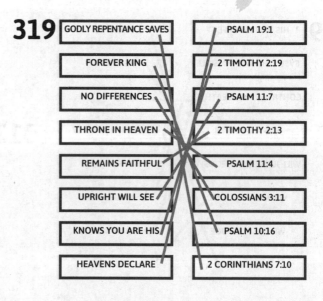

GODLY REPENTANCE SAVES	PSALM 19:1
FOREVER KING	2 TIMOTHY 2:19
NO DIFFERENCES	PSALM 11:7
THRONE IN HEAVEN	2 TIMOTHY 2:13
REMAINS FAITHFUL	PSALM 11:4
UPRIGHT WILL SEE	COLOSSIANS 3:11
KNOWS YOU ARE HIS	PSALM 10:16
HEAVENS DECLARE	2 CORINTHIANS 7:10

PAPAL CROSS

320

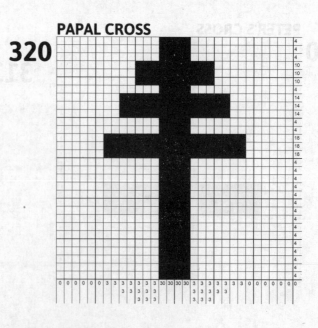

SOLUTIONS

Exodus 20:18-19

321

```
S M S Q W I T N E S S E D T C
P O L S W L O H G Q W W D L W
E U L U X B Z N U W I I O B Q
A N P D Q T I X O N B G O D P
K T U R X N G Q V L D R D L E
D A E R T M I O M U D E P R O
L I X H M O S E S K D D R I P
K N G M Z S K J U N N N S L L
D I S T A N C E U U A L L E E
L E Q B D N G O O T S V S T H
G D V O K X R S E Q A K E N W
S M O K E R D H M O I N P E H
W T A R U S A W R H D I E N E
S Q O S T R U M P E T H B O N
T R E M B L E D B A K T H E Y
```

NAMED BY GOD

322

```
        J
  J O H N T H E B A P T I S T
        S
M       U           L
A       S O L O M O N
G       J           R
O   J A C O B       U
R   E   E           H
M   Z   P       A D A M
I   E   H       B   M
S A R A H   L   R   A
S   E   A   O   A
M A H E R S H A L A L H A S H B A Z
A   L       M   H
B           M   A
I           I
B               I S H M A E L
```

323

9	2	4	8	5	3	1	7	6
8	5	7	1	6	2	4	3	9
1	3	6	4	7	9	5	2	8
4	8	5	3	1	6	2	9	7
7	1	3	9	2	4	8	6	5
2	6	9	7	8	5	3	4	1
5	9	1	2	3	7	6	8	4
3	4	8	6	9	1	7	5	2
6	7	2	5	4	8	9	1	3

324
ANTIPAS = LIKE HIS FATHER
APOLLOS = YOUTHFUL GOD OF MUSIC
ARIEL = LION OF GOD
AUGUSTUS = SACRED
BATHSHEBA = SEVENTH DAUGHTER
BERNICE = VICTORIOUS
BILHAH = TIMID
CANDACE = QUEEN

325 **RABBONI**

326 **Fasts Pt.1**

1. Moses' 40-day fast. (Deuteronomy 9:9)

2. Israelites fast after defeat. (Judges 20:26)

3. Israelites repent and fast. (1 Samuel 7:3-6)

4. Saul's soldiers fast. (1 Samuel 14:24-27)

5. Saul's fast. (1 Samuel 28:20)

6. Jabesh-gilead people fast. (1 Samuel 31:11-13)

7. David's fast over Saul. (2 Samuel 1:12)

8. David's fast over Abner. (2 Samuel 3:35)

9. David's fast over child. (2 Samuel 12:16)

10. Elijah's 40-day fast. (1 Kings 19:7-8)

11. Ahab's humbling. (1 Kings 21:27-29)

12. Jehoshaphat proclaims fasting. (2 Chronicles 20:1-4)

327 Saint Francis of Assisi
Pope John Paul II
Dwight L. Moody

SOLUTIONS

328
1. DAVID = ABIATHAR
2. NAHASH = DAVID
3. DAVID = ITTAI
4. HIRAM = DAVID

329

WORLDWIDE WORSHIP	1 PETER 3:22
FOREVER THE SAME	PSALM 22:27
BLESS WITH PEACE	PSALM 56:9
DOES NOT TEMPT	HEBREWS 13:8
MAKES WARS CEASE	JAMES 1:17
EVERY GOOD GIFT	PSALM 29:11
FOR ME	PSALM 46:9
AT THE RIGHT HAND	JAMES 1:13

330 ANCHOR

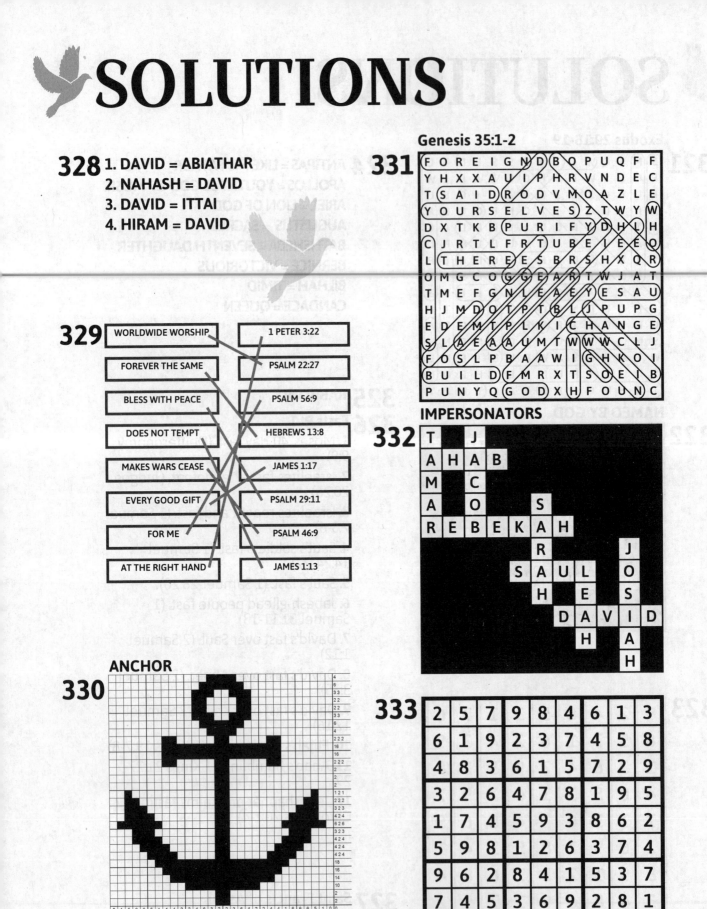

331 Genesis 35:1-2

IMPERSONATORS

332

333

SOLUTIONS

334 BARAK = THUNDER
BARNABAS = SON OF PROPHECY
BARTHOLOMEW = SON OF TOLMAI
BARUCH = BLESSED
BELA = DEVOURING
BENJAMIN = SON OF THE RIGHT HAND
CHLOE = GREEN HERB
CLAUDIA = LAME

335 STEPHEN

336 Fasts Pt.2
13. Ezra's fast. (Ezra 10:6)
14. Nehemiah's fast. (Nehemiah 1)
15. Esther's preparation. (Esther 4:13-16)
16. Darius' fast over Daniel. (Daniel 6:18-24)
17. Daniel's fast for Judah's sins. (Daniel 9:1-19)
18. Daniel's fast over a vision. (Daniel 10:1-3)
19. Ninevite's fast. (Jonah 3)
20. Anna's fast. (Luke 2:37)
21. Jesus' 40-day fast. (Matthew 4:1-11)
22. Paul's 3-day fast. (Acts 9:9)
23. Church elders' fast. (Acts 13:1-3)
24. Paul's 14-day fast. (Acts 27:33-34)

337 Anthony N. Groves
E. M. Bounds
Saint Polycarp of Smyrna

338 1. JOB = ELIPHAZ
2. BILDAD = JOB
3. JOB = ZOPHAR
4. DANIEL = SHADRACH

339
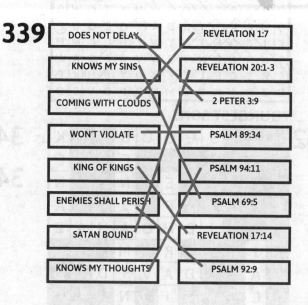

DOES NOT DELAY	REVELATION 1:7
KNOWS MY SINS	REVELATION 20:1-3
COMING WITH CLOUDS	2 PETER 3:9
WON'T VIOLATE	PSALM 89:34
KING OF KINGS	PSALM 94:11
ENEMIES SHALL PERISH	PSALM 69:5
SATAN BOUND	REVELATION 17:14
KNOWS MY THOUGHTS	PSALM 92:9

340 IX MONOGRAM

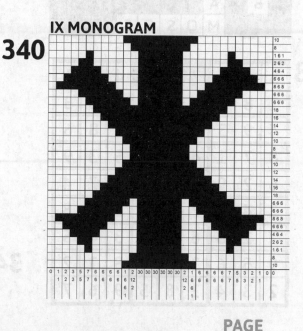

SOLUTIONS

341 Numbers 21:7-8

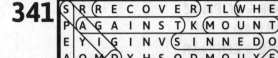

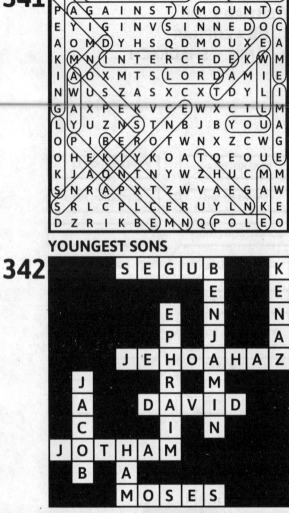

YOUNGEST SONS

342

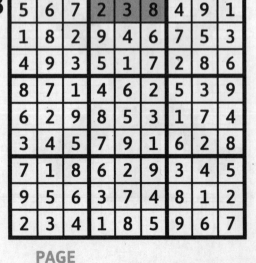

343

5	6	7	2	3	8	4	9	1
1	8	2	9	4	6	7	5	3
4	9	3	5	1	7	2	8	6
8	7	1	4	6	2	5	3	9
6	2	9	8	5	3	1	7	4
3	4	5	7	9	1	6	2	8
7	1	8	6	2	9	3	4	5
9	5	6	3	7	4	8	1	2
2	3	4	1	8	5	9	6	7

344 BILDAD = SON OF CONTENTION
BUNNI = MY UNDERSTANDING
BUZ = CONTEMPT
CAESAR = ONE CUT OUT
CAIAPHAS = SEARCHER
CAIN = ACQUIRED
CALEB = BOLD
CEPHAS = ROCK

345 PENTECOST

346 Famines

1. Abraham migrates to Egypt. (Genesis 12:10)

2. Isaac migrates to Philistia. (Genesis 26:1)

3. Egypt's preparations. (Genesis 41)

4. Joseph's brothers go to Egypt. (Genesis 42:1-3)

5. Naomi goes to Moab. (Ruth 1:1-2)

6. Gibeonite genocide causes famine. (2 Samuel 21:1)

7. Ahab's sins cause famine. (1 Kings 17:1)

8. Seven-year famine. (2 Kings 8:1-2)

9. Nebuchadnezzar's siege. (2 Kings 25:1-3)

10. Chaldeans siege Jerusalem. (Jeremiah 32:24)

11. Agabus predicts Roman famine. (Acts 11:28)

347 John Nelson Darby
John of Damascus
Saint Francis of Sales

BIBLE POWER PUZZLES

SOLUTIONS

348
1. DANIEL = MESHACH
2. ABEDNEGO = DANIEL
3. ESTHER = MORDECAI
4. JESUS = MARY

349

HIS LOVE ENDURES	PSALM 100:5
CAST INTO FIRE	PSALM 103:8
COMPASSIONATE	PSALM 103:8
INHERIT THE EARTH	REVELATION 20:7-10
GRACIOUS	MATTHEW 24:14
GREAT REWARD	MATTHEW 5:11-12
SLOW TO ANGER	PSALM 103:8
THE END SHALL COME	MATTHEW 5:5

350

ICXC NIKA (JESUSCHRIST CONQUERS)

351

1 Samuel 1:26-28

352

DREAMERS

353

5	3	9	2	6	1	8	7	4
6	1	8	7	9	4	5	2	3
4	2	7	8	3	5	1	9	6
3	5	6	1	2	9	4	8	7
7	9	4	5	8	3	2	6	1
1	8	2	6	4	7	3	5	9
2	6	1	3	7	8	9	4	5
9	7	5	4	1	2	6	3	8
8	4	3	9	5	6	7	1	2

SOLUTIONS

354 CORNELIUS = SUNBEAM
CRISPUS = CURLED
CYRUS = HEIR
DAMARIS = HEIFER
DANIEL = GOD IS MY JUDGE
DARIUS = HE INFORMS HIMSELF
DAVID = BELOVED
DEBORAH = BEE

355 PASSOVER

356 Taxes
1. Joseph's 20% tax. (Genesis 41:34)
2. Half-shekel census tax. (Exodus 30:12-16)
3. Samuel's warning. (1 Samuel 8)
4. Solomon's kingdoms tribute. (1 Kings 4:21)
5. Solomon's yoke. (1 Kings 12:1-14)
6. Menahem's tax. (2 Kings 15:19-20)
7. Hoshea's evasion. (2 Kings 17:3-4)
8. Jehoiakim's tax. (2 Kings 23:33-35)
9. Philistines' tribute. (2 Chronicles 17:11)
10. Persian toll, tribute, and custom. (Ezra 4:13)
11. Artaxerxes excempts clergy. (Ezra 7:24)
12. Asahuerus' tribute. (Esther 10:1)
13. Joseph and Mary's census tax. (Luke 2:1-7)
14. Fish's coin. (Matthew 17:24-27)

357 George Fox
R. A. Torrey
Saint Pachomius the Great

358 1. MARTHA = JESUS
2. JAMES = JOHN
3. ELIZABETH = MARY
4. JOSEPH = PHARAOH

359

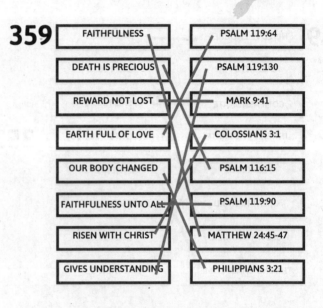

FAITHFULNESS	PSALM 119:64
DEATH IS PRECIOUS	PSALM 119:130
REWARD NOT LOST	MARK 9:41
EARTH FULL OF LOVE	COLOSSIANS 3:1
OUR BODY CHANGED	PSALM 116:15
FAITHFULNESS UNTO ALL	PSALM 119:90
RISEN WITH CHRIST	MATTHEW 24:45-47
GIVES UNDERSTANDING	PHILIPPIANS 3:21

360 OSTRICH EGG

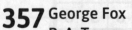 BIBLE POWER PUZZLES

SOLUTIONS

361

Ezra 9:9

```
F G X Z L R A B A N D O N E D
T O O K I N G S S O L E R I W
V G J D W I D R W T V Z E I H S
P R S L A V E R Y A I P X L D A E
R H Z F R O N H G C V S I E A G X
E J M S C K T F Y R E E E L I T
S Q U W Y F S J X E U E F C T E E
E C M D P K L T G B S D I Z E N
N E F G A W A L L U Q E G L D
C J K I U H V X O I R U A R E
E O Z X O W E H O L U K R J E
M G Q I Y Z S D Z D I N E N D
O C O P P E R S I A N M A M Z
I L U G T H O U G H S C L R X
J E R U S A L E M R E P A I R
```

ANCIENT PEOPLES Pt.1

362

```
            E
      H I T T I T E S        H
            H                U
C A N A A N I T E S          R
I     K     O                R
L     K     P        M       I
I     A     I        I       A
C H A L D E A N S     D       N
I     M     I        I       A
A     O     N        A       N
N     R     A S S Y R I A N S
S     I     N        N
      T              T
        E D O M I T E S      S
      S
```

363

```
4 6 9 | 1 2 8 | 3 7 5
1 7 5 | 4 3 9 | 6 2 8
3 8 2 | 5 6 7 | 4 9 1
------+-------+------
5 2 3 | 6 8 1 | 7 4 9
6 1 8 | 9 7 4 | 2 5 3
9 4 7 | 3 5 2 | 8 1 6
------+-------+------
2 5 4 | 8 1 3 | 9 6 7
7 3 6 | 2 9 5 | 1 8 4
8 9 1 | 7 4 6 | 5 3 2
```

364
DELILAH = DELICATE
DEMAS = RULER OF PEOPLE
DEMETRIUS = BELONGS TO DEMETER
DIDYMUS = TWIN
DINAH = JUSTICE
DIONYSIUS = TOUCHED BY GOD
DODO = LOVING
DORCAS = GAZELLE

365 BAPTISM

366 Signs
1. The rainbow. (Genesis 9:13-17)
2. The 10 plagues. (Exodus 10:1-2)
3. Unleavened bread. (Exodus 13:7-9)
4. The Sabbath. (Exodus 31:13)
5. Two censers. (Numbers 16:36-40)
6. Twelve stones. (Joshua 4:4-7)
7. Fleece. (Judges 6:17-21)
8. Torn altar. (1 Kings 13:1-5)
9. Slow sundial. (2 Kings 20:8-11)
10. Virgin birth. (Isaiah 7:14)
11. Jonah. (Matthew 16:4)
12. Wrapped baby. (Luke 2:12)
13. Tongues. (1 Corinthians 14:22)

367 James Nayler
Margaret Fell
Joseph John Gurney

SOLUTIONS

368
1. DEBORAH = BARAK
2. PAUL = PRISCILLA
3. AQUILA = PAUL
4. PAUL = LUKE

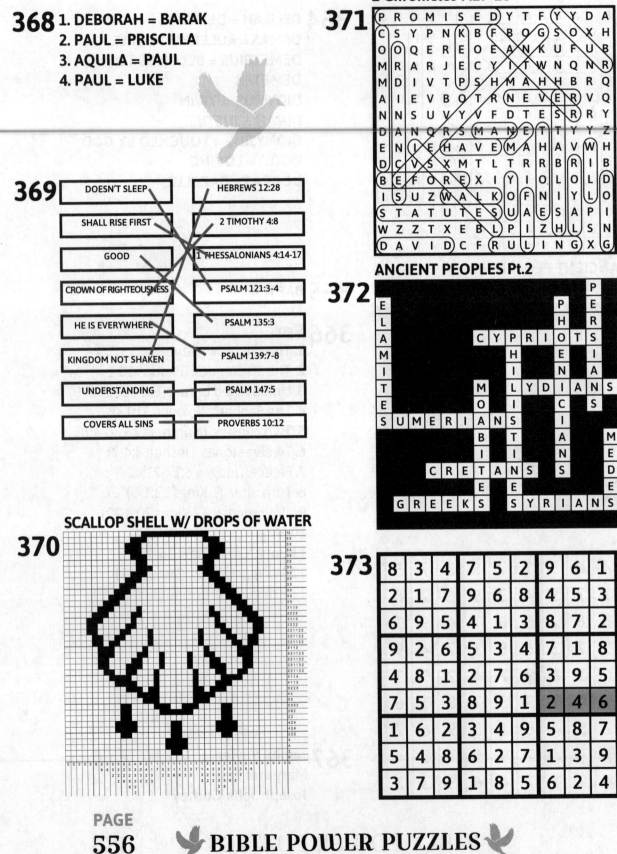

369

DOESN'T SLEEP	HEBREWS 12:28
SHALL RISE FIRST	2 TIMOTHY 4:8
GOOD	1 THESSALONIANS 4:14-17
CROWN OF RIGHTEOUSNESS	PSALM 121:3-4
HE IS EVERYWHERE	PSALM 135:3
KINGDOM NOT SHAKEN	PSALM 139:7-8
UNDERSTANDING	PSALM 147:5
COVERS ALL SINS	PROVERBS 10:12

370 SCALLOP SHELL W/ DROPS OF WATER

371 2 Chronicles 7:17-18

372 ANCIENT PEOPLES Pt.2

373

8	3	4	7	5	2	9	6	1
2	1	7	9	6	8	4	5	3
6	9	5	4	1	3	8	7	2
9	2	6	5	3	4	7	1	8
4	8	1	2	7	6	3	9	5
7	5	3	8	9	1	2	4	6
1	6	2	3	4	9	5	8	7
5	4	8	6	2	7	1	3	9
3	7	9	1	8	5	6	2	4

BIBLE POWER PUZZLES

SOLUTIONS

374 DRUSILLA = WATERED BY THE DEW
DUMAH = SILENCE
EDEN = DELIGHT
EGLON = CIRCLE
ELEAZAR = GOD IS HELPER
ELI = MY GOD
ELIJAH = GOD HIMSELF
ELISHA = GOD IS SAVIOR

375 BETHSAIDA

376 Baptisms
1. Jesus baptized by John. (Matthew 3:13-17)
2. 3,000 baptized. (Acts 2:41)
3. Simon the sorcerer baptized. (Acts 8:12-13)
4. Ethiopian eunuch baptized. (Acts 8:38-39)
5. Paul's baptism. (Acts 9:18)
6. Cornelius and friends baptized. (Acts 10:44-48)
7. Lydia and household baptized. (Acts 16:14-15)
8. Jailor and household baptized. (Acts 16:25-33)
9. Crispus and many more baptized. (Acts 18:8)
10. Twelve Ephesians baptized. (Acts 19:1-7)

377 Saint Teresa of Avila
J. R. R. Tolkien
Billy Sunday

378 1. TIMOTHY = PAUL
2. PAUL = EPAPHRODITUS
3. JEHOSHAPHAT = AHAB
4. SAMUEL = DAVID

379
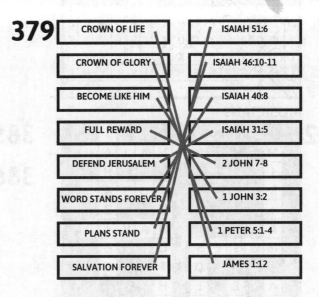

CROWN OF LIFE	ISAIAH 51:6
CROWN OF GLORY	ISAIAH 46:10-11
BECOME LIKE HIM	ISAIAH 40:8
FULL REWARD	ISAIAH 31:5
DEFEND JERUSALEM	2 JOHN 7-8
WORD STANDS FOREVER	1 JOHN 3:2
PLANS STAND	1 PETER 5:1-4
SALVATION FOREVER	JAMES 1:12

380 FLEUR-DE-LIS

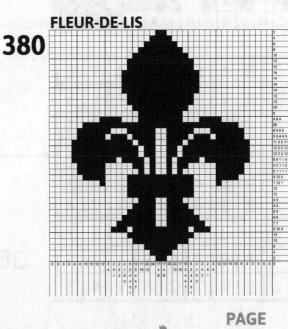

SOLUTIONS

Psalms 13:4-6

381

B Y B I S T R E A T E D T J V
E O Q K H H E X D H O I V R Y
C U U N I H A N R Y M C G O B
A B I O F T W K M C F B C M H
U F R O L E I D E R T Q C E T
S F E E P B X S N R K E U R S
E E A S R E U V V S I N G E U
H T F I D O T G L P U D I T J
B P S P T E U R A X M V B E O
L N O C H H Q Y Y B P O S D I
W L Y T T E F M X A H V M Z C
I B O R H X E U Z U E E Z Z E
L S A V S N P K L M D R Z Y H
L E A G E N E R O U S L Y B E
H U Y Y D E L I V E R A N C E

MUSICIANS

382

J
M B E N A I A H
I H
R J U B A L L
I E A
A D A V I D Z
M O S E S O U I
O T E
A E L H L
S T O U
A H E M A N
P A O
C H E N A N I A H

383

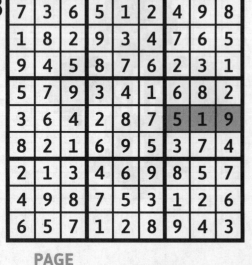

7	3	6	5	1	2	4	9	8
1	8	2	9	3	4	7	6	5
9	4	5	8	7	6	2	3	1
5	7	9	3	4	1	6	8	2
3	6	4	2	8	7	5	1	9
8	2	1	6	9	5	3	7	4
2	1	3	4	6	9	8	5	7
4	9	8	7	5	3	1	2	6
6	5	7	1	2	8	9	4	3

384 ELIZABETH = WORSHIPER OF GOD
ELON = STRONG
ENOCH = TEACHER
ENOS = MANKIND
EPHRAIM = DOUBLY FRUITFUL
ESTHER = STAR
EUNICE = CONQUERING WELL
EVE = LIFE

385 EPHESIANS

386 Exile Pt.1
1. Adam and Eve out of Eden. (Genesis 3:23-24)
2. Cain exiled to Nod. (Genesis 4:13-16)
3. Noah and family displaced by the flood. (Genesis 7:23)
4. Abraham left Ur. (Genesis 12:1-5)
5. Hagar and Ishmael banished (Genesis 21:10-14)
6. Jacob ran from Esau. (Genesis 27:41-45)
7. Joseph brought to Egypt. (Genesis 39:1)
8. Moses flees to Midian. (Exodus 2:15)
9. Israelites in Egypt. (Exodus 12:40)
10. Forty years in the wilderness. (Joshua 5:6)

387 J. C. Ryle
Henry Drummond
Saint Ignatius of Loyola

SOLUTIONS

388
1. ABRAHAM = MAMRE
2. ESHCOL = ABRAHAM
3. ABRAHAM = ANER
4. MELCHIZEDEK = ABRAHAM

389

WOUNDED FOR US	MALACHI 3:6
TREE OF LIFE	REVELATION 2:11
PROMISED GOOD	MALACHI 1:11
CROWN OF LIFE	ZEPHANIAH 3:17
WARRIOR SAVIOR	REVELATION 2:7
UNCHANGEABLE	ISAIAH 53:5
NO SECOND DEATH	REVELATION 2:10
GREAT AMONG GENTILES	JEREMIAH 32:42

390 CANTERBURY CROSS

391 Isaiah 37:26-27

INSTRUMENTS

392

393

2	6	1	7	9	3	4	5	8
5	3	7	8	4	6	1	2	9
4	8	9	2	5	1	3	7	6
1	4	2	5	7	9	8	6	3
3	9	5	6	8	4	7	1	2
6	7	8	3	1	2	9	4	5
7	5	3	4	6	8	2	9	1
8	1	6	9	2	7	5	3	4
9	2	4	1	3	5	6	8	7

SOLUTIONS

394 ETHAN = PERPLEXITY
EZEKIEL = GOD IS STRONG
FELIX = PROSPEROUS
GABRIEL = GOD IS MY STRENGTH
GAIUS = I AM GLAD
GAMALIEL = GOD'S REWARD
GEHAZI = VALLEY OF VISION
GIDEON = GREAT WARRIOR

395 BOANERGES

396 Exile Pt.2
11. Jephthah left for Tob. (Judges 11:3)
12. David flees from Saul. (1 Samuel 27:1-7)
13. Absalom in Talmai. (2 Samuel 13:37-39)
14. Jeroboam in Egypt. (1 Kings 11:40)
15. Assyria exiles Israel. (2 Kings 17:6)
16. Exile in Babylon. (2 Kings 24:14-16)
17. Jeremiah exiled to Egypt. (Jeremiah 43:5-7)
18. Joseph, Mary and Jesus flee to Egypt. (Matthew 2:13-15)
19. Early church persecuted. (Acts 8:1)
20. John in Patmos. (Revelation 1:9)

397 Mary Baker Eddy
Saint Augustine
Saint Ignatius of Antioch

398 1. ELI = SAMUEL
2. MOAB = JUDAH
3. EDOM = MOAB
4. EGYPT = CUSH

399

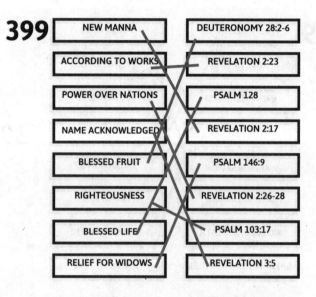

NEW MANNA	DEUTERONOMY 28:2-6
ACCORDING TO WORKS	REVELATION 2:23
POWER OVER NATIONS	PSALM 128
NAME ACKNOWLEDGED	REVELATION 2:17
BLESSED FRUIT	PSALM 146:9
RIGHTEOUSNESS	REVELATION 2:26-28
BLESSED LIFE	PSALM 103:17
RELIEF FOR WIDOWS	REVELATION 3:5

400 PRESBYTERIAN CROSS

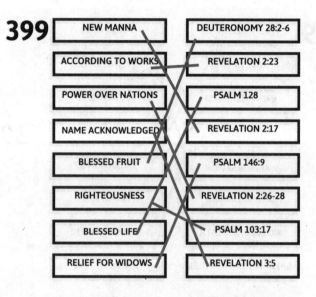

 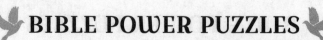 **BIBLE POWER PUZZLES**

SOLUTIONS

Zephaniah 3:8-9

401

```
F X T H E R E F O R E P O U P
H S V L C S M A S S E M B L E
K P L C W E B Y R U C L I N Z
J E A L O U S Y Q T S C O D W
N E K I N G D O M S H I I E B
U C O N S U M E D S T D Q C U
U H R R I S E S N A W J Z I R
L A C E C I E O N T H I M S N
O N V S S R I G Z T O C F I I
R G L Y U T I L G T L Y S O N
D E S P A D O R T A E Q E N G
M R J N N L B R Z Z T R R X H
B W A I T S Z K E M U H V X R
D E C L A R A T I O N T E K O
P L U N D E R C P F I R E R Z
```

GIANTS

402

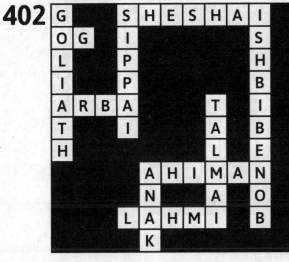

```
G       S H E S H A I
O G     I           S
L       P           H
I       P           B
A R B A             I
T       I     T     B
H             A     E
        A H I M A N
        N     A     O
        L A H M I   B
        K
```

403

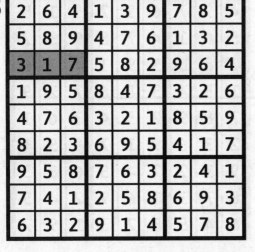

```
2 6 4 1 3 9 7 8 5
5 8 9 4 7 6 1 3 2
3 1 7 5 8 2 9 6 4
1 9 5 8 4 7 3 2 6
4 7 6 3 2 1 8 5 9
8 2 3 6 9 5 4 1 7
9 5 8 7 6 3 2 4 1
7 4 1 2 5 8 6 9 3
6 3 2 9 1 4 5 7 8
```

404 GILEAD = MASS OF TESTIMONY
GOLIATH = EXILE
GOMER = COMPLETION
HADAD = MIGHTY
HAGAR = FUGITIVE
HAMAN = WELL DISPOSED
HANNAH = GRACIOUS
HERODIAS = HEROIC

405 CORINTHIANS

406 Kisses Pt.1
1. Isaac kisses Jacob by mistake. (Genesis 27:26-27)
2. Jacob kisses Rachel on sight. (Genesis 29:11)
3. Laban kisses Jacob. (Genesis 29:13)
4. Laban kisses Jacob's kids. (Genesis 31:55)
5. Esau and Jacob reunite. (Genesis 33:4)
6. Joseph and his brothers reunite. (Genesis 45:15)
7. Israel blesses Joseph's sons. (Genesis 48:10-20)
8. Jacob kisses his dead father. (Genesis 50:1)
9. Aaron greets Moses. (Exodus 4:27)

407 Shusaku Endo
Saint Francis Xavier
Samuel Hopkins

SOLUTIONS

408
1. LIBYA = PUT
2. ABIMELECH = ABRAHAM
3. ISAAC = ABIMELECH
4. LABAN = JACOB

409

WICKED PUNISHED	REVELATION 3:21
MADE A PILLAR	PROVERBS 11:21
INHERITANCE	PROVERBS 13:22
PLACE BY THE THRONE	REVELATION 3:12
WILL BE BLESSED	GENESIS 12:3
HUNGER NO MORE	REVELATION 20:4
BLESSED IN ABRAHAM	GENESIS 18:18
1,000 YEAR REIGN	REVELATION 7:15-17

Matthew 11:28-30

411

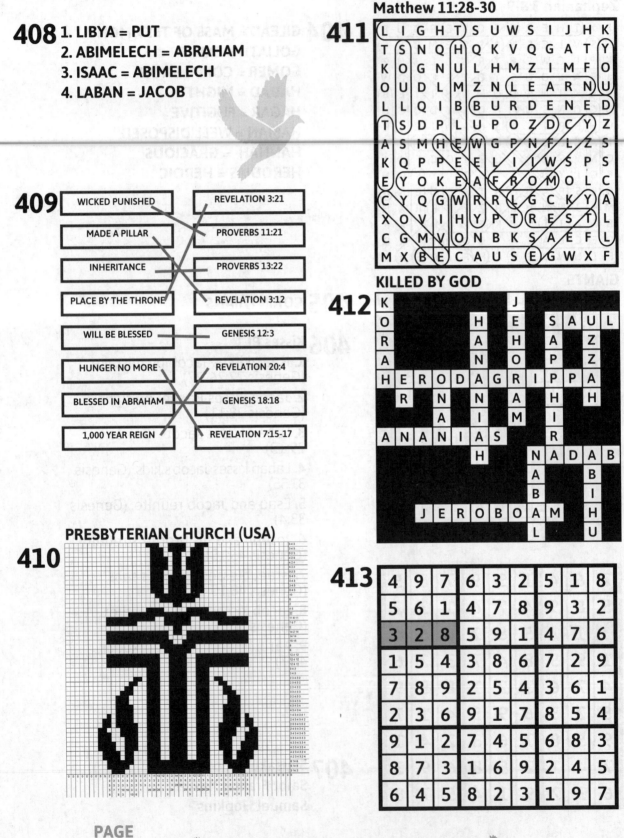

KILLED BY GOD

412

410
PRESBYTERIAN CHURCH (USA)

413

4	9	7	6	3	2	5	1	8
5	6	1	4	7	8	9	3	2
3	2	8	5	9	1	4	7	6
1	5	4	3	8	6	7	2	9
7	8	9	2	5	4	3	6	1
2	3	6	9	1	7	8	5	4
9	1	2	7	4	5	6	8	3
8	7	3	1	6	9	2	4	5
6	4	5	8	2	3	1	9	7

BIBLE POWER PUZZLES

SOLUTIONS

414 HEMAN = FAITHFUL
HERMES = GAIN
HERMOGENES = BEGOTTEN OF HERMES
HEROD = SON OF A HERO
HILLEL = GREATLY PRAISED
HIRAM = CONSECRATION
HORAM = ELEVATED
HUR = NOBLE

415 HARVEST

416 Kisses Pt.2
10. Moses kisses Jethro. (Exodus 18:5-7)
11. Naomi kisses Orpah and Ruth. (Ruth 1:9)
12. Samuel kisses and anoints Saul. (1 Samuel 10:1)
13. David and Jonathan kiss. (1 Samuel 20:41)
14. David kisses Absalom. (2 Samuel 14:33)
15. Absaloms steals hearts. (2 Samuel 15:5-6)
16. David kisses Barzillai. (2 Samuel 19:39)
17. Joab kills Amasa. (2 Samuel 20:9-10)
18. Judas kisses Jesus. (Matthew 26:47-50)

417 R. A. Torrey
Dietrich Bonhoeffer
Gilbert K. Chesterton

418 1. DAVID = ACHISH
2. ABNER = DAVID
3. DAVID = HIRAM
4. TOI = DAVID

419

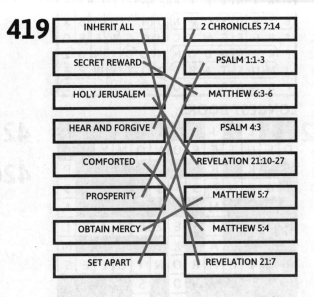

INHERIT ALL	2 CHRONICLES 7:14
SECRET REWARD	PSALM 1:1-3
HOLY JERUSALEM	MATTHEW 6:3-6
HEAR AND FORGIVE	PSALM 4:3
COMFORTED	REVELATION 21:10-27
PROSPERITY	MATTHEW 5:7
OBTAIN MERCY	MATTHEW 5:4
SET APART	REVELATION 21:7

NOAH'S ARK

420

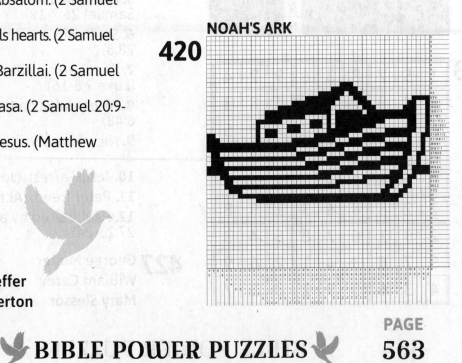

SOLUTIONS

Mark 4:30-32

421

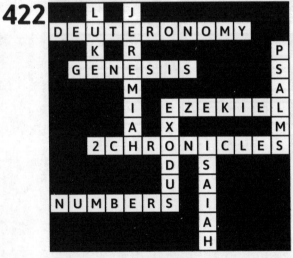

LONGEST BOOKS

422

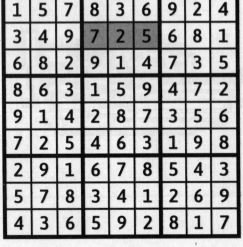

423

1	5	7	8	3	6	9	2	4
3	4	9	7	2	5	6	8	1
6	8	2	9	1	4	7	3	5
8	6	3	1	5	9	4	7	2
9	1	4	2	8	7	3	5	6
7	2	5	4	6	3	1	9	8
2	9	1	6	7	8	5	4	3
5	7	8	3	4	1	2	6	9
4	3	6	5	9	2	8	1	7

424 **IMMANUEL = GOD WITH US**
IRA = WATCHFUL
ISAAC = LAUGHING ONE
ISHMAEL = GOD HEARS
ISRAEL = RULING WITH GOD
ITHAMAR = PALM TREE
IZRI = CREATIVE
ISCAH = SHE WILL LOOK OUT

425 **GAMALIEL**

426 **Nighttime visits**
1. Jacob wrestles with a man. (Genesis 32:24-31)
2. Angel of death visits Egypt. (Exodus 12:29-31)
3. Gideon attacks the Midianites. (Judges 7:19-21)
4. Samuel is called. (1 Samuel 3:1-14)
5. David and Abishai visit camp. (1 Samuel 26:7-12)
6. Saul visits a witch. (1 Samuel 28:8)
7. Shepherds visited by angels. (Luke 2:8-16)
8. Jesus walks on the sea. (Mark 6:48)
9. Nicodemus visits Jesus. (John 3:1-2)
10. Jesus' arrest. (John 18:3-12)
11. Peter freed. (Acts 12:6-17)
12. Paul visited by an angel. (Acts 27:23-24).

427 George Muller
William Carey
Mary Slessor

SOLUTIONS

428
1. ONESIMUS = PAUL
2. PAUL = TYCHICUS
3. ARISTARCHUS = PAUL
4. PAUL = JOHN MARK

429

SWEET SLEEP	JAMES 4:6
JOINT-HEIRS	ISAIAH 40:31
SINS CLEANSED	ROMANS 8:17
CONFESS AND BE SAVED	ROMANS 10:9
WALK AND NOT FAINT	ISAIAH 1:18
JUSTIFIED	PROVERBS 3:21-24
NOT LABOR IN VAIN	ISAIAH 65:23
GRACE	GALATIANS 2:16

430

SEVENTH-DAY ADVENTIST CHURCH

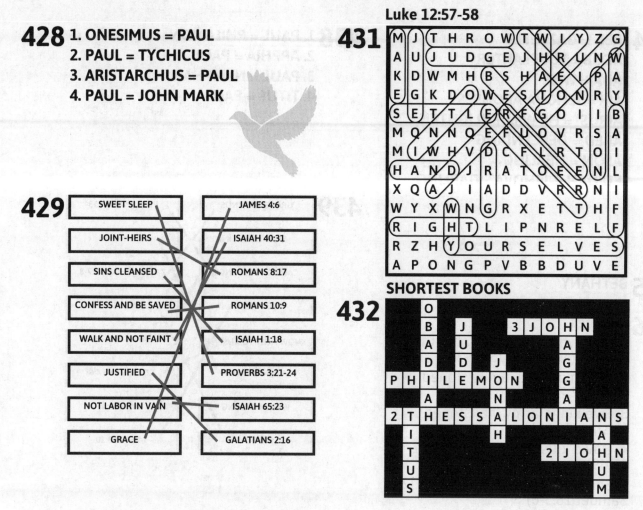

431 Luke 12:57-58

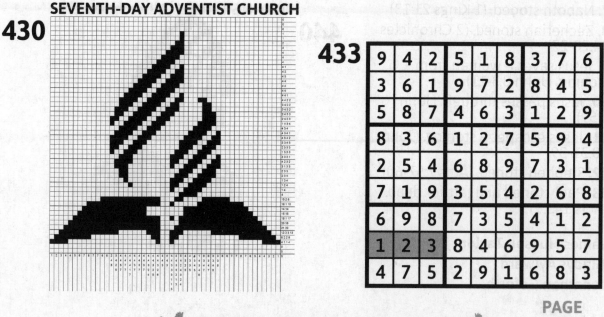

SHORTEST BOOKS

432

433

9	4	2	5	1	8	3	7	6
3	6	1	9	7	2	8	4	5
5	8	7	4	6	3	1	2	9
8	3	6	1	2	7	5	9	4
2	5	4	6	8	9	7	3	1
7	1	9	3	5	4	2	6	8
6	9	8	7	3	5	4	1	2
1	2	3	8	4	6	9	5	7
4	7	5	2	9	1	6	8	3

SOLUTIONS

434 JAEL = GAZZELLE
JACOB = SUPPLANTER
JADA = WISE
JAIR = JEHOVA AROUSES
JAIRUS = HE WILL ENLIGHTEN
JARED = DESCENDING
JASON = HEALING
JEDIDAH = JEHOVA'S DARLING

435 BETHANY

436 Stonings

1. Man who broke the Sabbath stoned. (Numbers 15:32-36)

2. Achan and his family stoned. (Johua 7:24-25)

3. Five kings' army "hailstoned". (Joshua 10:11)

4. David kills Goliath. (1 Samuel 17:49)

5. Shimei casts stones at David. (2 Samuel 16:5-6)

6. Adoram stoned. (1 Kings 12:18)

7. Naboth stoned. (1 Kings 21:13)

8. Zecheriah stoned. (2 Chronicles 24:20-22)

9. Jesus saves a woman from stoning. (John 8:3-11)

10. Jesus passes through. (John 8:59)

11. Jesus escapes a stoning. (John 10:31-39)

12. Stephen stoned. (Acts 7:57-60)

13. Paul stoned and left for dead. (Acts 14:19)

437 James Hudson Taylor
Gladys Aylward
Jonathan Goforth

438 1. PAUL = PHILEMON
2. APPHIA = PAUL
3. PAUL = NYMPHAS
4. TITUS = PAUL

439

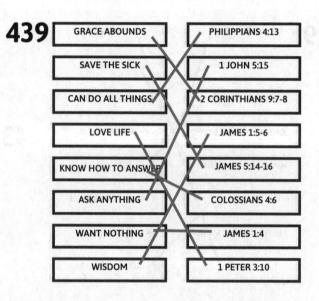

GRACE ABOUNDS	PHILIPPIANS 4:13
SAVE THE SICK	1 JOHN 5:15
CAN DO ALL THINGS	2 CORINTHIANS 9:7-8
LOVE LIFE	JAMES 1:5-6
KNOW HOW TO ANSWER	JAMES 5:14-16
ASK ANYTHING	COLOSSIANS 4:6
WANT NOTHING	JAMES 1:4
WISDOM	1 PETER 3:10

440 **PRAYING HANDS (Albrecht Dürer)**

SOLUTIONS

Luke 13:24-25

441

```
E N T E R H B L A Q U G O H D
H K X N A R R O W G N Q U N F
T X D C B A A M E I Y U T S D
J E K A L N A G Y O N C S A J
S Z N T E S I A X L N N T N Y
A M O T H W S F B T Z C D A N
U K W N B E C A U S E M E D M
W H E R E R N M A S A Q Z L A
T H R O U G H E P K F H L Z K
X F T W P U G F B O N I S S E
T E R Y K E I F D S W O O S R
R F N O J D N O O H N M C Q E
Y A V O W N E R O U O A X K R
M X V L W A R T R T Q P C W Y
G U V C F R O M P S L O R D X
```

LOST BOOKS

442

```
                    J
      J A S H E R
          H     H
  A H A S U E R U S
          M
  R E M E M B R A N C E
          I
      W   D A V I D
N A T H A N   H   D
          R       D
      S O L O M O N
```

443

9	2	1	6	8	3	4	7	5
3	6	5	7	4	1	9	2	8
7	4	8	5	9	2	6	1	3
2	1	6	4	3	8	7	5	9
8	9	7	1	2	5	3	6	4
4	5	3	9	6	7	1	8	2
5	7	4	2	1	9	8	3	6
6	3	2	8	7	4	5	9	1
1	8	9	3	5	6	2	4	7

444 **JEREMIAH = EXALTED OF GOD**
JESSE = JEHOVA IS
JETHRO = EXCELLENCE
JEMIMA = LITTLE DOVE
JEZEBEL = CHASTE
JOANNA = THE LORD IS GRACIOUS
JOB = WEEPING
JOEL = JEHOVA IS GOD

445 SANHEDRIN

446 **Court trials**
1. Moses judges by himself. (Exodus 18:13-24)
2. Judged for cursing. (Leviticus 24: 10-23)
3. Moses appoints judges. (Deuteronomy 1:9-17)
4. Jesus before Caiaphas. (Matthew 26:57-66)
5. Jesus before Pilate. (Luke 23:1-5)
6. Peter and John on trial. (Acts 4:5-21)
7. Paul judged for exorcizing a possessed girl. (Acts 16:16-24)
8. Paul before the priests council. (Acts 22:30-23:10)
9. Paul before Felix. (Acts 24:1-23).
10. Paul appeals to Caesar. (Acts 25:1-12)

447 Jerry Dunn
André Frossard
Sam Childers

SOLUTIONS

448
1. ALVAH = ESAU
2. ESAU = TIMNA
3. JETHETH = ESAU
4. ESAU = OHOLIBAMAH

449

THE KINGDOM	MATTHEW 5:8
REWARDED	PSALM 18:19
SEE GOD	MATTHEW 10:32
MERCIFUL	MATTHEW 5:9
CHILDREN OF GOD	PSALM 23:1
NOT WANT	MATTHEW 5:3
ACKNOWLEDGED	PSALM 18:20
DELIVERED	PSALM 18:25

450 SAINT CHRISTOPHER

451 John 11:25-27

452 RECORDS Pt.1

453

3	6	8	2	1	5	4	7	9
7	2	4	8	9	3	5	6	1
1	5	9	4	7	6	8	3	2
4	1	3	5	8	9	7	2	6
6	8	7	1	2	4	3	9	5
2	9	5	3	6	7	1	4	8
8	7	6	9	4	1	2	5	3
9	3	2	7	5	8	6	1	4
5	4	1	6	3	2	9	8	7

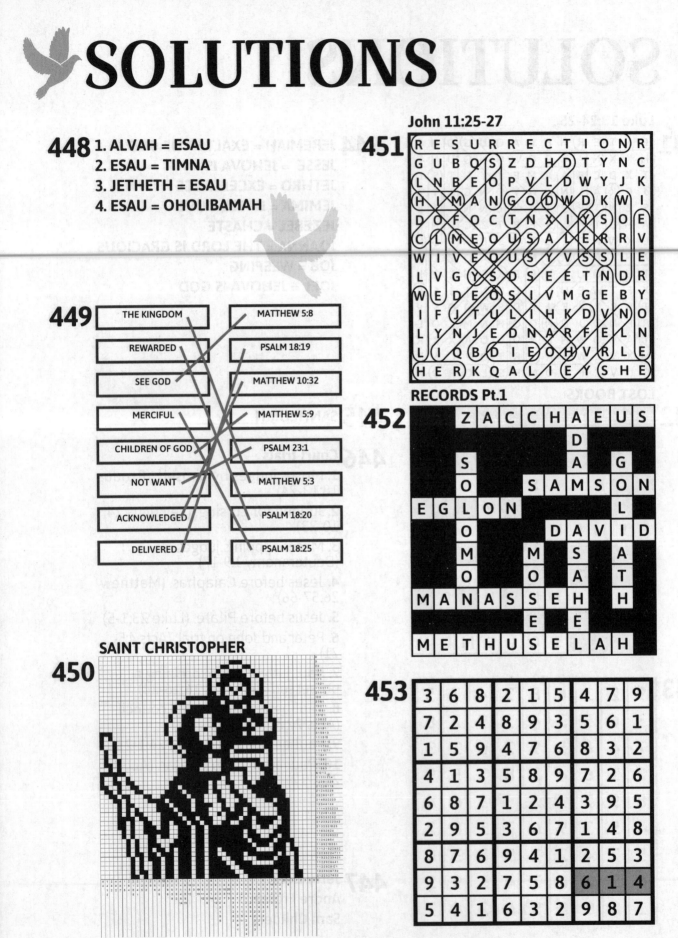

BIBLE POWER PUZZLES

SOLUTIONS

454 JOHN = JEHOVA IS GRACIOUS
JONAH = DOVE
JONATHAN = THE LORD GAVE
JOSEPH = HE WILL ADD
JUDITH = THE PRAISED ONE
JULIA = CURLY-HAIRED
JUNIA = BELONGING TO JUNO
JUDE = PRAISE THE LORD

455 ECCLESIASTES

456 Miraculous Pregnancies
1. Abimelechs' household fertile again. (Genesis 20:17-18)
2. Sarah conceives at age 90. (Genesis 21:1-5)
3. Abraham fathers more children. (Genesis 25:1-6)
4. Rebekah gives birth to twins. (Genesis 25:21-26)
5. Rachel gives birth to Joseph. (Genesis 30:22-24)
6. Manoah's wife bears Samson. (Judges 13:3-5)
7. Hannah gives birth to Samuel. (1 Samuel 1:1-20)
8. Shunnamite woman bears a son. (2 Kings 4:13-17)
9. Mary conceives while a virgin. (Luke 1:34-38)
10. Elizabeth gives birth to John (Luke 1:57-64)

457 Pope Francis
Rick Warren
J. C. Ryle

458
1. ESAU = ELAH
2. PINON = ESAU
3. ESAU = KENAZ
4. TEMAN = ESAU

459

LIFE RESTORATION	PSALM 23:4
ENTER THE KINGDOM	PSALM 23:3
FEAR NO EVIL	PSALM 23:6
THE GREATEST	MATTHEW 18:3
GOODNESS AND MERCY	MATTHEW 18:4
RECEIVE JESUS	PSALM 24:4-5
BLESSING	MATTHEW 18:20
IN OUR MIDST	MATTHEW 18:5

460 MATTHEW THE EVANGELIST

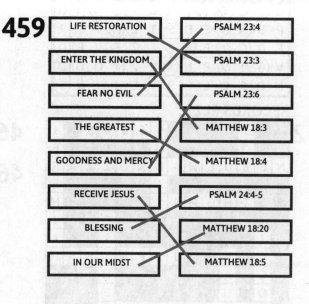

SOLUTIONS

John 17:20-22

461

RECORDS Pt.2

462

463

9	7	8	4	6	3	2	5	1
2	3	1	5	8	9	7	4	6
4	5	6	2	7	1	8	3	9
5	2	7	6	3	8	9	1	4
6	8	3	9	1	4	5	7	2
1	4	9	7	5	2	6	8	3
3	1	5	8	9	6	4	2	7
7	9	2	3	4	5	1	6	8
8	6	4	1	2	7	3	9	5

464 KENAN = SMITH
KETURAH = INCENSE
LAMECH = OVERTHROWER
LAZARUS = GOD HAS HELPED
LEAH = WEARY
LEVI = JOINED
LOIS = DESIRABLE
LUKE = LIGHT GIVING

465 IMMANUEL

466 Angelic Encounters Pt.1
1. Hagar told to return. (Genesis 16:1-12)
2. Lot rescued. (Genesis 19:1-22)
3. Abraham stopped. (Genesis 22:1-18)
4. Jacob's hip disjointed. (Genesis 32:24-30)
5. Balaam stopped. (Numbers 22:22-35)
6. Joshua instructed. (Joshua 5:13-15)
7. Gideon commissioned. (Judges 6:11-23)
8. Samson's mother promised a son. (Judges 13:1-21)
9. Elijah strengthened. (1 Kings 19:1-8)
10. Zacharias visited. (Luke 1:5-22)

467 J. I. Packer
Tyler Perry
George Whitefield

SOLUTIONS

468
1. JOSEPH = BENJAMIN
2. REUBEN = JOSEPH
3. MOSES = JETHRO
4. MIRIAM = AARON

469

SAVED	JOHN 3:16
EVERLASTING LIFE	MATTHEW 28:19-20
WHATEVER YOU DID	JOHN 8:31-32
ETERNAL LIFE	LUKE 11:13
ALWAYS WITH US	JOHN 8:12
NO DARKNESS	JOHN 6:54
HOLY SPIRIT GIFT	MATTHEW 24:13
SET FREE	MATTHEW 25:40

470 MARK THE EVANGELIST

471 Acts 10:4-6

472 ANIMALS

473

6	4	1	9	5	2	7	8	3
2	9	7	6	8	3	5	4	1
3	5	8	7	4	1	6	2	9
8	1	5	2	6	7	3	9	4
9	7	2	4	3	5	8	1	6
4	6	3	8	1	9	2	7	5
5	3	9	1	2	8	4	6	7
1	2	4	3	7	6	9	5	8
7	8	6	5	9	4	1	3	2

SOLUTIONS

474 LYDIA = BENDING
MARK = POLITE
MATTHEW = JEHOVA'S GIFT
MARA = BITTER
MARTHA = MISTRESS OF THE HOUSE
MICHAL = WHO IS LIKE JEHOVA?
MOSES = TAKEN FROM THE WATER
NAOMI = MY JOY

475 REDEMPTION

476 Angelic Encounters Pt.2
11. Mary visited. (Luke 1:26-38)
12. Shepherds visited. (Luke 2:8-15)
13. Christ strengthened. (Luke 22:43)
14. Resurrection announced. (Luke 24:4-7)
15. Apostles freed. (Acts 5:17-20)
16. Philip instructed. (Acts 8:26)
17. Cornelius instructed. (Acts 10:1-8)
18. Peter freed. (Acts 12:6-10)
19. Paul reassured. (Acts 27:21-25)

477 Dwight L. Moody
Origen of Alexandria
Charles G. Finney

478 1. RAHAB = JOSHUA
2. JABIN = JOBAB
3. RUTH = BOAZ
4. JEROBOAM = AHIJAH

479

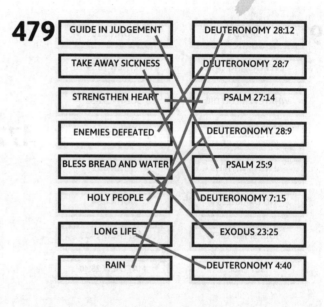

GUIDE IN JUDGEMENT	DEUTERONOMY 28:12
TAKE AWAY SICKNESS	DEUTERONOMY 28:7
STRENGTHEN HEART	PSALM 27:14
ENEMIES DEFEATED	DEUTERONOMY 28:9
BLESS BREAD AND WATER	PSALM 25:9
HOLY PEOPLE	DEUTERONOMY 7:15
LONG LIFE	EXODUS 23:25
RAIN	DEUTERONOMY 4:40

480 LUKE THE EVANGELIST

 BIBLE POWER PUZZLES

SOLUTIONS

Acts 22:25-26

481

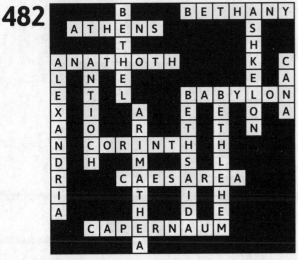

```
C O M M A N D E R I C O L K Q
S O N R O M A N H R M E J H K
Y D M E L A C S A U I W H A T
Q G O P E N E Q C B G N E U I
V N C Q R C N J R N M C Y N B
D T Q R A S T A N D I N G C T
S J E T L N U B U L T G H O U
C H C E S T R E T C H E D N H
O I D S Y I H D K E E C A E E
U S I T I P O V U E Y K N M A
R A R M I L N J D T S G A M R
G I K Q P Z A Q L S H B V M D
E D C L E A E S Z D V I T E N
R D X O U T U N H L O X S D O
N X G Q P W P L W H E N Q W H
```

CITIES Pt.1

482

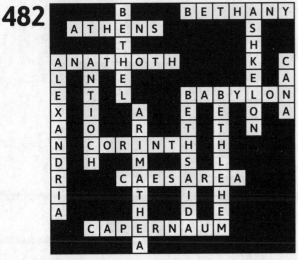

483

8	7	6	2	3	5	4	9	1
9	2	1	6	4	7	5	3	8
5	3	4	8	1	9	7	6	2
3	6	8	7	2	4	9	1	5
7	4	5	9	8	1	3	2	6
2	1	9	3	5	6	8	4	7
6	5	2	4	7	3	1	8	9
1	8	3	5	9	2	6	7	4
4	9	7	1	6	8	2	5	3

484
NOAH = COMFORT
OG = LONG-NECKED
OMAR = MOUNTAINEER
OREN = FINE TREE
PAUL = LITTLE
PEREZ = BREACH
PHOEBE = PURE
PRISCILLA = WORTHY

485 TABERNACLE

486 Prophecies fulfilled by Jesus Pt.1

1. He wouldn't see corruption. (Psalms 16:10)

2. His clothes would be parted. (Psalms 22:18)

3. His bones wouldn't be broken. (Psalms 34:20)

4. A friend would betray Him. (Psalms 41:9)

5. He would ascend. (Psalms 68:18)

6. He would be hated without cause. (Psalms 69:4)

7. He would drink vinegar. (Psalms 69:21)

8. He would speak parables. (Psalms 78:2)

9. He wouldn't be understood. (Isaiah 6:9-10)

10. He would be born of a virgin. (Isaiah 7:14)

11. He would live in Galilee. (Isaiah 9:1)

12. He would try to keep a low profile. (Isaiah 42:2-3)

487 J. Vernon McGee
Tertullian
John Calvin

 BIBLE POWER PUZZLES

SOLUTIONS

488
1. SOLOMON = HIRAM
2. REHOBOAM = ABIJAH
3. ASA = BEN-HADAD
4. NEHEMIAH = EZRA

489

SHALL BE LOVED	JOHN 15:5
STRONGER	ACTS 1:8
MUCH FRUIT	PROVERBS 2:7
PROSPEROUS	JOHN 14:21
POWER	JOB 36:11
SUCCESS	PROVERBS 3:5-6
REMISSION OF SINS	ACTS 10:43
DIRECT PATHS	JOB 17:9

490 JOHN THE EVANGELIST

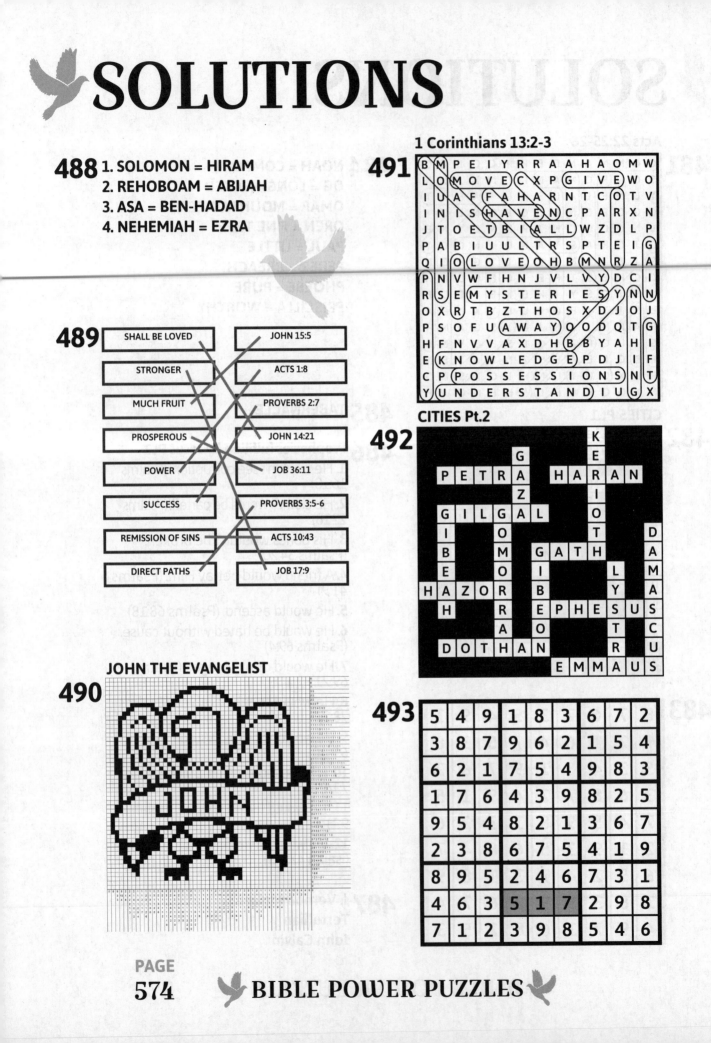

491 1 Corinthians 13:2-3

492 CITIES Pt.2

493

5	4	9	1	8	3	6	7	2
3	8	7	9	6	2	1	5	4
6	2	1	7	5	4	9	8	3
1	7	6	4	3	9	8	2	5
9	5	4	8	2	1	3	6	7
2	3	8	6	7	5	4	1	9
8	9	5	2	4	6	7	3	1
4	6	3	5	1	7	2	9	8
7	1	2	3	9	8	5	4	6

SOLUTIONS

494 RACHEL = EWE
REBECCA = CAPTIVATING
RHODA = ROSE
SALOME = PEACE
SAMUEL = ASKED OF GOD
SARAH = QUEEN
SETH = APPOINTED
STEPHEN = WREATH

495 COMMUNION

496 Prophecies fulfilled by Jesus Pt.2
13. They wouldn't believe in Him. (Isaiah 53:1)
14. He would bear mankind's suffering. (Isaiah 53:4)
15. He would be crucified with sinners. (Isaiah 53:12)
16. He would be anointed to preach. (Isaiah 61:1-2)
17. He would live in Egypt. (Hosea 11:1)
18. He would be born in Bethlehem. (Micah 5:2)
19. He would enter Jerusalem. (Zechariah 9:9)
20. He would be betrayed for silver. (Zechariah 11:12-13)
21. He would be pierced. (Zechariah 12:10)

497 Blaise Pascal
John Donne
Saint Clement of Alexandria

498 1. DANIEL = DARIUS
2. JESUS = NICODEMUS
3. JOSEPH OF ARIMATHEA = JESUS
4. JESUS = YOU

499
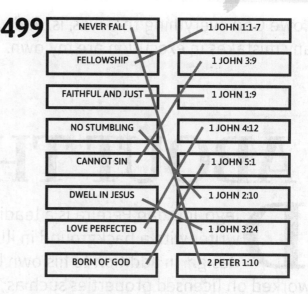

NEVER FALL	1 JOHN 1:1-7
FELLOWSHIP	1 JOHN 3:9
FAITHFUL AND JUST	1 JOHN 1:9
NO STUMBLING	1 JOHN 4:12
CANNOT SIN	1 JOHN 5:1
DWELL IN JESUS	1 JOHN 2:10
LOVE PERFECTED	1 JOHN 3:24
BORN OF GOD	2 PETER 1:10

500 THE HOLY BIBLE

ACKNOWLEDGMENTS

This book wouldn't have been possible without Jesse McHugh's belief in the project, while editor Jessica Burch's time-intensive reviewing and correcting made it shine. I love you both!

Tip of the proverbial hat to authors Albert Haase, C. S. Lewis, Joel L. Meredith, Moisés Silva, and Harold L. Willmington, whose works never fail to keep the lamp alight.

I owe God everything that was, is, and will ever be. His Word being flawless, any mistakes in execution are my own.

ABOUT THE AUTHOR

Diego Jourdan Pereira is a leading puzzle designer and nonfiction writer with a background in illustration, comic-books, and graphic design. In addition to his own books for children and adults, he has worked on licensed properties such as Teenage Mutant Ninja Turtles, Transformers, Donald Duck, Grumpy Cat, LEGO, Mars Attacks!, Regular Show, Sesame Street, Star Wars, Toy Story, and WWE, for an international clientele including DC Comics, DC Thomson Media, Dover Publications, IDW Publishing, Skyhorse Publishing, and The Topps Company.

BIBLE POWER PUZZLES

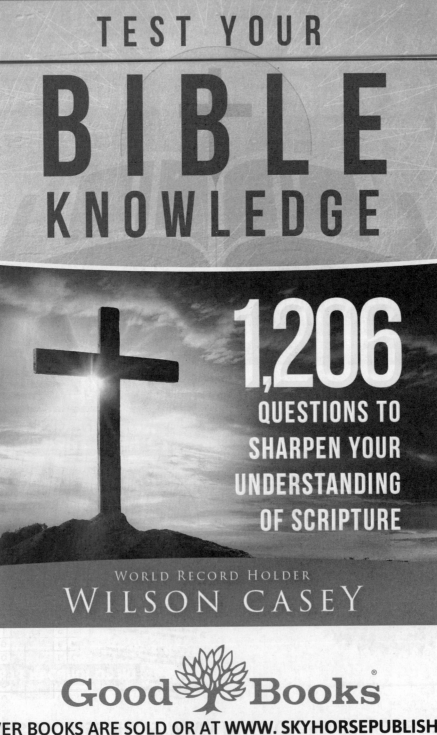

ALSO AVAILABLE

FROM AUTHOR LINDA PETERS

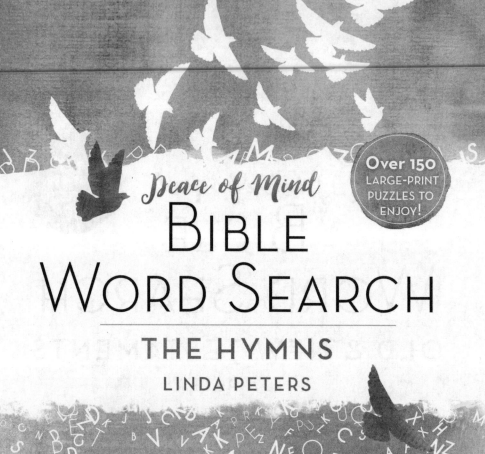

VOLUME 2

Over 150 LARGE-PRINT PUZZLES TO ENJOY!

Peace of Mind

BIBLE WORD SEARCH

THE HYMNS

LINDA PETERS

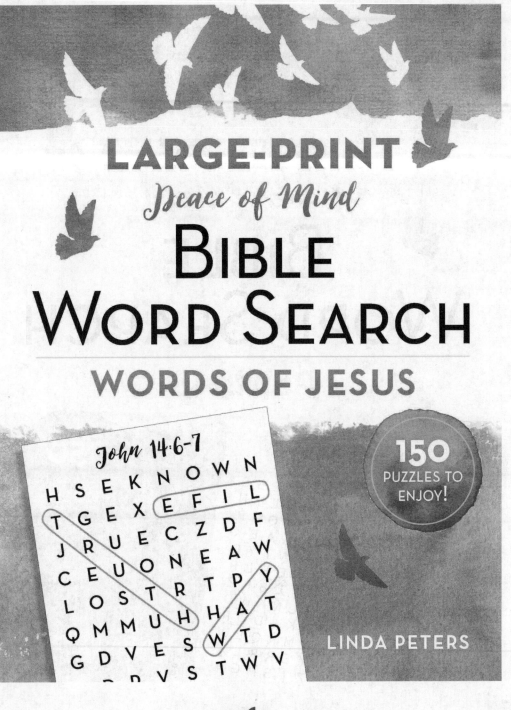

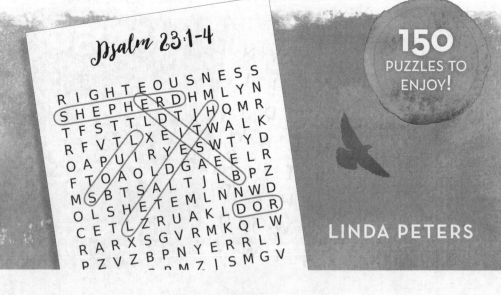

2